Open Your Eyes

OPEN YOUR EYES

DEAF STUDIES TALKING

H-DIRKSEN L. BAUMAN, EDITOR

 University of Minnesota Press
Minneapolis
London

Chapter 17 was previously published in *Sign Language Studies* 2, no. 4; copyright 2002 Gallaudet University Press; reprinted by permission.

Published by the University of Minnesota Press
111 Third Avenue South, Suite 290
Minneapolis, MN 55401-2520
http://www.upress.umn.edu

Library of Congress Cataloging-in-Publication Data
Open your eyes : deaf studies talking / H-Dirksen L. Bauman, editor.
     p.   cm.
Includes index.
Deaf Studies Think Tank : (2002 : Gallaudet University)
ISBN: 978-0-8166-4618-0 ISBN-10: 0-8166-4618-X (hc : alk. paper)
ISBN: 978-0-8166-4619-7 ISBN-10: 0-8166-4619-8 (pb : alk. paper)
1. Deaf. 2. Deaf—Social conditions. 3. Sign language. 4. Sign language.
I. Bauman, H-Dirksen L., 1964– II. Title.
HV2380.D43 2002
305.9'082—dc22   2007033907

Printed in the United States of America on acid-free paper

The University of Minnesota is an equal-opportunity educator and employer.

15   14   13   12   11   10   10   9   8   7   6   5

Contents

Part V. Intersections and Identities

Part VI. The Question of Disability

Preface

THIS BOOK WAS BORN out of the Deaf Studies Think Tank, a three-day symposium in the summer of 2002 sponsored by the National Endowment for the Humanities, Gallaudet University's Provost's Office, and the Gallaudet Research Institute. The Deaf Studies Think Tank convened twenty scholars to debate, discuss, and explore the issues and implications of the field of Deaf Studies. The Think Tank was scheduled in the three days preceding Deaf Way II, an international celebration of Deaf scholarship, arts, performance, advocacy, and development attended by more than nine thousand people from 121 nations.

We met in the circular Gallaudet University Board Room, designed specifically for the visual orientation of signing. Yet we would not remain in that room for the duration of the event. Just after the opening address of the Think Tank, the power went out. We hoped this was nothing more than a blink in the local power grid, but it was no blink: the local grid was asleep. The entire campus was out of power and would remain that way for the following thirty hours. So we made do. Plans changed.

We wandered in the hazy, sweltering heat to the nearby Washburn Art Building, which was bathed in afternoon light and featured a great number of works by Deaf artists from all over the world. In one work by Chuck Baird, welded pipes contorted into handshapes, resembling a language of hieroglyphic copper just out of reach of decipherment. In its own enigmatic way, Baird's work, titled *fingerspelling,* seemed to make sense of the blackout. These medusa-like fingers pointed in new and unexpected directions. They reminded us that taking an unexpected path may lead to new sights and new insights.

The blackout became a living symbol of the emerging field we had all convened to discuss. For one, when the power is out, the value of light increases. As Ben Bahan's chapter in this volume discusses, more than most other human cultures, Deaf Culture is keenly aware of in the value of light and vision. Light is often cited as a cultural value in itself, figuring prominently in stories, poems, and even in company names. The media production company LightKitchen, for example, takes its cue from the tendency of Deaf folk to flock to what is usually the brightest room in the house. But there were no bright rooms in the conference center. Like moths, we were drawn to any scrap of light, candles, and emergency lights. Unlike moths, we reflected on our relationship to light, to the ways that signers move through the world according to the conditions of a visual language.

Indeed, you start to see differently when the power goes out. You start to see, for example, that the power would never be out for thirty hours in nearby Capitol Hill or Georgetown, but in northeast Washington, D.C.—in an African American and Deaf neighborhood—the sense of urgency does not seem quite the same.[1] This local power outage was but a microcosm for the historical predicament of the Deaf world. While it might take a long time to restore light in northeast Washington, D.C., it has taken centuries for light to be shed on the lives, languages, and cultures of Deaf individuals. Deaf people have always been out of sight of the hearing majority. For centuries, deaf individuals were largely scattered across an agrarian globe without another visual language user to spark the eyes and hands into grammatical action. Not until the later eighteenth century in France and early nineteenth century in America did deaf individuals come into view as a collective group as a result of formal educational and medical establishments. Yet, even though deaf people became visible as a group, they still remained mostly out of sight. What hearing people saw, instead, was their own "projection of cultural prejudice, fear and hope, faith and ideology" on the blank screen of deaf people.[2] Instead of trying to view deafness through the eyes of Deaf people themselves, the hearing majority has largely inferred and determined the meanings of deafness on their own. All the while, Deaf people have been living their Deaf lives, generation after generation, forming their own schools, families, churches, clubs, businesses, and national and international political organizations, as well as their own bodies of literary and artistic production—all this without speech.

The darkness often associated with deafness, then, is not the horror of hearing loss that most presume, but instead the inability or unwillingness of hearing people to actually *see* what goes on in the Deaf world. This oversight has not only been detrimental to members of the Deaf world, but it has also left us with a legacy of incomplete understanding about the nature of human language, ability, and cultural formations.

This collection of essays is intended to open the eyes of many to the insights in the Deaf world and Deaf Studies. The majority of authors in this volume are Deaf themselves, though others are children of Deaf parents, and others, like myself, are hearing. I was not born that way, however. I was born as a *person who could hear*, which is different from being born *hearing*. Like any identity, hearing identity is a social construction. I became *hearing* at the age of twenty-one, when I was hired as a dormitory supervisor for the Colorado School for the Deaf and the Blind (CSDB). Suddenly, my world changed: it was no longer *my* world. I was an outsider, a foreigner in my own land. My identity was constructed for me; long before I ever began working at CSDB, a whole discourse on the meanings of being hearing had evolved in the Deaf world. Growing up, the thought that I was a hearing person never crossed my mind; hearing was so normal it went unnoticed. It was just the way things were. Only after a ten-year-old Deaf boy told me that I was hearing did the realization strike me. This is more than a residential school I have wandered into; this is a profoundly different way of being in the world. Though I could pass freely through the stone and wrought-iron fence surrounding the campus, I could never fully pass through the larger epistemological and cultural border that separates the Deaf and hearing worlds.

Things appear different on either side of this border. For example, as Carol Padden and Tom Humphries have pointed out, when hearing people say that someone is "very hard of hearing," they mean that the person is almost deaf. When Deaf people refer to someone as "very hard of hearing," they mean that the person is almost hearing.[3] After I began working at the Colorado School for the Deaf and the Blind, I found myself on the borderlands and began to see myself from a perspective I never imagined. This dual vision afforded me a critical perspective through which I could interrogate myself and the phonocentric ideologies in the world in which I was raised. I am now perpetually reminded, for example, of the audist ideologies that inform fundamental aspects of hearing society—its views on language, literature, culture, ability, disability, and identity.

It has been more than twenty years since I became hearing, and I am still inquiring into the meanings of hearing as well as d/Deaf identities in my role as a professor of Deaf Studies at Gallaudet University. Indicative of the different center of the Deaf world, I often joke about being a token as the only hearing member of my department. Indeed, there is a different orientation when a white, hearing, able-bodied, straight, middle-class male brings diversity to an academic department.

I am perpetually honored and humbled to serve as the only hearing member of the Deaf Studies program at the world's only liberal arts university for Deaf and hard-of-hearing students. I owe my colleagues and students my deepest gratitude for their welcoming attitude and enlightening exchanges. In particular, I wish to thank my colleague and friend Ben Bahan for originally suggesting that I move from the English department to the Deaf Studies department to assist in creating the graduate program. I also thank my department chair, MJ Bienvenu, for her support and leadership, and my colleagues in the Department of ASL and Deaf Studies: Arlene B. Kelly, Gene Mirus, Carolyn McCaskill, Lynn Jacobowitz, Flavia Fleischer, and Mike Kemp. The Deaf Studies Think Tank would not have been possible without assistance from Will Garrow and Jennifer Clifford. The Gallaudet University Office of Sponsored Programs was helpful in securing the National Endowment for the Humanities funding, and the Gallaudet Research Institute, under the leadership of Michael Karchmer, provided support for an ongoing research project, of which the Deaf Studies Think Tank was a part. We also received generous support from Gallaudet University's Provost, Jane K. Fernandes, who was able to participate in the Think Tank and manage a university during a power outage. I also thank the anonymous reviewers of the book and my editor, Richard Morrison, for his belief in its value. Andrew Jones is also to be thanked for his significant contribution to the preparation of the manuscript. Finally, I wish to thank Nicole Salimbene for the preparation of the visual images and for her support and encouragement while I prepared this project.

Notes

1. Lennard Davis made this observation as it became evident that the power was not going to come back for some time.
2. Douglas Baynton, *Forbidden Signs: American Culture and the Campaign against Sign Language* (Chicago: University of Chicago Press, 1996), 1.
3. Carol Padden and Tom Humphries, *Deaf in America: Voices from a Culture* (Cambridge, Mass.: Harvard University Press, 1988).

Introduction: Listening to Deaf Studies

H-DIRKSEN L. BAUMAN

> My line of work obliges me to go into many homes. Once inside I am invariably questioned about the deaf. But most often the questions are as laughable as they are absurd; they merely prove that almost everyone has gotten the falsest possible ideas about us; few people have an adequate notion of our state, our resources, or our way of communicating with each other in sign language.
>
> —Pierre Desloges, deaf bookbinder, 1779

> What does it matter, whether one speaks or signs, as they both pertain equally to the soul?
>
> —St. Augustine

AMONG THE SEISMIC SHIFTS in culture brought about in the 1960s was a much quieter but nonetheless profound revolution in our understanding of human language and culture: the validation of the fully linguistic nature of sign languages and the subsequent rewriting of deaf identity from deaf to Deaf, that is, from a pathological state of hearing loss to the cultural identity of a linguistic minority. Prior to this time, prevailing wisdom perceived signed languages as primitive communication systems limited to iconographic representations. Even worse, their use was thought to pose a grave danger to society, as it encouraged defective individuals to socialize, form associations, and ultimately intermarry and increase their numbers. In the spirit and momentum of the eugenics movement in the late nineteenth and early twentieth centuries, an all-out campaign was waged to remedy what Alexander Graham Bell warned against: the formation of a "deaf variety of the human race."[1] By the 1920s, "oralism"—the method of instructing deaf people through the exclusive use of speaking, lip-reading, and hearing—had become the dominant method of teaching, making it virtually impossible for Deaf individuals to maintain teaching positions that they held since the creation of American residential schools for the deaf in 1817.[2] To ensure purely oral environments, schools banned the use of sign language, often physically punishing anyone caught signing. It is common for Deaf adults of today to recount stories of their hands being beaten with rulers and sticks, while others tell of more calculated punishments such as being forced to kneel on a broomstick while holding dictionaries with outstretched arms.[3]

This literal and figurative shackling of deaf students and sign language may now be placed in stark relief against what we now know—that these deaf children were beaten for behaving as humans do, for exercising the indomitable human will to communicate. We now know, after four decades of linguistic research, that "language" may just as well be visual-manual as aural-spoken. We know that infants—whether hearing or deaf—may just as easily babble their way into a fully grammatical signed language as they would a spoken language. Now that we can spy on the neuroanatomical structure of language through brain imaging technology, we see that the regions once thought to process speech in the right hemisphere also light up like a city at night when processing sign language.[4] Whether ignited by sound or by sight, neurons ferry the electric luggage of language along a matrix of pathways that ultimately lead toward full linguistic and cognitive development. Long before the supple linguistic capacity of humans was verified by extensive research, Jean Jacques Rousseau intuited this deeper conception of language in the eighteenth century: "the invention of the art of communicating our ideas depends less upon the organs we use in such communication than it does upon a power proper to man, according to which he uses his organs in this way, and which, if he lacked these, would lead him to use others to the same end."[5] In other words, language behaves a lot like running water. If one way is blocked, it will well up and find another.

Given prevailing wisdom, readers most likely assume that such blockage is due to deafness; I want to suggest the counterintuitive position—that our historic disregard for manual languages has formed its own blockage. Not coaxed down the pathway of signing, language has opted for speech. The road less traveled, however, is still a road and is becoming more and more traveled as time goes on.

In retrospect, we may now see that the historic misunderstanding of sign languages is one of the longest enduring errors of human thought, leaving us with an incomplete understanding about the nature of human language—the implications of which have rippled throughout the centuries.[6] While effects of such a misalignment of thought can be traced throughout the history of Western thought, they have been felt most profoundly by deaf individuals whose intellectual abilities have been grossly misunderstood and their full humanity put into question. Indeed, the history of deaf individuals, like that of women, African Americans, Native Americans, gays and lesbians, and persons with disabilities, has been one of marginalization and misrepresentation. Nineteenth-century science did not treat deaf individuals any kinder than these maligned minority groups; the same scientific apparatus that proved their inferiority and deviance determined the pathological meanings of deafness and relegated sign languages as outcasts from the family of human languages.[7]

In the 1970s, however, the intellectual and cultural climate began to change. Not long after sign languages were accepted into the fold of human languages, Deaf people began to see themselves as belonging to the fold of human cultures. If Deaf people belonged to a culture, they would require a very different set of educational, legal, economic, political, and creative relations to the world.[8] This wholesale recategorization was the catapult that sent Deaf politics into a whole new direction. "The modern age for Deaf people," writes Tom Humphries, "did not begin until the 1970s,"[9] and it began through a rhetoric of culture.

The emergence of the cultural model came on the heels of the 1960s civil rights movements, which brought about a chorus of political and cultural voices that spoke out against systemic social injustice. Deaf activists were eager to join in this chorus, yet they faced a dilemma at ground zero of resistance: While "vocal" minority groups used the rhetoric of "gaining a voice" and "speaking out" without a second thought, the Deaf community faced the fact that the hegemony of the "voice" and "speaking" was precisely what they wanted to "speak out" against. This metaphorical incongruity magnifies the crux of Deaf political activism: how to seize a public voice that commands attention, how to speak out without speaking.

To complicate matters further, this public voice has had a daunting rhetorical task given the entrenched logic of normalcy buttressed by massive biopower institutions that promote medicalized constructions of deafness. It quickly became evident that the Deaf community and its allies would have to develop a body of knowledge about its ways, values, literature, politics, arts, and history. That is, Deaf Culture needed Deaf Studies to articulate, explore, and promote the phenomenon of Deaf Culture, both to the hearing world and to Deaf individuals themselves. Through this process, which Tom Humphries (in this volume) calls "talking culture," Deaf Studies has sought to gain control over the politics of representation by "speaking for itself" instead of being spoken for, which has been the case throughout history.

As a result of Deaf Studies' thirty years of "talking culture," the meanings of *deaf* have indeed changed. Nearly any dictionary includes the definition of Deaf as referring to "the community of deaf people who use American Sign Language (ASL) as a primary means of communication."[10] Today, the existence of a social formation of Deaf people is largely accepted. Deaf Studies may now move on beyond proving that a Deaf Culture exists to ask what it is about Deaf Culture that is valuable to human diversity. It asks what the previously obscure history of sign languages and their communities reflects and magnifies about the linguistics and cultural possibilities of the human character. If *language* is not what it used to be, then what about our constructions of *literature* and *literacy*? As language is a principle means of knowing the world, and as some would contend, of *producing the world,* then what sort of world have we made? How has the assumption that language = speech burrowed itself within the fields of education, anthropology, psychology, medicine, history, and the philosophy of language? As it engages questions fundamental to a deeper understanding of human language, communication, and cultural formations, Deaf Studies is relevant not only to members and allies of this community; anyone interested in questions of language, culture, identity, disability, and critical theory will have something to gain from engaging the field of Deaf Studies.

Historically speaking, however, few have listened to the insights from Deaf Studies. This book, *Open Your Eyes: Deaf Studies Talking,* intends to compel a variety of audiences to listen—from eavesdroppers to longtime residents of the Deaf world. *Open Your Eyes* hopes to encourage readers to consider new ways of listening, new ways of thinking, new ways of seeing the world through Deaf eyes. Throughout this volume, readers will be provided with a wide array of critical lenses that will magnify aspects of the world often overlooked in the peripheries of the phonocentric focus of the West. In this sense, the peripheral is both literal and metaphorical. As Ben Bahan documents in this volume, Deaf eyes have the uncanny ability to process simultaneous information through enhanced peripheral vision. Whereas hearing people depend on sound for information along the outskirts of their sight, Deaf people's vision pushes the boundaries of the peripheral, affording them the ability to entertain nuanced sensory input across a wide field of vision. Deaf vision, in other words, disperses the single-point perspective along a spectrum of perception, allowing the viewer to process multilayered, divergent information simultaneously.

Such acute visual practices can be extrapolated to deeper ways of seeing the world; it may lead toward a cultural and political vision in which the periphery is not so peripheral, in which the spectrum of focus is widened, becoming less hierarchical and more horizontal and democratic. The ability to bring the peripheral out of hiding serves as a model for Deaf critical lenses as well. *Open Your Eyes: Deaf Studies Talking* hopes to widen the spectrum of the humanities, to magnify ways that this peripheral area of study contains insights that affect how those in the "center" see the world. *Open Your Eyes,* like James Fernandez's chapter on "Peripheral Wisdom," "proceeds from the assumption that the experience of being in the peripheries shapes the sense of identity and the way of thinking, and also it assumes that centres have need of peripheries, not only for their own identity because there is always something to be learned from the peripheries."[11] Indeed, there is much to be learned from the peripheries, as this volume attests, but readers must open their eyes wide to entertain the world through Deaf lenses.

Open Your Eyes: Deaf Studies Talking features leading and emerging Deaf Studies scholars from a variety of subject positions, from Deaf of Deaf families to hearing of hearing families, and all points in between. This collection offers the long overdue opportunity to reflect on the development of Deaf Studies as an academic field, assess where it is, and suggest future directions for inquiry. While a wide range of topics are covered—colonialism, visual culture, transnationalism, literacy, philosophy of language, place, critical pedagogy, race, gender, sexual orientation, and disability—all the essays explore, critique, and reflect on the unique phenomenon of the language, culture, and identities of a visual-tactile minority living in a phonocentric world.

For many, this will be an eye-opening experience where sensory lack becomes phenomenological plenitude, where the peripheral becomes central, where Deaf becomes desirable. Deaf Studies has been trying to explain such counterintuitive positions for decades now. The difficulty has been in gaining an audience that truly listens. "To compel listeners, yes," Tom Humphries writes. "A self cannot exist if it is not heard. Deaf people have had to create voices, learn to hear their own voices, and now it remains to compel others to listen."[12] *Open Your Eyes* intends to compel an audience to listen in on the issues and insights gained from the unique perspectives in Deaf Studies.

Readers who do take the time to listen to Deaf Studies talking may sense that they have entered a conversation that began a long time ago. Indeed, some catching up is needed. Hence, in what follows, this introductory essay will back up and listen in on what Deaf Studies has been talking about for quite some time.

A Pre-History of Deaf Studies

As with any field of study, specific origins are difficult to pinpoint.[13] Long before there was a Deaf Culture or Deaf Studies per se, there was a long and sporadic philosophical fascination with sign languages and deaf individuals. Tracing this early Deaf history is a bit like tracing the paths of fireflies: the field is mostly dark, except for scattered moments of illumination. The darkness results in part because manual languages have had no written system, no way of preserving thoughts beyond the moment of utterance. One is always haunted by how much may have occurred among deaf individuals and communities throughout history but was never recorded. What we do have, however, are sightings of signing communities over the past two and a half millennia. These sightings appear as hearing philosophers, poets, and artists have come into contact with deaf individuals and their communities and then pondered about this alternative way of being-in-the-world. Two and a half millennia ago, for example, Plato referred to a group of signers in Athens in the *Cratylus* (see Bauman, this volume). Since then, a number of philosophers and writers—including St. Augustine, da Vinci, Cardamo, Descartes, Rousseau, Leibniz, Diderot, Condillac, and others—have mused about deafness and manual languages.[14] For nearly two hundred years, travel writers noted with great curiosity that the famous Topkapi Palace in Constantinople was populated with signing mutes.[15] In the end, we are left to connect the dots from one sighting of deafness to the next to form a ventriloquist historiography, where the actual lives of deaf people and signing communities are known only through the writings of others.

It was not until 1779 that a deaf person, Pierre Desloges, seized control of a public voice—through written French—that commanded the attention of Parisian society and its intellectuals.[16] When Desloges took up pen and paper, little did he know that he would lay the rhetorical foundation for Deaf Studies some two hundred years later: catalyzed by the widespread misunderstandings of sign languages and their communities, he provided insights into the social, cultural, and intellectual livelihood of the Deaf community.

> There are congenitally deaf people, Parisian laborers, who are illiterate and who have never attended the Abbe de l'Epee's[17] lessons who have been found so well instructed about their religion, simply by means of signs, that they have been judged worthy of admittance to the holy sacraments, even those of the eucharist and marriage. No event—in Paris, in France, or in the four corners of the world—lies outside the scope of our discussion. We express ourselves on all subjects with as much order, precision, and rapidity as if we enjoyed the faculty of speech and hearing.[18]

Desloges's insider perspective testifies to the fact that Deaf people do what any other human would do in similar circumstances—develop a natural language and social discourse. Yet, Desloges goes even further to claim that sign language is not only good for deaf people, but that it could be of immense value to all of humanity. "I cannot understand how a language like sign language—the richest in expressions, the most energetic . . .—is still so neglected and that only the deaf speak it (as it were). This is, I confess, one of the irrationalities of the human mind I cannot explain."[19] Over two hundred years later we are now beginning to realize the broader cognitive and psychological benefits of sign language for all humans—whether hearing or deaf. Desloges would be vindicated to learn about the lucrative industry that encourages hearing parents to sign to their hearing babies in order to stimulate cognition, social behavior, and language skills.[20]

A contributing factor to this "irrationality" may be that hearing people don't actually *see* sign language, even when they look directly at it. It is not only a foreign language, but a profoundly foreign concept that a language could exist outside the full presence of sound. This leaves defenders of sign language to explain themselves in print, rendering sign language lost in translation. Desloges was quick to admit that "My presentation of sign language is limited to a simple outline of it, with no claim to a full explanation of its mechanism. That would be an immense enterprise requiring several volumes. Indeed, sometimes a particular sign made in the twinkling of an eye would require entire pages for a description of it to be complete."[21] Desloges and the generations of Deaf activists after him would have to resort to print to defend something that cannot be rendered in print. Yet, print would have to be the voice of self-representation throughout the nineteenth century.

In the tradition of Desloges, Deaf Americans began to claim their own meanings, identity, and language. While there were Deaf communities prior to the founding of the residential school in 1817,[22] the American Deaf community formed in numbers like never before as residential schools spread across the land, bringing with them "the sign language" and a growing sense of solidarity and shared experiences. Throughout the nineteenth century, the Deaf world[23] grew into a transnational cultural phenomenon with residential schools, clubs, and local, national, and international associations; it argued its rights in education and employment; it created new literary genres; it made films, art, literature, and published a national network of newspapers known as the "Little Paper family" forming what Benedict Anderson calls an "imagined community."[24] The title of the newspaper from the Mississippi Institution for the Education of the Deaf and Dumb during the years 1882–1910—*The Deaf-Mute Voice*[25]—sums up the rhetorical position of the Deaf community: its lack of a literal voice would by no means stop its members from speaking out by any means necessary.

As technology advanced in the early twentieth century, Deaf activists sought another means for the real Deaf-mute voice to speak out: film. In 1913, the National Association of the Deaf (NAD) collected funds to produce a series of short films with the intention of defending, preserving, and promoting sign language use.[26] These films included samples of master signers engaging in political oratory, storytelling, songs, translations, and historical events. Today, they are regarded as cultural classics, leaving behind a signed history and insight into the evolution of "the sign language" that was to become American Sign Language.

In addition to creating films, the NAD would work through the first half of the twentieth century to defend Deaf workers' rights, the right to drive cars, and the right to intermarry.[27] Despite such organized resistance, Deaf issues remained peripheral to American cultural consciousness. Only those who happened to be involved in Deaf education, churches, or employers' families would have taken notice of the Deaf world and its concerns. The hearing world's ignorance of Deaf ways of being has had particularly deleterious effects on the majority of deaf people as they are born into hearing households and are therefore cast into a medicalized version of deafness that will indelibly mark their lives as disabled. The "Deaf-mute voice" has been no match for the ideological mega-phone of the biopower institutions designed to fix deafness and discourage the forma-tion of a deaf variety of the human race. Just as Desloges faced a public that had the "falsest possible ideas" about deaf people, the Deaf community generations later would still be plagued with the common misunderstandings promoted by medical and educa-tional experts. Rarely would the public listen to Deaf people themselves explain what it is like to live Deaf lives. Clearly, it would take more than renegade writers like Desloges and films by the NAD. It would take a formalized area of study and inquiry: it would take the scientific validation of sign language and the subsequent formation of Deaf Studies to gain a wider audience to hear Deaf political and cultural voices.

Deaf Studies in the Academy

The first known public mention of the term "Deaf Studies" came in 1971, from the execu-tive director of the NAD, Frederick Schreiber. "If deaf people are to get ahead in our time, they must have a better image of themselves and their capabilities. They need concrete examples of what deaf people have already done so that they can project for themselves a brighter future. If we can have Black studies, Jewish studies, why not Deaf studies?"[28] Soon after, the 1970s saw the first Deaf Studies articles, such as Robert Panara's "Deaf Studies in the English Curriculum" in 1974, the first courses, "The Deaf in Literature" (1972), and the first master's thesis, Dennis Hoffmeyer's "The Rationale for Developing a Deaf Studies Curriculum" (1975).[29] The Deaf Studies movement was also advanced by the Linguistic Research Laboratory, directed by William Stokoe at Gallaudet,[30] and the journal he founded, *Sign Language Studies,* which published early works on the socio-logical and cultural aspects of sign languages.

Deaf Studies curriculum was indeed under development in the 1970s, but came to greater fruition in the early 1980s with the first degree-granting programs: Boston Uni-versity established its Deaf Studies program in 1981[31] and California State University at Northridge in 1983.[32] In addition to these programs, which examined the Deaf commu-nity from sociological, cultural, and linguistic perspectives, there was a proliferation of seminars and workshops on American Sign Language and Deaf Culture. The primary agenda during these years was the defense of Deaf Culture, defining attributes of Deaf identity, and the development of a bilingual/bicultural model for Deaf education.

It would not be until 1994 that Gallaudet University, the world's only liberal arts uni-versity for deaf and hard-of-hearing individuals, would establish a Deaf Studies pro-gram. This is partially due to the fact that Deaf Studies was already taught across the curriculum at Gallaudet University and partially due to resistance within Gallaudet Uni-versity, for fear that such a program would foment resistance and activism. In any event, the solidification of a department was an important moment in the field's history, as was the formation of its graduate program in 2002.[33]

Despite there being no program in the 1980s, Gallaudet was an important site for Deaf activism. No event galvanized the Deaf world as much as the Deaf President Now (DPN) movement at Gallaudet University in 1988 when students, faculty, staff, and community members shut down the university in protest of the hiring of a hearing president. The protest seized international media attention and led to a new visibility of the Deaf world as a political group.[34] Deaf President Now has been referred to as the Selma and the Stonewall of the Deaf rights movement. The visibility of this protest was an impetus for the groundbreaking Americans with Disabilities Act, which followed DPN by two years.

One year after DPN, Gallaudet University sponsored the international Deaf Way conference in 1989, convening over six thousand people from more than eighty countries.[35] This festival gave way to an international Deaf art movement, known as DeVIA, or Deaf View/Image Art.[36] The 1990s then saw the first academic conferences to focus on Deaf Studies. Gallaudet sponsored the first two Deaf Studies conferences in 1991 and thereafter conferences took place every two years from 1993 to 2001.[37] While not directly referred to as Deaf Studies conferences, Gallaudet University Press Institute has sponsored several conferences on specific topics of genetics, deaf people in Hitler's Europe, Deaf life-stories, and sign language linguistics, literature, and literacy. Thirteen years after the first Deaf Way celebration, in 2002, Gallaudet University hosted Deaf Way II, which brought nearly 9,700 people from 121 countries.[38] Beginning in 2004, Utah Valley State College has taken up the biennial Deaf Studies Today conference and has published the proceedings.[39] These Deaf Studies conferences featured the majority of panels on issues of education, art, literature, anthropology, history, sociology, linguistics, and psychology.

In addition to these conferences, the number of publications within Deaf Studies has grown rapidly. Deaf Studies has grown over the past two decades with many texts focusing on the multidisciplinary aspects of the Deaf world—including Deaf cultural studies and critical theory,[40] American Deaf history,[41] international Deaf history,[42] the Holocaust and Deaf people,[43] collections of Deaf writers,[44] philosophy of signed languages,[45] and sign language literature.[46]

Not only has Deaf Studies grown in its academic output, students are lining up to take American Sign Language classes. According to an MLA survey, the number of students enrolling in ASL classes over the past five years has increased 435 percent.[47] Currently, American Sign Language is the fifth most taught language in American colleges and universities and the second most taught language in community colleges. ASL was offered for the first time in 187 universities between the years 1998 and 2002.[48] Many new ASL programs leave hundreds of students on waiting lists every semester. There is a growing, multimillion-dollar industry to learn American Sign Language and Deaf Studies.

Such growth and exposure is undoubtedly positive insofar as it increases public awareness of the Deaf world. Yet one of the great social contradictions of Deaf Studies is that while hearing individuals are being encouraged to sign in unprecedented numbers, from infancy through higher education, deaf people are being discouraged from signing, also from infancy through higher education. This contradiction—that sign languages are good for hearing people but bad for deaf people—is indicative of the historical situation of deaf people being spoken about and spoken for in the institutions designed to serve them. Even within the field of Deaf Studies, perspectives of Deaf people are often not valued. Many programs call themselves Deaf Studies but are actually based on an audiological model or are focused on deaf education and the strategies for acquiring English. The same is true for publications. The *Journal of Deaf Studies and Deaf Education* and the *Oxford Handbook of Deaf Studies, Language and Deaf Education,* for example, provide important research primarily on deaf education, but focus very little on the cultural dimensions and theoretical critiques of existing social structures. The struggle over the contents of Deaf Studies is symptomatic of larger battles over self-determination that have been a part of the critical work of Deaf Studies since its inception. The field of Deaf Studies originally developed along the model of other minority studies; yet it would be unthinkable for African American Studies or Women Studies journals to focus almost exclusively on empirical educational research. Instead, African American Studies, Women's Studies, Deaf Studies, and other allied fields critique existing social arrangements that have served to marginalize their kind; they explore the complexities of identity construction within a political context, and they celebrate what is most unique to their ways of being. As such, Deaf Studies has explored a wide spectrum of topics, many of which which fall under the more general notions of *identity, power,* and *language.*

In what follows, the reader will be provided with an overview of some of the principle discussions that have taken place in the field. Having such a background will help provide context for the discussions that take place in the following chapters.

Deaf Identity and Cultural Politics

It should come as no surprise that the concepts of identity and culture have been a central preoccupation of Deaf Studies since its inception. This focus is not unique to Deaf Studies, but to all minority studies, especially in their formative stages. Power over defining and developing identity is itself the battleground of the most important ideological battles of the past thirty years. Rewriting deaf to Deaf is about disowning an imposed medicalized identity and developing an empowered identity rooted in a community and culture of others who share similar experiences and outlooks on the world. As soon as the orthographic proclamation of "big D" Deaf was made, Deaf Studies scholars had to describe what made someone Deaf as opposed to deaf. Carol Padden was one of the earliest to ask and answer the question, "Who are *Deaf* people?"[49] "Deaf people can be born into the culture, as in the case of children of Deaf parents. They begin learning the language of their parents from birth and thus acquire *native competence* in that language."[50] This early model clearly favored those who enter the Deaf world at birth, who are themselves deaf, and, most importantly, who share the cultural values of Deaf people. These values, according to Padden, are, first and foremost, use and respect for ASL, as opposed to speech, for face-to-face communication. Deaf people also value their social and family ties within the Deaf world and they learn values of the culture through literature. Padden then makes further distinctions of the cultural boundaries of Deaf people by how difficult it is for outsiders, such as those raised orally, to assimilate to the ways of Deaf people—from eye gaze to cultural patterns of introductions and value systems.

As a means of bringing further relief to the ways of Deaf Culture, Padden distinguished the *deaf community* from *Deaf Culture.* The Deaf community "may include persons who are not themselves Deaf, but who actively support the goals of the community and work with Deaf people to achieve them" while Deaf Culture is "more closed than the deaf community."[51] With the focus on the most "native" Deaf individuals, the notion of the "center" or "core" became an important feature of cultural discourse. In *Deaf in America,* Padden and Humphries explained the distinct ways that Deaf people described their experiences as a result of being aligned toward a "different center" than hearing people, a center where sign language use and not relying on sound was the norm, not the deviation.[52] Similarly, Cokely and Baker reinforce the model of a strong Deaf center in their Venn diagram to demonstrate four attributes of being culturally Deaf—audiological deafness, use of ASL, social affiliation, and political involvement (see Figure I.1).[53] When in alignment, these attributes create a strong Deafcentric identity. This diagram was often used to describe the phenomenon of Deaf identity affiliation.

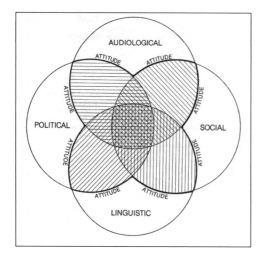

Figure I.1. Diagram of Deaf cultural identifications. Reprinted with permission from Dennis Cokely and Charlotte Baker-Shenk, *American Sign Language: A Teacher's Resource Text on Curriculum, Methods, and Evaluation* (Washington, D.C.: Gallaudet University Press, 1991), 18. Copyright 1980 by Dennis Cokely and Charlotte Baker-Shenk.

In addition to the model of a Deaf Culture, the concept of ethnicity was introduced as a means of explaining the nature of Deaf people's identities.[54] The model of ethnicity deepens the ontological connection between Deaf people and their identity. Harlan Lane adopts A. D. Smith's definition that ethnicity consists of a collective name, feeling of community, norms for behavior, distinct values, knowledge, customs, social structure, language, arts, history, and kinship in order to demonstrate the ethnic status of Deaf people.[55] Ethnicity has also been used to denote the "core" group of those who are natively Deaf. As Lawrence Fleischer writes, "Deaf Ethnicity consists of Deaf people of Deaf parents whose lives were entrenched in traditions. It can also include CODAs (Children of Deaf Adults)."[56] Along with belonging to a Deaf ethnicity come self-identification and -esteem. "The members within the Deaf Ethnicity circle feel right about themselves as Deaf people. However, the Culture group is somewhat less sure about its understanding of what it means to be Deaf. The Community is much more unsure and more diverse in its understanding. Finally, those in isolation are completely outside."[57] Such descriptions of Deaf Culture and Deaf ethnicity serve to describe that a group of people who were once considered a social group have deeper ties connected to their language, history, and traditions—a culture or ethnicity like any other in most important respects.

While the discourse of Deaf Culture and ethnicity in the 1980s and early 1990s was largely about defining Deaf as a single axis of identity, the 1990s brought about recognition of the complex relationship with the wider world. Rutherford noted that the concept of "subculture" would be more accurate if only the term would not be taken negatively, while Turner suggested the model of a Deaf "microculture" that coexists within a larger cultural world.[58] Padden noted that the 1980s discourse of Deaf Culture had begun to shift toward the "bicultural" model. "To talk of the 'bicultural' is not to talk about an additive state, to be of two cultures, but more about states of tensions. Deaf people coexist, indeed work, with hearing people in different ways today than they did thirty or forty years ago."[59] This evolving cultural identification was the impetus for MJ Bienvenu and Betty Colonomos to form The Bicultural Center in 1987, an activist organization dedicated to promote understanding of bicultural education and qualified ASL teaching and interpreting. The *Bicultural News* was published quarterly until 1994, featuring articles and opinion pieces on the politics and realities of Deaf bicultural life.

The shift from the cultural to the bicultural is indicative of the dynamic nature of identity construction. Where there was once the central focus on the right way to be Deaf, the complexities of Deaf identity could not be ignored. "The reality of the 'authentic' Deaf person is one that holds for just about any modern individual—it is an ideal. Not surprisingly, such individuals are not numerous."[60] In fact, their numbers may be shrinking since, in reality, less than 4 percent of deaf children are born to one or more deaf parent, and further, the commanding majority of deaf children are educated in mainstream schools instead of separate deaf residential schools.[61] In 1989–90, 23 percent of deaf children were educated in residential schools compared to 13.6 percent in 2003–4.[62]

Increasingly, the disconnect became more obvious between the rhetoric of an authentic Deaf identity and the reality that most people do not fit this model. The majority of Deaf people do not come from Deaf families. There are those who are Deaf of hearing families, Deaf of mixed families, hard of hearing from Deaf families, hard of hearing from hearing families, hearing of Deaf families, spouses, siblings, friends, and as many points and variations in between as befitting the astounding variety of human experiences. As Lennard Davis notes, this move toward recognition of the diversity of d/Deaf experiences parallels that of most forms of identity politics.

> The first wave of any struggle involves the establishment of the identity against societal definitions that were formed largely by oppression. In the first phase, the identity—be it blackness, or gayness, or Deafness—is hypostasized, normalized, turned positive against the negative descriptions used by the oppressive regime. In a second wave, the principals are comfortable about self-examining, finding diversity within the group, and struggling to redefine the identity in more nuanced and complex ways. Often this phase will produce conflict within a group rather than unity.[63]

Indeed, the 1990s have seen efforts at moving beyond the notion of an autonomous cultural identity to one that is more aware of the various ways of being Deaf along a complex assembly of borders as d/Deaf people will be found in every race, ethnicity, tribe, nationality, economic class, gender, sexual orientation, and geographic region.[64]

As the Deaf community is not immune to ideologies of oppression, it should come as no surprise that the first models of Deaf Culture have been critiqued as being from a default white Deaf Culture. On a cultural level, however, groups within the Deaf community have long felt the need for organizations of their own. Despite the formation of the NAD in 1880, African Americans were not admitted until 1965; despite the founding of Gallaudet University (formerly known as the National Deaf-Mute College) in 1864, African Americans were not admitted until 1951.[65] As a result of the dominant white Deaf discourse and political activism, the Rainbow Alliance of the Deaf was founded in 1977, the National Black Deaf Advocates in 1982, Deaf Women United in 1986, and the Intertribal Deaf Council in 1994.[66]

Amid the tensions of reifying a culturally Deaf identity and the recognition of diversity within the Deaf world, the question of essentialist features arises. Invariably two factors combine to form the common ground of a Deaf identity: audiological deafness and use of sign language. These two factors of identification meet in an intriquing question: Can a hearing person such as a Coda be more Deaf than a nonsigning deaf person? If so, then language use would trump audiological deafness. However, if this is the case, then how can one explain the argument for the desire of Deaf people to have deaf babies, since hearing children can become just as fluent in ASL as deaf children?[67] Initially, audiological deafness was disavowed as a factor in the Deaf world, and the word *deafness* today still carries negative connotations in the Deaf world.[68]

A recent example of the wholesale dismissal of deafness and "deaf" as the ground of identity is to refer to the "signing community." The British Deaf Association now calls itself the *Signing Community* followed by the smaller "British Deaf Association" underneath.[69] By shifting the focus to sign language use, this move makes clear distinctions between oral deaf and signing Deaf. Ironically, this move opens the cultural borders to hearing signers who participate in the community. For some, this undermines the nature of the Deaf community, but for others, the notion of "signing community" depathologizes deafness by removing it from the equation of identity, focusing instead on language use.

A similar move had been made in defining Deaf people as "visual people." Ever since George Veditz referred to deaf people "as first and foremost and for all time, people of the eye,"[70] Deaf people have been referring to themselves through visual metaphors. Ben Bahan wonders about referring to Deaf people as "seeing people,"[71] and in his contribution to this volume he further explores the visual orientations unique to Deaf ways of being. Like the notion of "signing community," "visual people" focuses on the plenitude of Deaf experience rather than on auditory lack. Critics, however, note that such a label effectively dismisses Deaf-Blind people from the community and does little to distinguish Deaf people from sighted hearing people insofar as they all share the sense of vision. Clearly differences exist in Deaf and hearing vision—as pointed out in Bahan's chapter in this volume—but no consensus exists to adopt the visual label as the essential defining character of Deaf identity.

In addition to these constructions, Paddy Ladd's concept of *Deafhood* appears to be gaining wide usage in the Deaf community as witnessed through Web sites and vlogs (video blogs).[72] Ladd writes, "Deafhood is not seen as a finite state but as a process by which Deaf individuals come to actualize their Deaf identity, positing that those individuals construct that identity around several differently ordered sets of priorities and principles, which are affected by various factors such as nation, era and class."[73] Further explanation of Deafhood in historical perspective is presented in Ladd's contribution to this volume.

These newer conceptualizations of Deaf identity seek to find ways to avert the dead end of identity politics and instead forge a broad construction that encompasses the myriad ways of being d/Deaf, yet while maintaining some critical features that distinguish the existential state of being Deaf from other identities. Addressing the complexities of Deaf identity construction, Guy McIlroy proposes the term "DeaF" where the capitalized F indicates a *fluidity* of identities, not essentially rooted in either Deaf or hearing worlds, but in the cultural agility that "handles the interface/tension between both worlds."[74] The DeaF position is to be aspired to where one's identity is bilingually and biculturally fluid and fluent.

From *deaf and dumb* to *DeaF*, intense battles have been fought, not only over the power to name oneself, but over what sort of self should be named. Each label is a specific lens ground through the heated debates over the meaning of bodily difference within a context of unequal power-relations. Deaf Studies has provided a field in which these debates may be discussed and debated; it has also brought these concerns from the peripheries of social concern directly into the discourse of civil and human rights. *Open Your Eyes* features several chapters that discuss the myriad ways that people are Deaf, as well as the profound impact that oppression—in this case, audism—has on the lives of Deaf individuals. As audism is a new concept for many, some background information will be helpful for those listening to Deaf Studies talking.

Power: Audism and the Critique of Normalcy

Before there was *racism,* there was racism; before the word there was the practice.[75] Yet, after the word was coined, it has become a powerful tool to collect the diverse practices of oppression and compress them into a single lens through which we can see just how deeply racism structures societal arrangements and identities. While the concept and word *racism* has shaped how we see the world, the discriminatory treatment of deaf individuals throughout history had no name until 1975 when Tom Humphries coined the term *audism,* based on the Latin *audire,* meaning "to hear." In his original article, Humphries defined audism as "the notion that one is superior based on one's ability to hear or behave in the manner of one who hears."[76] Despite the usefulness of having a name for oppression, Humphries did not publish his article on audism, and the word remained dormant throughout the 1980s, despite the explosion of Deaf activism. It was not until Harlan Lane's 1992 *The Mask of Benevolence* that *audism* gained further definition and usage. Lane discussed the systemic nature of audism, defining it as "the corporate institution for dealing with deaf people, dealing with them by making statements about them, authorizing views of them, describing them, teaching about them, governing where they go to school and, in some cases, where they live; in short, audism is the hearing way of dominating, restructuring, and exercising authority over the deaf community."[77] Thanks to Lane's development of the concept, awareness of audism began to spread through the 1990s. A few years later, Lennard Davis alerted readers to pay attention to the "audist assumptions that readers tend to make about texts. The conflict may not be between a conception of language as oral versus written. Rather these assumptions of Western culture may be related to the originary point of language—the mouth or the hand—and the receptive point of language—the ear or the eye."[78] As such, audism influences some of the most fundamental orientations that humans have toward language and textuality—so fundamental that they go undetected. Davis's discussion of audism as an ideological orientation would be discussed further in the twenty-first century as Bauman discussed the roots of audism in the metaphysical orientation of phonocentrism that conflates a full human identity with speech.[79] Given audism's presence on individual, institutional, and ideological levels, Deaf individuals cannot help but internalize aspects of oppression, a phenomenon Genie Gertz labels "dysconscious audism."[80] Lindsay Dunn also explores the effects of audism on identity construction, likening it to the impacts of racism.[81] Despite these academic discussions of audism, the word did not enter Deaf cultural consciousness until the first decade of the twenty-first century, thanks in part to the documentary film *Audism Unveiled.*[82]

The dynamics of audism principally take the form of colonial relations. Ladd and Lane have both explored parallels between colonization and the Deaf experience, through the eradication of indigenous language, education, values, and history.[83] The claim of a hearing-colonialist regime may seem extreme on the outset, but once the history of deaf people comes to light, we see that it is bound up in the historical practices of normalization, and thus linked with institutional practices of ableism, racism, and sexism. The same scientific apparatus that "proved" the hysterical nature of women and the intellectual inferiority of African Americans also proved the deleterious effects of allowing deaf people to congregate, mate, and spread the use of manual languages. There is perhaps no more telling example of audism than the targeting of deaf people in the Holocaust.[84] For some the atrocities of the Holocaust are of a different era, and deaf people are no longer threatened by forces of genocide. However, it is revealing that while the German government has paid restitution to Jewish families of persons persecuted in the Holocaust, it refuses to pay restitution to deaf individuals who were sterilized because it is still considered justified to sterilize deaf and disabled people.[85]

While the critique of the eugenics movement can be chalked up to the "history of a bad idea" as one scholar puts it,[86] the ideology remains intact despite different labels, what Black refers to as "newgenics."[87] The question of what lives are worth living is now answered in doctors' offices instead of in the Nazi's T-4 program. Currently, parents have the option of aborting their fetus based on amniocentesis results indicating deafness and many other disabilities.[88] The forces of normalization seem to be gaining ground, particularly in cases like Australia, where one researcher predicts the death of Australian Sign Language (Auslan) within the next few generations due to high rates of mainstreaming, cochlear implantation, and genetic testing and counseling that discourages parents from carrying deaf babies to birth.[89] With whole signing communities in danger, the stakes over medical versus cultural models of Deaf people are quite high and are being waged over the ideological terrain of normalcy, oppression, disability, identity, and culture.

Being on the defensive, however, is nothing new to Deaf people. From Desloges to

Veditz to the formation of Deaf Studies, Deaf people have been defending the right to use sign language, the right to intermarry, and the right not to be subjected to medical and religious cures, the right simply to be left alone. Yet, increasing numbers of parents opt for surgical cures to deafness. The argument of cultural genocide, however, often falls on deaf ears. While Deaf Studies has proven the existence of Deaf Culture, the cultural argument is often not enough to convince hearing doctors and parents to cease their endless search for a cure. Why should society want to keep and promote Deaf people? What good are Deaf people to society? What good are deaf children to a family? These difficult questions must now be explored if the Deaf world is to continue in the face of biopower institutions intent on the eradication of the Deaf community. In addition to arguments on the grounds of cultural defense, arguments about the need for cultural, cognitive, and linguistic diversity need to be developed. How would the world be affected negatively by the loss of Deaf communities? What do Deaf communities teach us about epistemology, about reading the visual/tactile world, about literature, about the human capacity for language?

This last question has received the majority of research attention over the last forty years as research on sign language has brought about a paradigm shift in human understanding of our capacity for language—not just for deaf people but for the very nature of language—its origins, acquisition, and neurological basis. The following is a brief background on the role that language has played in Deaf Studies since its inception, so that readers may listen in to what Deaf Studies has been talking about for the last few decades.

Language

Along with *identity* and *power, language* is a key concept in Deaf Studies, perhaps *the* key concept as it was the revelation of the linguistic nature of sign languages that opened the way for Deaf Studies to enter the public discourse within wider civil rights and cultural studies movements. Though others before William Stokoe have asserted the linguistic status of sign languages,[90] Stokoe was the first to validate that signs, like spoken words, could be broken down into smaller parts, which he initially referred to as *cheremes* to distinguish them from their spoken counterparts, phonemes.[91] Linguists, however, opted instead to expand the meanings of *phonology* beyond sound-based units to include the visual/kinetic/tactile units of signs, which include particular handshapes, movements, movement paths, palm orientations, and nonmanual markers.[92] Once these sign parts were documented and observed, sign languages were seen, like all other human languages, to be complex systems operating according to an intricately governed structure.

When Stokoe proposed the linguistic nature of signed languages, the idea was so radical that even native Deaf signers thought it preposterous. Yet, the weight and clarity of his vision soon caught on, and Stokoe's Linguistics Research Laboratory (established 1971) at Gallaudet University became the epicenter of a paradigm shift in the understanding of human language.[93] Soon after, Stokoe formed the journal *Sign Language Studies,* which began to collect the first articles on a wide variety of topics regarding sign languages.[94] In addition to the East Coast work on signed languages, Ursula Bellugi formed the Laboratory for Cognitive Neuroscience in 1970 at the Salk Institute in California where she and colleagues began exploring the neurological underpinnings of sign language to find out, as the title of her book with Howard Poizner and Edward Klima puts it, *What the Hands Reveal about the Brain*.[95] From these two centers of exploration, collections of articles followed, and a growing body of literature began to form by the late 1970s and early 1980s.[96]

One of the early tasks of early sign linguistics was to dispel centuries of misunderstandings regarding sign languages.[97] Principle among these misunderstandings is that sign language answers the historic yearning for a pre-Babel era of a universal language. Sign languages, however, are as diverse as spoken language, with migration patterns all their own. Though Deaf Americans and Deaf Britons live in English-speaking societies, their sign languages—ASL and British Sign Language (BSL)—are mutually unintelligible; in fact, fingerspelling English words to each other would only deepen miscommunication as BSL and ASL use completely different manual alphabets (BSL uses a two-handed alphabet while ASL uses a single-handed one). An ASL user would instead be more likely to recognize some aspects of French Sign Language (LSF) due to the particular historical circumstances that brought a French Deaf man and his language to the United States to help establish American deaf education.[98]

Though not the case in America, sign language migration often follows colonial rule. Australian Sign Language (Auslan) and New Zealand Sign Language (NZSL), for example, have both evolved from the original importation of BSL. However, in other instances, sign languages from developed countries, such as ASL, are often imported through missionaries, educators, and development projects rather than through political rule. This explains why sign languages in the Philippines, Costa Rica, Thailand, and Nigeria are deeply influenced by American Sign Language, although there has been no overt American government installed in these countries.[99] The importation of ASL at the expense of local sign languages creates conflicts in countries that are all too familiar with linguistic colonialism. In the Western African nations of Burkina Faso and Benin, hearing educators insist on using ASL signs while mouthing French words. Not only does this make for a dubious language-learning practice for students, it is a dramatic example of the ways that neocolonialism and global power continue to discipline the bodies and minds of a nation's youth.

The growing dominance of ASL, though, is being countered with movements to recognize and encourage the growth of local sign languages.[100] We cannot be precisely sure how many local and national sign languages exist in the world. In Thailand and Viet Nam alone there are at least seven different sign languages, each developing for historically and geographically specific reasons.[101] Iranian Deaf use the Tea House Sign Language and Persian Sign Language,[102] and Canada has both American Sign Language and Quebecois Sign Language (LSQ). A map of all the sign languages in the world would most likely have to also include sign languages and sign communication systems of indigenous people. The Australian Aboriginal Sign Language has over thirteen different dialects, while North America has been home to various incarnations of manual languages and communication systems as well.[103]

It should now be clear: sign languages do not form a single, reductive brand of Esperanto. This point needs to be made explicit, for even language experts such as those who edit the Modern Language Association Bibliography categorized sign languages as "Invented Languages" next to Klingon and Esperanto as recently as 1996. While the MLA has since recategorized sign languages on par with other natural human languages, the fact that those allegedly most knowledgeable about languages were so unknowledgeable means that there remains much explaining to do.

Another means of setting the record straight is to compare natural sign languages of Deaf communities with intentionally contrived communication systems. While there is no single, universal sign language, there is, however, a system of International Sign used in international deaf gatherings.[104] The system of International Signs is a pidgin language formed through a lexicon used in the contact of several languages, especially taking advantage of a visual, iconic logic inherent in signed languages.[105] While Deaf people have guided the formation and uses of International Sign, they have largely resisted artificially constructed manual codes for spoken languages, such as forms of Manually Coded English (MCE).[106] Ever since the inception of formalized deaf education, teachers like the Abbe de l'Epee sought to transform the sign language into a manual version of spoken language, replete with articles and verb conjugations. The cognitive disconnect between the properties of a natural sign language and these systems provides clear testimony to the widely divergent grammatical logic required of a visual as opposed to a spoken language.

The differences between speech and sign are also magnified through the practice of Simultaneous Communication (referred to as SimCom) where one speaks and signs at the same time. This popular educational practice is akin to producing divergent languages, say Navajo and English, simultaneously. Clearly the accuracy and integrity of each language is nearly impossible to maintain, and given the heavy presence of the voice in the phonocentric loop of hearing oneself speak, the speaker is often under the illusion that she is communicating. SimCom, more often than not, produces signs that are misshapen, misplaced, or missing altogether.

These communication practices, which may have been developed with the most benevolent of intentions, often result in diminished communication between teacher and students. Seeing the need for the use of a fully developed and intelligible language in the classroom, educators and activists called for a revolution in deaf education, toward a bilingual model that would use ASL and written English. The 1980s saw the first bilingual programs founded along with curriculum developments.[107] The fight for bilingual education has been central to Deaf activism from the 1980s to the present. Despite the long-standing recognition of the linguistic status of ASL, many state residential schools do not consider themselves bilingual/bicultural programs. Protests continue to call attention to the need for bilingual education for deaf children.[108] In addition to incorporating ASL into the K-12 classroom for deaf children, activists and scholars have called for the recognition of ASL as a foreign language in American colleges and universities, where considerable headway has been made, making ASL the fifth most taught language in American higher education.[109]

By the 1990s, the case for the linguistic status of sign language had long been made.

The implications of sign language research began to extend beyond educational policies to encompass the fundamental questions of human identity and language-making capacity. Old questions could be asked in new ways, such as the eternally perplexing problem of the origin of language. Though it was a widely debated topic during the late eighteenth century, the Linguistic Society of Paris banned discussion of language origins in 1866, claiming that no evidence could be found to prove any one point of view.[110] The emergence of sign language linguistics, however, began to shed new light on this age-old problem. The hand, it seems, must have been present in order for signs to be linked with the world. How else could the link between sound and the world be forged? "Visible human movements," writes Stokoe, "are not merely sufficient for language but were absolutely necessary for making that first solid connection between sign and meaning."[111] If this is the case, then the implications of manual languages extend beyond—but never lose sight of—the Deaf community, to reach into the very core of our humanity.

The study of sign language also afforded researchers the rare opportunity to study just how languages are born and evolve. The founding of a deaf school in Nicaragua and the discovery of an emerging signing community using the Al-Sayyid Bedouin Sign Language in the Negev desert have allowed researchers to witness the emergence of a new language and to study its evolution in the first generations of use.[112] On another scale, researchers have redefined our understanding of the neurological basis of language. As noted earlier, we now know that language processing is not dependent on sound, but rather on deeper neuronal patterning, whether triggered by sight or sound or touch. Without the emergence of sign language studies, these insights would not have been revealed to us with such clarity.

The insights into the nature of human languages revealed by sign language studies and Deaf Studies have led to a popularity of sign language not experienced since the end of the eighteenth century. Ironically, while hearing individuals become enamored with the aesthetic and cognitive benefits of signing, deaf children are systematically denied access to sign language, creating the strange message that sign language is good for hearing people but bad for deaf. As William Stokoe notes, increased knowledge of ASL should directly affect deaf children: "The status of deaf people, their education, their opportunities in life, and the utilization of their potential—all these could be much enhanced if we understood that the way deaf people still make language may be the way the whole human race became human."[113]

While the epicenter of the cultural and linguistic revolutions brought about by Deaf Studies was in the field of linguistics, it was soon felt in the fields of literature and literacy. A growing body of criticism has developed around sign language literature, exploring its poetics, genres, and the ways sign literature challenges fundamental notions of literature and textuality.[114] Similarly, traditional definitions of literacy are being challenged from Deaf Studies, as can be found in Marlon Kuntz's chapter in this volume, "Turning Literacy Inside Out." So entrenched are conceptions of literacy based in reading and writing phonetic languages that Deaf Studies scholars and sign language linguists have much work ahead.

These prove to be exciting years as increased opportunities to publish sign language on the Web will broadcast sign languages as never before, something akin to advancements of the printing press and the dissemination of print.[115] American Sign Language literacy will rise with increased publication of academic ASL, replete with standardized citation format. Sign language publishing will continue the tradition since the initial writings of Desloges—of defending sign language and educating the public about the Deaf world. Only now, Deaf Studies may begin to publish bilingual texts where the Deaf-mute voice—the voice of sign language—may be listened to with wide open eyes, loud and clear.

For the time being, though, the voices of Deaf Studies scholars are speaking through print in this volume. With the background presented here, readers may now tune in and listen to the wide array of voices presented in *Open Your Eyes*. Below is a synopsis of the book's sections and chapters.

Open Your Eyes: Deaf Studies Talking

The first section, Framing Deaf Studies, features three articles that reflect on the state of Deaf Studies, putting the field into perspective. Humphries begins with a reflective essay on the past forty years of "talking culture" in Deaf Studies—of connecting "deaf peoples all over the world to the notion of 'culture.'" This talking culture involved the search for a public voice. Humphries reflects on what was said about culture, the anxiety of having to prove a culture. Yet, Humphries notes, "Before we talked culture, culture talked. Without mentioning the word 'culture,' Deaf people have historically maintained a discourse that was about themselves, their lives, their beliefs, their interpretation of the world, their needs, and their dreams." Humphries advocates that Deaf Studies scholars need "to achieve a balance between the rhetoric of talking culture that too often seeks to 'prove' something and talking culture that is about the circulation and acceleration of culture. . . . Put simply, we need to move on from 'How are we different?' to 'How are we being?'" Humphries's distinction is borne out through the book. Many of the articles engage in listening to "culture talking" and then draw out the implications that such "talk" has on ways of being human.

What Tom Humphries refers to as getting back to "culture talking" Paddy Ladd refers to in his chapter, "Colonialism and Resistance: A Brief History of Deafhood," as a "second phase" of Deaf Studies: "We now face the challenge of bringing about the second phase, to search for more explicit Deaf epistemologies and ontologies that can frame these developments in a more holistic way, so that Deaf Studies can become a more conscious model for Deaf-centered praxis." Ladd conducts this search, beginning with the lofty and proud rhetoric of nineteenth-century French Deaf Banquets, and then through the colonialist assault of oralism in twentieth-century England, and finally to the "Deaf Resurgence," the coming to a greater activist and liberatory engagement evident in Deaf Studies. This is a story about the way that the culture has talked and has searched for a "Deafhood" that Ladd defines as the existential state of Deaf "being-in-the-world."

Like Tom Humphries and Paddy Ladd, Frank Bechter's chapter, "The Deaf Convert Culture and Its Lessons for Deaf Theory," advocates a full-hearted listening to Deaf Culture talking—and he does so through two genres of traditional ASL storytelling. Bechter suggests that such talking through indigenous cultural forms is the very voice that is most transformative. Deaf Studies needs not to prove that it is a culture like any other, but to argue for what is most unique and instructive about this culture and its language. "Standing on the public stage is not enough," Bechter writes. "For deaf life truly to be heard there (for a subaltern voice truly 'to speak' and no longer be subaltern), the very terms of discourse on that stage—its very 'alphabet'—would need to be transformed. Deaf Studies should strive to be a producer of theory, rather than a consumer of it—to penetrate contemporary discourse at its fundamentals, in both content and form."

Together, these three articles call for a deeper listening to Deaf Culture talking—to its internal and indigenous ways of being that are themselves powerful means of "speaking out" with a Deaf public voice that speaks on its own terms.

The following section, Deaf Perception and Community, carries out Ladd's search for Deaf epistemologies as it examines the visual orientation of the Deaf world and its impact on the formation of Deaf communities, leading to the larger question of the relation of sensory perception and community affiliation. Long before they ever called themselves a culture, Deaf people referred to themselves as "people of the eye." The notion of visual plenitude has always stood in contrast to audiological lack. Ben Bahan's chapter, "Upon the Formation of a Visual Variety of the Human Race," is the first time the various perspectives of Deaf visual-culture talking have been assembled into a single story. Bahan takes an interdisciplinary approach to Deaf visual practices through sign language linguistics, storytelling, pedagogy, cognition, proxemics, art, and literature. Through this interdisciplinary inquiry, we see how the Deaf world pushes the boundaries of vision beyond other cultural groups.

If, as Bahan suggests, vision is a primary dimension of being in the Deaf world, then this way of being would logically transcend national and linguistic boundaries, opening the possibility for a transnational affiliation based on common ways of perception and experience. As Joseph Murray writes, Deaf people have historically "shared a common experience of living as members of a visual community in an auditory world, an experience transcending local contexts and national boundaries." In his chapter, "Co-equality and Transnational Studies: Understanding Deaf Lives," Joseph Murray listens to another aspect of Deaf cultural talking—the talking that took place over the centuries between Deaf individuals from across the Atlantic. By moving beyond the nation-state narrative, Deaf Studies may better see the bonds that draw Deaf people together—to see what is most Deaf about being Deaf.

Hilde Haualand's essay, "Sound and Belonging: What Is a Community?" turns the gaze in the opposite direction: toward the deeply influential role that sound has played in dominant constructions of belonging and community. Haualand describes how the physical properties of sound and light operate differently and thus disclose a different sensory grasp and metaphysical relation with the world. The perceived bond between sound and being may have profound cultural, linguistic, and cognitive consequences. "Confusing language with speech," Haualand writes, "may thus be a consequence of the metaphysics of sound." Such an approach marks a new direction for Deaf Studies that would parallel the turns in Black Studies to investigate the constructions of whiteness or in Women's Studies the construction of masculinity. Now, the notion of *hearing* can be placed in relief through the perspective of a Deaf anthropologist for its difference.

When read together, this section advances previously described notions of Deaf Culture by delving into Deaf epistemological orientations as a formative element in community affiliation, which adds new insights into the relations of sensory perception, embodiment, and cultural formation.[116]

The following section, Language and Literacy, extends the previous section's critique of dominant ideas regarding vision, community, and language. While Deaf Studies has long discussed language as the fundamental cultural marker, this section expands the discourse on language to examine the fundamental construction of *language* in the Western tradition, and therefore of *literacy*. In his chapter, "On the Disconstruction of (Sign) Language in the Western Tradition: A Deaf Reading of Plato's *Cratylus*," Bauman critiques the *disconstruction of language;* that is, the notion that categories of *language, being, nature,* and *human identity* have been constructed within a fundamental oversight: the inability to see language in all its modes. Bauman explores one of the West's earliest and most influential oversights in Plato's *Cratylus,* the only Socratic dialogue to focus on the question of names and language. When read through a Deaf Studies lens, the contradictions in the *Cratylus* become magnified and the implications on Western thought and the denigration of signed languages made explicit.

If the encompassing category of language has been *dis*constructed, then the implications ripple outward, touching all other aspects of language—including literature and literacy. While the implications of sign literature have been explored elsewhere,[117] the concept of literacy remains entrenched in the common wisdom of meaning "reading and writing." In this volume, Marlon Kuntze calls for "portraying literacy in a radically new way." Kuntze illustrates how the essentialized connection between writing and literacy ignores the broader relation of language and cognition in the manual mode that produces characteristics of literate thought. Kuntze shows how studying ways that deaf children acquire the properties of literate thought provides a strong argument for renovating literacy's basic definition. This call exemplifies what Frank Bechter calls for in Deaf Studies, "to penetrate contemporary discourse at its fundamentals, in both content and form."

One of the difficulties, however, of arguing for literacy in sign language is the paucity of texts. Lawrence Fleischer's "Critical Pedagogy and ASL Videobooks" addresses this problem through a case study of one project that sought to create hundreds of ASL texts for children to "read." Through Fleischer's argument, we see a case study of the hegemony of English, even within attempts to create texts in ASL. Fleischer shares his correspondence with the Director for the Clearinghouse for Specialized Media and Technology under the auspices of the Department of Education that coordinates the "ASL Videobooks" project with the California School for the Deaf, Riverside (CSDR). As Fleischer notes, such a project has enormous potential for an engaged critical pedagogy, yet the result is a reinscription of dominant notions of literacy and textuality. Allowing us to listen in on this case study affords us insight into a continuum of disconstruction that has been traced in this section—from the Western disconstruction of language in an important text in the fifth century BC, to a rethinking of literacy, to a specific instance where change was attempted. The long arm of speech does not let go of its grasp easily.

As these discussions on visual language and communities show, the critiques of

Deaf Studies work to redraw previously drawn borders, widening them to include the broad and more complex ways that being human is illuminated through Deaf lives and a Deaf lens. While Deaf Studies expands the boundaries of the hearing world's categories, it encounters a complex set of its own. The next section, Places and Borders, inquires into these internal borders—from the physical and cultural boundaries of Deaf places to the boundaries around and between the wide variety of d/Deaf identities. The issues of where to draw the line are complicated for any minority group, yet perhaps even more difficult for the Deaf world as there is no indigenous homeland, no territorial boundaries to circumscribe "a people." However, the visual ways of being and the visual language of the Deaf world discussed in the previous two sections have emerged in bastions of educational institutions and Deaf clubs throughout America since the nineteenth century. Despite their longevity, these spaces are rapidly decreasing. Fewer than 10 percent of deaf children now attend residential schools and Deaf clubs are closing all around the country. In her essay, "The Decline of Deaf Clubs in the United States: A Treatise on the Problem of Place," Carol Padden suggests that the clubs' demise is due to larger shifts in the economic structure of the Deaf community, the rise of a professional Deaf class, and a recognition of the diversity of Deaf identities. "The story about American Deaf clubs should be told as a narrative about how Deaf people's work lives changed, and how their relationships with each other changed, introducing new tensions of class, race, gender, and ethnicity, in the end rendering the Deaf club irrelevant to the new social realities." Through Padden's essay we can see the broad cultural shift in the Deaf world and a new dispersal of Deaf cultural life, where attachment to place is temporary and nomadic. This problem of a physical place is now a question of shifting borders in a postmodern world.

Brenda Brueggemann's essay, "Think-Between: A Deaf Studies Commonplace Book," extends Padden's discussion of the relation of place and identity, only she engages in a very different type of "place"—that is, the metaphorical notion of the place *between* allegedly fixed identities. The "Think-Between" in her title plays off of the ASL sign THINK-HEARING in which the handshape and movement of the sign HEARING is placed not on the mouth, but on the forehead, denoting a deaf person who thinks in the manner of one who hears—that is, who prefers to speak, use the phone, and take advantage of hearing ways. Brueggemann suggests that the binary thinking inherent in Deaf Studies rhetoric—that one is either hearing or deaf—would be enriched by exploring the space between the two. "What I am suggesting," Brueggemann writes, "is that we might begin in Deaf Studies to push beyond the mere recitation of the 'd/Deaf' pledge in our footnotes and to explore, instead, all the rhetorical situations that arise from the d/D distinctions, that bring the distinctions to bear, and that, most importantly, keep shifting them like an identity kaleidoscope in our own hands." In her "commonplace book" Brueggemann notes a series of rhetorical situations in which it would behoove Deaf Studies to "think between" the rhetorical positions of Deaf and hearing.

Robert Hoffmeister's chapter, "Border Crossings by Hearing Children of Deaf Parents: The Lost History of Codas," explores just such a "between" space described by Brueggemann. Children of Deaf parents grow up straddling a myriad of borders, as they are often culturally Deaf but physiologically hearing, creating the odd circumstance in which they may be "more Deaf" than some people who cannot hear at all. Hoffmeister examines the multifaceted situation of Codas whose identities are created along a constant negotiation of physiological and cultural borders. The insights into the particular positionalities of Codas offer a new set of angles from which to view Deaf and hearing cultural and political lives.

Taken together, these three chapters illustrate the complexities involved in the Deaf world in its search for a place and in defense of an identity they are frequently taught to disavow. Yet the act of drawing boundaries is no simple task and perhaps in this difficulty we gain insights into the complexities of identity formation.

The following section, Intersections and Identities, extends the discussion of borders and Deaf identity politics by looking at Deaf identity within the context of audism. It also seeks to move beyond the discussion of Deaf identity as a single axis of identity, and seek a more complex notion of identity as being always formed at the nexus of multiple intersections.

In her chapter, "Dysconscious Audism: A Theoretical Proposition," Genie Gertz builds on the notion of Joyce King's "Dysconscious Racism" that implies the internalization of oppression that impedes one's critical consciousness that detects and critiques the systemic nature of oppression. Gertz listens to Deaf Culture talking through the narratives of Deaf individuals from Deaf families to explore just how deeply embedded audist ideologies may be in the allegedly "most Deaf" individuals. She focuses on these individuals' perceptions of language and finds that there are a host of conflicting views, some of which reveal the presence of dysconscious audism.

Lindsay Dunn's chapter, "The Burden of Racism and Audism," also explores the impact of institutionalized oppression on the creation of privilege and identity formation. Dunn engages in a dialogue about the twin circumstances of racism and audism, confronting such issues as the social pressures to conform to white standards and hearing standards. Dunn muses, for example, on whether hair straightening, melanin treatment, and cochlear implants could have similar sources in the social arrangement of power and normalcy. Dunn then draws parallels between theories of Black Identity Development and Deaf Identity Development, providing a sense of just how pervasive institutional oppression can be. By placing audism and racism in the same dialogue, Dunn reminds us that discrimination follows similar patterns though it may be focused on particular identities.

Arlene Kelly's chapter, "Where is Deaf HERstory?" takes a critical look at Deaf Studies' elision of feminist perspectives. Kelly's call for a more gendered Deaf Studies signifies an important moment in the field that, like other areas of identity politics, realizes the exclusions that take place when movements coalesce around a single identity. Identities, however, do not come in singular packages: no one can be exclusively Deaf, but is always Deaf *and* a complex host of other identities including one's gender, race, class, ethnicity, ability, and so on. Looking at Deaf Studies through a feminist lens, Kelly draws attention to the notion of the "feminist standpoint epistemology" and asks whether there is a Deaf standpoint and further, a Deaf feminist standpoint.

Similarly, MJ Bienvenu illustrates the particular positions that Deaf and Queer people face—issues of dueling identities, allegiances, and cultures. Bienvenu listens to the culture talking that has taken place at the cultural intersection of Queer and Deaf over the past thirty years. Often there have been collisions between competing agendas and pathologized identities—homophobia within the Deaf community and audism within the Queer community. Bienvenu critiques the mindset that attempts to hierarchize identities (Are you Deaf first or a Lesbian first?). There have been improvements and advances made as each identity gains greater public acceptance. Bienvenu looks at these changes through language use and the negotiations of the intersections at social and political gatherings of either affiliation. Taken together, this section adds to the growing discourse about the inherent diversity of the Deaf world.

The final section of the book, The Question of Disability, addresses the politics of the disability label and identification in Deaf Studies. Deaf Studies began in the first place largely as a disavowal of the disability label. Deaf individuals have traditionally sought to distance themselves from the notion of disability. In their efforts to demonstrate their lack of disability, they have shown how other persons with disabilities do not share a common language and culture. Historically, this lumping together has created profound misunderstandings, especially in the early years of the inclusion movement, with the notion of integration into the "least restrictive environment." While early disability movements sought greater inclusion, Deaf advocates wanted greater seclusion; this set up a difficult agenda between Deaf and disability agendas. For many deaf people, the residential school is the "least restrictive environment" where access is in a visual language and their peers share the same language, rather than being in a mainstream school where their interaction is mediated through an interpreter, which often restricts their social and extracurricular activities. With different agendas, Deaf and disability communities have had a contentious relationship, though they do share similar forms of oppression. The chapters in this section debate the implications of either dismissing or accepting the disability label.

Harlan Lane explores the social construction of disability at length in his essay, "Do Deaf People Have a Disability?" Lane answers the title's question by noting that the question ultimately does not make sense, for a disability is not something to have but a label one acquires. The question then becomes whether or not Deaf people should openly acquire and accept this label. Lane proceeds to make the case for rejecting the disability label, noting that *culture,* like *disability,* is also a social construction and that Deaf people may have more power to construct the meanings of "Deaf" in cultural ways precisely by rejecting the disability label. To accept the disability label would be a great detriment, as it, among other things, "encourages the technologies of normalization in their eugenic and surgical programs aimed at eliminating or severely reducing the ranks of culturally Deaf people." Clearly, no culture wants to intentionally hasten its demise.

Doug Baynton's chapter, "Beyond Culture: Deaf Studies and the Deaf Body," begins by noting that the "existence of a deep, rich, and longstanding culture of American Deaf people is now beyond reasonable dispute"; however, he argues that "the concept of Deaf culture increasingly appears inadequate by itself as an explanation of the Deaf community and the experiences of Deaf people." Unlike other cultures, Baynton notes that Deaf people align themselves along sensory differences (i.e., as people of the eye); they form unusually strong transnational bonds and exhibit wholly unique enculturation patterns. Baynton agrees with Lane that the medical model of disability is an inappropriate label for Deaf people, and he goes on to note that it is also precisely this model that disability studies and activists also reject. The social model of disability, on the other hand, "is entirely compatible with an understanding of Deaf people as a cultural minority group and, as a complement to the cultural model, accounts for much about Deaf experience that the cultural model cannot." Together, Baynton argues, Deaf Studies would have a more accurate description of the unique phenomenon of living lives in d/Deaf bodies.

In "Postdeafness," Lennard Davis critiques Deaf identity politics by asking why Deaf people would want to tie themselves to an increasingly suspect model of identity based on cultural ethnicity. "The very idea of a singular, unproblematic identity is crumbling. . . . So, given these complexities and attacks on identity, why should Deaf people now choose to see themselves as fitting into the kind of identity politics now being reexamined by society at large?" Counter to Lane's position, Davis notes that clinging to the ethnic model of Deaf identity may actually be complicit in a labeling practice with negative effects. "The ethnic argument sets up a model of the true or 'pure' Deaf person, in imitation of the worst aspects of racially defining a people." In an age where we have witnessed the deleterious effects of a politics based on ethnic purity—think Darfur, Uganda, Rwanda, Bosnia, Serbia—any celebration of the ethnic basis of Deaf identity needs greater scrutiny. "A better course for Deaf Studies would be to examine the situation in identity politics now, learn from the past, think about the beyond-identity issues floating in the public sphere, come up with flexible and nonhierarchical models of being, and lead the way out of the dead end of identity thinking."

This volume of essays then concludes with an editor's postscript that reflects on the issues circulating throughout this volume—identity, power, language, and the struggle for a Deaf public voice—as they played out in the Gallaudet University protests of 2006. As many of the contributors to this volume were involved in the protest—on both sides and in the middle—it thus seems only fitting that a postscript be added to clarify the context and consequences of the protest that garnered widespread media attention.

Conclusion

As these chapters demonstrate, the meanings of Deaf extend far beyond the medical notion of hearing loss, and the possibilities of Deaf Studies extend into the very reaches of how we see the world. Taken together, the essays collected in *Open Your Eyes* hope to compel readers to listen to previously marginalized voices, with wide-angle lenses that draw the peripheral out of historical blind spots and put them clearly on display. Just as sign language studies have revealed that neuronal plasticity rather than sound is the hallmark of human language, Deaf Studies and this volume hope to show that there are a great number of ways to be human, and that Deaf ways of being human are not only valid, but are worth preserving and promoting.

Notes

I would like to thank Tom Humphries, Lennard Davis, Nicole Salimbene, and Richard Morrison for their feedback on drafts of this chapter. The organization and content of this chapter evolved through ongoing discussions with Ben Bahan. I take full responsibility for the contents.

1. Alexander G. Bell, *Memoir upon the Formation of a Deaf Variety of the Human Race*, Paper presented to the National Academy of Sciences, November 13, 1883 (Washington, D.C.: National Academy of Sciences, 1885).

2. See Harlan Lane, *The Mask of Benevolence: Disabling the Deaf Community* (New York: Alfred Knopf, 1992); Douglas Baynton, *Forbidden Signs: American Culture and the Campaign against Sign Language* (Chicago: University of Chicago Press, 1996); Robert Buchanan, *Illusions of Equality: Deaf Americans in School and Factory, 1850–1950* (Washington, D.C.: Gallaudet University Press, 1999); Susan Burch, *Signs of Resistance: American Deaf Cultural History, 1900 to 1942* (New York: New York University Press, 2002).

3. This particular story is told in the documentary film *Audism Unveiled* along with several other stories of disciplining the body into a speaking, nonsigning body. *Audism Unveiled*, executive producer H-Dirksen L. Bauman, directed by Ben Bahan, H-Dirksen L. Bauman, and Facundo Montenegro (Washington, D.C.: BlackMountain Films, 2006). *Audism Unveiled* is distributed by DawnSignPress, http://www.dawnsign.com.

4. See L. A. Petitto, M. Katerelos, B. Levy, K. Gauna, K. Tétrault, and V. Ferraro, "Bilingual Signed and Spoken Language Acquisition from Birth: Implications for Mechanisms Underlying Bilingual Language Acquisition," *Journal of Child Language* 28 (2001): 453–96. See V. Penhune, R. Cismaru, R. Dorsaint-Pierre, L. A. Petitto, and R. Zatorre, "The Morphometry of Auditory Cortex in the Congenitally Deaf Measured Using MRI," *NeuroImage* 20 (2003): 1215–25.

5. Jean-Jacques Rousseau, *Essay on the Origin of Languages*, trans. John Moral and Alexander Gode (Chicago: University of Chicago Press, 1966), 10.

6. See H-Dirksen L. Bauman, "On the Disconstruction of (Sign) Language in the Western Tradition: A Deaf Reading of Plato's *Cratylus*," this volume.

7. See Baynton, *Forbidden Signs*; Lane, *Mask of Benevolence*; Nicholas Mirzeoff, *Silent Poetry: Deafness, Sign and Visual Culture in Modern France* (Princeton: Princeton University Press, 1995); Lennard Davis, *Enforcing Normalcy: Disability, Deafness, and the Body* (London: Verso, 1995).

8. Padden and Humphries, *Deaf in America*; Carol Padden and Tom Humphries, *Inside Deaf Culture* (Cambridge, Mass.: Harvard University Press, 2005).

9. Tom Humphries, "Of Deaf-mutes, the *Strange*, and the Modern Deaf Self," in *Deaf World: A Historical Reader and Primary Sourcebook*, ed. Lois Bragg (New York: New York University Press, 2001), 349 (repr. from *Culturally Affirmative Psychotherapy with Deaf Persons*, ed. Neil S. Glickman and M. Harvey [Hillsdale: Lawrence Erlbaum Associates, 1996]).

10. *The American Heritage Dictionary of the English Language*, 4th ed. (New York: Houghton Mifflin, 2000).

11. James Fernandez, "Peripheral Wisdom," in *Signifying Identities: Anthropological Perspectives on Boundaries and Constested Values* (Florence, Ky.: Routledge, 1999), 117. I originally encountered this quote in Jan-Kåre Breivik, *Deaf Identities in the Making: Local Lives, Transnational Connections* (Washington, D.C.: Gallaudet University Press, 2005).

12. Humphries, "Of Deaf-mutes," 353.

13. This beginning has been adapted from a book review: H-Dirksen L. Bauman, "A Mighty Change: An Anthology of Deaf American Writing 1816–1864 (review)," *Sign Language Studies* 2 (2002): 452–59.

14. Harlan Lane, *Wild Boy of Averyon: Foundations of Special Education* (Cambridge, Mass.: Harvard University Press, 1979); Jonathan Rée, *I See a Voice: Deafness, Language and the Senses—A Philosophical History* (London: Metropolitan Books, 1999); Sophia Rosenfeld, *A Revolution in Language: The Problem of Signs in Late Eighteenth-Century France* (Stanford: Stanford University Press, 2001).

15. M. Miles, "Signing in the Seraglio: Mutes, Dwarfs and Jestures at the Ottoman Court 1500–1700," *Disability and Society* 15 (2000): 115–34.

16. Pierre Desloges, "A Deaf Person's Observations about *An Elementary Course of Education for the Deaf*," in *The Deaf Experience: Classics in Language and Education*, ed. Harlan Lane, trans. Franklin Philip (Cambridge, Mass.: Harvard University Press, 1984), 30.

17. The Abbe de l'Epee was the founder of the first formalized school for deaf children that would become Institut Nationale des Jeunes Sourds. Most histories of deaf education assert that French Sign Language largely began at Epee's school. Desloges's account relates that sign language existed prior to the founding of the school.

18. Desloges, "Deaf Person's Observations," 36.

19. Ibid., 46.

20. Companies like BabySigns, Eensy Weensy Signers, and Signing Baby all compete for a growing market of hearing parents who want to enhance their hearing baby's cognitive and social behavior. For research on the effects of early signing, see Susan Goodwyn, Linda Acredolo, and Catherine Brown, "Impact of Symbolic Gesturing on Early Language Development," *Journal of Nonverbal Behavior* 24, no. 2 (2000): 81–103.

21. Desloges, "Deaf Person's Observations," 30–31.

22. For further reading on signing communities prior to the founding of residential schools, see Nora Ellen Groce, *Everyone Here Spoke Sign Language: Hereditary Deafness on Martha's Vineyard* (Cambridge, Mass.: Harvard University Press, 1985), and Harlan Lane, Richard Pilliard, and Mary French, "Origins of the American Deaf-World: Assimilating and Differentiating Societies and Their Relation to Genetic Patterning," *Sign Language Studies* 1 (2000): 17–44.

23. Before there was any talk of a Deaf Culture, Deaf people were referred to through the sign DEAF-WORLD. It is unclear as to when the use of the sign DEAF-WORLD came about, but it clearly dates back generations. "Deaf people in the U.S. use the sign DEAF-WORLD to refer to . . . the social network they have set up and not to any notion of geographical location." Harlan Lane, Robert Hoffmeister, and Ben Bahan, *A Journey into the Deaf-World* (San Diego: DawnSignPress, 1996), 5.

24. Benedict Anderson, *Imagined Communities: Reflections on the Origin and Spread of Nationalism* (London: Verso, 1991).

25. I thank Ben Bahan for bringing this title to my attention.

26. These films have been collected in one video: *Preservation of Sign Language: The Historical Collection* (Burtonsville, Md.: Sign Media, 1997).

27. Burch, *Signs of Resistance*.

28. Quoted in Charles Katz, "A Partial History of Deaf Studies," in *Deaf Studies VI Conference Proceedings: Making the Connection* (Washington, D.C.: College for Continuing Education, Gallaudet University, 1999), 120.

29. Ibid., 121.

30. The Linguistics Research Laboratory produced groundbreaking work in linguistics from scholars such as Carol Padden, Harry Markowicz, Robbin Battison, Charlotte Baker, Dennis Cokely, James Woodward, and Robert Johnson.

31. This program was founded by Stephen Nover and Dr. Robert Hoffmeister.

32. This program was founded by Drs. Larry Fleischer and Ray Jones.

33. The undergraduate program was founded by Dr. Yerker Andersson and the graduate program by Drs. Ben Bahan, H-Dirksen Bauman, and MJ Bienvenu.

34. Jack Gannon, *The Week the World Heard Gallaudet* (Washington, D.C.: Gallaudet University Press, 1989). Sharon Barnartt and John Christiansen, *Deaf President Now! The 1988 Revolution at Gallaudet* (Washington, D.C.: Gallaudet University Press, 1995). Gallaudet University was also the site of another protest in 2006 when the Board of Trustees announced Dr. Jane Fernandes as the ninth President of Gallaudet. Faculty, students, staff, and alumni coordinated a protest to voice their displeasure over flaws in the search process and the selection of an unpopular, though deaf, candidate.

35. Carol Erting, Robert C. Johnson, Dorothy Smith, and Bruce Snider, eds., *The Deaf Way:*

Perspectives from the International Conference on Deaf Culture (Washington, D.C.: Gallaudet University Press, 1994).

36. For more information on this Deaf art movement, see http://www.deafart.org/. Also Patricia Durr, "Deconstructing the Forced Assimilation of Deaf People via De'VIA Resistance and Affirmation Art," *Visual Anthropology Review* 15, no. 2 (1999/2000): 47–68.

37. See Paddy Ladd, "Colonialism and Resistance: A Brief History of Deafhood," this volume, for a political context for these conferences.

38. Harvey Goodstein and Laura Brown, eds., *Deaf Way II: An International Celebration* (Washington, D.C.: Gallaudet University Press, 2004).

39. *Deaf Studies Today: A Kaleidoscope of Knowledge, Learning, and Understanding,* ed. Bryan K. Eldredge, Doug Stringham, and Minnie Mae Wilding-Diaz (Orem: Utah Valley State College, 2005).

40. Padden and Humphries, *Deaf in America;* Mirzeoff, *Silent Poetry;* Owen Wrigley, *The Politics of Deafness* (Washington, D.C.: Gallaudet University Press, 1996); Davis, *Enforcing Normalcy;* Lane, Hoffmeister, and Bahan, *Journey into the Deaf-World;* Brenda Brueggemann, *Lend Me Your Ear: Rhetorical Constructions of Deafness* (Washington, D.C.: Gallaudet University Press, 1999); Jan Branson and Don Miller, *Damned for Their Difference: The Cultural Construction of Deaf People as Disabled* (Washington, D.C.: Gallaudet University Press, 2002); Paddy Ladd, *Understanding Deaf Culture: In Search of Deafhood* (Clevedon, UK: Multilingual Matters, 2003); Ila Parasnis, ed., *Cultural and Language Diversity and the Deaf Experience* (Cambridge: Cambridge University Press, 1998).

41. John Van Cleve and Barry Crouch, *A Place of Their Own: Creating the Deaf Community in America* (Washington, D.C.: Gallaudet University Press, 1989); Baynton, *Forbidden Signs;* John Van Cleve, *Deaf History Unveiled: Interpretations from the New Scholarship* (Washington, D.C.: Gallaudet University Press, 1999); Burch, *Signs of Resistance;* Buchannan, *Illusions of Equality.*

42. Renate Fischer and Harlan Lane, eds., *Looking Back: A Reader on the History of Deaf Communities and Their Sign Languages* (Hamburg: Signum Verlag, 1993).

43. Horst Biesold, *Crying Hands: Eugenics and Deaf People in Nazi Germany,* trans. Will Sayers (Washington, D.C.: Gallaudet University Press, 1999); Donna Ryan and John Schuchman, eds., *Deaf People in Hitler's Europe* (Washington, D.C.: Gallaudet University Press, 2002).

44. Christopher Krentz, ed., *A Mighty Change: Deaf American Writing, 1817–1864* (Washington, D.C.: Gallaudet University Press, 2000); Bragg, ed., *Deaf World.*

45. Rée, *I See a Voice.*

46. H-Dirksen L. Bauman, Jennifer Nelson, and Heidi Rose, eds., *Signing the Body Poetic: Essays in American Sign Language Literature* (with DVD) (Berkeley and Los Angeles: University of California Press, 2006).

47. Elizabeth B. Welles, "Foreign Language Enrollments in United States Institutions of Higher Education, Fall 2002," in *Profession 2004* (New York: Modern Language Association, 2004), 128–53. Originally published in *ADFL Bulletin* 35, nos. 2–3 (2004): 7–26 (http://www.adfl.org/resources/enrollments.pdf).

48. Ibid., 153.

49. Carol Padden, "The Deaf Community and the Culture of Deaf People," in *Sign Language and the Deaf Community,* ed. Charlotte Baker and Robbin Battison (Washington, D.C.: National Association of the Deaf, 1980), 89–104.

50. Ibid., 95.

51. Ibid., 92–93.

52. Padden and Humphries, *Deaf in America.*

53. Dennis Cokely and Charlotte Baker, *American Sign Language: A Teachers Resource Text on Curriculum, Methods, and Evaluation* (Silver Spring, Md.: T.J. Publishers, 1980), 18.

54. Carol Erting, "Language Policy and Deaf Ethnicity in the United States," *Sign Language Studies* 7 (1978): 139–52; Robert E. Johnson and Carol Erting, "Ethnicity and Socialization in a Classroom for Deaf Children," in *The Sociolinguistics of the Deaf Community,* ed. Ceil Lucas (San

Diego: Academic Press, 1989), 41–84; Amy Terstriep, "Ethnicity, Social Theory, and Deaf Culture," in *Deaf Studies III: Bridging Cultures in the 21st Century, Conference Proceedings* (Washington, D.C.: College for Continuing Education, Gallaudet University, 1993), 231–44; Davis, *Enforcing Normalcy.*

55. Harlan Lane, "Ethnicity, Ethics and the Deaf World," *Journal of Deaf Studies and Deaf Education* 10, no. 3 (2005): 291–310.

56. Lawrence Fleischer, "Communication Issues: ASL and English," in *Deaf Studies: What's Up?* trans. Arlene B. Kelly (Washington, D.C.: College for Continuing Education, Gallaudet University, 1991), 139.

57. Ibid., 140–41.

58. Susan Rutherford, "The Culture of American Deaf People," in *Academic Acceptance of American Sign Language,* ed. Sherman Wilcox (Burtonsville, Md.: Linstok Press, 1992), 21–42. Graham Turner, "*How* Is Deaf Culture? Another Perspective on a Fundamental Concept," *Sign Language Studies* 83 (1994): 103–25.

59. Carol Padden, "From the Cultural to the Bicultural: The Modern Deaf Community," in Parasnis, *Cultural and Language Diversity and the Deaf Experience,* 94–95.

60. Ibid., 87.

61. Ross Mitchell, "National Profile of Deaf and Hard of Hearing Students in Special Education from Weighted Survey Results," *American Annals of the Deaf* 149 (2004): 344.

62. Ross Mitchell and Michael Karchmer, "Demographics of Deaf Education: More Students in More Places," *American Annals of the Deaf* 151 (2006): 95–104.

63. Lennard Davis, *Bending over Backwards: Disability, Dismodernism, and Other Diffficult Positions* (New York: New York University Press, 2002), 11. I thank Chris Krentz for important discussions regarding the politics of d/Deaf identity; an e-mail posting of his reminded me of Davis's discussion of identity politics.

64. See Parasnis, *Cultural and Language Diversity and the Deaf Experience;* Leila Monaghan, Constanze Schmaling, Karen Nakamura, and Graham Turner, eds., *Many Ways to Be Deaf: International Variation in Deaf Communities* (Washington, D.C.: Gallaudet University Press, 2003).

65. See Lane, Hoffmeister, and Bahan, *Journey into the Deaf-World,* 164. Women were admitted into the NAD and Gallaudet (the Deaf-Mute College); however, they were prevented from attending soon after, in 1865. A letter-writing campaign was led by Georgianna Elliott and Angeline Fuller Fischer in 1886–87 to argue for admission for women. Fischer threatened Edward Miner Gallaudet, the President, that she would start a college for deaf women elsewhere. In response, Gallaudet admitted six women in 1887. Only one of the six actually graduated: Alto May Lowman (Maryland); Fischer, however, never enrolled. Arlene B. Kelly, personal correspondence, June 12, 2006.

66. For more information about these organizations visit National Black Deaf Advocates at http://www.nbda.org/; Deaf Women United at http://www.dwu.org/; Intertribal Deaf Council at http://www.deafnative.com/; Rainbow Alliance of the Deaf at http://www.rad.org/.

67. See H-Dirksen L. Bauman, "Designing Deaf Babies and the Question of Disability," *Journal of Deaf Studies and Deaf Education* 10, no. 3 (2005): 311–15.

68. MJ Bienvenu, "Can Deaf People Survive 'Deafness'?" in *Perspectives on Deafness: A Deaf American Monograph,* ed. Mervin Garretson (Silver Spring, Md.: National Association of the Deaf, 1991), 21–28.

69. See Sign Community at http://www.bda.org.uk/.

70. George Veditz, "President's Message," in *Proceedings of the Ninth Convention of the National Association of the Deaf and the Third World's Congress of the Deaf, 1910* (Philadelphia: Philocophus Press, 1912).

71. Ben Bahan, "Notes from a Seeing Person," in *American Deaf Culture: An Anthology,* ed. Sherman Wilcox (Silver Spring, Md.: Linstok Press, 1989), 29–32.

72. Originally developed at length in Ladd, *Understanding Deaf Culture,* the concept of Deaf-

hood has been the focus of various conferences and Web sites. For example, the Deafhood: Meeting the Challenges of a Changing World conference, London, July 12–14, 2001; see also Web sites that further explain and explore this concept, such as Patrick Boudreault's at http://www.csun.edu/~patrickb/DH/DH.html.

73. Ladd, *Understanding Deaf Culture*, xviii.

74. Guy McIlroy, "Deaf Identities: A Range of Possibilities" (paper presented at the Deafness and Mental Health conference, Worcester Cape Town, De La Bat Institute for the Deaf, August 2005).

75. "Racist" was originally used to describe the race-hygiene politics of Hitler in the 1930s.

76. Tom Humphries, "Audism: The Making of a Word," unpublished paper, 1975.

77. Lane, *Mask of Benevolence*, 43.

78. Davis, *Enforcing Normalcy*, 102–3.

79. H-Dirksen L. Bauman, "Audism: Exploring the Metaphysics of Oppression," *Journal of Deaf Studies and Deaf Education* 9, no. 2 (2004): 239–46.

80. See Genie Gertz, "Dysconscious Audism: A Theoretical Proposition," this volume. Also, Eugenie Nicole Gertz, "Dysconscious Audism and Critical Deaf Studies: Deaf Crit's Analysis of Unconscious Internalization of Hegemony within the Deaf Community" (PhD diss., University of California, Los Angeles, 2003).

81. See Lindsay Dunn, "The Burden of Racism and Audism," this volume.

82. *Audism Unveiled*, documentary film. See note 3 above.

83. Lane, *Mask of Benevolence*; Ladd, *Understanding Deaf Culture*.

84. Beisold, *Crying Hands*; Ryan and Schuchman, *Deaf People in Hitler's Europe*; see also Douglas C. Baynton, "Beyond Culture: Deaf Studies and the Deaf Body," Brenda Jo Brueggemann, "Think-Between: A Deaf Studies Commonplace Book," Lennard J. Davis, "Postdeafness," and Harlan Lane, "Do Deaf People Have a Disability?" this volume.

85. Henry Friedlander, "Introduction," in Beisold, *Crying Hands*, 11–12.

86. Elof Carlson, *Unfit: History of a Bad Idea* (Cold Spring Harbor, N.Y.: Cold Spring Harbor Press, 2001).

87. Edwin Black, *War on the Weak: Eugenics and America's Campaign to Create a Master Race* (New York: Four Walls Eight Windows, 2003).

88. For more on genetics and the Deaf community, see John V. Van Cleve, ed., *Genetics, Disability and Deafness* (Washington, D.C.: Gallaudet University Press, 2004).

89. Trevor Johnston, "W(h)ither the Deaf Community? Population, Genetics, and the Future of Australian Sign Language," *American Annals of the Deaf* 148 (2004): 358–75. See also the special issue of *Sign Language Studies* that features a reprint of Johnston's article with commentary by an international group of scholars who generally concur with Johnston's prediction of the falling numbers of the signing population in Australia; the rates of decline and ultimate result of language death remain in dispute. *Sign Language Studies* 6 (2006).

90. Before William Stokoe and his fellow researchers in the Linguistics Research Laboratory at Gallaudet University in the 1970s, a few insightful scholars also recognized that sign languages were languages in every sense of the word. In 1779, Pierre Desloges wrote, "In sign language we find verbs, nouns, pronouns of every kind, articles, genders, cases, tenses, modals, adverbs, prepositions, conjunctions, interjections and so on. Finally, there is nothing in any part of speech that cannot be expressed in sign language." Desloges, "Deaf Person's Observations," 37.

91. William Stokoe, Carl Croneberg, and Dorothy Casterline, *A Dictionary of American Sign Language on Linguistic Principles* (Washington, D.C.: Gallaudet College Press, 1965). The root of *chereme* refers to the Greek "hand."

92. Nonmanual markers consist of facial expressions and other bodily movements that serve a crucial phonological and grammatical function. For a basic overview of ASL linguistics, see Clayton Valli, Ceil Lucas, and Kristin Mulrooney, *Linguistics of American Sign Language*, 4th ed. (Washington, D.C.: Gallaudet University Press, 2005).

93. The Language Research Lab employed many Deaf and hearing researchers, including Robbin Battison, Charlotte Baker, Dennis Cokely, Harry Markowicz, Carol Padden, and James Woodward.

94. *Sign Language Studies* was initially published semiannually with the support of Thomas Sebeok through Mouton and Indiana University (1972–75) and was then published quarterly by Linstok Press from 1975 to 1996. Today Gallaudet University Press publishes *Sign Language Studies,* with David Armstrong as the journal's editor.

95. Howard Poizner, Edward Klima, and Ursula Bellugi, *What the Hands Reveal about the Brain* (Cambridge, Mass.: MIT Press/Bradford Books, 1987).

96. See, for example, Edward Klima and Ursula Bellugi, *The Signs of Language* (Cambridge, Mass.: Harvard University Press, 1979). William Stokoe, ed., *Sign and Culture: A Reader for Students of American Sign Language* (Silver Spring, Md.: Linstok Press, 1980).

97. In 1977, Harry Markowicz published a primer on correcting the myths of sign language that can now be accessed on the Web at http://facstaff.gallaudet.edu/harry.markowicz/asl/.

98. Thomas Hopkins Gallaudet was sent to England by Mason Cogswell, a wealthy doctor and father of a deaf girl, Alice, in order to learn the best practices in deaf education. Rather than being trained in the oralist practices prevalent in England, Gallaudet was drawn to Paris after witnessing a performance of sign language education in London. Within a year, he returned to America along with Laurent Clerc, a Deaf French teacher who would bring LSF and sign language–based education to the United States. The first school, the Connecticut Asylum for the Education and Instruction of Deaf and Dumb Persons, opened in 1817. For more on the history of deaf education, see Van Cleve and Crouch, *A Place of Their Own.*

99. Constanze Schmaling, "ASL in Northern Nigeria: Will Hausa Sign Language Survive?" in *Signed Languages: Discoveries from International Research,* ed. Valerie Dively, Melanie Metzger, Sarah Taub, and Anne Marie Baer (Washington, D.C.: Gallaudet University Press, 2001), 180–93. See also James Woodward, "Modern Standard Thai Sign Language, Influence from ASL, and Its Relationship to Original Thai Sign Varieties," *Sign Language Studies* 25 (1996): 225–52.

100. The Deaf Empowerment Foundation was founded, in part, to encourage development work in which local sign languages have to be equally respected and encouraged. For more information, see http://www.def-intl.org/.

101. James Woodward, "Sign Languages and Deaf Identities in Thailand and Viet Nam," in Monaghan, Schmaling, Nakamura, and Turner, *Many Ways to Be Deaf,* 283–301.

102. For a background on Iranian Deaf communities and their languages, see Ali Behmanesh, "Deaf Way II Presentation on Iranian Deaf Culture," at http://www.geocities.com/abehmanesh/IranDeaf.htm.

103. While indigenous sign languages are generally seen as not as grammatically sophisticated as native Deaf sign languages, they nevertheless indicate the human will to communicate manually. See Adam Kendon, *Sign Languages of Aboriginal Australia: Cultural, Semiotic and Communicative Perspectives* (Cambridge: Cambridge University Press, 1988). Brenda Farnell, *Do You See What I Mean? Plains Indian Sign Talk and the Embodiment of Action* (Austin: University of Texas Press, 1995). Melanie McKay-Cody, "Plains Indian Sign Language: A Comparative Study of Alternate and Primary Signers" (master's thesis, Kansas State University, 1996).

104. Such transnational events have been a hallmark of deaf people since the nineteenth century as Joseph J. Murray, "Coequality and Transnational Studies: Understanding Deaf Lives," this volume, describes and are increasing now given globalization and development forces and the founding of the World Federation of the Deaf (WFD) and the European Union of the Deaf (EUD).

105. International Deaf events are extraordinary sights of multilingualism in practice, with a display of interpreters from across the globe and an International Sign interpreter. For more on the linguistic properties of International Sign, see Rachel Rosenstock, "The Role of Iconicity in International Sign," *Sign Language Studies* 8 (forthcoming).

106. Manually Coded English (MCE) takes the shape of various systems developed that essentially replicate English word order and vocabulary through signs.

107. See, for example, Robert E. Johnson, Scott Liddell, and Carol Erting, "Unlocking the Curriculum: Principles for Achieving Access in Deaf Education," Research Institute Working Paper 89–3 (Washington D.C.: Gallaudet University Press, 1989). Also see the Center for ASL/English Bilingual Education and Research (CAEBER) at http://www.nmsd.k12.nm.us/outreach/aslresearch.html and The Signs of Literacy (SOL) project, sponsored by Gallaudet University, at http://sol.gallaudet.edu/.

108. In November 2005, Ryan Commerson garnered international attention to focus on the implementation of bilingual education at the Michigan School for the Deaf, broadcasting his hunger strike through a blog: http://starvingforaccess.blog.com/. See also Lawrence Siegel, "The Argument for a Constitutional Right to Communication and Language," *Journal of Deaf Studies and Deaf Education* 7, no. 3 (2002): 258–66.

109. See Welles, "Foreign Language Enrollments"; Sherman Wilcox and J. Peyton, "American Sign Language as a Foreign Language," in *ERIC Digest* (Washington, D.C.: ERIC Clearinghouse on Languages and Linguistics, 1999), at http://ericdigests.org/1992-4/asl.htm; Wilcox, ed., *Academic Acceptance of American Sign Language*. A helpful resource can also be found at Sherman Wilcox's Web site, http://www.unm.edu/%7ewilcox/aslfl.html.

110. Gordon Hewes, "A History of the Study of Language Origins," in *Handbook of Human Symbolic Evolution,* ed. Andrew Lock and Charles Peters (Oxford: Oxford University Press, 1996), 571–95. Also cited by David Armstrong, "Language Origins: Introduction," in *The Study of Signed Languages: Essays in Honor of William Stokoe,* ed. David Armstrong, Michael Karchmer, and John Vickery Van Cleve (Washington, D.C.: Gallaudet University Press, 2002), 85.

111. William Stokoe, *Language in Hand: Why Sign Came before Speech* (Washington, D.C.: Gallaudet University Press, 2001), 21. See also William Stokoe, David Armstrong, and Sherman Wilcox, *Gesture and the Nature of Language* (Cambridge: Cambridge University Press, 1995); David Armstrong, *Original Signs: Gesture, Sign and the Sources of Language* (Washington, D.C.: Gallaudet University Press, 1999); Michael Corballis, *Hand to Mouth: The Origins of Language* (Princeton: Princeton University Press, 2003).

112. See Laura Polich, *The Emergence of the Deaf Community in Nicaragua* (Washington, D.C.: Gallaudet University Press, 2005). See Wendy Sandler, Irit Meir, Carol Padden, and Mark Aronoff, "The Emergence of Grammar: Systematic Structure in a New Language," *Proceedings of the National Academy of Sciences* 102, no. 7 (2005): 2661–65.

113. Stokoe, *Language in Hand,* 16.

114. See Bauman, Nelson, and Rose, *Signing the Body Poetic.* Rachel Sutton-Spence, *Analysing Sign Language Poetry* (London: Palgrave Macmillan, 2004). Cynthia Peters, *Deaf American Literature: From Carnival to Canon* (Washington, D.C.: Gallaudet University Press, 2000).

115. One example of increased ASL presence on the Web can be seen through vlogs, or video blogs. See also Christopher Krentz, "The Camera as Printing Press," in Bauman, Nelson, and Rose, *Signing the Body Poetic,* 51–70.

116. Kathyrn Guerts, *Culture and the Senses: Bodily Ways of Knowing in an African Community* (Berkeley and Los Angeles: University of California Press, 2003). Thomas J. Csordas, ed., *Embodiment and Experience: The Existential Ground of Culture and Self* (London: Cambridge University Press, 1994).

117. Bauman, Nelson, and Rose, *Signing the Body Poetic.*

PART I *Framing Deaf Studies*

1. *Talking Culture and Culture Talking*

TOM HUMPHRIES

THAT THERE IS A DISCIPLINE of Deaf Studies today is probably in large part due to the fact that there has been a lot of "talking" in the past forty years and even before that. Many of today's Deaf Studies scholars have been part of this talking, and many were among those who actually started it, or at least poured fuel on the fire to get it going. But a lot of the talking had nothing to do with scholars and researchers and had everything to do with Deaf people all over the country, and the world for that matter. The "talking" I am referring to has two forms, "culture talking" and "talking culture."

First, talking culture. Many of us have been talking Deaf Culture for quite some time. Many of us have built our careers around it, built bodies of literature and research around it. I think anyone who has been involved with Deaf people over the past four decades knows well the subject and form of this talk that has been central to a theory that connects deaf peoples all over the world to the notion of "culture." It is through those of us who could not and would not stop talking culture that there grew a rich national and world discourse in which talking about Deaf Culture is the frequent subject.

But before we talked culture, culture talked. Without mentioning the word "culture," Deaf people have historically maintained a discourse that was about themselves, their lives, their beliefs, their interpretation of the world, their needs, and their dreams. It is this internal process of "culture talking," probably one of the strongest of cultural processes, that forms the basis for both private and public expressions of what we know today as "Deaf Culture." We would not be talking culture if we had no clue as to what Deaf people think or know or what their behaviors or artifacts (such as American Sign Language [ASL]) mean. So we depend on private expressions of self or culture "going public" to be able to talk culture in relation to Deaf people.

It is this relationship between private and public expression of culture that fascinates me, this process of revealing the inner workings of Deaf people's lives that is so attractive to me both on a personal level and as a student of what Greg Urban calls "metaculture" or "culture that is about culture."[1] Thinking about culture and, subsequently, talking about culture, or talking culture, aids in the circulation of meaning and, in that way as Urban proposes, is a process of acceleration of culture. Culture talking is an unbelievably powerful trait of humans. We express to each other all the meaning and knowledge of our worlds and in doing so create kinds of "imagined communities."[2] We express a world that emanates from "me" but includes "we." We express the kind of communities that we wish to have but also reveal what we don't intend.

I view the discourse and rhetoric of the past forty years among Deaf people as a search for "voice." Having written elsewhere about the problem of voice for Deaf peo-ple[3] I don't want to go into it here, but I do want to state the obvious: culture talking for Deaf people was not always about "culture," and we began talking culture only recently (first in the 1960s) when we began to desire to call our private world a "culture." And when we began to want our public image to be more like our private image of ourselves. Thus we needed a new way of talking about ourselves. This new voice was heavily em-bedded within a discourse of culture.

There were some struggles in this process. After an early "wrong" path, telling our story to hearing people and having them tell it back to us, we have been getting the "secret" out ourselves. At first, it was mostly hearing people who articulated our story in the language of culture (too many to cite here). Most early works that attempt to de-scribe ASL and a culture of Deaf people were by hearing people reporting what they had learned from us. Predictably this did lead to some resentment and ultimately to more and more Deaf people telling our story ourselves. But first, we had to overcome the pres-sures from within that constrained our expression of our private world.

Those pressures were quite strong and self-suppressing. Some may remember the reluctance to teach ASL to strangers and a suspicion of hearing people's motives in wanting to learn ASL that led us to a reticence to share our language. After all, they had never expressed much interest in it before and what good could come of their learning our "secret" language? Was it a good idea to let them know it, and know us? Would that be safe?

Another pressure constraining the projection of the private into public space was the pressure to conform in our writing to a writing tradition that only allowed us space to write autobiographies in the frame of "overcoming deafness." For most of our history, when Deaf people took up the pen and decided to write in English, it was invariably about themselves and their lives. This was basically the only genre open to them. The only genre in which they would be welcomed and their writing found to be interesting and, therefore, publishable. This is not unlike the experience of other ethnic writers who found that the writing tradition of telling one's life story was a first, and sometimes only, path to public expression. This writing tradition, being the only one accessible, served as a constraint on other kinds of creative expression.

Related to the pressure to write only in a limited tradition, was the pressure to "make nice" with hearing people and not offend, the pressure to "tell stories" or little white lies about everything from our desire to have Deaf babies (we said we didn't want them) to denying that we were actually reproducing them. We wanted them but we could not say that we wanted them so we lied. Many Deaf families have stories of how they or their children became deaf due to illness or trauma. Many Deaf adults today can remember their Deaf parents telling them and others that their deafness was not genetic. Common were our attempts to reconcile our internal desires with the horror that hearing people expressed about knowingly having deaf babies. Despite these attempts to "make nice" with hearing people's demanding stance that deafness is "bad," Deaf people, of course, continued to secretly desire Deaf babies and reproduce them unabated.

In short, we silenced ourselves. We reacted to these pressures as many other ethnic minorities did. We stifled self-expression, self-pride, and our true voice. But for the past forty years we have been constantly thinking about how we are talking. We have had to reexamine everything we say and analyze every word in light of a new idea, how to express our private world without the constraint of others' cultural bias. Our task, and the one that concerns the field of Deaf Studies so strongly at this time, has been to understand what the voice of this "new" Deaf Culture is.

Coming to voice, as I see it, is not about coming out. It is about the subsistence of individual and group sensibilities. Finding ways to talk about our selves may be a process of affirmation and confession, as coming out often is, but it is a different process, it involves developing a sustaining voice, one that sustains the individual and the group alike. For one thing, coming to voice often reaches the level of rhetoric and literature and art and is embedded in the artifacts of each of these genres. So, while talking culture may be about revealing or creating identities as some people say, it seems to me that it is as much about *processing identities* and *creating artifacts* in the process that help us to hold and circulate among us and among others those notions that we wish to project into public space.

But when we began this process of talking culture back in the late 1960s and early 1970s, we had a problem. We had little idea what to say. And it turns out, crucially, that if we were to claim that there is such a thing as "Deaf Culture" we must quickly find some artifacts of it. There must be art and literature that is "Deaf." Those of you who are Deaf may remember the near panic that we felt when we realized that we would be asked to produce these examples of our difference. And they had to be darn good examples too. Well, first we produced the best cultural artifact of all, our language, ASL. But that wasn't enough; we needed to present, for public scrutiny, a literature. A few pieces of ASL poetry would not do the trick; we needed to collect as much as we could as fast as we could.

As a result of public insistence that we produce evidence of culture, I believe, for forty years we have been "collecting ourselves."[4] We have spent all this time searching for *the* authentic literature and art of ourselves. We have been trying to assemble the material of our world that is unique to us. This has been an incredible task as most Deaf Studies scholars know.

As hard as this task has been (this simple act of trying to find and identify material representations of our cultural lives), harder has been the task of identifying what it is in our private world that we want to be consumed in the public world. In a sense this is a useless endeavor because, ultimately, we may not have any control whatsoever over what is revealed or what is seen by others. But in another sense, it is a useful and important aspect of our forty years of talking culture. If we think of our attempts to collect and catalog our art and literature (as well as interpret and analyze it) as a first step in the distribution of our culture for public consumption, then we are involved in the distribution of our private world and we ought to think about that as an important activity.

We began by identifying what we considered to be "high" examples of Deaf art and literature. The 1970s marked the emergence of the "great" ASL poets, Dorothy Miles, Ella Lentz, Clayton Valli, to mention a few. It also was a time of confusion about what constituted Deaf literature. Was poetry composed by Deaf poets who worked in English and not ASL to be considered as artifacts of a culture of Deaf people? Poets like Mervin

Garretson, Will Madsen, Robert Panara, and even Dorothy Miles in the beginning, composed their poetry in English. Since they were all Deaf people, were their English works then to be considered Deaf literature? For that matter, were Deaf authors who wrote in English in other genres to be included? Or did Deaf literature have to be ASL literature? This question still tends to be a bit problematic even today.

A problem of collection immediately arose in regard to ASL literature. With little recording of ASL literature to be found before the spread of videotape, how could one argue that a rich ASL literature existed? This was a serious issue at many colleges and universities as they began to offer ASL courses and deal with issues of whether to allow the use of ASL to meet various language and humanities requirements for graduation. Proposals to have ASL meet the language requirement of a university almost always ran head-on into a challenge: show us the literature. The few and contemporary examples of ASL literature that existed on videotape during the 1970s and even today often proved insufficient to convince traditional academicians. I remember getting frequent requests from colleges and universities around the country for help in identifying a literature of sufficient weight to convince skeptical faculty committees or, at least, for a convincing argument that would explain why more ASL literature was not readily available. A common explanation that went around was that one had to think of ASL literature in terms of an "oral tradition" or like those many other world languages that had no printed forms.

Locating such treasures as the cache of films produced for the National Association of the Deaf in 1913 including the George Veditz speech "The Preservation of the Sign Language" was probably the most significant outcome of our early efforts to collect ASL literature. Not because it contained examples of scintillating literature but because it was old. We needed to establish not just that ASL literature existed but that it had existed a long time ago. It seemed that "literature" had to be old in order for it to have cachet. We have struggled to find circumstantial and indirect evidence of the existence of ASL literate forms earlier than 1913. The best evidence that we have besides early films is the performance of our older generations and the histories told and written about community life that sometimes describe vibrant Deaf community theaters and club performance.

In the visual arts, we have tended, I think, to seek out Deaf art that explicitly promotes the notion that we can *see* the "Deaf" in the work. At the early stage of talking culture, we needed to stand up and name the artists and name their works and come up with the numbers and weight to impress those who argued there could be no Deaf Culture without a Deaf art. But what was Deaf art? Was it defined by who the artist was? How "Deaf" did an artist have to be? Did Goya qualify? As far as we know he didn't use a sign language, so what did that make his art? Or did there have to be something in the work of art itself that defined it as "Deaf." We quickly embraced the works of artists like Betty Miller, Harry Williams, Morris Broderson (he had fingerspelling in his art!), and others because we could clearly identify either themes that were considered to be Deaf themes or qualities that we could point to and say, "this symbolizes the Deaf experience, this art could only have been done by a person who is Deaf." I fear to think back to how much we stretched this categorization. But at the time we needed a very elastic definition of Deaf art because we had not yet figured out who we were and, therefore, did not know what the boundaries of Deaf art might be. Hopefully we will never completely get comfortable with the boundaries. After all, it is art, and art redefines itself every second. No, it has not been an easy task, this collecting of ourselves.

In literature and in art, we will continue to collect and catalog and analyze. However, I am hoping that we will achieve something more. In fact, I think we have to if we hope to realize an aesthetic that is something more than just appreciation of the fact of production. We all know Deaf poets that we like and don't like. We all know Deaf artists that we like and don't like. We are less sure *why,* and we are very unsure what the "why" should be. I think we are still unsure what the qualities are that constitute criticism of Deaf art and literature.

Many years ago when we still had the annual "Celebration" art festivals in Berkeley, one year a group of the attending artists stayed after the festival to spend a day together discussing art. I was asked to facilitate this meeting. I prepared an agenda, and one of the items near the end that I raised was the question of art criticism within the Deaf community. I was not prepared for the response. I think in my naïveté I expected that we would be able to talk about the contribution that art criticism could make to the development and enrichment of an entity that I then thought of as "Deaf art." I recall that I was thinking about how much I found some art I was seeing to be totally lacking in any redeeming value, while other works were compelling, and that it would be good to have a discussion about the distinction. But, unfortunately, the timing was obviously wrong. Clearly, at that early stage of the emergence of Deaf art as a genre, criticism was a luxury we would not afford. At just the point when we were starting to go public with our art, it seemed I was a bit nuts to become discriminating. We needed all we could get as fast as we could get it . . . and damn the aesthetics.

So that discussion at Celebration didn't get very far. As I recall, it quickly got to the question of how a community that is as small and intimate as the Deaf community could sustain Deaf critics of Deaf works of art. It seemed difficult to imagine how any of us could openly critique the work of Deaf artists without the risk of offending on a more personal level. Given the nature of the Deaf community, would not personal motivations rather than aesthetics color all criticism? Would not such criticism be too harmful to the ecology of artistic thought and production? No one could seem to get beyond that concern, and the sense I got is that it might be impossible.

But, I'm back today with this issue because I think it's important. A field of criticism is not yet emergent for Deaf art or literature and, inasmuch as criticism plays multiple roles in the arts—making important challenges to notions of aesthetics, influencing public consumption, and influencing production—it is not meaningfully present today.

This is troubling because the alternative to continuing without a strong critical examination of art and literature is that both will be driven by market forces. We will end up with little else on the market but what is useful for sign language students, for interpreter training, or for teachers to use in Deaf education classrooms. Because this is where consumption of Deaf art occurs most frequently. I don't believe we can afford an aesthetic driven by what is popular and marketable. Let me remind you that the most popular piece of art collected in the United States is a painting of dogs playing poker. I think that's all I need to say to make that point. It is unfortunate to me that Deaf literature and art are still at the stage of finding and cataloging and perhaps analyzing to some extent. We need to talk culture to elevate the greatness in our art and literature, starting from within with the development of a notion and a process of art and literary criticism.

If we view art and literature as ways we express a collective consciousness, we can view both as forms of culture talking. One of the things we have to guard against (and could guard against if we had a stronger field of art criticism) is the compulsion to talk culture in our art and literature instead. If all of our art and literature is about convincing the rest of the world that we have a culture or about telling the world how much pain it has caused us, we are bound by our relationship to the other and not free. Of course, I understand that we are bound by our relationship to the other probably forever, but that should not prevent us from seeking to be more than just reactionary. We need to do more than just explain ourselves to the other in our art and literature. Culture talking is what we do, unlike talking culture, which is what we *have* to do in order to project the private into public space. As good and valuable as our art and literature has been, we need to elevate into public consciousness more than just a "liberation" art or literature.

It seems to me that the challenge we face, now that we have so successfully talked culture for forty years, is to get back to culture talking. I hear many of you talking about "what can Deaf Culture teach the world," and I have also raised that question. In fact, in my teaching, I use Deaf people and their lives to ask students to rethink language and to rethink culture. I ask them to examine notions of groups and intergroup relationships that go beyond the particular case of Deaf people that we happen to be studying. But I suggest that we also need to study what is "cultural" about Deaf people for its own sake. In other words, we need to better understand, to use Urban again, how Deaf Culture moves through the world.[5] We are nowhere near finished with this work.

We have some promising examples of emerging work that seeks to understand how Deaf Culture moves through the world in different disciplines. In education, we have a focus on what constitutes a Deaf practice in the classroom. We are talking culture in our research on classroom practice, and our focus is on how culture talks, that is, what indigenous practices find their way into the classroom when Deaf adults are the teachers? In history, we have moved beyond early studies of the "history of Deaf people in education" to study the evolution of ideas and practices within Deaf communities. In other areas of study it seems likely that the future will see studies that are more inclined to look at cultural processes rather than "the culture," an important orientation for avoiding the trap of "what is and what isn't" Deaf Culture, and thus understanding our world from the inside out.

In Deaf art and literature, we can do and should do more. To encourage contemporary artists and writers, poets and performers, we need to offer them a concept of Deaf art and literature that is not about collecting or producing art for public display for the purpose of exhibition of ourselves. We are at a point where exhibiting ourselves does not have to be all-consuming; we can afford to let culture talk about something other than ourselves and transcend our relationship with the other.

Malcolm X told his story to Alex Haley and called it an "autobiography."[6] While one can argue that it is not one, no one can doubt that it is a powerful work and no one can doubt the truths in it. When you read Haley on the work of preparing this book—feeling each other out, developing a way to talk to each other, agreeing on parameters—and read Haley's introduction on Malcolm's obvious self-consciousness about the whole process, you sense very strongly that these two men tacitly agreed to "talk race." We have tacitly agreed to talk "Deaf Culture" for forty years. Like Malcolm, we have been effective.

The best sign of this is that deaf children, actually even young deaf adults in college these days, do not seem to share our compulsion to talk culture, and perhaps that is a wonderful sign. But I think that we, and especially those of us in Deaf Studies, now need to achieve a balance between the rhetoric of talking culture that too often seeks to "prove" something and talking culture that is about the circulation and acceleration of culture. When we free ourselves in this way, our art and literature will have survived and thrived after the cathartic period of hyper self-definition we have gone through in the last half of the twentieth century. Put simply, we need to move on from "How are we different?" to "How are we being?"

Notes

1. Greg Urban, *Metaculture: How Culture Moves through the World* (Minneapolis: University of Minnesota Press, 2001), 3.

2. Benedict Anderson, *Imagined Communities: Reflections on the Origin and Spread of Nationalism* (London: Verso, 1991).

3. Tom Humphries, "Of Deaf-mutes, the *Strange,* and the Modern Deaf Self," in *Culturally Affirmative Psychotherapy with Deaf Persons,* ed. Neil S. Glickman and M. Harvey (Mahwah, N.J.: Lawrence Erlbaum Associates, 1996), 99–114. Tom Humphries, "The Modern Deaf Self: Indigenous Practices and Educational Imperatives," in *Literacy and Deaf People: Cultural and Contextual Perspectives,* ed. Brenda J. Brueggemann (Washington, D.C.: Gallaudet University Press, 2004), 29–46. Carol Padden and Tom Humphries, *Inside Deaf Culture* (Cambridge, Mass.: Harvard University Press, 2005).

4. James Clifford, *The Predicament of Culture: Twentieth-century Ethnography, Literature, and Art* (Cambridge, Mass.: Harvard University Press, 1988).

5. Urban, *Metaculture.*

6. Malcolm X and Alex Haley, *The Autobiography of Malcolm X* (New York: Ballantine, 1992).

2. Colonialism and Resistance: A Brief History of Deafhood

PADDY LADD

THE FIRST PHASE in the emergence of Deaf Studies as a discipline has been characterized by remarkable developments across a wide range of domains, from linguistics to psychology, from history to culture. We now face the challenge of bringing about the second phase, to search for more explicit Deaf epistemologies and ontologies that can frame these developments in a more holistic way, so that Deaf Studies can become a more conscious model for Deaf-centered praxis. In this chapter I will utilize the new concepts of postcolonialism and Deafhood to examine aspects of the Deaf Culture concept and suggest how these can be used to ground just such a liberatory praxis.

Colonialism and Deaf Communities

Lane and Wrigley were the first to draw attention to parallels between the Deaf experience and colonialism.[1] Ladd presents the first sustained examination of the idea and provides a tentative frameworking.[2] Four forms of colonization can be identified: *economic, welfare, linguistic,* and *cultural.*[3] This chapter is concerned primarily with the latter two features.

Linguistic and cultural colonization can be understood as a formal, structured network and set of processes whereby, as Merry has it, one group "not only controls and rules the other, but also endeavours to *impose its cultural order* on the subordinate group."[4] In the case of Deaf communities, traditional ideas concerning the superiority of majority (spoken and written languages) over sign languages developed into a worldwide policy of active suppression of the latter during the late nineteenth and twentieth centuries. One of the central agents of colonialism is its education systems; in the Deaf domain this was embodied in the concept of oralism, taking two forms. One was the banning of sign language from education with its subsequent high rate of illiteracy,[5] and the other was the virtual removal of the prime means of transmission of Deaf cultural traditions—Deaf principals, teachers, and auxiliary staff.[6] The consequent diminished confidence and achievement levels, together with the delayed entry into Deaf community life and exposure to the Deaf cultural heritage, left the community vulnerable to refinements in the development of welfare and economic colonization that were then used to administer the Deaf colonies.

Colonization and Deaf Cultures

Seen from this perspective, and mindful of the extent to which this pattern of cultural suppression intensified as generation succeeded generation, one can understand that Deaf Cultures experienced a diminution in the scope and range of their cultural beliefs and visions. One way to begin to appreciate this is to adopt a simple exercise—imagining what the Deaf world would look like if oralism had never happened.

It is not impossible to assume that there would have been one hundred years of literate, strong, proud Deaf people, many Deaf superintendants and administrators, teachers and professionals. Or that there would have been many more interpreters, that many more hearing people would have been using British Sign Language (BSL) and be part of the Deaf community. As a consequence, Deaf public prominence and the ensuing political issues would have attained much greater recognition, and a larger amount of sign language and Deaf presence would be seen in film and on television. Relationships with parents of deaf children would have been very different indeed. Deaf arts would also be far more developed. Such a listing could continue, amounting effectively to a different world, one consisting not of a few elite Deaf people with better jobs, but whole communities living another dimension of existence, with very different relationships to majority cultures.

Instead of this, as Ladd describes, one finds Deaf communities positioned defensively, operating with an almost "underground" mentality via cultural patterns formed in reaction to that oppression, and with the loss of an overt and positive vision of the Deaf state of being, both in the communities and among most of their leaders.[7] Although the last twenty-five years have witnessed a Deaf Resurgence, at least in the West, the process and effects of that colonialism have not been directly addressed, leading to the continuation of cultural patterns that are counterproductive to a full decolonization.

"Deaf Culture" vis-à-vis "Deafhood"

A simple way to summarize the process above in respect to decolonization is therefore to draw a metaphorical line under *Deaf Culture,* acknowledging that this represents Deaf traditions, which must be learned, understood, and respected. But they should not prevent us from the search for our largest Deaf selves, which I term *Deafhood.* These distinctions form the basis for the explorations of the rest of the chapter. Holding such a dual focus enables Deaf peoples to open up new worlds of meaning, while still maintaining awareness of our traditions, both negative and positive, how they still operate on us, and which aspects of each we might wish to attempt to change in the decolonization process.

These larger Deaf selves can be observed beginning to manifest themselves during the last twenty years of the Deaf Resurgence. However, for a fuller understanding of Deafhood it is vital that we seek examples from history, notably the eras before oralism.

Deafhood in Precolonial History

Because sign languages could not be recorded, much evidence has been lost. But there do exist examples of Deaf discourses that encompassed such questions as "What is 'Deaf'?" "Who are we and why are we here on earth?" "What might our roles here on earth be?" which developed positive answers and drew powerful conclusions.

Although there are traces of such discourse within the United Kingdom,[8] the most prominent examples can be found in the printed records of the thoughts and perceptions of French Deaf people, from just before the French Revolution in 1789 through the postrevolutionary period to the "Paris Banquets" inaugurated by Berthier and colleagues from the 1830s onward.[9] All these reveal an elevated sense of self and community, much of which appears to have been lost during the oralist century.

Berthier and his colleagues' belief in what we now call bilingual education saw them involved in an intense struggle with the Parisian deaf school that was taking its first steps toward oralism. One of his group's political and cultural strategies was to establish annual banquets to which the press were invited. These became so famous—in an age of limited international communication—that Deaf people travelled from as far away as the United States to attend. Indeed as we shall see, this international-signing dimension represents an important aspect of Deaf epistemology. At those banquets, speeches were given in sign that were conveyed to print and thus have remained (potentially) accessible ever since.[10] The tone of these speeches is very impressive:

> [Sign language] easily wins out over all the separate limiting languages of speaking humanity. . . . Our language encompasses all nations, the entire globe.[11]

Berthier and those like him were clear about their own ontological status:

> The language of Deaf-mutes, that sublime universal language given to us by Nature.[12]

The Nature trope is vital because the group's concept of "the Supreme Being" stressed that Nature was in effect a manifestation of that Being in all its varied forms. Thus, all that was "natural" existed because it was intended to exist. It would appear that they perceived themselves in some ways as akin to what we now call First Nation peoples, who were viewed as equally "natural," or living in harmony with Nature or their "natural state."

An earlier example occurs in de Ladebat's account of Massieu and Clerc's visit to London in 1815, which is centered around the lectures they gave there. When Clerc was asked to compare English and French ladies, his lengthy reply surprised them in its frankness, to which he replied:

> It [such a frank reply] is the privilege of a Man of Nature.[13]

Clearly "Nature" was not merely an abstract concept, but one that was enacted in daily cultural praxis.[14]

Mottez draws attention to a report from a non-Deaf newspaper reporter at the 1849 banquet:

> None of the orators we most admire could even remotely compete with Berthier, Forestier or Lenoir for the grace, the dignity, and the correctness of their gestures. In truth, seeing the speeches that these three young men deliver is enough, I think, to make us wish we could unlearn speech.[15]

The Deaf were very clear in how they perceived this reporter:

> An "incomplete man" according to these gentlemen, a "wretch," deprived of the language of mimicry. . . . An expression of ineffable pity could be read on their faces at his approach. "The hapless one," the celebrants said. "He won't be able to make himself understood."[16]

What can be extrapolated from such examples of Deaf discourse? I suggest that seven basic principles can be identified that give an indication of what Deafhood meant to those Deaf participants.

1. Deaf communities possess a gift of languages so special that they can be used to communicate things that speech cannot.
2. They are even more special because they can be adapted to cross international boundaries where spoken languages fail.
3. Consequently, Deaf people manifest *in potentia* the ability to become the world's first truly global citizens, and thus serve as a model for the rest of society.
4. Deaf people were intentionally created on earth to manifest these qualities, and the value of their existence should not be called into question.
5. Non-Deaf people unable to use these languages are effectively incomplete, "sign-impaired" citizens.
6. The languages are to be offered to non-Deaf people, so that if they joined with Deaf people and learned them, the quality of their lives would be improved.
7. Although the banqueteers represented what might seen as a Deaf elite, they were well aware that most Deaf people had not yet had the chance to attend Deaf education or develop their talents within Deaf communities. Instead of being content to be an elite, they instead pledged themselves to continue to fight to ensure that all Deaf people had the right to such opportunities—in effect, they perceived all Deaf people as of equal worth.

This belief in "Naturalism" became Deaf communities' downfall during the rise of science, industrialization, imperialism, and colonialism, where they were seen merely as "natural" as all the other "savage" races of the earth, as not fully human, and thus fit only to serve the western non-Deaf colonialist interest.[17] As yet, however, modern Deaf communities have not indicated an overt awareness of these ontological dimensions, which is unsurprising given that many of the Deafhood principles above have been lost during the oralist century.

The importance of the "discovery" of these dimensions lies in the extent to which they disrupt the subsequent colonialist narratives, in particular, their implicit assertion that, far from being the passive recipients of medical treatment and social welfare charity, Deaf peoples actually embody skills that the non-Deaf world can learn and benefit from. Confirmation of this can be found in the recent research by Garcia that use of sign language with non-Deaf babies enhances their cognitive skills and the speed of spoken language acquisition.[18] Further research will almost certainly reveal other benefits.

Likewise further research into precolonialist Deaf discourses, not only in France, but in the United States and elsewhere, will enable us to identify whether other Deafhood characteristics existed. Finally, we should note that Berthier and his colleagues also posited the concept of the "Deaf-mute Nation," and a belief that this Nation should be able to elect its own members of Parliament, far-sighted ideas that also have the potential to disrupt colonialist policies. From this basis we can move forward to examine other aspects of Deafhood in the oralist century and beyond.

Deafhood in the Twentieth-Century United Kingdom: Deaf Children's Acts of Resistance

The rise of oralism was initially resisted by an international Deaf movement but gained hegemony by 1900 in some parts of Europe and the United States, while other Deaf communities resisted up until the 1920s.[19] However, once the number of Deaf teachers declined, and Deaf illiteracy spread, the quality of Deaf leadership diminished and the maintenance of earlier Deafhood principles became increasingly difficult.

My research into early to mid-twentieth-century Deaf Culture, centered around the two key sites of enculturation, schools and Deaf clubs, indicated that the existence of all seven principles could no longer be confirmed. In the case of deaf schools, this was hardly surprising given that the children had to virtually re-create their own language and culture with minimal access to Deaf traditions. However, it was possible to identify characteristics of resistance that could be interpreted as strategies by which deaf children tried to create their Deaf selves, and maintain a semblance of Deafhood, one of which I identify as "1001 (small) Victories."

Chapter 7 of my *Understanding Deaf Culture* illustrates the range of these strategies, as well as indicating the extent to which oralism negatively influenced the Deaf Culture that those children then brought into their adult lives. These strategies and their subsequent effects indicated that although the range of meanings deaf children were able to give to their actions was more limited than in preoralist times, they were nevertheless able to hold fast to a sense of collective identity through which they could implicitly or explicitly define themselves from, as Padden and Humphries put it, a "different centre,"[20] which is the core requirement for cultural survival, however diminished, and thus a basis for a similarly diminished, but nonetheless valuable, Deafhood.

Deafhood in the Twentieth Century: Deaf Resistance to Missionary Colonialism

Examination of UK Deaf clubs and Deaf social and cultural life during the period of missionary/welfare-officer colonialism up to 1970 revealed sets of patterns through which some Deaf people kept their Deafhood alive.

In the UK, Deaf clubs operated on three levels. The first was the Management Committees, which consisted almost solely of hearing people. The third level was the Deaf social club committees. In between these two levels, the second, the missionary level, was the sole link between the two committees and their cultures. The missionaries surrounded themselves with a small group of Deaf people, mostly of middle-class parentage. As part of their strategy, they invited some of these parents onto the Management Committees, in order to help attract funding and support to the club. The missionaries relied on this Deaf comprador class to carry out their decisions and impose their ideas on the third level, the ordinary Deaf members whom I term the "Deaf subalterns." It is important to remember that the missionaries were all powerful. If one crossed them or their Deaf acolytes, one could be punished in a variety of ways, including banning them from the club or from the missionaries' services—both terrifying prospects for Deaf people back in those days.

Chapter 8 of my *Understanding Deaf Culture* showed that there were major differences in how those two "classes" of Deaf people behaved. The subalterns, known to the others as "the Deaf," consciously or semiconsciously maintained their Deafhood by the "1001 Victories," in their interaction with hearing people, with the missionaries, and with the middle-class Deaf. By challenging hearing people as they did, they in effect fought to make life better for all Deaf people, not just themselves—an essentially *collectivist* cultural response.

They saw the middle classes as "hearing," in that on leaving school and coming under more direct influence from their wealthier hearing families, they gave up much of their own Deafhood, avoided social challenges, and tended more toward *individualist* cultural patterns. Their behavior was not conventionally middle class, however. Because of their particular situation, their reactions to being caught between two cultures manifested in essentially petit bourgeois behavior, full of fear of what others might think of them and with a striving for respectability. What was interesting about these classic social patterns was the rendering of them in the terms of "Deaf" and "Hearing": clearly each group had their own ideas of what constituted appropriately "Deaf" beliefs, values, and behavior. Both groups were undoubtedly culturally Deaf persons, both were BSL users and both equally ill educated; there was none of the later social divisions along axes such as "more/less educated," "BSL/Signed English users," or "Deaf/hard of hearing." Therefore the most helpful way to construct their self-image may be to say that each operated from *different beliefs of what constituted Deafhood.*

Finally it is important to make clear that these differences did not prevent the development of a powerful social and cultural unity. Indeed, such differences provided both groups with the implicit challenge to ensure that their own social interaction was positive and fruitful, because unlike most members of majority society, where different classes were not forced to occupy the same social spaces, let alone the same rooms, Deaf people had to find positive ways to creatively coexist. And indeed they did so, so that Deaf life, in the clubs through strategies like reciprocity,[21] in Deaf sports, and elsewhere, became a powerful positive cultural resource for future generations of Deaf school–leavers.

Deafhood in the Twentieth Century: The Pub Rebels

During the same time period, there was also a small number of Deaf people who did get banned from the clubs, or who chose to rebel against the missionaries. They met in local pubs (perhaps importantly, these were often "rough" ones) and developed meaningful relationships with the hearing people they met there, via writing and fingerspelling. (It was much easier to teach people twenty-six "signs" than several thousand.)

However, for many reasons, there were still conflicts and misunderstandings between the club subalterns and the pub rebels. Much of this had to do with different ideas about Deafhood. The subalterns still kept up the model learned at school: "1001 Victories." The pub groups had a different focus. Some of them wanted to enlarge the idea of what the Deaf world might become. So they brought to club members ideas they had learned about hearing struggles and rebellions in history, or ways in which Deaf clubs could become a more lively and outward-looking place via different activities and debates. But when they brought those ideas into the clubs, they found them dismissed as "hearing ideas" or "hearing ways." Their own response was to say, effectively, "If you call these hearing ways, what about about you? You're the ones who follow the hearing ways of the missionaries." But the subalterns also had a good point. Many of the pub rebels had good English skills, and the others were very sensitive to any sense that they might be being looked down on, which in some instances seems to have been the case.

This issue is crucial for our understanding of Deafhood, because it illustrates two different approaches to Deafhood. One is based on trying to *maintain* Deafhood within the boundaries of the oppressive Deaf world as it then was. The other is based on trying to stretch the boundaries, to *enlarge* the idea of what Deafhood might mean, taking ideas from anywhere and adapting them to Deaf life.

It is especially interesting to note that Deaf families (who were rarely members of the petit bourgeois group) did not join the pub groups, feeling that if they did so they would be abandoning their parents, uncles and aunts, cousins, and so on. They had to stay in the clubs and contest the issues arising there. Their fight was important, but nonetheless embodied a confusion between what might be interpreted as Deafhood and the changing, perhaps even diminishing, Deaf Culture. This was because over time, as oralism bit deeper and the missionaries gained more power, the vision of what being Deaf meant was shrinking. Thus by the 1970s, even the norms and values of both the petite bourgeoisie and the subalterns became identified as *true Deaf ways.*

Deafhood and the Deaf Resurgence in the 1980s

The UK Deaf Resurgence of the late 1970s and 1980s appears to confirm the cultural patterns identified above. Once transportation and communication became easier, the groups of pub rebels made regional, then national contact with each other. By 1976, they formed the radical National Union of the Deaf (NUD)—Deaf run but with active hearing allies—whose first convention took place above a pub.

Similarly when BSL was first acknowledged, Deaf families from the subaltern Deaf club members found their skills and heritage recognized for the first time and obtained posts as BSL tutors, university researchers, television presenters, and so on. By 1980 the British Deaf Association (BDA, which had been run along the same lines as Deaf clubs—controlled nationally by the missionaries and locally by the Deaf petite bourgeoisie—for most of the twentieth century) appointed a radical Coda as CEO. He took on board the NUD agenda and began the process of changing the BDA accordingly. Thus the two "rebel" groups had started to make good, albeit very separate, progress in redefining Deafhood.

However, between 1981 and 1983, the "old guard" of missionaries and the petite bourgeoisie tried to resist the changes and forced the CEO to resign. This resulted in the first successful national UK Deaf rebellion—the first time both rebel groups became consciously aware of each other as groups. Working together, by the BDA Congress of 1983 they were so well organized that they defeated the old guard. The CEO was reinstated, the first Deaf chair was elected, and the Executive Council became all Deaf from that point onward.

And thus two streams of Deafhood came together, using their very different skills to create a combined force that raised many possibilities for what "Deaf" could mean in the future. Nevertheless, these steps toward Deaf decolonization revealed a further set of distinctions.

Colonialism and Modern Deaf Culture

My research found that by 1996, even though the BDA was Deaf run, its range of sociopolitical actions and "depth" of cultural activity were still very constrained. I was able to trace backward and forward the cultural patterns, as described earlier, and found that, even though the missionaries had gone, the limited Deaf cultural values and Deafhood self-definitions of that era still lived on inside those prominent Executive Council members of the BDA who had willingly taken part in the first wave of changes.

It is important to note that the BDA (or in the United States, the National Association of the Deaf [NAD]), unlike national colonialist organizations "for the deaf" in the UK, such as the Royal National Institute of the Deaf, is a *culturally Deaf entity*. As such it cannot change its organizational culture as swiftly as the latter, who with each new CEO simply brings in a new administration of "expert" hearing professionals. Culture is of course a living, breathing, organic force that can only change slowly. In this sense, the BDA or the NAD are the *embodiment* of traditional Deaf Cultures—our cultural heritage as it manifests itself politically.[22] Change can only be accelerated when a culture examines itself, learns to understand the forces acting upon it, and initiates changes based on its findings—in other words, employs essential features of the decolonization process such as found in the Black Consciousness Movement in South Africa during the 1970s.[23]

In this respect the concept of Deafhood is again helpful. By schematizing the influence of oralism and the missionaries as colonialist cultural characteristics that then negatively influenced Deaf Cultures, it is possible to confirm the idea that some majority cultural features became part of Deaf Cultures.[24] Moreover, aspects of the colonizing culture that were not widely practiced in their own majority culture, but were used on the Deaf-colonizing "front-line" itself, were also absorbed into Deaf Culture. There are many examples, but a few may suffice here.

Informants made reference to the characteristics of praise and criticism in Deaf Culture. "It's the Deaf way to criticize rather than praise" was a common theme, and a few were even able to identify this as a cultural feature learned under oralism. Another common "Deaf way" feature is known both in the UK and the United States as the "crab theory," wherein Deaf persons who appear to be moving into a position of leadership or engaged in other potentially "separating" developments are subjected to severe internal criticism and restraint. Similar features can also be identified in other colonized groups.[25]

Another set of examples concerns the widespread defensive or negative cultural attitudes toward hearing people. These become more understandable when we note that for almost a century Deaf people were largely unaware that oralists were actually not typical of hearing people, and that there were in fact many thousands of other hearing people not directly involved in the colonizing process who were either fascinated by sign languages or willing to engage in friendship.

Colonialism also severely affected Deaf languages and art forms. One set of examples can be found in Deaf club–based theatre, where very few plays were set within the Deaf community, utilized Deaf characters, portrayed Deaf cultural themes, or even used "strong BSL." Examples such as Bergman and Bragg's (1981) *Tales from a Clubroom* are very much the exception.[26] The Deaf gaze is clearly outward toward majority culture, indicating an inability to conceive of their own lives as valid cultural material for art.

It is perhaps noteworthy that the Deaf cultural forms to survive relatively intact, such as storytelling, are those that do not require interaction with majority society art-form concepts. But in the UK even today many of the best storytellers and comedians, usually "strong Deaf" community members, lack confidence in their own skills and do not believe those who praise them. This contrasts with others who are more English-orientated, with less impressive signing skills, but who take the lead in any domains concerning formal theatrical art.

Deaf Cultures and Colonized/Minority Cultures

Although I identify Deaf Cultures as colonized cultures, I posit also that certain Deaf cultural patterns suggest that a new concept of minority cultures can be developed. Space does not permit a detailed exploration, but the essence of the concept lies in the fact that members of minority cultures have to deal with enculturation into two unequal cultures, whereas members of majority cultures have only the one to contend with. One key aspect of this process is bipolar tension for minority members—between resistance to or compliance with that majority culture. This process plays itself out constantly on many levels—within individuals in everyday situations, within groups of those individuals, and indeed across the whole range of both minority and majority cultural domains. In the absence of conscious, formal examination of these relationships, minority cultural members contend with what Bhabha has termed *hybridity,* an existential condition containing a mixture of characteristics of both cultures without a clear understanding of how these processes work upon us and within us.[27] Thus the idea that we might find Deafhood in a clearly comprehended biculturality is not as yet explored, let alone understood.

Internationalist Aspects of Deafhood

However, one site in which we can locate some of the deepest manifestations of Deafhood is on the international level, remembering that this was a key theme in the nineteenth-century scenarios described earlier. On that level, for maximum communicative effectiveness, signed discourse must be kept as visually clear, as "pure" as possible. If one uses too many features that are specific to one's own national culture, communication breaks down. Linguistic examples of these are fingerspelling and much of one's own national sign vocabulary, while ethnocentric examples of names and concepts from one's own culture also have to be watched for and guarded against.

In setting aside one's own two national cultures in this way, one enters what has been characterized elsewhere in postmodernist writing as a Temporary Autonomous Zone.[28] In these settings, one's national identity begins a process of "enlarging" itself into a transnational commonality of Deafhood. As yet we know very little in the formal sense about this phenomenon, although we are aware that the remarkable syntactic similarities between sign languages is a crucial factor. It is possible to understand such linguistic similarities as implying a set of deeper existential similarities; if languages do indeed shape our thinking processes, then it is possible to recognize powerful similarities within Deaf people from different nations. Moreover we can factor in other sets of similarities, Deaf peoples' existential living situations in audist and oralist societies, which also enable them to relate to each other across international boundaries.

In considering this construction, we should note another key linguistic feature. Sign linguistics, in what we might term the "first wave" of Deaf Studies, concentrated on identifying how sign languages displayed linguistic equivalents of spoken language features, an inevitable first step toward validation and thus decolonization. However, if we are to progress further, a formal move toward identifying the *differences* between signed and spoken languages (especially the positive powers within signed languages) is necessary if we are to delineate the full dimensions of the Deafhood experience. Nineteenth-century Deaf writers wrote of sign languages as an *art* rather than a science, making reference to the *plasticity* of the language, its unique mutability. It is this plasticity that engages with the syntactic similarities to enable communication beyond national cultures.

This potential cannot be fully realized unless one leaves behind the national culture and reaches within into a "Deaf place" that exists beyond them. In this respect, therefore, it is possible to identify that deep "Deaf place" as being the repository of an equally deep Deafhood. If internationalist Deafhood is properly researched, it may well be that, in years to come, the genius of sign language may be appreciated for its underpinning of the remarkable feelings of global citizenship that can be felt in the "new" dimension of transnational Deaf interaction. And to reiterate, it was precisely this internationalist dimension that fuelled the Deafhood principles developed by the Paris Banquets.

Specific National and Continental Deafhoods

Comparative Deaf cultural research has barely begun, but there are extensive unrecorded Deaf discourses around such themes. Some of the themes I have noted indicate that much of this discourse is ethnocentric. Thus one hears from Europeans that "American Deaf people are not really [behaving] Deaf. At international gatherings they do not mix, and their communication remains firmly within American Sign Language (ASL). They seem to be Americans first and Deaf second." Deaf Americans on the other hand observe that European Deaf people seem to be more "oral," and as a consequence somehow less "Deaf."

Such comments suggest that both sets of Deaf people construct the meaning of "Deaf" differently. Rather than become compelled to concur with either perspective, we can utilize the Deafhood concept to posit that the *Deafhood of each Deaf nation is constructed around different cultural priorities.* Thus to the Deaf foreigner visiting the United States, the most obvious cultural difference is a greater "Deaf pride," a greater self-belief and confidence in the idea that "Deaf people can do anything but hear." The foreigner who stays for any length of time knows that continued exposure to this experience results in a feeling of internal Deaf growth, a larger Deafhood developing.

A major priority within American Deafhood is the much greater appreciation of "good signing" or "beautiful signing," which is so extensive that people can become Deaf leaders to some extent simply *because* they are powerful signers. By contrast, this feature is a very low priority within UK Deafhood. One effect of this priority is that many young Deaf Americans work hard to improve their signing skills, possibly in accordance with nationally understood models. Another effect is that Deaf signing art has many more skilled formal and semiformal practitioners, in poetry, storytelling, cabaret, theatre, and so on. Clearly for Deaf Americans, the deeper one's ASL skills, the deeper one's Deafhood.

Returning to the international gatherings, the observations of the non-Americans can now be interpreted as a belief that for their own Deaf nations, their Deafhood is based on acting out their identity as global Deaf people—in effect their commitment to the global Deaf world. This is clearly not a cultural priority for most Deaf Americans. Such beliefs of course involve ranges and degrees of meaning, for some European Deaf people have opined that British Deaf people are not that different from Americans in resisting immersion into international Deafhood.

Further examples can be found in the political arena, in which it appears that Deaf Americans have little involvement. The Gallaudet Deaf President Now campaign of 1988 was almost a one-off, in that direct action has rarely been subsequently utilized, in contrast to numerous other Deaf nations.[29] It would seem that U.S. Deafhood is not strongly linked to political action.

This stands in contrast with the UK and much of Deaf Europe, where national struggles, including marches to obtain official recognition of sign languages, are a significant feature of the cultural landscape. There, Deafhood seems to be much more closely linked to political service to the community, and the quality of one's signing skills (or school background) can become secondary to what else one can bring to the struggle.

We know from Philip and elsewhere that American Deaf cultural values were once centered on active work for and responsibilities to the local community, through the Deaf clubs.[30] At one time, therefore, it seems that both U.S. and UK Deafhoods were similar in this respect. In the UK the pattern still continues in the present day, but in the United States there appears to be a growing influence from the majority culture of a belief in individualism and certain patterns of status, rather than the older models that either stressed or paid lip service to Deafhood concepts of equality and community. Thus, to give one simple example, it appears that if in the United States one is born to a Deaf family, one inherits a "cultural crown." In the UK the same offspring still have to earn their cultural capital by working hard to serve the Deaf (club) community. Again these can be read as different types of Deafhood—the latter being focused on the idea of individuals having to work to achieve Deafhood, and the former almost seeing Deaf-hood as an inscribed status.

Another example is the European Deafhood prioritizing of the struggle for sign language TV programming. In the United States, the equivalent battle is only for English captions. One might ask with mock innocence whether this means that all Deaf people in the United States can read English unproblematically. Since this is clearly not the case then it would appear that in Europe Deafhood cannot (or will not) countenance the idea of taking action that does not include all sign language monolinguals—another manifestation of the strength of the cultural feature of collectivism. By contrast one either labels the U.S. practice as elitist or, using the Deafhood concept, posits that U.S. Deafhood gives a lower priority to these kinds of collectivist beliefs.

The observations above represent just the beginnings of what might be learned about Deafhood through cross-cultural research, and we can anticipate that these tentative conclusions will be greatly refined in the years to come.

Deafhood and the Future of Deaf Studies

The opportunity in this volume to reevaluate Deaf Studies, to assess its development since its inception twenty-odd years ago, and to suggest future directions for its development is not only timely, but indeed somewhat overdue. I will apply the principles utilized above to such an initial analysis.

One can begin by observing the contrast between "Deaf Studies," that is, the domains of Deaf communities, culture, arts, and history, and the other discourse domains around the Deaf experience, namely sign linguistics, education, mental health, and social welfare.[31] Each of the latter (which traditionally are constructed as existing "for" rather than "of" "the Deaf") are characterized by international journals, formal bodies, national and international conferences, and semiformal Internet groupings.

By contrast, with the exception of Deaf history, Deaf Studies itself exhibits almost none of these characteristics. There are no journals, formal bodies, or international conferences. (There has never been a conference on "Deaf Cultures," for example.) Moreover, the only regular national conference, organized from 1991 to 2001 by Gallaudet University, produced a wealth of thought and data in its postconference publications, yet remained virtually unknown throughout much of the United States and abroad.

Such an apparently low status is reflected in the proceedings themselves being published, not by the main arm of the Gallaudet University Press, but by the now defunct College of Continuing Education. Moreover it appears that this consequent lack of recognition and respect has actually led not only to the cessation of publication from 1997, but the demise of the conferences themselves.[32] By contrast, the other domains above go from strength to strength.

The significance of this contrast is that Deaf Studies represents the only site where the collective experience of Deaf persons and Deaf nations can gather together to form a systematic reflexive praxis, *without which decolonialism cannot take place*. The striking differences between the two sets of domains thus reflect the extent to which colonialism still holds sway above and within Deaf Studies.

Yet, as with other minority studies, it is the task of Deaf Studies to formally establish Deaf and Deafhood epistemologies and ontologies, based on traditionally understood "Deaf Ways," yet sensitive to the degree to which these themselves have been diminished by colonialism. Such work cannot be achieved by our present levels of self-understanding as expressed within the extant literature—considerable research into Deaf communities is required to identify those epistemologies and ontologies. Thus it is at precisely this point that we can come to realize and belatedly appreciate the significance of the sheer paucity of research into Deaf communities themselves.

It is perhaps no coincidence that numerous participants in Deaf Studies discourses have in the last few years been decrying the lack of epistemological progress within the discipline, for that lack of progress precisely correlates with that absence of research. To some extent this is because we Deaf scholars, few in number because we are the first generation to emerge from what I have termed the oralist holocaust,[33] have had to deal with numerous other struggles toward decolonization in other domains, not least in resisting the considerable neocolonialist backlash of the past decade (as manifested in the spread of oralist mainstreaming and cochlear implant experimentation). It is also exacerbated by the colonial relationship as manifested in the institutionalized discrimination of academia—the immense barriers imposed with respect to obtaining research funding, and the lack of career paths within Deaf Studies. And it has been prolonged also because the other domains named earlier, such as education, mental health, and sign linguistics, have formed a significant proportion of what we understand by "Deaf Studies."

We need to understand that the vast majority of the work produced in those domains still casts Deaf communities as the *object* of the gaze. This is itself a pattern inherited from colonialism and raises the question as to whether large areas of Deaf Studies itself are in fact sites of neocolonialism. Work on Deaf Culture, arts, community, and history generally posits Deaf peoples as *subject*. And decolonization cannot be achieved until the subject replaces the object.

During my decade-long examination of Deaf Culture and Deafhood, it has become clear to me that it is culture and language that are the epistemological "core" of the collective Deaf subject. It has often been said that sign languages alone form that core, but in fact recognition of the languages without the culture can actually lead to a subversion of Deaf community beliefs.

To give one example. When sign languages were linguistically recognized and the basis for bilingual education established, many Deaf people thought that radical change, as opposed to piecemeal liberal reform, would inevitably follow. What has happened instead is that sign languages have been relegated to the status of "educational tools," in order that (consciously or unconsciously) non-Deaf teachers and administrators could justify their continued control of the deaf education system.

The threat to colonialism that lies within Deaf cultural recognition is that along with the language comes *collective* cultural ways of seeing, being, thinking, and strategizing. These form a profound basis upon which, for example, a deaf child–centered education system can be constructed, one that explictly rears the children to take their place primarily within their own language community, while equipping and encouraging the children to operate from this center to achieve in majority society also. And although all cultures, like all languages, are objectively equal in value, minority cultures often have an iron-clad case in asserting the primacy of their own cultural values in rearing their own children.

To formally recognize Deaf Culture therefore immediately calls time on non-Deaf colonial administrations, not just in education, but in Deaf welfare services, in medical and political domains, in Deaf television, in Deaf organizations, and in the academy. Such change can be delayed if research into Deaf communities is left unfunded, because it is precisely this next phase of research that will inform the paradigm shift needed to attain decolonization.

To continue the previous example, until Deaf educational personnel are formally observed in daily practice, interviewed to enable them to express their understanding of the rationales by which they operate and the problems they observe with non-Deaf educational strategies, and the consequent results published and disseminated widely, we are not yet properly engaged with decolonizing praxis. More than that, it must be firmly understood that such research must move beyond individualism to seek the collective cultural commonality that lies within this praxis. In the absence of such research we find the discourse still limited to theoretical cliches such as "Deaf role models" and a concept of "bilingual education" where the bicultural dimension is almost completely ignored and where each Deaf staff member must struggle on alone, operating chiefly from their own intuition, often on a lower or a nonteaching grade, and frequently without professional respect.[34]

Similar patterns can be found right across the colonized professions. This brings us back to Deaf Studies once more and the apparent paradox that the very area of research that is most needed, research into Deaf community and culture, is the very area that has the least formal academic discourse, as we have described earlier.

Deaf Studies and Minority Studies

These patterns can be more easily understood by a comparison with other minority studies. Most of these were founded and administered by minorities themselves. Moreover each discipline was consciously conceived as a central plank of the liberation strategy for their "community."[35] By contrast, Deaf Studies was and is run primarily by non-Deaf academics.

Even where Deaf academics are in pole position, there has been very little thought given to the question of decolonization per se. The rationale, priority, or financial imperative they have inherited in most institutions is one of training non-Deaf people to become professionals in the Deaf domain, and there is little time or space to reflect upon how this situation might be changed.

A similar pattern could be observed in Gallaudet University's own resistance to establishing a Deaf Studies department; there was for years a very tangible fear that this would somehow bring together the most "radical" of Deaf faculty and by implication threaten the colonial control over the rest of the university.

Anti-intellectualism, Colonialism, and Deaf Studies

Classic radical decolonization strategies conceive of the newly emerging nation as a holistic entity, holding the entire society within their gaze, and from that position conceive of policies that will remove the negative effects of colonialism and replace them with cultural values and beliefs that they consider central to their precolonized societies.[36] In so doing, a reflexive praxis that identifies the place of the intellectual classes in relation to other classes is established. This may manifest conservatively in that it seeks to maintain class divisions in its ruling policies, or radically as in the field of Subaltern Studies. But for both, social analysis and historical awareness are central motivating forces that impel their policies and actions. The danger that exists for Deaf Studies entering decolonization is that, without such reflexivity, it may continue to replicate inherited oppressive patterns from colonialism.

The simplest example that can be offered from Deaf cultural study is that of individualism and collectivism. Deaf Cultures are increasingly being recognized as among the world's 70 percent collectivist cultures.[37] However, most Western Deaf Cultures operate within individualist cultures. The temptation for the Deaf academic is therefore to pledge intellectual allegiance to the latter rather than the former. This combined with the ahistoric stance of individualism can result in a disregard for a Deaf community concept that recognizes traditional social classes. In the present time this stance is most often manifested as a belief that, since the traditional Deaf club-and-school cultural basis is rapidly declining, examination of the tradition in a postmodern era is of little value.

This form of postmodern individualism with its reduced valuation of collectivism as a daily praxis thus enshrines an academic elitism in which the everyday lives of groups of subaltern Deaf people are seen as deserving of little attention. However, a Deaf Studies that cuts itself off from its roots, that is content to teach and market a simple model of historicity, is a culture in danger of continuing to reify only the external struggles with the non-Deaf world, unable to describe what Raymond Williams calls the "smell and taste" of a culture—the internal cultural life full of grit and grime, the blood, sweat, and tears of the daily struggle, as well as its triumphs.

It is precisely the blandness of this "whitebread" diet that lies unrecognized at the root of the dissatisfactions felt by some Deaf Studies practitioners. A simple comparison with Black Studies may be useful here. By valuing black history and the everyday details of survival, suffering, and joy, by embracing rather than hiding from the several controversial historical dimensions of black life, whether these be the liberal/conservative discourses of black churches, the contrasting traditions of Booker T. Washington and W. E. B. Dubois, the "house nigger-field nigger" discourses, or the range of competing modernist discourses from black conservatism to black Muslims to the radical/Panther wings, and by tracing the historical traditions of black arts, African American communities have emphasized the concept of *soul*, so that participation in a Black Studies course brings just such a grittiness of smell and taste, blood, sweat, and tears of joy into epistemological awareness.

The oralist colonization of Deaf communities has been focused on a sustained attempt to sever the intergenerational lineage. However this is not unique to them; the same patterns were enacted not just on African Americans but on First Nation tribes. What has been noticeable in the case of the latter is that when the process of decolonization has begun, their first concern is to locate their historical traditions and cultures. They have not given priority to theories about their contemporary postmodern existence; rather they sense a deeper need for their peoples' psychic health that can only be met by regenerating as much of their precolonized belief systems as is possible.[38]

Deaf Studies, Deaf Ontologies, and Deafhood

Perceptions of the psychic health of a colonized people as a crucial element in true decolonization have led to in-depth investigations of their philosophies, spiritualities, and religions originating from their own cultures. It is noticeable within Deaf Studies that such ontological dimensions have been more or less ignored.[39] Indeed it would be true to say that, unlike other minority studies, Deaf Studies remains largely unaware of these dimensions, whether stemming from the present day or the preoralist past, as in the Deafhood principles of the Paris Banquets. This too can be attributed to the colonial process that has turned the Deaf gaze outward. If Deaf Studies is to make a meaningful contribution to decolonization, it must extend its gaze to these ontological dimensions both past and present.

Ironically the emergence of the genetic engineering movement suggests that in the near future both Deaf communities and Deaf Studies will be placed in a position where the value of the continued existence of Deaf peoples will come under question, and justification for that existence will be demanded. Deaf Studies may well be compelled to embrace the ontological dimensions of Deaf existence in order to locate a basis for that justification. In so doing, we may well find that locating precolonialist ontologies, such as the Deafhood principles of the Paris Banquets, and exploring their present-day manifestations are necessary for the survival of Deaf communities and thus Deaf Studies itself.

Notes

1. Harlan Lane, *The Mask of Benevolence: Disabling the Deaf Community* (New York: Random House, 1993). Owen Wrigley, *The Politics of Deafness* (Washington D.C.: Gallaudet University Press, 1996).
2. Paddy Ladd, *Understanding Deaf Culture: In Search of Deafhood* (Clevedon, UK: Multilingual Matters, 2003).

3. Economic: Lane, *Mask of Benevolence*. Welfare: Quentin Beresford and Paul Omaji, *Our State of Mind: Racial Planning and the Stolen Generations* (South Fremantle, Wash.: Fremantle Arts Centre Press, 1998). Linguistic: Lane, *Mask of Benevolence*. Cultural: Susan Merry, "Law and Colonialism," *Law and Society Review* 25 (1991): 889–922.

4. Ibid., 894. Italics mine.

5. Reuben Conrad, *The Deaf School Child, Language and Cognitive Function* (London: Harper and Row, 1979).

6. Harlan Lane, *When the Mind Hears: A History of the Deaf* (New York: Random House, 1984).

7. Ladd, *Understanding Deaf Culture*.

8. Ibid.

9. Pierre Desloges, "A Deaf Person's Observations about an *Elementary Course of Education for the Deaf*," (1779) in *The Deaf Experience: Classics in Language and Education*, ed. Harlan Lane, trans. Franklin Philip (Cambridge Mass.: Harvard University Press, 1984), 28–48. Laffon De Ladebat, *A Collection of the Most Remarkable Definitions of Massieu and Clerc* (London: Cox and Baylis, 1815). Bernard Mottez, "The Deaf Mute Banquets and the Birth of the Deaf Movement," in *Looking Back: A Reader on the History of Deaf Communities and Their Sign Languages*, ed. Renate Fischer and Harlan Lane (Hamburg: Signum Verlag, 1993), 143–56.

10. In actuality, such accessibility has for the most part been hypothetical. The library of St. Jacques's Deaf School in Paris contains many volumes of these speeches beautifully bound, with collections of these volumes also being republished (evidence itself of their perceived importance at the time). However, as of 2003, there is no sign that anyone apart from Lane, Mottez, and Bernard have examined them. Given that the school is the oldest and most impressive of all the Deaf schools left in the world, such neglect tells its own tale of colonization.

11. Mottez, "Deaf Mute Banquets," 151.

12. Ferdinand Berthier, "The Deaf Before and Since the Abbe de L'Epee," in Lane, *The Deaf Experience*, trans. Philip, 112.

13. De Ladebat, *A Collection*, 11.

14. This frankness is one Deaf cultural feature that survives to the present day, although it is impossible to conceive of it now being stated from such an enlarged philosophical perspective. It is worth noting also that in contrast to his teacher Massieu, Clerc generally adopted a much more diplomatic tone in public, which makes this assertion the more remarkable.

15. Mottez, "Deaf Mute Banquets," 149.

16. Ibid., 147.

17. The last twenty-five years have witnessed an ever-widening "Green movement"—back toward the "natural," toward appreciation of the richness and diversity of Earth's manifestations, and concerned about the paths that the trope of "Science" has taken in negatively affecting those manifestations. It is not a coincidence that Deaf communities have been able to reemerge and become more positively regarded during this same time period. Indeed, extricating the philosophical, cultural, and political connections between the two is one of the more urgent tasks before us, given the advent of the Cochlear Implant and Green Movement industries.

18. Joseph Garcia, *Sign with Your Baby: How to Communicate with Infants before They Can Speak* (Seattle: Northlight Communications, 1999).

19. Robert Buchanan, "The *Silent Worker* Newspaper and the Building of a Deaf Community, 1890–1929," in *Deaf History Unveiled*, ed. John Van Cleve (Washington, D.C.: Gallaudet University Press, 1993), 172–97.

20. Carol Padden and Tom Humphries, *Deaf in America: Voices from a Culture* (Cambridge, Mass.: Harvard University Press, 1988), 33–55.

21. Marie Philip, *Cross-Cultural Comparisons: American Deaf Culture and American Majority Culture*, Workbook (Westminster, Colo.: Front Range Community College, 1993).

22. We should note that some would question the extent that this can be applied to the NAD, inasmuch as the organization's emergence and development is closely tied to Gallaudet College (as it

was known for almost a century), and thus further removed from Deaf subaltern than most other national Deaf organizations. Nevertheless this does not detract significantly from the argument advanced here.

23. See Barney Pityana, Mamphela Ramphele, Malusi Mpumlwana, and Lindy Wilson, eds., *Bounds of Possibility: The Legacy of Steve Biko and Black Consciousness* (Cape Town: David Philip, 1991).

24. Another simple example from the United States: the refusal (until the 1960s) to allow black Deaf persons to become members of the NAD. This is clearly an example of Deaf Cultures absorbing majority-cultural values. Deafhood values, by contrast, would welcome all Deaf persons, irrespective of racial/gender/etc. differences.

25. Toni Morrison, ed., *Race-ing Justice, Engendering Power* (New York: Pantheon, 1993).

26. Bernard Bragg and Eugene Bergmann, *Tales from a Clubroom* (Washington, D.C.: Gallaudet University Press, 1981).

27. Homi Bhabha, *The Location of Culture* (London: Routledge, 1994).

28. Hakim Bey, *The Temporary Autonomous Zone: Ontological Anarchy, Poetic Terrorism* (Brooklyn: Autonomedia, 1991).

29. It is interesting to note the extent to which Deaf President Now has been consistently promoted since that time, in what appears to be self-celebratory rhetoric, yet the U.S. Deaf nation appears not to notice its own inability or unwillingness to apply these apparently highly successful tactics to the many other political challenges that have faced it since.

30. Marie Philip, *Deaf Culture and Interpreter Training Curriculae: New Dimensions in Interpreter Education* (Silver Spring, Md.: RID Publications, 1987).

31. Space limitations prevent me from exploring an issue that urgently demands our attention, namely how one conceives of and defines the discipline of "Deaf Studies" itself, and why that might be important. Sign linguistics and Deaf education are at the core of some domains and situations, as the title of the journal *Deaf Studies and Deaf Education* attests. Given that these two disciplines already have their own existence and traditional discourse, their approach to Deaf Studies is essentially "studying Deaf people from the outside," that Deaf people are the *objects* of their gaze. Thus it follows that Deaf Studies departments built around these (or some of the other "external" disciplines) will conceive of Deaf Studies itself as necessarily meaning "Deaf communities as objects." They will find it difficult to conceive of another way of constructing Deaf Studies—from the "inside." In other situations, such as at Gallaudet, these two departments and even Deaf History are actually separate departments from Deaf Studies. It is possible to argue that a genuinely decolonizing approach would be to reconstitute the discipline from the "inside" outward, and that either Deaf Cultural Studies or Deafhood Studies might more accurately reflect the basis on which it would be rebuilt. Explorations of these two opposing positions have much to teach us.

32. The impulse to continue such work exists (cf. the Deaf Studies Think Tank of 2002, or the Deaf Studies Today conferences in Utah in 2004 and 2006), but it appears that Gallaudet itself lacks the will to lead the conference-organizing process and the publication of the creditable research that is still emerging.

33. Ladd, *Understanding Deaf Culture.*

34. In parts of Latin America, where decolonization is an issue for all peoples, Deaf or hearing, an equivalent critique is emerging but is confined at present to writings in Spanish and Portuguese. See Carlos Skliar, *La Educacion de los Sordos* (Mendoza: EDIUNC, 1997).

35. Maulana Karenga, *Introduction to Black Studies* (Los Angeles: University of Sankore Press, 1993).

36. That they do not always succeed in this has much to do with the strength of the forces of neocolonization that continue to operate on them.

37. Anna Mindess, *Reading Between the Signs: Intercultural Communication for Sign Language Interpreters* (Yarmouth, Maine: Intercultural Press, 2000).

38. See Eduardo Duran and Bonnie Duran, *Native American Postcolonial Psychology* (Albany: State University of New York Press, 1995).

39. Though note Padden and Humphries, *Deaf in America.*

3. The Deaf Convert Culture and Its Lessons for Deaf Theory

FRANK BECHTER

IN THIS CHAPTER, I suggest an integrated conception of Deaf Studies, animated by the overarching pursuit of "deaf public voice."[1] I argue that deaf public voice is vital to the discipline, not merely a worthy goal.

Two narrative genres orient the chapter: personification stories and ABC stories.[2] Most fundamentally, they suggest a view of deaf culture based on the inherent intersection of deaf and nondeaf worlds, a view that departs from the classic anthropology of "autonomous" cultures. While the classic view has underwritten the emergence of Deaf Studies, I show that it does not reflect the logic of these genres, an impressive logic from the standpoint of critical social theory. The genres frame "deaf life" in terms of relative constraints and relative recognition, not in terms of autonomous properties. They suggest a theory of "voice."

Building on this, the genres thus help to model Deaf Studies. "Subalternity," they teach, is no fluke of oversight but rather a direct product of accepted values, pursuits, and modes of thinking, very likely one's own. To understand deaf disenfranchisement is not to see a mere glitch of history, easily remedied with a call for recognition; rather, it is to see the logical outcome of an overall social-discursive orientation, a system whose material and ideological character are interwoven. Indeed, even standing on the public stage is not enough. For deaf life truly to be heard there (for a subaltern voice truly "to speak" and no longer be subaltern), the very terms of discourse on that stage—its very "alphabet"—would need to be transformed. Deaf Studies should strive to be a producer of theory, rather than a consumer of it—to penetrate contemporary discourse at its fundamentals, in both content and form.

"Deaf Culture"

"Deaf Culture" is sometimes used as a synonym for "the deaf community"—as in "I'm a part of Deaf Culture." In what follows, however, I use the phrase "deaf culture" in the sense of asking, "In what way does the world *make sense* to deaf signers? In what terms is it *intelligible?*" In such a reckoning, we are of course concerned with what signers say and consciously value, but we are more concerned with principles that can be inferred from what signers do, though these principles may never be spoken of directly. Thus, when anthropologists talk of "culture," they are concerned with a level of social reality that is, by definition, relatively unavailable to conscious reflection.

Deaf Storytelling as a First Principle of Deaf Theory

ASL storytelling and poetry may seem to contribute to Deaf Studies merely by rounding out the picture of the deaf signing community as "a cultural community," i.e., a community with the categories of folk expression that all cultural communities are said to have, along with all other expected traits. Thus, as a deaf undergraduate at the University of Virginia recently commented, "Deaf culture is a culture like any other, and it has its own language. There are poetry and stories, but it's signed, not written."[3] In this way of viewing things, deaf narrative analysis might be regarded as a secondary concern in Deaf Studies, of interest to those with a special taste for the artistic side of deaf life, but secondary to more pressing issues of "deaf politics." However, I would like to suggest that deaf narrative analysis lies at the very core of Deaf Studies, grounding all other political considerations, and therefore provides the logic by which Deaf Theory can be elaborated and, indeed, by which Deaf Studies can understand itself.

When one looks at the signing community in the abstract, one thing seems central: most signers are not born to signers. One might say, therefore, that the deaf community is a community of "converts," at least in large part. Hence, whatever is true of the "culture" of this social collective—i.e., whatever is true of deaf signers' practical orientation to the world and the unconscious principles of categorization that underlie this orientation—must presumably relate in some way to this unorthodox pattern of socialization. Also, movement from the hearing world to the Deaf World is not a one-time affair, where all ties are cut. Far from it. Despite early isolation in hearing homes, deaf signers maintain profound, albeit conflicted, ties to their nondeaf families and to nondeaf society. Indeed, all deaf signers participate in multiple mainstream cultural forms (e.g., they enjoy mainstream books, magazines, television, movies, electronic games, the Internet, restaurants, parades, etc.). Thus, it seems clear that "deaf cultural consciousness" does not exist autonomously (certainly, it would be difficult to explain how it could), but rather is constituted in pervasive contact with nondeaf ways of understanding the world. Indeed, this is a world of which deaf signers are still a part.

I study deaf culture through the lens of deaf narratives. That is, I study the way a particular "worldview"—a basic intuition of the natural order of things—is reproduced through deaf narrative practices. Before giving details, let me jump ahead to several key conclusions, and then I'll backtrack and explain.

Above, I said that the deaf signing community is a community of converts, "at least in large part." But let me go further than that. The stronger claim is that deaf culture is *about* conversion. That is, far from being "a culture like any other," deaf culture is what we might call a *convert culture,* with narrative forms that function differently than those of most cultures with which we are familiar. By speaking of a deaf "convert culture," I do not mean that all deaf signers come to the community from outside it, but rather that the culture itself (the worldview itself) is "conversionary," and, as such, all signers in the cultural community engage in inherently conversionary forums that reproduce this worldview. These forums cannot be viewed as mere conduits through which one comes to the signing community and never looks back. Rather, they are the stuff of deaf cultural life itself, and hence are always in play, most particularly through narrative/discursive practices. Before clarifying, let me add another major claim: in the deaf cultural worldview, *the world is made of deaf lives.* The task of deaf narratives, or perhaps of deaf culture itself, is "to see deaf lives" when others—even one's deaf friends—do not.

On Seeing the Invisible: Personification Stories

Everyone knows, of course, that signers tell stories about their lives, and about other deaf people's lives. And, indeed, the particulars of such stories are significant in understanding how deaf society is constituted as a cultural community, and what a "deaf life" really seems to mean. However, the logic of "deaf lives" is best illustrated with "personification stories."

The most impressive personification story I have ever seen is Paul Johnston's "The Pinball," which he performed at the TISLR conference in 1998.[4] Indeed, this story's title suggests the principle of the genre as a whole. In this unique deaf narrative form, the signer's head plays the role of a sentiently rendered ball or other object trapped inside a totalizing system, such as a pinball game, to whose violent vicissitudes it is subject. In a word, personification stories are "subaltern" stories—by which I mean, following Gayatri Spivak's famous characterization,[5] that personification stories feature protagonists who fundamentally "cannot speak." Thus, the pinball. While the story's protagonist has feelings, nonetheless *it has not been given hands*—and hence *cannot sign,* cannot speak for itself or protest its plight. Nor can the pinball control its own destiny in any way, having no limbs. It is a locus of systematic abuse, subalternity personified.

Indeed, the pinball does not even realize that it is a pinball—that the forces impacting it are, in fact, part of a coherent, purposeful system in which it plays the most unlucky role. Neither do narrators state this. Personification stories are generally not introduced, and so it is the task of the audience to discern these facts—to grasp the external logic that gives sense to the series of representations. "Aha! It is a pinball," audience members realize. And to some, the comedy's never-stated lesson is clear: it is not good to be a pinball. Indeed, that the lesson is not stated is intrinsic to the genre's cultural function. Seeing deaf lives when they are pointed out is easy; what is essential, rather, is seeing deaf lives "when others do not."

Note that deaf signers are not, in principle, opposed to the game of pinball. We'll find no deaf picket lines at pinball arcades. Deaf signers, just like hearing people, may very much enjoy pinball, and the genre's conversionary lesson depends on this. What the genre teaches is that for every system—even cherished systems that "no one would ever dream of opposing"—there is always a radically disenfranchised position upon which that system mechanically depends. Since systems can be found everywhere, this logic corresponds to the notion that "the world is made of deaf lives," as well as to our hypothesis that deaf cultural consciousness is constituted in pervasive contact with the nondeaf world, and with nondeaf ways of understanding the world.

That is, the subject matter of Johnston's story is not taken from an autonomous realm where deaf culture is constituted by its own private mythical elements. To the contrary, personification stories refer to elements in the *nondeaf* world, revealing lives that are "invisible" there. It is in this sense that we see the "conversionary" nature of the worldview itself. Elements of the dominant interpretive framework (e.g., the compelling dazzle of pinball) are converted, "flipped"—*reinterpreted* as defining (and hence revealing) lives of radical subalternity.

Indeed, this narrative genre sheds new light on the meaning of "deaf" and "nondeaf." In the *Live at SMI* series, for example, Mary Beth Miller brilliantly construes ASL itself as an oppressive system that her left (nondominant) hand suddenly refuses to participate in.[6] What is deaf becomes a relative phenomenon, a question of how one sees the systematicity of the world, not of how various elements in the world are independently sorted.

Johnston's pinball story is a simple story in principle, but it reveals a dynamic of deaf storytelling that is highly relevant to the formulation of Deaf Theory. *Personification stories are a native mode of ontological critique.* They are exercises in ontological critique for the sake of ontological critique itself. They are, in other words, "studies"—*études*—in seeing and valuing the world differently, and in narrating lives that cannot speak for themselves. (Of course, they are also *études* in particular signing skills, a key dimension of analysis that space does not permit me to address.) What seems to be important is not pinballs, golf balls, coffee cups, or 747s themselves, but rather the ability to understand and relate to, and ultimately give voice to, these objects' particular kind of position in the world, and to do so in front of others with great thoroughness and skill. (Does the narrator really, *really* know . . . what it's like to be deaf?)

Transcending Constraints: The Pinball's Opposite

I have used the notion of "deaf lives" to describe that aspect of the world that personification stories convey, but certainly there are deaf lives out there that are not so utterly disenfranchised as this—no? Indeed, we can better understand the notion of deaf lives employed here by looking at the best-known genre of deaf storytelling, the "ABC story,"[7] which I doubt anyone has ever compared to a personification story. However, the tight relation of these two forms can be seen by reference to the notions I have thus far introduced. Personification stories and ABC stories are, in fact, both *études* (studies) and define two extreme poles of deaf life. The genres are exact opposites. But to see this, we must understand the genres in social-theoretical terms—that is, in terms of their role in deaf sociocultural reproduction—so that we feature not only the story in our analysis, but also the storyteller and the audience.

If the pinball is the protagonist of the personification story, then who is the protagonist of the ABC story? What drama is the audience paying attention to? Interestingly, it is none other than the ABC storyteller him- or herself whose predicament is featured for audience appreciation. Like the pinball, the ABC storyteller faces constraints; but, unlike the pinball, the ABC storyteller penetrates and masters these constraints. Indeed, he or she seems even to make these constraints "disappear." It is the *audience's* task to realize the constraints are there; which is to say, it is audience members' task to realize they have just witnessed a "deaf life" in action.

The ABC storyteller's constraints are the arbitrary shapes of the manual alphabet and their strict arbitrary order, and he or she transcends these constraints in two key ways. First, like an audience member viewing a personification story, the ABC story-teller *recognizes the deaf life trapped within the manual alphabet* (life made invisible by a dominant interpretive framework). "B is for *door*," as Ben Bahan once concisely put it to me. That is, the storyteller *steps outside of a particular "nondeaf" way of viewing things* and is enlightened, demonstrating the conversionary epiphany that all deaf audi-ences are enjoined to experience. But, beyond this, the ABC storyteller actually liberates these deaf lives, and can do so precisely because he or she has hands and knows how to "speak" with them.

Thus, whereas the pinball is confined within a game, the ABC storyteller is outside of the game and able to engage with it at will. Whereas the pinball is alone, without the deaf community, the ABC storyteller is the center of attention, the veritable defining point of the deaf community. And whereas the pinball does not know who it is, the ABC storyteller knows exactly who he or she is.

From a certain perspective, the entire deaf community is one big pinball trapped within a game it didn't design. And how is this pinball to liberate itself? The answer, of course, is that it must grow arms and legs, wrench its way out of the machine, find an audience for itself on the public stage, and then speak and be heard. Or, to put it an-other way, it must create a new kind of storytelling game for the public stage where it itself becomes the ABC storyteller. The brilliance of a personification story—the degree to which it is a good example of the genre—lies in the degree to which the storyteller captures the full mechanical operation and rationale of the environment in which the protagonist is trapped. This, presumably, is precisely the goal of Deaf Studies—inter-rogating, for example, the foundations and operations of audist institutions, but going far beyond this, as well, to grasp the logic and force of all systems in which deaf people's lives are implicated, such as the deep and multifaceted logic of the parent-child bond in mainstream American culture.

After hearing my analysis of personification stories, Dirksen Bauman brought a very interesting Peter Cook story to my attention, a variation on this genre. Perhaps taking Gil Eastman's masterful story "The Tree" (from the Green Book series) as his starting point,[8] Cook figures a tree as the protagonist. But, strangely in this case, the tree manages to jump out of the ground to avoid being felled by an ax. This, of course, foregrounds the premise of the genre by defying that premise. Pinballs—*by their nature*—can't escape their mechanical trappings. Trees *by their nature* can't jump from the ground. They are rooted there. But the brilliance of the genre, and particularly of this recent variation (and I could cite several similar variations; take, for instance, Mary Beth Miller's per-formance just mentioned), is that *it puts the natural order of things into question*. If the deaf community is a tree, then it needs to be one very interesting sort of tree. It needs to be able to dislodge itself from the roots that, by nature of a particular system, strap it in place where all of the lumberjacks roam.

The above is the barest sketch of my endeavors in deaf narrative analysis, and omits all mention of the methodological principles by which such analysis proceeds, as well as a plurality of generic divisions the analysis discloses.[9] Nonetheless, I hope it conveys the idea that the best starting point for Deaf Studies as a field of critical inquiry—the best starting point for Deaf Theory—lies in foregrounding the conversionary logic of deaf culture itself. If Deaf Studies is a mode of cultural critique concerning deaf people's place in the world, then, indeed, Deaf Studies is an outgrowth of deaf culture, a development of deaf narrative's logic. A major aim of Deaf Studies should be the cultivation, collection, cataloging, aesthetically effective translation, and ready distribution of deaf narrative materials.

In the following sections, building on the above, I explore several questions concerning the general orientation of Deaf Studies and then work toward a specific proposal for "Deaf Theory." Oriented toward the problematics of achieving "voice," the proposal takes the real constraints of Deaf Studies as its starting point. Having mastery of constraints as its goal, the proposal envisions Deaf Studies as maximally responsive to the position of the deaf.

Why "Culture" and "Nature" Are Problematic Starting Points

A problem with studying deaf culture as a culture like any other is that this undermines the appeal of Deaf Studies to contemporary social theory. Cutting-edge fields of critical inquiry—feminist scholarship, gay/lesbian/bisexual/transgendered critique, disability studies, or, indeed, contemporary anthropology—are not based on a valorization of culture, but rather on a critique of culture. (Not all culture is good, after all. Nor are all cultures necessarily good.) Consequently, it cannot be deaf culture for deaf culture's sake that would enlist the involvement of critical scholarship, but rather the possibility that there is something particularly valuable or instructive about the content or the mechanics of deaf culture. If deaf culture's equivalence to all other cultures is made a first principle, this possibility is foreclosed.

Meanwhile, just as "culture" is a suspect category in contemporary social theory, so is the category of "nature."[10] Although "what's natural" is often invoked in deaf political discourse, this is a problematic construct for Deaf Studies. While "it's only natural" that deaf people want to sign and socialize with signers, so too "it's only natural" (someone might answer) that hearing parents want their children to speak the language of the family. The ground of nature is a theoretical impasse, leading not to critical engagement, but rather to a practical stand-off between a small and unfunded coalition of deaf culture advocates, and a large, well-funded, and institutionally backed population of speech/hearing advocates. Making *nature* a first principle does not provide a good ground for the expansion of Deaf Studies or for debaters in deaf politics. After all, is Deaf Studies willing to say that people should only do what's natural?

Participants in 2002's Deaf Studies Think Tank were presented with the sentence, "Deaf Theory magnifies _____," and asked to fill in this blank. My previous discussion of deaf narratives suggests that Deaf Theory magnifies issues of subalternity and "being-heard," as well as issues of conversion. These terms highlight what the literary theorist Mikhail Bakhtin would call the "dialogism" of social life through which human beings are constituted as social "subjects."[11] Understanding social life dialogically, cultural inheritance is seen not as a seamless path, but rather as a path fashioned by power and politics, and, in one way or another, marked by choices of whom to listen to. Issues of conversion and being heard are not constructs of nature, but rather constructs of subjectivity and citizenship.

The recent case of Sharon Duchesneau and Candace McCullough provides an illustration.[12] In this case (where a deaf lesbian couple brought two deaf children into the world with the help of a genetically deaf male friend), public debate has focused on the parent-child bond. Some say it's natural for parents to want a baby that resembles them; others say its unnatural to impose deafness on a child. What has not come to the fore in this debate, however, is a question like, "What does it mean to be an American citizen?" "What does it mean to live *in the land of the free, and the home of the brave?*" Do those who oppose the couple's decision (saying, for example, that they should be imprisoned) also oppose, in principle, the right of an American citizen to reproduce with whom he or she wants? By changing the debate to a debate on citizenship, it becomes possible to go on the offensive, rather than being forever on the defensive in an argument that one essentially cannot win. By instituting new terms to the debate—terms that have a claim on all citizens' attention—it becomes possible to implicate those who are speaking in the debate. One doesn't ask, "what is natural?" Rather, one asks, "Who are *you* and on what terms are you asking *us* ('Americans') to listen to you?"

Should Deaf Studies Abandon Universalism?

When we study deaf culture, we are said to learn about basic human needs, such as the need to socialize, to create art, to let off steam, or to interpret the world in a coherent way. This approach has been invaluable in the birth of Deaf Studies (challenging medical conceptions of the deaf) and is good as far as it goes. But, unfortunately, it really can't go much further. Indeed, to the extent that deaf culture is modeled simply as "human culture," this mitigates against any particular interest in it. ("Why look here, when we already know what we'll find?")

Further, the universalist construction leads Deaf Studies scholars to marginalize those aspects of deaf culture that seem atypical, though these may be the most developed aspects of the culture, and the most interesting ones for scholars cross-disciplinarily. Deaf families (clearly of key importance) are often foregrounded as the definition of deaf culture, and seen as the sole site for its study, ironically the places where the signing community's viability is *least* at risk.

More critically, there is a sense in which "Deaf Culture," under this conceptualization, looks very much like hearing culture—that is, what hearing culture would look like if hearing people were deaf. While hearing people speak, deaf people sign; while hearing people need a quiet place to talk, deaf people will talk in the kitchen where there's light; while hearing people use cell phones and doorbells, deaf people use pagers and flashing lights. If not x, then *x*. Perhaps signing would help hearing people when scuba diving, but what seems particularly good about deaf culture, under this basic reckoning, is that it is good *for deaf people;* there is no profound sense (under this reckoning) in which deaf culture is good for *hearing* people—good in principle rather than simply in adaptation. Consequently, while it does provide cautions against inappropriate parental expectations and educational methods in the world as it is, this perspective achieves no real force, in principle, against the *goal* of curing deafness. "Sure, you can have your culture if you want it," a hearing parent or a hearing scholar might say, "but I see no compelling reason that I should support it or hope for it to last, provided it's not necessary—provided, in short, that there are other ways to meet the deaf child's basic human needs."

The argument I have put forward concerning deaf narratives essentially makes the claim that there is something *better* about deaf culture, or particularly worthwhile about its study, some sense in which deaf people, by virtue of their culture (not by virtue of their deafness), are fundamentally more enlightened than their hearing peers, fundamentally deeper thinkers. It is not simply that we learn something about ourselves as human beings from the deaf—rather, we learn about the nature of the world in which we live, the *political* world, a world we all *need* to learn about, not simply might enjoy learning about.

Similarly, if ASL is merely "just as good as" English, and ASL storytelling merely "literature for signers," there is no deep sense in which these forms *ought* to be studied by the nondeaf. Perhaps they can be valued for diversity, but is there any sense in which intellectually engaged world citizens would be better off knowing sign language? Because of the steep hill that Deaf Studies has to climb, it is well worth considering whether ASL and ASL storytelling mastery ought to be presented as, in some sense, *more* worth studying than other languages.

On the Virtues of "Critical Exchange"

Deaf people have long been told "who they are." The notion of Deaf Studies engaging with other disciplines, therefore—such as feminist studies or GLBT studies, as per the Think Tank's design—may seem deeply problematic. Shouldn't Deaf Studies be a bounded space where scholars can theorize without outside influence? As I see it, such a project, while promising in certain respects, would be unproductive as a total model for Deaf Studies. Indeed, investigation of markedly native forms such as deaf narrative finds deaf identity being framed in dialogic relation to "nondeaf" forms. In light of this, a Deaf Theory making no reference to nondeaf discourse seems at odds with deaf culture.

Insofar as deaf people have long been told they are "disabled," this makes exchange with Disability Studies seem especially suspect. Isn't "the disability model" a thing of the past? Shouldn't Disability Studies literature be eschewed in principle? While I believe that scholars of disability are correct to argue that this sentiment may follow from a misconception of their field (and, indeed, I favor consideration of disability politics in Deaf Studies), I believe that a deeper issue lies in conceptions of "critical exchange" itself.

Useful engagement with related discourses need not be based on identification with them. Rather, critical exchange, as the name suggests, is in the first instance "critical." The ideal aim is not to borrow precrafted insights in order to apply them elsewhere, but rather to create them in the moment of critical encounter itself—to create them for *both* fields, precisely because they are different. Perhaps this point can be illustrated with the most contentious sort of example: a Disability Studies article that happened to be assigned to Think Tank participants.[13]

Rosemarie Garland-Thomson argues that "the disabled female figure occupies an intragender position; . . . she is not only defined against the masculine figure [because she is female], but [because she is disabled] she is imagined as the antithesis of the normative woman as well."[14] Garland-Thomson argues that this underlying logic motivates mainstream judgments of the disabled woman's body as "asexual and unfeminine."[15] This is an elegant argument and seems to account for the absence of disabled women in popular media.

And yet, what happens if we apply this model to a film like *Children of a Lesser God?*[16] The main character, Sarah, and her relation to the camera, is in fact radically "bodily" and sexual in character, perhaps far more so than female protagonists are often portrayed. Sexuality is a key plot element, with James's attraction to Sarah being experienced by the audience as entirely intuitive, without need of explanation. Upon further reflection, one begins to suspect that, far from being "the antithesis" of the eroticized Western female, the "deaf female figure" may well even hold a privileged position in this regard. Marlee Matlin didn't simply play the part; she won the Oscar for it. Heather Whitestone became Miss America. That Maureen Amy Yates's deaf signing body "IS BEAUTIFUL" could be straightforwardly announced on the cover of The *New York Times Magazine*[17]—thought-provoking, it would seem, only in its uncanny obviousness. (The magazine's recent cover featuring Harriet McBryde Johnson in her wheelchair certainly makes no similar claim.)[18] If these examples seem to reflect only refined opinions, one might consider a *Maxim* article on "How to Pick Up a Deaf Chick"[19]—a piece that is not flattering to deaf women, but that fits, or even underscores, the feminist model of female sexual objectification in terms of which Garland-Thomson makes her argument.

These examples suggest that, while the deaf are ideologically construed as disabled, nonetheless, at a deeper (cultural) level, deaf people (at least deaf women) seem to occupy a very different sort of place in the mainstream mind, perhaps being even *more female,* as it were, than "the normative woman." Pursuing this construction of deafness further, one finds that ASL itself is eroticized by hearing authors. In Leah Hager Cohen's *Train Go Sorry,*[20] one of the most popular outsider accounts of deafness (a *New York Times* "Notable Book of the Year"), Cohen construes her journey into sign language fluency with her deaf teacher in sexual terms: "Threads that had previously bound my thoughts to the rigid, linear grid of English loosened and came undone; I began to trust what I could see. Tactile and explicit, with language passing like liquid between us, we engaged in uncommon communion."[21]

Thus, by productive engagement with Disability Studies' own theorizations of the cultural landscape, a principled distinction can be maintained between deaf signers and "the disabled." To ignore Garland-Thomson's paper is to ignore an open invitation to publish a related study—of considerable interest to several fields (feminism, critical gender, Disability Studies, anthropology)—that not only introduces a new range of questions to Deaf Studies, but also makes the very case that many Deaf Studies scholars champion.

What Must Deaf Studies Be for It to Survive?

The long-term viability of Deaf Studies cannot be assumed. This distinguishes the discipline in an elemental way from feminist scholarship, African American Studies, GLBT critique, and even Disability Studies. What are the institutional preconditions of the survival of Deaf Studies? And in what way can Deaf Studies itself support or create them?

In what follows, I pursue an understanding of Deaf Studies as a material discursive formation. While the discipline's material character might seem supplementary to abstract formulations of "Deaf Theory," I suggest that an intrinsic relation should bind the two. Unlike students in the above critical fields, Deaf Studies students are in no position to sit back and take in the discipline's primary and critical texts, since, by and large, these texts do not yet exist. I suggest, therefore, that the discipline's curricular character should embrace this fact as its animating force. In as many ways as possible, students' scholarly activities should generate Deaf Studies' material requisites, which, ultimately, are the requisites of a viable deaf public voice.

The Constraints of Deaf Studies

In exploring the possibility of "Deaf Theory," it makes sense to consider the constraints facing Deaf Studies, and then to conceptualize Deaf Theory within an entire Deaf Studies paradigm designed to penetrate and master these constraints. It is in this sense that Deaf Studies could be conceptualized as "a new kind of storytelling game," spoken of earlier, where the deaf signing community would now be "the ABC storyteller" at center stage. As with an ABC story, mastery would not consist of bowing at the altar of constraints and speaking in their language (one does not tell an ABC story by fingerspelling), nor certainly could it consist of skipping letters whenever it is convenient. Rather, mastery would consist of penetrating and reconstituting the very logic of these constraints, and thereby teaching a higher-order language to all. The constraints of Deaf Studies seem to be of two major types.

First, Deaf Studies faces a discursive landscape that was not designed for it. The discourses of linguistics, anthropology, literary theory, literacy theory, multiculturalism, etc., are the very platforms for being seen and heard on the public stage; they are the "language" offered to Deaf Studies for writing itself. But, insofar as these discourses were designed for nondeaf people, and have evolved in harmony with nondeaf values, the story seems rigged from the start. Indeed, it is as if these discourses had been designed specifically to exclude deaf signers—via major dumping-ground terms such as "gesture" and "disability" and discursive formats which, indeed, cannot even accommodate deaf expression.

Thus, even if Deaf Studies were to talk only to its friends, it could not entertain them by speaking in this language. Nor, in fact, can it claim the attention of critical scholarship by doing so. When it merely consumes the defining logics of these discourses, logics that make no real place for the deaf, Deaf Studies essentially figures itself as a spectator in the language games of an alternate cultural tradition, rather than as a player or official in them. While Deaf Studies cannot enter these discourses except by engaging their forms (their "alphabet") in some way, nonetheless it cannot tell its own story except by giving these forms new content and inventing a new logic of their relation. If the deaf are to be heard for what they are, Deaf Studies must be a producer, not a consumer, of theory.

Second, as an institutional formation, Deaf Studies has the constraints of any academic discipline: (1) it must have "objects of study," and, more specifically, *materials* to study; (2) it must have students; (3) it must have places for those students to take classes; and (4) its students must receive jobs upon graduating—constraints that bear upon one another reciprocally. If the long-term viability of Deaf Studies "cannot be assumed," as stated above, it is because these basic preconditions of the discipline cannot be assumed.

Leaving aside the complex question of objects of study for the moment, we can consider the interrelation of a continuing supply of Deaf Studies students, places to teach Deaf Studies students, and places to hire Deaf Studies graduates. The Think Tank generating this volume, for example, was held at Gallaudet University, and this is where most deaf students in the discipline will be found. And yet, it is clear from recent closings of deaf schools one after the other that the permanence of Gallaudet is by no means guaranteed. Gallaudet is mostly funded by taxpayers, only a very small percentage of whom are deaf signers. Thus, as with most signers being born to nondeaf families, this is another major example of how the deaf signing community does not produce the institutions necessary for its own reproduction, a fact that belongs at the center of any Deaf Theory. Considering this, and considering that Gallaudet, deaf schools, and other similar institutions are major potential employers of Deaf Studies graduates, it would behoove Deaf Studies to include within its own curricular apparatus a mechanism for engaging the nondeaf world (e.g., an ongoing seminar or think tank), functioning to ensure the vitality and support of institutions upon which it directly or indirectly depends.

But the issue runs deeper. After all, the existing deaf academy (Gallaudet, National Technical Institute for the Deaf, etc.) cannot possibly hire *all* of Deaf Studies' top graduates—that is, those with mastery in "Deaf Theory." These top graduates—if they are to have any real reason for studying Deaf Theory and developing its cutting edge—clearly must be hired at institutions of higher learning (either after graduating, or after graduating from PhD programs elsewhere); but the current deaf academy has only so many students to teach. Deaf Studies must therefore *grow*. Its institutional expansion, that is, is not simply a worthy goal, but rather a condition of viability.

This need for disciplinary expansion might be illustrated with the case of critical gender studies, a discourse that has permeated the humanities and social sciences, and whose scholars are hired at ever-increasing numbers of universities. Indeed, it is not that critical gender theory has been "added on" to time-honored disciplines such as anthropology—patted on the head and given a chair in the corner. Rather, it has changed these disciplines' basic terms of discourse.

And yet, critical gender has depended on one key fact that Deaf Studies cannot. While advancing as a wave of insight, it has more crucially advanced as if *upon* a wave. Essentially, critical gender theory's principles are "in demand" at colleges and universities by force of a student body that is largely and increasingly comprised of its object population. Thus, a basic constraint of Deaf Theory is that, while it must expand, nonetheless it must do so without depending upon an academic system biased in its favor.

But there is luckily a third constraint facing Deaf Studies—one that is the antidote to the other two, and that has the advantage of being the most obvious object of the discipline. By this constraint I mean *the realities of deaf cultural life*. These realities are the best friends of Deaf Studies (one might say as an overarching theoretical principle) because they are, in fact, precisely what is recalcitrant to the "alphabet"—the ascendant theoretical paradigms—of the mainstream academy. Rather than steering clear of these theoretically problematic forms (forms that are readily investigable by empirical study), Deaf Studies should pursue them tenaciously.

Thus, as Lon Kuntze suggests in this volume: in order to understand deaf literacy, literacy theory itself must change. Kuntze's argument, of course, is not that we must arbitrarily change a perfectly good literacy theory so that we can be nice to deaf kids. Rather, it is that literacy theory with respect to *all* kids is misconceived, and that we learn this by means of studying deaf literacy—deaf literacy for what it actually is. Or, if I may borrow terms from Tom Humphries's discussion, it is not by "talking culture" but rather by letting deaf culture *talk*—that is, by investigating it empirically—that Deaf Studies can contribute valuable insights to anthropology, literary theory, linguistics, and a host of other fields.

Indeed, Deaf Studies' investigations of ASL literary forms should certainly not fail to ask the most fundamental question: Is ASL literature "ASL"? One might consider, for example, whether personification stories are "ASL." Since in their most refined form, personification stories include no linear syntax and no citation form signs, it is clear that linguistics has no tools to model this form. And yet the form is based entirely upon what signers routinely cite as definitive of ASL: classifier expression, spatial regimentation, facial affect. Conversely, one might imagine producing an ASL literary form that, like an English novel, would match the bedrock principles of linguistic theory. This form would have no spatial regimentation, no classifiers, no facial affect, and, very likely, no audience. Such a form is precisely what sign language storytellers avoid in constructing a powerful narrative, and likewise what ASL teachers tell their students to avoid, describing such signing as "Englishy." Calling sign language "language" is not the same as theorizing it as such from top to bottom—a task that can only require *the theorization of language itself*. Indeed, if champions of Universal Grammar are so keen on citing "ASL" by name, then let them come up to bat for it in all its substance.

Empirical realities, investigated rigorously, theorized forcefully, and published loudly, are Deaf Studies' best friends because, when numbers are lacking, these are the only real weapons against ascendant modes of thought. In this sense, the goal should not be for Deaf Studies simply to tell its own story well, but rather to present this story as especially in need of telling. *Everyone* should want to tell the deaf story, so that they may better learn to tell their own.

A Proposal for Deaf Theory

Following the above, Deaf Theory's unifying logic can be modeled as *the pursuit of deaf public voice*. But to claim such a pursuit is immediately to beg the question: What would "deaf public voice" be? What should it consist of if it is truly to be a *deaf* public voice? This question can be answered only through ongoing discussion, but I suggest the following as fundamental:

First, deaf public voice would express what deaf signers value. It would not contort itself to fit the value schemes of others, but rather, as a voice to be reckoned with, it would discover, claim, and convey that which is intrinsic to deaf value schemes. Meanwhile, it would be responsive to issues impacting the deaf, at center stage in any such discourse. Second, deaf public voice would consist, in very large part, of deaf people doing the talking (theorists, artists, and lay people)—a condition amply suggested by the NAD's 1997 monograph *Who Speaks for the Deaf Community?*[22] And third, deaf public voice would reach a deaf audience—or else what would be the point?—while it would also reach a nondeaf audience (the larger, the better), lest the discourse not be institutionally consequential; lest it, indeed, not be a "public" voice.

These conditions concern the content, context, speakers, and addressees of deaf voice, but what of its form? This is the heart of the issue. Supporting all of the above, a truly *deaf* public voice would consist, in very large part, of signed expression—literary, scholarly, and general registers. Clearly, in the very effort to champion the value of sign language, Deaf Studies cannot allow itself to become an instrument of sign language's de facto suppression, an ultimate validation of the premise that "after all, it's a hearing world." English is clearly crucial for any deaf discourse in the public sphere, but no more crucial than richly constructed ASL there. Indeed, the goal is deeply practical: any lesser achievement of voice would radically inhibit not only the deaf community's access to such discourse, but also the number of deaf signers who could produce it. ASL composition, and high standards thereof, should be the heart of Deaf Studies publication and academic practice, with the translation of ASL being likewise developed as a high art of the discipline—a high art of "deaf voice."

Finally, a viable deaf public voice would require durable sign language *materials*—primary and secondary text artifacts (e.g., literary works and critical discussions)—that are widely available, *very inexpensive,* accessible to all, and aesthetically engaging, functioning to recruit deaf and nondeaf audiences. Indeed, without such texts being widely distributed and consumed (downloadable? on DVD?), a critical scholarly discourse on these objects would not be possible, or would essentially be meaningless. (One can hardly imagine foreword essays to classic novels being written without a significant readership. Meanwhile, such essays themselves are text artifacts and thus catalyze further discourse, further essays, and indeed further novels.) In terms of this, it makes sense to conceive of deaf public voice as developing over time, recruiting advocates, scholars, and signers cumulatively in stages. It would begin in contexts where it is most invited—for example, the signing community itself, and in university ASL courses, where critical sign language essays to accompany canonical Deaf Studies texts would be cheered. Then, it would build from there.

The obvious question, of course, is how such a state of affairs could be brought about? And there is essentially only one answer: Deaf Studies itself must bring this about. Indeed, Deaf Studies is in the uniquely disadvantaged position of having not only to produce critical discourse in a discursive field not designed for it, but, indeed, of having to rely entirely upon itself to produce the text artifacts on which such discourse would be based. In a field such as African American Studies or Women's Studies, for example, no one need worry that there will be a publisher and significant readership for Toni Morrison's next novel. Neither do these fields need to worry about translating such work. Nor, certainly, is there the least concern that the technology required for rendering Morrison's work in an accessible and enjoyable form might not yet even exist. The entire development of Western discursive technologies and post–civil rights consumer capitalism supports the funding, and ready and inexpensive distribution, of Morrison's work, as well as any critical publications concerning it, mainstream or scholarly. Professors in these fields need only put in orders at campus bookstores and all will follow. Deaf Studies cannot rely on *any* of the above. It must pull itself up by the bootstraps.

Deaf Theory, in this sense, consists of the full comprehension and modeling of what Deaf Studies faces. To "pursue deaf public voice" is thus to require a unified conceptual vocabulary for understanding what would be necessary—starting from the world as we know it and proceeding from there—for the deaf community to achieve the place it requires on the public stage, "to wrench its way out of the machine and then speak and be heard." Reflexively, Deaf Studies itself would figure as a key element in this theory. In a model of such a transformation, that is, Deaf Studies would fill the role—since there is no other entity to fill it—of that center of activity that facilitates necessary changes.

Thus, technically, the discipline would have three "objects of study." First, as suggested in the previous section, Deaf Theory would model "the realities of deaf cultural life." As an "inward" focus, it would approach the signing community empirically in order to understand its principles and its people, sometimes requiring theoretical innovation. Second, in an "outward" focus, Deaf Theory would model the nature of public voice in general. What is required for any group to maintain voice in the public sphere? What are the institutions, discourses, and theories that inhibit deaf voice intrinsically? What are those that stand in its favor? And, finally, as a third "reflexive" object, Deaf Studies would query its own role in facilitating deaf public voice. What discourses must it penetrate? What ideas must it theorize? What resources must it secure? What materials must it produce? And what organizational structure must it have in order to do so?

Another way of stating the matter is that the discipline, as modeled here, would have two orientations: *understanding* and *doing*. Deaf Studies would seek to *understand* the deaf, the authoritative world, and its own relation to the two, and would *do* that which enables deaf discourse. The latter would include (1) generating scholarly and creative materials on video that can be studied and appreciated by both deaf signers and beginning signers, and that are easily available and affordable; (2) securing major funding for this; and (3) developing translation and presentation technologies that, in an aesthetically engaging way (for deaf and nondeaf), would generate interest in and effectively "teach" sign language, thus recruiting new signers. Further, it would (4) monitor public and scholarly discourses and create ways of intersecting with such discourses in a timely fashion; (5) establish coursework to cultivate deaf scholarly expression in ASL, used in every aspect of coursework; (6) secure funding for pursuing ethnographic methods as a staple of coursework so that students are always cultivating primary materials; and (7) develop expertise in theoretical paradigms that exclude realities of deaf life, doing so in order to retheorize these paradigms.

Before closing this formulation of Deaf Theory and "deaf voice," particular attention should be given to the question of video. Indeed, in a key narrative by David Supalla, "The Deaf Mountain Climber Alone," it is perhaps no coincidence that the deaf protagonist is saved by none other than a video camera.[23] Coming to life and recognizing the injured and stranded deaf mountain climber as "my good friend," it treks down the mountain on its tripod legs and offers up its tape to the public.

Video is clearly the friend of the deaf. And, as far as salvation goes, it makes great sense for Deaf Studies to put nearly every egg it has into this basket. While written English is an important modality for deaf discourse, the reader will note that I have made no mention of sign language transcription systems in the above discussion. This is because an orientation toward transcribing sign language onto paper can only be retrograde in the pursuit of deaf public voice. Rather than making research in the deaf community maximally inviting to researchers and maximally engaging to readers (be they hearing or deaf), transcription systems such as *SignWriting* and *Labanotation* function to institutionalize the subaltern position of the deaf yet further, making their study contingent upon mastering obscure notation systems that, for all their difficulty, are fundamentally incapable of representing masterful signed expression. Indeed, to the extent that deaf signers would employ such systems themselves for pedagogical or other purposes, they would necessarily speak a radically impoverished form of the language.

But beyond introducing hurdles, and beyond being an inadequate medium for representing the form of deaf voice, such transcription systems in fact directly subvert the value of deaf voice. Rendering relatively clear and relatively nonarbitrary forms as opaque and arbitrary, these transcription systems undermine precisely what signers routinely celebrate about sign language. While linguists value sign arbitrariness, it is a very rare deaf signer that speaks of ASL in these terms. To the contrary, deaf signers valorize the "naturalness" and "clarity" of masterful signing, citing facial expression and classifier forms in particular—i.e., signing modes which specifically exploit degrees of transparency.

As I have suggested above, a truly *deaf* public voice would be able to convey what deaf signers value; it would not need to contort itself to fit the value systems of others. While nontransparency is a value of linguistics, sign iconicity is a major hallmark of deaf humor, and, indeed, deaf ASL instructors commonly tell students to "think in terms of pictures." Deaf Studies should keep in mind that many impressively impenetrable languages ("agglutinative-polysynthetic" languages, to which ASL has been compared) have gone extinct without the Western world blinking an eye. In the pursuit of deaf public voice, it is not sign arbitrariness, but rather sign language's brilliance, its rigorous "clarity" and immediate appeal, that should be brought to the people—much as Albert Ballin championed years ago.[24]

Ultimately, it is not linguistics, or any form of expert argumentation, that can sufficiently buffer the goals of the deaf signing community. Mainstreaming and cochlear implantation have skyrocketed during the rise of sign language linguistics. It is only "the people," the strength of numbers, that can support Deaf Studies. Three quarters of a century after Albert Ballin, with the burgeoning of computer-graphics technology (the answer to ASL translation), decreasing costs of video production, and ease of video distribution, Deaf Studies has far more resources at its disposal for projecting deaf voice into the public and teaching its aesthetic genius.

Conclusion

One way of looking at Deaf Studies is that it should explore materials that already exist in libraries and elsewhere and use accepted discursive practices—e.g., written English—to propound the findings of this research in a legitimate scholarly way. This conception problematically assumes, however, that Deaf Studies can exist "in the world as it is," employing only the materials that have been made available to it in the world as it is, and using the accepted modes of discourse that have themselves shaped the world as it is. A founding question of the discipline, however, should be whether these very research practices and discursive forms are not themselves part and parcel of the exclusion of Deaf Studies, heretofore, from legitimate discourse.

Most archival research, for example, does not require deaf researchers. Nor does it require the researcher to interact with deaf people, or even to know sign language. Nor does its publication usually reach a deaf audience, or require, in and of itself, that nondeaf audiences encounter sign language in any way. For these reasons, research into written texts or archives in general—even when they concern deaf history—is problematic as an emphasis of Deaf Studies. Though certainly of importance for many reasons, nonetheless, this mode of research in its fundamental form—a form that is consistent, say, with classic studies of ancient Greece—does not actually require that a viable deaf signing community exist, or that deaf schools or Gallaudet exist. Consequently, the successful pursuit of deaf historical research holds no guarantee for the signing community's survival, having no intrinsic relation to signers that are alive today.

Rather than aiming students primarily toward libraries and the written word, I suggest that the methods of Deaf Studies should be oriented in the opposite direction. "Deaf Method," one might say, should always require the "visibility" of signers. Such methods, in their very nature, would thus constitute achievements of deaf voice, always putting deaf signers (as researchers, or as objects of research) in contexts where they have hitherto gone unseen or unheard. One might imagine a "Deaf Historical Project" in which students conduct interviews with a particular contact or group of contacts in the community, leading to a final edited "documentary" with an introductory essay arguing the relevance of the data. In a single course, the amount of materials available for future Deaf Studies research—including the student's essay—would increase dramatically. One might also imagine sending students into the field to record a wide range of narratives and poetic pieces. This (particularly if the pieces could be published online) would increase the possibility of deaf literary study exponentially.

Rather than looking to the world as it is for its methods of exposition, Deaf Studies should be interventionist, working rather to create a world in which deaf voice is possible. If the world is to take sign language seriously, then, indeed, Deaf Studies should take sign language *extremely* seriously, devoting an ongoing seminar to ASL Composition, a course which may, for example, develop "foreword" essays for texts commonly assigned in ASL classes, as spoken of earlier. Meanwhile, if these essays are truly to be heard, Deaf Studies should develop translation techniques where the meaning and combinatoric place of every single form that the viewer sees is made clear directly on the video (i.e., at the press of a button), as also suggested earlier. A seminar devoted specifically to this goal would, in addition to everything else, define the cutting edge of sign language study.

For every "problem" that emerges in Deaf Studies' critical purview, it is Deaf Studies itself that should provide some type of solution, no matter how preliminary. Doing so is to make Deaf Studies an eminently *meaningful* exercise, worthy of students' utmost exertion. And, indeed, by clearly defining what "Deaf Studies" actually *needs,* the discipline would make itself meaningful to, and worthy of the funding of, numerous granting agencies or large corporations. In July of 2003, the National Institutes of Health awarded a five-year grant of *$1.78 million* to a communications professor at the University of Texas to research the "mental dictionaries" developed in hard-of-hearing children.[25] If this scale of grant is available for deaf-related research of such uncertain benefit, it is likely that Deaf Studies, an enterprise of immediate import, can secure similar grants, particularly if it devotes its own curricular energy to this pursuit (e.g., an ongoing student-faculty "think tank"). Video-graphic translation of ASL, for example, would have obvious links to the Information Technology industry (telecom, data networking, entertainment), whose philanthropic budgets are large.

Thus, far from seeing "constraints" as interrupting the possibility of Deaf Studies, the discipline should understand its constraints as yielding its real purpose. If Deaf Studies students should have a grasp of contemporary critical paradigms, the discipline should institute a course in which these fields' principles are advanced and their relation to Deaf Studies considered and problematized. On a larger scale, for Deaf Studies to project itself directly to the fore of contemporary critical discourse, it would be relatively straightforward to design a quarterly colloquium, inviting a paper and presentation each quarter from a leading scholar in a select field. Such written essays (plus ASL translation), with critical response essays (signed and translated), could well be published annually, giving a particular coherence to the academic year.

In a personification story, we see the constraints of an otherwise invisible protagonist, and we must guess the system these constraints define, though the protagonist (comic as it all is) remains uncomprehending. In an ABC story, meanwhile, it is now the constraints that have become invisible—made so by the protagonist's mastery of them—and only a keen observer realizes they are there. It is this observer who knows something "Deaf" has just taken place. It may well be that all academic disciplines are defined by their constraints, but that, given their smooth functioning and their seemingly undisputed place in the world, only keen observers see what these constraints are. In some far-off time, perhaps Deaf Studies will seem this way. In the meantime, however, if "deaf life" is defined always through a structure of constraint and relative recognition, it may be that the most meaningful deaf act is to face constraints with one's companions and with all of one's ingenuity. Regardless of the outcome, regardless of whether its constraints are ever fully mastered, Deaf Studies encountered as this type of "project" will always be an engaging story.

Appendix

ABC Stories

Signers use a manual alphabet for spelling names and terms without common signs ("psychology" has a well-known sign, but "cathexis" does not). An ABC story takes the arbitrary handshapes of the manual alphabet and makes a story out of them. The letter "A" (a fist with the thumb to the side) might be used to knock on an imaginary door. The "B" hand (a flat hand with all of the fingers together) is, in fact, part of the sign meaning "door" (two B hands positioned next to each other, one pivoting), and so the signer might represent the door opening mysteriously. The "C" hand is part of a sign meaning "to search" (etymologically, as if holding a telescope), and so the character might then cautiously enter the room and begin to search for something. Then there are the letters D, E, F, G, etc., all the way to Z. No letters may be omitted, and no other handshapes can be inserted between the letters. A *good* ABC story is one in which the audience doesn't realize that it's an ABC story. The signer is so fluent that some audience members, at least temporarily, do not realize that the story's plot is radically constrained in form.

Personification Stories

Personification stories represent an entity's environment moving around it, and the audience must guess what the entity is on this basis. The narrative is not over when the audience has guessed; rather, the full "life" of the entity (such as a tea cup or a pinball) is shown. Like ABC stories, personification stories exploit iconicity. But unlike ABC stories—which use signs like DOOR and SEARCH—personification stories typically use no citation-form signs. The signer's head represents the entity, and various shapes and surfaces move with respect to it. The entity (the protagonist) has "eyes," and can see what is happening, and has a "brain," and thus attempts to make sense of its situation, and can feel the impact of the surfaces. The signer shows this via facial expression. If the protagonist were a water bottle, it might "hold its breath" when being filled with water. A surface of liquid would be represented as rising from the bottle's belly to its chin, and then over its nose. When finally it is tipped and drained slightly, the bottle might gasp for air with the water now at its chin, all the while not understanding what is happening.

Notes

I adopt the lowercase spelling "deaf" as an unmarked term paralleling usages such as "d/Deaf" and "DEAF" in signers' online discourse (as well as in Deaf Studies discourse) and the sign "DEAF" in ASL. Terms such as these allow reference to deaf people without respect to whether they sign, and reference to deaf signers without respect to their degree of affiliation with the orientation designated by the capitalized spelling, "Deaf." It is not that these phenomena and distinctions are not of extreme importance, but only that it is convenient to have a term that does not foreground them at every point in the discussion. With a construction such as "to grasp the logic and force of all systems in which deaf people's lives are implicated," it is clear that not only deaf signers' lives are at issue, and certainly not only those signers affirming a "Deaf" identity, but rather the lives of all audiologically deaf people (particularly prelingually deaf people)—viewed especially insofar as they could be (or could have been) signers, and insofar as the world could ideally welcome them as such. These are considerations that would be artificially separated through the "deaf" and "Deaf" opposition. Further, in arguing that "the ABC storyteller recognizes the deaf life trapped within the manual alphabet," the referent is no longer defined by audiology or by signing, but by a manner of perceiving the world. The lives at issue here would often be counterposed to what is usually meant by the capital-D spelling.

In signing the above constructions, signers would use the ASL sign "DEAF," or perhaps fingerspell the English word "D-E-A-F," and rely on further signs to convey the meaning at issue. Likewise in this chapter, when referring to audiologically deaf signers, I write "deaf signers," and when referring to the culture pertaining to them, I write "deaf culture." Spellings such as "Deaf" and "Deaf Culture" are used to quote or make reference to the discourses in which such spellings appear. A signer describing such developments of contemporary deaf discourse might, in like fashion, use the marked sign in ASL referring to "CAPITAL-D" identity, or simply to the capital-D spelling.

I have used capitalization in referring to deaf disciplinary formations throughout.

1. A discussion of the spelling conventions adopted for "deaf" and "Deaf" in this chapter can be found in the chapter's first (unnumbered) note, above.

2. A brief overview of these forms can be found in the Appendix.

3. *Inside UVA,* May 17–23, 2002, 3, http://www.virginia.edu/insideuva/2002/18/smith.html.

4. Theoretical Issues in Sign Language Research conference (Gallaudet University, Washington, D.C., November 12–15, 1998).

5. Gayatri C. Spivak, "Can the Subaltern Speak?" in *Marxism and the Interpretation of Culture,* ed. Cary Nelson and Lawrence Grossberg (London: Macmillan, 1988), 271–313.

6. *Mary Beth Miller, Live at SMI* (VHS) (Burtonsville, Md.: Sign Media, 1992).

7. Susan Rutherford, *A Study of American Deaf Folklore* (Burtonsville, Md.: Linstok Press, 1993).

8. Gilbert Eastman, "The Tree," in *Tales from "The Green Books"* (VHS), ed. Charlotte Baker-Shenk and Dennis Cokely (Washington, D.C.: Gallaudet University Press, 1980).

9. For a treatment integrating five additional genres, see my article "Deaf Narratives and 'Deaf Life': An Integrated Look," in *Deaf Studies Today: A Kaleidoscope of Knowledge, Learning, and Understanding,* ed. Bryan K. Eldredge, Doug Stringham, and Minnie Mae Wilding-Diaz (Orem: Utah Valley State College, 2005), 76–95.

10. Donna Haraway, *Simians, Cyborgs, and Women: The Reinvention of Nature* (New York: Routledge, 1991).

11. Mikhail Bakhtin, *The Dialogic Imagination: Four Essays,* ed. Michael Holquist, trans. Caryl Emerson and Michael Holquist (Austin: University of Texas Press, 1981).

12. Liza Mundy, "A World of Their Own," *Washington Post,* March 31, 2002, W22, http://www.washingtonpost.com/ac2/wp-dyn/A23194-2002Mar27.

13. Rosemarie Garland-Thomson, "Feminist Theory, the Body, and the Disabled Figure," in *The Disability Studies Reader* (New York: Routledge, 1997), 279–92.

14. Ibid., 288.

15. Ibid., 285.

16. *Children of a Lesser God,* directed by Randa Haines (Hollywood: Paramount Pictures, 1986).

17. *New York Times Magazine,* August 28, 1994.

18. *New York Times Magazine,* February 16, 2003.

19. "How to Pick Up a Deaf Chick," *Maxim,* January 2002, 40–41.

20. Leah Hager Cohen, *Train Go Sorry: Inside a Deaf World* (New York: Houghton Mifflin, 1994).

21. Ibid., 217; see also 219, 230.

22. A. B. Farb, ed., *Who Speaks for the Deaf Community? A Deaf American Monograph* (Silver Spring, Md.: National Association of the Deaf, 1997).

23. David Supalla, "The Deaf Mountain Climber Alone," in *Short Stories in American Sign Language* (VHS), by Clarence Supalla and David Supalla (Berkeley: ASL Vista Project, 1991).

24. Albert Ballin, *The Deaf Mute Howls* (1930; repr., Washington, D.C.: Gallaudet University Press, 1998).

25. "Professor Gets Funds for Communications Study," *Dallas Morning News,* August 5, 2003, 5B.

PART II   *Deaf Perception and Community*

4. *Upon the Formation of a Visual Variety of the Human Race*

BENJAMIN BAHAN

IN NEW YORK CITY, a father and daughter sat in a café people-watching out the window and drinking coffee.

"Look across the street," signed the father.

His daughter quickly scoped the busy street packed with people hustling to and fro before quizzically looking back at her dad.

"One of them is deaf . . . which one is it?" he asked.

She looked back and scanned the crowd. She noticed one man's eyes glancing from side to side. "The one with the brown overcoat," she guessed.

"I agree. Let's watch and see," he suggested.

The man in the brown overcoat was about to cross the street, but sensed the sudden shift in the crowd of people around him as they simultaneously looked in the same direction. He decided he too should check in that direction and saw sirens and flashing lights accompanying a speeding ambulance. After the commotion subsided, he crossed the street and continued walking past the café. The father waved his hands in the man's periphery. In the middle of a bustling city, the man in the brown overcoat noticed a flutter of hands through the window and quickly turned to see the father and his daughter.

"You deaf?" signed the father.

The man was astounded and asked, "How did you know?"

People of the Eye

The characters in this short story are unique in that they inhabit a highly visual world. They use a visual language to communicate and have developed a visual system of adaptation to orient them in the world that defines their way of being.[1] This is not an unusual story. Episodes like this have been shared and reported all over the world. The claim that deaf people are highly visual and tactile is not a new concept. It has been stated time and time again in various sources—both in writing and through the air ("orally"). The most notable statement came from George Veditz, who eloquently commented at the National Association of the Deaf convention in Colorado in 1910, "[Deaf people] are first, last and of all time the people of the eye."[2]

The strongest support for the notion put forward by Veditz (and others) is the emergence of a visual-gestural language. Since the dawn of time, whenever and wherever there were deaf people[3] on earth, a visual communication system (using gestures, mime, and home signs) would be developed to convey thoughts, feelings, desires, and ideas. Although there is no written record of this phenomenon from ancient times, one of the earliest recorded observations of deaf people using gestures and signs is found in Plato's *Cratylus*.[4] In ensuing dialogue between Socrates, Hermogenes, and Cratylus on issues of names and language, Socrates made an observation in reference to deaf people using gestures/signs in Athens around 400 to 350 BCE:

> Suppose that we had no voice or tongue, and wanted to communicate with one another. Should we not, like the deaf and dumb, make signs with the hands and head and the rest of the body?[5]

Observations of deaf people creating visual-gestural communication do not only occur in major metropolitan areas but also in isolated places around the globe from the jungles of the Amazon[6] to the many islands scattered all over the world's oceans.[7] In essence this discussion highlights what Veditz also said a few years later in 1913, "As long as we have deaf people on earth, we will have signs."[8]

The desire and drive to create signs is deeply rooted in our fundamental human need for communication. The truth is "we cannot be truly human apart from communication . . . to impede communication is to reduce people to the status of things."[9] Deaf people, being of a human variety, have refused to be reduced to the status of things and have found ways to communicate visually and developed visual languages.[10] That is the essence of their being. All other things are constructed around this, channeled through and by vision.

The roots in visual-gestural languages have pushed the boundary of vision far beyond other human groups known.[11] This essay will draw from various bodies of research and observations to further demonstrate the significance of "vision" to the Deaf world.

The Use of Eyes in Language and Culture

Before looking at the role that vision and the use of eyes play in the language and culture of deaf people we need to realize two things: (1) there are people who are not deaf but are highly visual in the way they think, behave, and express themselves, and (2) unlike the ears, human eyes have communicative functions, which play a role in sending and receiving information. Almost all humans are able to display this duality. The size of pupils sends information on whether one is scared, interested, and so on. Droopy eyes send the signal of drowsiness.[12] However, among signing deaf people, the role of vision and the use of eyes expands exponentially. We must bear in mind that when using signed languages signers manifest many different kinesthetic features that are depicted visually: the body, head, hands, arms, facial expressions, and the physical space surrounding the signer and his/her eyes. The focus here will be on the role the eyes and vision have in linguistic and discourse exchanges and ways they are extended to other cultural and literary functions.

Various Eye Behaviors in Language

When signing, the signer's eyes are always moving in a saccadic manner—rapid eye movements to and from fixation points—to signal various linguistic information in different layers. The eye movement may occur over a single word[13] to convey specific meaning, appear in sentences to indicate the spatial position of the object, signal constituent boundaries, bring the addressee in and out of a story world, and/or play a role in turn-taking. All saccadic movement happens in one brief exchange.

At the lexical level, the eye gaze may shift to correlate with the manual portion of a sign and convey additional meaning to the word. Sentence 1 shows an example of this co-occurrence with an adjective. In this sentence the signer looks at the addressee, then quickly shifts his gaze to the hands where the shortness of the cute boy is conveyed, and then shifts his gaze back to the addressee.

Sentence 1

gaze down
BOY CUTE SHORT.

Translation: The boy is short and cute.
(Note: No eye gaze transcription over a sign means the signer is looking at the addressee.)

At the syntactic level, the eyes play a critical role in relations to syntactic constituents, such as noun phrases and verb phrases in simple sentences. They have different functions depending on where in the sentence the eyes are being used. In noun phrases, the eyes can have function to convey the location and distance of an entity.[14] Eye gaze frequently accompanies the indexical sign that expresses definite determiners in ASL. The eyes gaze to the same location in space where the finger points: the location in space associated with the referent that is being referred back to, as seen in sentence 2.

Sentence 2

gaze left
IX-left MAN WANT BUY YOUR CAR

Translation: The man (over there) wants to buy your car.

Indefinite reference in American Sign Language (ASL) is associated with a broader region in space than just a single point. So, for example the indefinite determiner SOME-THING/ONE is articulated by an upward pointing index finger moving in quick circles within a small region in space. The eye gaze that accompanies the indefinite determiner is also more diffused within that region of space. So, sentence 3 illustrates the distinction in that the definiteness/indefiniteness of the noun is reflected in the different types of eye gaze used.

Sentence 3

diffused gaze
SOMEONE MAN WANT BUY YOUR CAR

Translation: A man wants to buy your car.

In the verb phrase, the eyes used in transitive constructions serve as nonmanual markers of syntactic object agreement.[15] In sentence 4, the direction of the eye gaze (to the left) marks the location associated with the object and augments the sentence by functioning as a nonmanual object agreement marker as it spreads across the verb phrase.

Sentence 4

gaze left
JOHN LOVE MARY.

Translation: John loves Mary.

When engaging in discourse, the listener usually fixes and maintains his gaze on the signer's face, particularly the eyes, thus creating a conversational partnership in regulating different discourse functions. As previously mentioned, the signer's eyes are constantly moving in a saccadic manner to convey various linguistic purposes. This eye movement continues throughout the exchange. The signer gazes away from the addressee (– gaze) for various linguistic and discourse-related reasons and gazes back to the addressee (+ gaze) to check on him/her, to keep him/her involved, and/or to give a turn.[16] This "checking mechanism" often happens at points that are identified as constituent boundaries or lines.[17] In a situation where the addressee wants to initiate a turn, he will place his hands in the signer's visual field, wait until the signer is gazing at him (+ gaze), and then start signing. In a heated exchange, the signer can maintain his role by minimizing the number of times he performs + gaze. By doing this he minimizes the chances of being interrupted.[18]

The dynamics of a classroom involve more complex turn-taking strategies where the teacher usually assumes the role of a regulator. In the case of signing classrooms, this equation has been observed: the more fluent the teacher is with visual communication signals, the more fluid classroom discourse will be. These teachers maintain a clear distinction between two forms of gazes: individual gaze (I-gaze) and group gaze (G-gaze).[19] In a classroom, the two different gazes serve different functions, for instance, when the teacher wants to address a particular student he employs the I-gaze at that student, by keeping his eyes transfixed to that student (with allowance for saccadic linguistic markers), and maintains mutual eye contact while engaging in questions and answers. When the teacher wants to talk to the class as a whole his gaze is less transfixed and more diffused as he addresses the whole group. The teacher will also sweep his gaze and head around the group to address all of the students. Handling this distinction between the two types of classroom eye gaze has been problematic for nonfluent signing teachers and has caused misunderstandings between the teacher and student. For example, a teacher used an I-gaze at one particular student when he was actually addressing the whole class. Signing "Please pay attention when I am talking" with the eye gaze at one particular student will likely result in the student responding "I have been paying attention; why are you picking on me?"[20]

While telling a story, a signer typically does not relinquish his/her turn to the audience. Instead the expectation is that the storyteller maintains his/her turn until the story is completed. Thus, the role of eye gaze, while still vital to engaging the listener/audience, takes a somewhat different form. In addition to the constant saccadic shifts that fall within the categories described above (e.g., using eye gaze for lexical and syntactic purposes), the teller uses eye gaze in constructed action/dialogue, to present information from the point of view of a character in the story. This type of eye gaze serves a major function in storytelling. The teller assumes various characters' gazes while signing his/her actions and incorporates reciprocal gazes to clearly represent dialogues between two or more characters in a story. At a more global level, the teller brings the story world up right before the addressees' eyes, and eye gaze serves to modulate between the narrator's perspective, the story world, and the more "direct" depiction of events through the eyes of a character.[21] In addition, closer scrutiny allows one to see that the teller's rhythmic gaze from the story world to the audience serves as a device for demarcating narrative units in a formulaic sense.[22]

There are eye behaviors, other than gaze directions or saccadic movements, that play additional roles in the language that are worth mentioning here. While accompanying various spatial-related signs the aperture of the eyelids can also convey a sense of nearness or farness. When the eyelids widen in association with a lexical item it conveys closeness, whereas the squinting of the eyelids conveys distance. Another behavior includes the way the closure of the eyes with a word conveys an emphasis; this has been identified as emphatic eye closure.[23]

Another type of eye behavior involves eye blinks in sentences. If one looks at the site where eye blinks occur with regularity one will find signers blink their eyes in constituent boundaries that are between the noun phrases and verb phrases and at the end of sentences as shown in sentence 5.[24]

Sentence 5

blink   *blink*

LAST NIGHT JOHN   VISIT MARY   .

Translation: Last night John visited Mary.

The proposition that the role of eyes used for signaling communicative function among signing deaf people is expanded exponentially is thus confirmed. The essence of what may appear as simple eye-gazing behavior is in fact part of a complex multilayered linguistic system in ASL. That is, the signer's eyes are always moving in a saccadic manner to signal various linguistic information in different layers from a single word to interactions with a large group.

Visual Language and the Brain

Oliver Sacks, a renowned neurologist and author, was astounded at the complexity and multilayered role that eyes play in conjunction with sign production.[25] He commented, "One can have a dozen, or a dozen-and-a-half, grammatical modifications, done simultaneously, one on top of the other, and when this came home to me, the neurologist in me was aroused. I thought: 'that's impossible. How the hell can the brain analyze eighteen simultaneous visual patterns?' I was filled with a sort of neurological awe. The answer to this, briefly, is that the normal brain can't make such visual analysis, but it can learn to do so."[26]

There are a number of neurological studies examining the interactive function of signed language, vision, and the brain that support Sacks's observation. In this essay the focus is on three research areas that portray this learned visual way of being: (1) peripheral vision, (2) spatial processing tasks, and (3) rapidly presented visual information tasks.

Since the 1980s several studies have looked at peripheral vision of deaf people through electroencephalograms (EEGs) and functional magnetic resonance imaging (fMRI) tests. The results have consistently shown that signers have superior attention to the peripheral visual space.[27] This scientific proof gave legitimacy to what has been known in the Deaf community for a long time. The story in the beginning of this essay showed how the man in the brown overcoat was able to use his peripheral vision to "navigate" his way in the world of sound. This attention to the periphery develops at a very early age in children. One personal observation concerns my daughter when she was three and a half. She was engaged in a conversation with an adult seated across from her at the dining room table. I was seated to her right (in her periphery). They were going over the names of her classmates in preschool. I supplied a name sign hoping to clarify and help out the adult. My daughter quickly looked away from the adult and corrected the way I produced that particular classmate's name. I was astonished that at age three and a half, she was able to recognize the name sign error I made out of her peripheral line of vision. Her facility using peripheral vision is further evidence in support of the claim that signers have superior attention in this area.

Several spatial processing tasks were also done comparing native signers of ASL with nonsigners. The tasks required subjects to recall, compare, and identify various mental and visual images. They include being able to quickly identify, generate, and transform mental and mirror images.[28] Tests include spatial cognition tasks in nonverbal IQ tests such as block designs, a subtest of the Wechsler Intelligence Scale for Children,[29] and recognition and matching an array of six faces oriented and shadowed differently with the target face.[30] These spatial processing tasks show that native signers of ASL performed better than nonsigners.[31]

Another task focused on the ability of deaf people to recognize rapidly presented visual information. Researchers created a videotaped test of invented Chinese characters written in the air with tiny light bulbs attached to a hand. The videotape was shown to a group of deaf and hearing Chinese first graders. The tasks required students to maintain in memory the path traced rapidly, analyze into component strokes, and finally reproduce on paper. The deaf signing first graders significantly outperformed their hearing counterparts.[32]

The perception tasks discussed above do not require knowledge or use of signed languages. However, comparative results show that the native signers had a consistent advantage when performing the tasks. These studies reinforce the notion that signing deaf people make better use of vision.

In Culture and Literature

The visual way of being in the world discussed thus far is carried over into the cultural lives, values, consciousness, social spaces, and literatures of signers.[33] Recall the story in the beginning of this essay, where the father and daughter were able to identify the man in the brown overcoat as deaf out of thousands of people on the bustling city street. They noticed the subtleties that only members of this culture (those who share the visual experience) can see. The first visual cue was the way the man in the brown overcoat was orienting himself in the streets of New York City by executing saccadic eye and head movements. The father and daughter knew from observing the synchrony of these movements that there was something uniquely familiar about this man; something that is visable only to deaf people. This man had what is known in the community as "deaf eyes." The daughter's guess that the man in the brown overcoat was "the" deaf man was confirmed by observing how he read the world.

Visual-Cultural Adaptations

There are different sets of learned behaviors and adaptive systems that are passed on with respect to "reading the world." One learns to engage in observing, looking, and eventually seeing that sound has ways of bouncing off visual cues. I remember my father's advice as I was growing up. He would sign, "Observe others around you; if you notice them looking in one direction, something is happening over there. This is not limited to people walking, but also driving. If cars in front of you slow down or stop at an intersection when the light is green, do not attempt to pass without checking around you because this is a telltale sign of an oncoming ambulance or police in the intersection." My father also noted that pets and/or other animals are able to broadcast auditory cues. My wife and I are able to "hear" our kids coming down the stairs or playing upstairs when they are supposed to be in bed by noticing our pets (cats and dog) perk up from their sleep and glance at the space behind us. When I walk my dog in the woods I often "hear" things by noticing her glances in particular directions. Another "visual rule" my father hammered into me as a child was the necessity of looking back every time you leave a room or place. "You never know if someone may need your attention, so it is a courtesy to look behind you to check with others before you leave." I also learned the significance of periphery as an integral part of reading the world. The man in the overcoat used it to respond to the father through the café window just as my three and a half–year-old daughter used it to correct me when I incorrectly produced her friend's name sign.

When we look at social spaces we see that the proxemics or social distance between interlocutors is at a distance that is comfortable for the eyes. When more than two people are involved, the spacing arrangement between signers becomes triangular. When additional signers join the conversation the circle becomes larger, and always maintains visual sight lines of one another. At conferences or sporting events it is common to see many circles forming throughout the lobby and people maintaining appropriate visual proxemics.

When participating in and/or joining a circle, signers need to be in synchrony with each other's body rhythms.[34] Listeners need to be in sync with the signer's pace of signs, body, and saccadic movements in order to take a turn. To join a conversation already under way, the newcomer needs to be in sync with the established interlocutors. When deftly done it appears as if the person was part of the initial conversation.

There appears to be symbiosis between native members of the signing community. Whenever native signers go to a location for the first time, whether it is a national or international site, they meet new people and hang out with new friends. Invariably these new friends are also native signers. It is remarkable that without actively seeking them out they naturally connect with other native signers. There is clearly a rapport, a synchronicity, and a subjective way of being that binds them. Having grown up in visual environments they learn to use the eyes and body for various functions related to language, discourse, and culture. When they meet someone else who has acquired and emits this way of being, synchronicity happens and a connection results.

Another related area is how signers naturally create or modify their habitat as exemplified by the phrase "this is a deaf house." This comment indicates that the particular house has earned the "seal of approval" for the way it is structured for vision. The floor plan of a "deaf house" is usually open and has fewer walls and many windows in the common area.[35] Additionally the line of sight to the second floor is not obstructed, and there are visual extensions of auditory signals such as flashing doorbell lights and phone and baby-cry signals. Some homes also have strategically placed lights to maximize vision at night and mirrors to allow for visual access in other parts of the house that are obstructed. The significant features of this type of habitat, a "deaf house," create minimal visual obstructions and enhance visual communication pathways.

Visual Symbolism in Arts and Literature

In this section we look at ways the visual experience permeates into the arts and literature by looking at some symbols: doors, windows, light, and night. Although the signing community shares many established symbols in various arts and literary works with the majority culture, there are some idiosyncratic representations that are indigenous among signers. Examination of these symbols provides insight into the consciousness that binds the community.

DOORS AND WINDOWS

The attributes of doors and windows are often tied to visual permeability, which for our purpose is connected to language modality.[36] A large number of "Deaf" narratives, especially narratives of personal experiences, have recurrent themes of protagonists being caught, shut in, or locked out behind doors. Conflicts arise because of the opaqueness of doors, which makes them inaccessible transporters of visual elements and language modalities. In seeking resolution, the protagonists try various visual extensions of sound to get the attention of the party "on the other side."[37] More conflicts arise when these extensions fail and the ultimate solution is almost always found through a window of some sort. Windows are permeable; protagonists wave through windows, throw objects at windows, and climb up to windows in order to communicate. As conveyors of light, windows are conveyors of visual communication.

In terms of communication permeability, doors are to hearing people what windows are to deaf people. Though they do impede the process, hearing people can communicate through closed doors because they allow the transmission of sound. Otherwise, there would be no "knock-knock" jokes. Their prevalence in the hearing community speaks volumes. There is even a Web site devoted exclusively to knock-knock jokes (www.knock-knock-joke.com). Here is an example of conversations happening through doors:

> Knock Knock!
> Who's there?
> Doris.
> Doris, who?
> Doris locked, that's why I had to knock![38]

Knock-knock jokes are almost nonexistent in the Deaf signing community; for Deaf people the exchange stops at "knock knock."[39] Windows, on the other hand, silence hearing people. Generally, hearing people have difficulty carrying on conversations through closed windows. One scene in the mockumentary film *This is Spinal Tap,* about a heavy metal band in decline, effectively demonstrates this point. There is a scene involving the heavy metal band riding in the back of a limousine whose driver incessantly and fanatically rambles about Frank Sinatra to them. An annoyed member of the band presses the button closing the power window behind the driver in order to shut him up. The impermeability and divisiveness of windows as a conductor of speech communication is echoed in "The Ebony Tower," by John Fowles: "The cruelty of glass: as transparent as air, as divisive as steel."[40] Thus, even though nondeaf people can see each other, communication is assumed to be blocked if the auditory channel is reduced as is the case with a closed window. In comparison, windows allow visual communication for signers as this story demonstrates:

> A Deaf couple stops by a supermarket to pick up a few items on their way home. As they pull into the shopping center, they realize that their two-year-old child has fallen asleep. Rather than waking up the child, they agree that the mother should stay in the car and the father goes in for the items they need. As he shops, the father realizes he is not sure which type of herbal tea his wife wanted. So, he goes to the front of the store, past the cashier and waves through the window to get the answer to his question. The mother notices someone waving inside the store and looks up. Through two sets of windows (the store window and car window) they clarify exactly the kind of tea she wants. As he turns to go back to the aisle where teas are shelved, he notices all the people around the cashier staring at him wondering what he was doing.[41]

The following story further illustrates the differences in the way a deaf man and a hearing man deal with windows and communication.

At a stoplight a deaf man noticed out of his periphery that the driver of the car to his left had rolled down the passenger window. The deaf man turned to find the driver asking, "May I have the time?" which the deaf man was able to lip-read.

The deaf man glanced at his wristwatch and gestured (by holding up five on one hand and an index finger on the other hand), "six."

The hearing driver shook his head and said, "Roll down the window."

The deaf man rolled down his window and repeated the gesture "six."

The hearing man finally got it.[42]

The humorous tale above is a spoof on hearing people and their helplessness when it comes to communicating through windows. There was no change in the way the deaf person expressed himself. The visual message was the same; it only became "louder" to the hearing person when the gesture was done through an open window.

There are also several poems that incorporate the use of doors and/or windows. Consider Ella Lentz's poem "The Door."[43] This creative work describes deaf people breaking free from the bondage of oralism, sheltering themselves in a room with a heavily secured door. Later in the poem, someone bangs on the door and the deaf people in the room wonder who it could be. Finally, one person goes to open the door, but the other cautions this person saying, "You don't know who it could be!" The role of the door as "a passage" takes on additional meaning here. In this case, as in other literary works, it represents taking a risk, opening the door to an inaccessible unknown.[44]

In a performance entitled "Doors for Sale: Audism in the Deaf World,"[45] I told various stories and talked about doors as a metaphor for oppression and barriers in the Deaf world and proposed their elimination. After all, unless you can hear, one never knows who stands on the other side. Soon after my presentation I received this e-mail from John Lee Clark.

I recalled a 1921 obituary in the Minnesota State Academy for the Deaf's school paper, "The Companion." You know, in those days deaf families would have hearing neighbors who they'd go to if they needed important calls made. Well, late one night this fellow's wife became very sick and urged her husband to go over to the next house to have the widow there call the doctor. He goes over there and knocks on the door. No reply. More knocking. Still no reply. More kno—BOOM!—The guy is shot dead. The widow was calling "Who's there?" and grew panicky when she got no response and she got the rifle and simply shot through the door. So you can say that at least one door killed a deaf person. A window would've saved his life. Even a small window, bullet-hole sized like a peephole, would've been enough to save his life. I've thought about that story now and then, but now it has a new significance for me.[46]

A similar application of these literary analyses to visual arts adds new perspectives on several paintings by the late Harry R. Williams. In these paintings, doors are featured in the middle of landscapes.[47] *Coffin Door* (Figure 4.1) is one example. In this picture, we see a door shaped like a coffin (resembling one at Gallaudet University) directly in the middle of beautiful seascape, blocking its visual continuity and obstructing the view. A hand enfolds (from behind) the top of the door suggesting that someone is behind it. This demystifies the situation, yet we never know who it is. To the left of the door in the distance is a picture window of the city of Los Angeles. In the foreground

Figure 4.1. Harry R. Williams, *Coffin Door.* Copyright Harry R. Williams. Used with permission of DawnSignPress.

is a rowboat, presumably ready to travel toward the window suggesting an orientation toward the visible.[48]

As we further extend the symbols it is important to note that doors and windows are parts of a dwelling. If we consider the human body "a dwelling" it creates an interesting metaphor related to particular signs that closely resemble doors and windows. The sign

Figure 4.2. DOOR.

Figure 4.3. DOOR.

Figure 4.4. DEAF.

Figure 4.5. DEAF.

DOOR (Figures 4.2 and 4.3) is done with the same "B" hand shape and palm orientation as the formal sign DEAF (Figures 4.4 and 4.5).[49] The sign for WINDOW (Figures 4.6 and 4.7) is made with the same hand shape and palm orientation as the signs EYES SHUT and EYES OPEN[50] shown in Figures 4.8 and 4.9 respectively. It is doubtful whether the association is intentional, but the natural relationships of these parallels are worth pursuing. It is beyond question that they further contribute to a pattern of symbolic representations of visual communication and opacity. But, interestingly, unlike real windows, the sign WINDOW cannot be seen through. Thus the abstract representation loses something that is in the real world.

LIGHT AND NIGHT

Light and absence of light (i.e., night) is another constant theme that's widely reported and acknowledged.[51] The theme of light is permeated in various forms of Deaf life from the way different organizations/companies name themselves (e.g., DawnSignPress, www.lightkitchen.com, etc.)[52] to the folk explanations of why Deaf people gather in the kitchen. The common saying is they do that because the lights are brighter in the kitchen. This may be true but it is also true for many hearing people of other cultures. The issue is deeper than that because light is a deeply ingrained value for those leading a visual way of being. Light, like windows, signifies the ability to communicate, and when one communicates one belongs. And when one belongs, one is at home in the world.

Figure 4.6. WINDOW.

Figure 4.7. WINDOW.

Figure 4.8. EYES-SHUT.

Figure 4.9. EYES-OPEN.

Ladd reports of Deaf people assembling around a lamppost long after clubs closed for the night in the UK.[53] Similar observations have been noted elsewhere. In fact, after the "Doors for Sale" performance in Minnesota, a security guard, apparently well advised, began to turn off the lights in the auditorium and then the lobby, managing to herd a bunch of deaf people out of the building. Instead of going home, as one would expect, they all congregated around a lamppost in the parking lot. As I was observing this procession, a young woman came up to me and asked this question, "What do Deaf people and moths have in common?"[54]

Peters noticed that the consistency of light as a theme and symbol is illuminated in various Deaf literary works—from the "birth of the community," light is prominent in the story of how Épée came upon the two young deaf sisters one night in front of a fireplace,[55] to the presence of and absence of light as symbol in various literary works from ASL Poetry (e.g., Valli's "Bright Windy Morning") to ASL narratives (e.g., Bahan's "Bird of a Different Feather").[56]

In the end of "Bird of a Different Feather," the surgically altered bird, unable to fit in either world (the eagle and the bird world), decided to fly away into the sunset followed by darkness. To many the symbolic interpretation of night in this context is death. There is another possible way of interpreting the end of the story. Using a lens from those leading a visually oriented way of life, night takes on additional meaning: unlike those who hear, the absence of light means there is no access to communication. In order to communicate one will have to resort to tactile means, and for those with no or limited experience with tactile communication it is like being removed from the world. Unhomed and alone in the world of night, as a theme or symbol in literature, one can say in the context of visual communication, night is to doors as light is to windows.

Reflection

The thoughts accumulated for this essay—though not comprehensive—show how signing Deaf people acquire this multilayered visual way of being in the world beyond the capacity of ordinary eyes. They inhabit a highly visual sensory world and appear to be pushing the boundaries of vision far beyond limits known by other human groups. The push springs from the innate human need to communicate. This desire is essential and powerful enough to cause a domino effect in the following areas:

- In language: We have seen the emergence and flourishing of visual languages (using space and physical phonological building blocks) as well as the role of eyes inside and outside the linguistic, discourse, and neurological system.
- In culture: We have discussed examples of ways the culture offers suggestions to lead a visually encompassed life.
- In arts and literature: We have examined some recurrent themes and symbols associated to vision.

This just scratches the surface of the potential for vision and visuality. And in terms of examining Deaf people's sensory worlds, we have not yet explored in depth or discussed another territory that has been told in countless life stories and anecdotes—on the ways Deaf people develop tactile minds. This is another dimension definitely worth exploring.

In retrospect I can't help but wonder about the "what ifs," because it has taken society so long to acknowledge the role of vision and signed languages in the lives of Deaf people. So many generations of signers have been handcuffed in a society intoxicated by the ideology that speech is language and vice versa. It is amazing that with these impositions, Deaf people have developed into one of the most visual groups of people on the face of the Earth. One wonders what the possibilities would be if they were allowed to proceed in life unbounded. How far would this human variety push the boundaries of vision?

Notes

Much thought and discussion with the following colleagues have led their way into this essay. I thank Dirksen Bauman, MJ Bienvenu, Todd Czubek, Janey Greenwald, John Lee Clark, Robert Lee, Flavia Fleischer, Sue Burnes, Steve Nover, Carol Neidle, Laura Petitto, Bob Hoffmeister, and Harlan Lane. I particularly thank Janey Greenwald, Robert Lee, and Dirksen Bauman for their editorial assistance, and Sue Burnes for appearing as sign model.

1. Edward Hall, *The Hidden Dimension* (New York: Anchor, 1982), states "people of different cultures not only speak different languages but, what is possibly more important, inhabit different sensory worlds" (2).

2. George Veditz, "President's Message," in *Proceedings of the Ninth Convention of the National Association of the Deaf and the Third Worlds Congress of the Deaf, 1910* (Philadelphia: Philocophus Press, 1912), 30. George Veditz used the phrase "people of the eye" at least twice. The first can be found in his president's message to the congress, "all-wise Mother Nature designed for the people of the eye, a language" (22).

3. The discussion here refers to those who were born deaf or became deaf in their infancy.

4. See H-Dirksen L. Bauman, "On the Disconstruction of (Sign) Language in the Western Tradition: A Deaf Reading of Plato's *Cratylus,*" this volume.

5. Plato, "Cratlyus," in *The Collected Dialogues of Plato Including the Letters,* ed. E. Hamilton and H. Cairns (Princeton: Princeton University Press, 1961), 457.

6. J. Kakumasu, "Urubu Sign Language," *International Journal of American Linguistics* 34, no. 4 (1968): 275–81; P. Farb, *Word Play: What Happens When People Talk* (New York: Vintage, 1973).

7. See, for example, James Woodward, "Attitudes toward Deaf People on Providence Island, Columbia," *American Anthropologist* 63 (1978): 49–68; Jane Poole, "A Preliminary Description of Martha's Vineyard Sign Language" (paper presented at the 3rd International Symposium on Sign Language Research, Rome, Italy, June 1983); Nora Ellen Groce, *Everyone Here Spoke Sign Language: Hereditary Deafness on Martha's Vineyard* (Cambridge, Mass.: Harvard University Press, 1985); W. Washbaugh, *Five Fingers for Survival* (Ann Arbor: Karoma, 1986). For further information on the development of home signs and gestures among deaf children in the contemporary world, see Susan Goldin-Meadow, *The Resilence of Language: What Gesture Creation in Deaf Children Can Tell Us about How All Children Learn Language* (New York: Psychology Press, 2003).

8. George W. Veditz, "The Preservation of the Sign Language," original version in *American Sign Language,* trans. Carol Padden and Eric Malzkuhn, reprinted in *Deaf World: A Historical Reader and Primary Sourcebook,* ed. Lois Bragg (New York: New York University Press, 2001), 83–85.

9. Paulo Freire, quoted in M. J. Wheatley, "The Power of Talk," *Utne Reader,* July–August 2002, 54–58.

10. Over the course of human history, the social perception of gestures and sign language swayed from being acceptable to not acceptable. In the later part of Western civilization (from the mid-nineteenth century to today) many have held that the uses of gestures and sign language were not language per se or have no significant social value, and have imposed restrictions on its development and use; see for example Douglas Baynton, *Forbidden Signs: American Culture and the Campaign against Sign Language* (Chicago: University of Chicago Press, 1996).

11. See for example C. Chamberlain, "Do the Deaf 'See' Better? Effects of Deafness on Visiospatial Skills" (masters thesis, McGill University, 1994), which argues that being deaf alone is not enough to see enhanced visual processing skills. The research suggests that it is the inclusion and use of sign language that enables this enhancement.

12. For more discussion of this function, see Hall, *Hidden Dimension,* and Martin Jay, *Downcast Eyes: The Denigration of Vision in Twentieth-Century French Thought* (Berkeley and Los Angeles: University of California Press, 1993).

13. The term "word" is used in this essay instead of "sign" to reduce the need for such distinction because there is no difference. A human utterance is a human utterance whether signed or spoken.

14. D. MacLaughlin, "The Structure of Determiner Phrases: Evidence from American Sign Language" (PhD diss., Boston University, 1997); Ben Bahan, "Non-manual Realization of Agreement in American Sign Language" (PhD diss., Boston University, 1996); Carol Neidle, Judy Kegl, Dawn MacLaughlin, Ben Bahan, and Robert Lee, *The Syntax of American Sign Language: Functional Categories and Hierarchical Structure* (Cambridge, Mass.: MIT Press, 2000).

15. In the case of first-person object, the eye gaze will mark the subject. For more information, see Ben Bahan, "Non-manual Realization of Agreement in American Sign Language," in Neidle et al., *Syntax of American Sign Language.*

16. Charlotte Baker, "Eye-openers in ASL" (paper presented at the California Linguistic Association Conference, San Diego State University, 1976); Charlotte Baker, "Regulators and Turn-Taking in American Sign Language Discourse," in *On the Other Hand: New Perspectives on American Sign*

Language, ed. L. Freidman (New York: Academic Press, 1977), 215–36; Charlotte Baker and Carol Padden, "Focusing on Nonmanual Components of American Sign Language," in *Understanding Language Through Sign Language Research*, ed. Patricia Siple (New York: Academic Press, 1978), 27–57; Ben Bahan and Sam Supalla, "Line Segmentation and Narrative Structure: A Study of Eye Gaze Behavior in American Sign Language," in *Language, Gesture and Space*, ed. K. Emmorey and J. Reilly (Hillsdale, N.J.: Lawrence Erlbaum Associates, 1995), 171–91.

17. Bahan and Supalla, "Line Segmentation"; Baker, "Eye-openers in ASL" and "Regulators and Turn-Taking"; Baker and Padden "Focusing."

18. Baker, "Eye-openers in ASL" and "Regulators and Turn-Taking"; Baker and Padden, "Focusing."

19. Susan Mather, "Eye Gaze and Communication in a Deaf Classroom," *Sign Language Studies* 54 (1987): 11–30; Susan Mather, "Visually Oriented Teaching Strategies with Deaf Preschool Children," in *The Sociolinguistics of the Deaf Community*, ed. by Ceil Lucas (San Diego: Academic Press, 1989), 165–87.

20. See Mather, "Visually Oriented Teaching Strategies," for more details about this phenomenon.

21. Bahan and Supalla, "Line Segmentation."

22. Ibid.

23. Baker, "Eye-openers in ASL."

24. See for example: Baker, "Regulators and Turn-Taking"; Baker and Padden, "Focusing"; Bahan and Supalla, "Line Segmentation"; R. Wilbur, "Eye Blinks and ASL Phrase Structure," *Sign Language Studies* 84 (1994): 221–40.

25. Most information in this section draws from Harlan Lane, Robert Hoffmeister, and Ben Bahan, *A Journey into the Deaf-World* (San Diego: DawnSignPress, 1996).

26. Oliver Sacks, "Seeing Voices: Lecture at Durham University," video transcript (Durham, UK: Deaf Studies Research Unit, 1990). Reported in Ernst Thoutenhoofd, "Vision | Deaf: Vision as a Constitutive Element of 'Deaf Communities,'" *DeafWorlds* 1, no. 13 (1997): 26.

27. H. Neville, "Cerebral Organization for Spatial Attention," in *Spatial Cognition: Brain Bases and Development*, ed. J. Stiles-Davis, M. Kritchevsky, and U. Bellugi (Hillsdale, N.J.: Lawrence Erlbaum Associates, 1988), 327–41; D. Bavelier, A. Tomann, C. Hutton, T. Mitchell, D. Corina, G. Liu, and H. Neville, "Visual Attention to the Periphery Is Enhanced in Congenitally Deaf Individuals," *Journal of Neuroscience* 20, RC93: 1–6 (2000).

28. Karen Emmorey, "Processing a Dynamic Visual-Spatial Language: Psycholinguistic Studies of American Sign Language," *Journal of Psycholinguistic Research* 22, no. 2 (1993): 153–88; Lane, Hoffmeister, and Bahan, *Journey into the Deaf-World*.

29. U. Bellugi, L. O'Grady, D. Lillo-Martin, M. O'Grady-Hynes, K. van Hoek, and D. Corina, "Enhancement of Spatial Cognition in Deaf Children," in *From Gesture to Language in Hearing and Deaf Children*, ed. V. Volterra and C. Erting (Berlin: Springer Verlag, 1994), 278–98; F. H. Sisco and R. J. Anderson, "Deaf Children's Performance on the WISC-R Relative to Hearing Status of Parents and Child-Rearing Experiences," *American Annals of the Deaf* 125 (1980): 923–30; Lane, Hoffmeister, and Bahan, *Journey into the Deaf-World*.

30. Bellugi et al., "Enhancement of Spatial Cognition"; Emmorey, "Processing a Dynamic Visual-Spatial Language"; Lane, Hoffmeister, and Bahan, *Journey into the Deaf-World*.

31. With the exception of several studies on nonverbal IQ tests that showed deaf children scoring higher than hearing children.

32. E. S. Klima, O. Tzeng, A. Fok, U. Bellugi, D. Corina, and J. Bettger, "From Sign to Script: Effects of Linguistic Experience on Perceptual Categorization," in *The Biological Bases of Language*, Journal of Chinese Linguistics Monograph Series 13 (Berkeley: University of California Berkeley, Project on Linguistic Analysis, 1999), 96–129; Lane, Hoffmeister, and Bahan, *Journey into the Deaf-World*.

33. Most of the observations discussed in this section are based on personal experience as a native member of this visual culture.

34. For some examples of synchrony of body rhythms, see E. T. Hall, "Deaf Culture, Tacit Culture, and Ethnic Relations," in *The Deaf Way: Perspectives from the International Conference on Deaf Cul-

ture, ed. Carol J. Erting, Robert C. Johnson, Dorothy L. Smith, and Bruce D. Snider (Washington, D.C.: Gallaudet University Press, 1994), 31–39.

35. One should take a look at houses or buildings designed by Olof Hanson, a deaf architect in the late nineteenth and early twentieth centuries.

36. Interestingly, the dichotomy of a window and a door as a metaphor for deaf signers was used as far back as 1776 in the preface of Épée's book on methods of educating the deaf through sign language. He stated, "The book will show, as clearly as possible, how to go about bringing in through the window what cannot come in through the door; namely, to insinuate into the minds of the deaf through the visual channel what cannot reach them through the auditory channel." Charles-Michel Épée, "Institution des sourds et muets par la voie des signes méthodiques," in *The Deaf Experience: Classics in Language and Education,* ed. Harlan Lane, trans. Franklin Philip (Cambridge, Mass.: Harvard University Press, 1984), 51.

37. In narratives of personal experiences persons are deaf by default, unless mentioned for emphasis. Those nondeaf are usually identified, e.g., hearing person.

38. Retrieved from http://www.knock-knock-joke.com.

39. There are some people who enjoy these jokes and translate them into ASL, but this is not widespread.

40. I thank John Lee Clark for bringing this to my attention.

41. This composite was told at several storytelling events by Ben Bahan.

42. This composite was told at several storytelling events by Ben Bahan.

43. Ella Lentz, *The Treasure: Poems by Ella Mae Lentz* (Berkeley: In Motion Press, 1995).

44. A hearing person would have simply asked, "Who's there?"

45. St. Paul College, Minn., May 7, 2004.

46. John Lee Clark, personal communication, May 7, 2004.

47. HRW, as he is known, has done several paintings that feature doors; one is featured on the cover of the text *Journey into the Deaf-World.* Near the end of his life he painted a series of coffin doors, which may have foreshadowed his coming demise.

48. Like all artworks, there may be different interpretations on this. I am merely applying what I have learned from various literary works to the painting. Unfortunately, I cannot confirm this analysis with HRW.

49. I thank Dirksen Bauman for this insight.

50. There are other signs used to depict the same concept.

51. See for example Carol Padden and Tom Humphries, *Deaf in America: Voices from a Culture* (Cambridge, Mass.: Harvard University Press, 1988); Cynthia Peters, *Deaf American Literature: From Carnival to the Canon* (Washington, D.C.: Gallaudet University Press, 2000); Paddy Ladd, *Understanding Deaf Culture: In Search of Deafhood* (Clevedon, JK: Multilingual Matters, 2003).

52. Peters, *Deaf American Literature,* 48.

53. Ladd, *Understanding Deaf Culture,* reports "It should be noted here that the lamp-post, a source of light at night for Deaf people, is a significant symbol within Deaf culture, one that carried even more weight in the era before homes were lit with electricity. It also rendered Deaf people and their signing highly visible to the public. Since most Deaf gatherings took place after work, willingness to be seen signing in public was symbolised by the lamp-post" (344).

54. They both are drawn to light.

55. Reported in Padden and Humphries, *Deaf in America.*

56. Peters, *Deaf American Literature,* 49.

5. Coequality and Transnational Studies: Understanding Deaf Lives

JOSEPH J. MURRAY

ON THE FIRST MONDAY *of July 1889, Deaf American Amos Draper mounted a platform in the chapel of St. Saviour's Church. Facing him was a crowd of more than one hundred largely working-class British Deaf men, all gathered at this Oxford Street meeting room in central London to greet a delegation of some twenty Deaf Americans en route to the first International Congress of the Deaf in Paris, France. Draper surveyed the audience and, quoting Shakespeare, declared, "One touch of nature makes the whole world kin."*[1]

This "touch of nature," the physical fact of deafness, manifested itself in a number of commonalities in the lives of nineteenth-century Deaf people from different nations. Deafness had long been a nexus around which transnational bodies of professionals incorporated. While a transnational body centered around a professional discourse is perhaps commonplace, a look at the late nineteenth- and early twentieth-century Western Deaf world shows Deaf people of this time created and maintained consistent contact with one another over national and continental boundaries, despite seemingly few similarities between their lives. After all, what could a Deaf American educated at the state-supported American Asylum for Deaf Mutes in Hartford, Connecticut, and employed as a professor at the National Deaf-Mute College in Washington, D.C., possibly see himself as having in common with a Deaf Briton educated at the privately funded Old Kent Road school in London and working as a draughtsman for the Imperial Admiralty? In other words, what incentive would a person living in one national and occupational context have to spend time and energy on interactions with someone living in a much different context?

Hints of an answer emerge from the St. Saviour's Church meeting. In his address, Draper noted that, despite vast geographical separation,

> in all essentials our experiences are probably the same. If you have troubles, we can sympathize with you, for we have the same troubles; or if you have joys, those joys are ours, and we rejoice with you.[2]

Deaf people, for good or bad, shared a common experience of living as members of a visual community in an auditory world, an experience transcending local contexts and national boundaries. This experience was supported by a shared rejection of larger social misconceptions and professional ideologies that homogenized them as deficient countrymen, ignoring the realities of their lives as members of a cultural community.

Draper's comments point to an area that has thus far lain outside the research frameworks used by scholars in Deaf Studies and related fields. To date, Deaf Studies has most often explored Deaf lives within the frameworks of single national communities.[3] One consequence of this restricted field of study is that Deaf Studies scholars often view Deaf people in a framework of comparison (whether explicit or implied) with other national minorities/oppressed groups. Why do we always reach for analogies with the African American civil rights movement or look to Women's Studies for ideas on how to interpret the experience of Deaf Americans? I do not want to suggest we cannot learn much from such comparisons, nor would I deny research within this framework has had a beneficial impact on the field of Deaf Studies and Deaf people's lives. Yet, is it possible that an adherence to theories and structures designed to explain the place of other minorities in specific nation-states not only unwittingly ties us to nation-specific narratives but also obscures just what it is that is most *Deaf* about being Deaf? Transnational studies of Deaf people may enable us to see beyond the classic nation-state-based "minority struggle for equality" narrative to explore how Draper's "touch of nature" illuminates commonalities in Deaf lives across national boundaries and what these commonalities mean for the world in which we live.

I would like to suggest Draper's sentiments, signed in 1889, are applicable to the current global Deaf community. This does not mean Draper's nineteenth-century Deaf world and our contemporary twenty-first-century Deaf world are alike in all respects, but that constructions of transnational spaces for articulating Deafhood exist/ed both in the nineteenth century and today.[4] Transnational interaction among Deaf people does not ignore national boundaries or national identities. Rather, I believe Deaf people in different locations share a common discursive field as Deaf people, a field existing alongside identities framed within the boundaries of specific nation-states and the cultures associated with those states. Living in a visual community stretching across national boundaries, while simultaneously participating in their auditory, national communities, Deaf people live uniquely structured lives.

Understanding Deaf Lives

The 1893 World's Congress of the Deaf at the Chicago World's Fair brought together over one thousand Deaf people from the United States and Europe. While the Congress was an event run by Deaf people for Deaf people, it was also part of the Chicago World's Fair's Congresses Auxiliary, an assembly of 225 Congresses on topics ranging from temperance to religion to "women's progress."[5] Deaf American George T. Dougherty, head of the World's Congress of the Deaf organizing committee, noted with satisfaction that the Congress of the Deaf "got recognition on a basis co-equal with all the great World's Congresses of other kinds."[6] Dougherty marveled at this fact, as did other Deaf people in attendance, proud of their ability to "meet the hearing world in congresses."[7] Participants listened to papers from Deaf men on the current state of Deaf lives in different Western countries and passed a resolution affirming their unanimous condemnation of the oral method in Deaf education. The Congress was not all work, however, as participants conversed well into the early morning hours at a lavish banquet in downtown Chicago, one among a number of well-attended social events during the week.[8]

Dougherty's use of the term "on a basis co-equal" points at a way of being Deaf that has not been fully explored in the field of Deaf Studies to date. When social scientists first began to study Deaf people as a distinct community, they presented an image of a community hindered by failed educational practices and limited vocational opportunities in its struggle for equality with hearing society.[9] Later work in the field of Deaf Studies has moved away from this focus to emphasize how Deaf people have managed to maintain a unique cultural community despite overwhelming ignorance, and at times outright hostility, to sign language and Deaf Culture.[10] Throughout much of the academic literature, a dichotomy of assimilation and resistance is predominant, with hearing society presented as a hegemonic force provoking resistance among inhabitants of the Deaf world.

The idea of coequality offers something different. Deaf people are not foreigners in their own country or solely oppressed minorities within their nation-states. The experience of being Deaf encompasses an expectation of participation in a society not tailored to Deaf norms as well as the articulation of a separate space of being Deaf, a space that, at times, transcends national boundaries. With coequality, the traditional binaries—of Deaf worlds and hearing worlds, of Deaf lives "segregated from" or "assimilated into" hearing societies—can be seen not in opposition to one another, but as mutually formative. Deaf people live simultaneously in hearing spaces and in Deaf spaces, are part of a Deaf community and active participants in non-Deaf social settings. Coequality presumes a distinct group acculturated to, but not assimilated in, larger society.

Take the exultation Dougherty and his counterparts felt on having their World's Congress presented alongside other international meetings at the great World's Fair. Not only was this a triumph in that it presented Deaf people as equal to hearing people (and on a global scale to boot), it was also, according to Dougherty, the culmination of a century's worth of Deaf people being educated and working together as a distinct community:

> Who would have dreamed one hundred years ago that this could ever be possible? Then the deaf were uneducated and widely scattered, unknown to each other; their influence, of course, was *nil.*[11]

Nineteenth-century Deaf people saw their consolidation into a single community through organizations and conferences as the best means to achieve not just equality, but coequality with larger society. Deaf people willingly sought to participate on an equal basis in the society around them, but refused to be submerged into it. In order to shape their terms of participation in non-Deaf society, it was necessary to have a Deaf world. Otherwise, "unknown to each other, their influence, of course, was *nil.*" Coequality highlights the ability of Deaf people to live successful, productive lives *as Deaf people,* moving within both the Deaf world and non-Deaf society at will.

Deaf American Olof Hanson, traveling in Germany in 1890, found himself sitting opposite a young Deaf German man in a Berlin café where "about a hundred" Deaf Germans were assembled. Hanson found this young man, educated orally and with only a rudimentary knowledge of German Sign Language, was on his first trip from the provinces to this metropolitan gathering of Deaf Germans. He had come for a single reason: "I am here looking for a wife."[12]

If coequality presumes a distinct community, where can this community be found in geographical space? Hanson's story of the young German man illustrates the fact that sites of cultural production and transmission in the Deaf world have not remained the same over time. Hanson would have pointed to the Berlin café as a site of entrance into the Deaf community. A few decades ago in America it would have been possible to give an equally simple answer: Deaf clubs and Deaf schools. Today, both schools and clubs are on the wane, and increasing numbers of young Deaf people do not participate in either arena of cultural production. It is time for Deaf clubs and residential schools for Deaf people to be historicized, to be understood as products of a specific historical moment and not as universal, singular vehicles of Deaf cultural transmission.

The major features of the new Deaf cultural landscape consist of gatherings at designated public or private spaces situated both in physical, geographical space and at virtual sites that exist only in moments of active creation and consumption. An example of the latter can be found in "Deafzone," a World Wide Web page created by young Deaf Swiss-Germans where Deaf parties in ever-shifting locations are advertised, e-mail and instant messaging addresses are exchanged, and ideas are debated in online discussion forums.[13] The inherently temporary nature of contemporary gatherings in physical space is illustrated by a Deaf New Year's Eve party in Amsterdam attended by a group of young Deaf people from different European countries, all jetting into a mutually agreed upon location to party with like-minded counterparts for several days. Contemporary sites for the manufacture, expression, and consumption of Deafhood are increasingly fluid, temporary, and situational.

Mobility and continuous community re-creation are emerging as the key characteristics of the twenty-first-century Deaf community, but they are not necessarily unique to this time, nor should we see community mobility and change solely determined by technology. Admittedly, e-mail and the Internet play an important role in current community interconnections that sometimes transcend national boundaries, just as railroads, steamships, and new global postage rates were also factors in transnational interconnections among nineteenth-century Deaf people. Technology may be an enabler, but it is not an originator of transnational contact. For changing social contexts over time also reveal a commonality across time: the desire for Deaf people to be with members of their own community and the continued significance of transnational sites for the articulation of Deafhood.

I had the pleasure of participating in the 1996 Nordic Deaf Youth Camp in Kinsarvik, a community of little over four hundred people located deep in the mountains and fjords of western Norway. During the weeklong camp, we seventy-odd Deaf young adults (ages eighteen to thirty) became a significant percentage of the town's population, transforming it into a Deafcentric space. On the final day of the camp, after the last busload of campers left, I wandered around the campsite, now a depleted shell. The campsite's hearing owners came out of the woodwork and set about tidying up the place for the next set of guests. My three travel companions, one Russian, one Dane, one Norwegian, and myself, an American, drove home with little left to say to one another; all sharing an unarticulated feeling of longing, a sense that something significant had ended and now we were back to the regular pattern of our lives.

This feeling of dislocation and longing after a large-scale Deaf event seems to be a fairly common phenomenon, as is the jarring feeling one experiences upon seeing a formerly Deaf physical space transformed into a hearing space. Sites of today's World's Congress of the World Federation of the Deaf (WFD), quadrennial meetings attended by several thousand people, are Deafcentric sites for several days, then emptied of their Deaf character immediately afterwards. Unlike diaspora populations, Deaf people do not live their lives in the expectation of some end point where all Deaf people will come together in a homeland.[14] Rather, Deaf people go to preselected geographical locations to establish temporary physical communities of Deaf people. These temporary spaces provide Deaf people an environment where being Deaf becomes a standard way of being.

The centrality of transnational Deaf spaces in maintaining a sense of coequality is important here. These spaces bring fresh insights into specific Deaf localities needing points of comparison for their own lives lacking in the larger society physically around them. Arjun Appadurai's use of the word *locality* seems to fit in with this type of inter- action. Appadurai conceives of locality as existing in a form that is "primarily relational and contextual rather than as scalar or spatial . . . constituted by a series of links be- tween the sense of social immediacy, the technologies of interactivity, and the relativity of contexts."[15] Within temporary localities constructed at Deaf events, Deaf people find a space to express Deafhood, fully aware that this space exists beside a contact zone containing philosophies with different degrees of understanding—and tolerance—of Deaf people.[16] It might be possible to call Deaf localities *translocal*, functioning as nodes in larger transnational flows of knowledge on Deaf people.[17] Interactions that are intensely localized in time and space exist alongside and are influenced by previously formed Deaf localities, potentially separated by one or both of the twin elements of time and geography. Attendees at the most recent WFD Congress bring together ideas from their home settings, from previous WFD Congresses or other transnational gath- erings, and from interactions with one another. All of these settings come together in one space, and interactions within this space bring together multiple viewpoints cen- tered around a common theme: the experience of being Deaf. Transnational Deaf lo- calities are continually changing articulations of coequality derived from a multiplicity of sources within the global Deaf world and from contact zone interactions with non- Deaf societies. Coequality positions Deaf people as being cognizant of (and incorpo- rating ideas from) discourse both from the societies in which they live and from their transnational Deaf counterparts.

Approaching Transnational Studies

So far I've tossed out some terms—coequality, contact zones, and (trans)localities—that I think may prove useful in understanding Deaf lives. While Martha's Vineyard may or may not have once been a sign language mecca, most Deaf people do not live their lives in anticipation of its return.[18] Rather, Deaf people aim for a state of coequality in which they participate in non-Deaf societies while simultaneously creating temporary, situ- ational localities in which to express their Deafhood. These localities, I contend below, cannot be seen as existing solely in the boundaries of a single nation-state. I offer below three points on Deaf transnationalism, with some questions.

DEAF EVENTS HIGHLIGHT DEAFHOOD

The Nordic Youth Camp and the WFD Congress examples above point to the significance of Deaf-centered events for Deaf lives. It is at these events that Deaf people can highlight the Deaf aspect of their identities. The Deaf community is a largely decentralized community that forms in specific geographical spaces only at prearranged times, most often at events enacted for Deaf people (often by Deaf people themselves). How does the inherently temporary nature of most Deaf events affect Deaf people's constructions of their lives? Are Deaf events a temporary respite from the process of living in a contact zone? Are these events constructed by individuals as the primary events in their lives, with their geographical microlocations (hearing workplace/neighborhoods) and contact zone interactions playing a lesser role in a hierarchy of importance they accord to events in their own lives? What similarities/differences emerge in the articulation of Deafhood/coequality in different localities? How does Deafhood change in explicitly transnational contexts (for example, WFD Congresses) as opposed to local contexts with transnational influences?

COMMON GLOBAL DISCOURSES SPUR TACTICALLY MOBILE RESPONSES

In 1883 Alexander Graham Bell addresses the U.S. National Academy of Sciences on the possibility of the "formation of a deaf-mute variety of the human race." Intense discussion ensued among scientists, educators, and the general public about the best way to prevent this from occurring, with a number of influential thinkers suggesting Deaf-Deaf marriages ought to be discouraged by a variety of means. Deaf Briton R. Armour, in his address to Deaf men from nearly a dozen countries at the 1889 Paris Congress, concluded his summary of British objections to restrictions on Deaf-Deaf marriages with the comment, "It is scarcely necessary for me to enlarge on any of these [objections] since I know that your own sentiments coincide with mine."[19]

Armour felt comfortable making such a claim because he and his contemporaries were responding to a single discourse perpetuated by people utilizing the same global grid of scientific knowledge—eugenic science—to advance their aims. The ideas used by Deaf people to respond to this discourse had what Ann Laura Stoler calls *tactical mobility*.[20] Tactically mobile ideas are those formed in one setting that are transferable to other settings. While specific national contexts may predicate specific local responses, these responses are then transmitted to other localities, to be adapted to and adopted by Deaf people experiencing similar mechanisms of control elsewhere. Tactical mobility thus highlights not only Deaf transnationalism but also commonalities in the experience of being hearing when faced with a Deaf world.

Of particular interest in this vein is that mechanisms devised by hearing people to control Deaf people's lives slip so easily from their points of origin to other sites. Technologies of hearing improvement are a classic example of a transnational phenomenon impacting Deaf people in different countries: the hearing aid and cochlear implant did not sit quietly within the nations in which they were invented, but quickly spread to all areas of the world.[21] With a transnational study of audism, for example, the task would not be limited to looking at the different trajectories audism takes in the United States and Britain, to pick two countries at random, but would explore which aspects of audism operate regardless of national boundaries, while paying attention to the forms audism adapts itself to in response to context-specific circumstances. Exploring the commonalties of Deaf lives across national borders may enable us to uncover previously overlooked transnational instruments of rule and resistance that may be obscured in single national contexts.[22]

TRANSNATIONAL CIRCUITS OF KNOWLEDGE PRODUCTION

In 1890, Deaf Briton Francis Maginn took a leading role in the "formation of an Association on American lines" that was to become the British Deaf and Dumb Association. His argument for the necessity of the association drew on the accomplishments of the Deaf American delegation to the International Congress in Paris. For their part, American Deaf people found themselves having to "follow instead of leading" when they discovered Maginn's conference was attended by representatives from different Deaf Societies, as opposed to the U.S. National Association of the Deaf conventions that were "heterogeneous gatherings of men and women who represent nothing but their individual opinions."[23]

A British conference, emerging from observations among British Deaf men at the Paris International Congress and following the American example, ended up influencing Americans themselves. Sometimes, ideas did not merely transmit; they ricocheted across transnational circuits into different localities.[24] Nineteenth-century Deaf people often wrote on issues of concern to their national communities in a framework that included frequent references to similar problems faced by Deaf people in other nations. Transnational networks produce knowledge on what it means to be Deaf in different translocalities, localities that serve in turn as nodes in which ideas from different sources intermingle, are reshaped, and are sent on (or not). Can we identify the nodes, institutions, and individuals operating on twenty-first-century Deaf circuits of knowledge production? How is coequality articulated in these circuits? Which localities (if any) lie outside these circuits and why? What are the possible consequences of participation in/exclusion from circuits of knowledge production in today's Deaf world?

Transnational work will no doubt uncover previously overlooked commonalities between Deaf communities situated in different national spaces. To give just two examples: Why does nearly every national association of Deaf people place official recognition of their sign language by the government high on its list of political aims? Likewise, why is it that—at least in every Western nation I have had the opportunity to test this out in—the standard Deaf to Deaf individual attention-getting method consists of precisely *two* taps on a shoulder? The task here is not really to explain "who came first" but to ask why these similarities occur. Because of a "touch of nature"? A shared experience of living as visual minorities? If these similarities are the result of cross-national pollination, why do extranational influences find such fertile ground in different Deaf localities? While exploring similarities, we should take care not to do our studies in a teleological model that presumes any one existing national Deaf community as a model to which others will inevitably evolve. Similarities should be studied as manifestations of specific phenomena that cut across national boundaries, not as inevitable steps in a historical evolution.

Of course, differences do exist. Most Deaf Malawians live lives very different from those of most Deaf Canadians. I emphasize similarities in this essay because it is easy to fall back into simplistic nation-based narratives of development with certain Deaf communities on an apex of successful integration into national societies ("We have the ADA/relay services, etc.") to which other countries need to catch up. Or comparisons that presume Deaf lives depend solely on the societies in which they live ("Scandinavian Deaf people are so lucky. Their socialist societies provide for everything!"). It is easier to find national differences in Deaf people's lives than to understand transnational similarities. Whether these differences are due to national/geographical factors or to some overlooked variations in Deafhood is another question for us to explore. In doing so, scholars should also keep in mind how social, ethnic, and economic hierarchies structure transnational interactions among Deaf people. Where were African American Deaf people at the 1893 World's Congress? Are Malawian Deaf people able to find their way into contemporary Deaf transnational conversations often dominated by developed countries? How do these exclusions hinder, even distort, the efficacy of transnational circuits of knowledge production among Deaf people?

The Future of Coequality: Some Questions Currently without Answers

The exhibit floor at the 2000 U.S. National Association of the Deaf convention presented a visitor with an array of Deaf-owned firms selling Deaf products from FRIENDS *earrings to teddy bears signing* ILY. *Next to these expressions of cultural distinctiveness were businesses marketing different forms of assimilation into non-Deaf society: computerized avatar interpreters, cochlear implants, and telecommunications relay services.*

Deaf people today still affirm the ability of Deaf people to live Deaf-centered lives while simultaneously exploring different forms of coequality with non-Deaf societies. This overlapping duality of cultural distinctiveness and individual assimilation is a dominant organizing principle of the contemporary Deaf world. Yet, with advances in genetic engineering progressing rapidly, we may face a time when the physical fact of deafness becomes not an accident of nature but the product of a conscious choice. Do individuals whose families made this choice still have a claim to state largesse (in the form of relay services, interpreter services, state-funded schools for Deaf people) largely based on a benevolence model? Are both sides of coequality sustainable?

If citizenship is predicated on participation in larger society, and participation in our contemporary society is now increasingly oriented toward the consumption of goods and services, then what does it mean to be Deaf in a consumerist society? We are seeing increasingly powerful corporate entities (some Deaf-controlled, many with Deaf employees) become major sponsors of events organized by political advocacy organizations for Deaf people. Dougherty claimed Deaf people found power through community organizations. How has commercialization affected Deaf community organizations built on notions of representative democracy? Today, corporations offer a variety of services centered around both conceptualizations of Deaf as a culture and of deaf as a disability, providing consumers with a menu of services ranging from American Sign Language classes to job-training services. Understandings of Deaf people based on both assimilation and cultural distinction are today being manufactured and sold, often by Deaf people themselves. How does coequality change when it becomes a commodity packaged and sold by businesses oriented toward institutional profit? What happens when ways of being Deaf are commodified and sold? Globalization may foster transnational meetings among Deaf people, but how do the discourses within these meetings change due to consumerism?

Beyond the Nation-State into . . . an Understanding of Deaf Lives?

Nkhata Bay, Malawi, 1998: I sit on a small beach on the shores of Lake Malawi, watching my laundry dry on the sand in front of the thatched hut I've rented for a few days. A thin Malawian approaches me. The dust on his pants indicates he has walked a long distance and the neat, but worn, clothes on his slim frame tell me he is either a farmer or fisherman, earning an income without resorting to the tourist trade. Our eyes meet and he lifts his right hand to his face to ask, "Deaf?"

What role can transnational studies play in understanding the structures of Deaf lives? I would suggest that restricting ourselves to nation-based narratives is not, on its own, sufficient for us to fully understand what it means to be Deaf. Utilizing a transnational field of study enables Deaf Studies to discover just what it is that is most Deaf about being Deaf. More than a mere "touch of nature," being Deaf is the dominant factor in ways of organizing individual and community lives that contain remarkable similarities across national boundaries. An aspect of this similarity no doubt comes about because of similar patterns of domination through global scientific and pedagogical discourses aimed against Deaf people's cultural expression. But there is something more—Deaf people find real value in the lived experiences of their Deaf counterparts in different nations, willingly incorporating extranational productions of Deafhood into their own translocal personas. Transnational studies of Deaf people may end up clarifying similarities in Deaf lives, similarities obscured by nineteenth- and twentieth-century ideologies privileging distinctiveness based on the imagined boundaries of nation-states. What does it mean to be Deaf—to live as a visual minority in an auditory world? Transnational Deaf Studies can guide us to multiple possible answers to this question.

Notes

1. Amos Draper, "Report to the President," in *Annual Report of the Columbia Institution for Deaf Mutes, 1889* (Washington, D.C., 1889), 34.

2. Ibid.

3. There are a growing number of essay collections that bring together essays on a range of national or regional groups under a single cover, but few individual essays in these collections work outside of a national framework. Examples abound in a range of disciplines. See Leila Monaghan, Constanze Schmaling, Karen Nakamura, and Graham Turner, eds., *Many Ways to Be Deaf: International Variation in Deaf Communities* (Washington, D.C.: Gallaudet University Press, 2003); Renate Fischer and Tomas Vollhaber, eds., *Collage: Works on International Deaf History International*

Studies on Sign Language and Communication of the Deaf, vol. 33 (Hamburg: Signum, 1996); Penny Boyes Braem and Rachel Sutton-Spence, eds., *The Hands Are the Head of the Mouth: The Mouth as Articulator in Sign Languages* (Hamburg: Signum, 2001); and selected volumes of essays in the Sociolinguistics in Deaf Communities series from Gallaudet University Press.

4. The term Deafhood was devised by Paddy Ladd to define "the existential state of Deaf 'being-in-the-world.'" I use the term here as a shorthand for naming the cultural experience of being Deaf, finding it a ready counterpart to the idea of coequality. See Paddy Ladd, *Understanding Deaf Culture: In Search of Deafhood* (Clevedon, UK: Multilingual Matters, 2003), xviii.

5. David F. Burg, *Chicago's White City* (Lexington: University Press of Kentucky, 1976), 235.

6. *Proceedings of the World Congress of the Deaf and the Report of the Fourth Convention of the National Association of the Deaf* (Chicago, 1893), 10.

7. Ibid., 20.

8. "1,000 participants," ibid., 11; "lavish banquet," 109.

9. Works in this vein would be Paul Higgins, *Outsiders in a Hearing World* (Beverly Hills: Sage Press, 1980); Beryl Lieff Benderly, *Dancing Without Music: Deafness in America* (Washington, D.C.: Gallaudet University Press, 1980); and Jerome Schein, *At Home among Strangers: Exploring the Deaf Community in the United States* (Washington, D.C.: Gallaudet University Press, 1989).

10. A number of works emerged in the late 1980s and 1990s. For a representative sample, see Harlan Lane, Robert Hoffmeister, and Ben Bahan, *A Journey into the Deaf-World* (San Diego: DawnSignPress, 1996); MJ Bienvenu and Betty Colonomos, *Introduction to American Deaf Culture,* videotape series (Burtonsville, Md.: Sign Media, 1992–93); Sherman Wilcox, ed., *American Deaf Culture: An Anthology* (Burtonsville, Md.: Linstock Press, 1989); Carol Padden and Tom Humphries, *Deaf in America: Voices from a Culture* (Cambridge, Mass.: Harvard University Press, 1988). Works in this vein are still being published today, a recent work of Deaf history being Susan Burch, *Signs of Resistance: American Deaf Cultural History, 1900 to 1942* (New York: New York University Press, 2002).

11. Emphasis in original. *Proceedings of the World Congress of the Deaf and the Report of the Fourth Convention of the National Association of the Deaf,* 10.

12. Olof Hanson, "Observations Abroad," *American Annals of the Deaf* 35 (1890): 270.

13. "Deafzone," http://www.deafzone.ch/.

14. There are scholars who deemphasize the place of a homeland in diasporic communities. James Clifford notes "transnational connections linking Diasporas need not be articulated primarily through a real or symbolic homeland. . . . decentered, lateral connections may be just as important as those formed around teleology of origin/return": *Routes: Travel and Translation in the Late Twentieth Century* (Cambridge, Mass.: Harvard University Press, 1997), 249–50.

15. Arjun Appadurai, *Modernity at Large: Cultural Dimensions of Globalization* (Minneapolis: University of Minnesota Press, 1996), 178. For more on localities, see chapter 9.

16. The term "contact zone" is drawn from Mary Louise Pratt, who describes them as "social spaces where disparate cultures meet, clash, and grapple with each other, often in highly asymmetrical relations of domination and subordination": *Imperial Eyes: Travel Writing and Transculturation* (New York: Routledge, 1992), 4.

17. Appadurai has a bleaker view of this term, using as an example of translocalities tourist sites where "local subjectivity is commodified, and . . . nation-states . . . erase internal, local dynamics through externally imposed modes of regulation, credentialization, and image production": *Modernity at Large,* 192.

18. For more on Martha's Vineyard, see Nora Ellen Groce, *Everyone Here Spoke Sign Language: Hereditary Deafness on Martha's Vineyard* (Cambridge, Mass.: Harvard University Press, 1985).

19. "Reminisces of the Deaf and Dumb Congress in Paris," *Deaf and Dumb Times* (November 1890), 83.

20. Ann Laura Stoler, "Tense and Tender Ties: The Politics of Comparison in North American History and (Post) Colonial Studies," *Journal of American History* 88, no. 3 (2001): 847.

21. Global distribution does not mean even distribution across the globe; wealth plays a large role in determining which areas of the world will receive the latest technology first, with developing countries getting the latest technology later than their developed counterparts.

22. This is an idea advanced by Stoler, "Tense and Tender Ties."

23. "Our Notes," *Deaf and Dumb Times*, April 1890, 122; Francis Maginn, "The Proposed National Association of the Deaf," *Deaf and Dumb Times* (January 1890), 73.

24. The term "circuits of knowledge production" is drawn from Stoler, "Tense and Tender Ties," 831.

6. *Sound and Belonging: What Is a Community?*

HILDE HAUALAND

What Is Sound?

Where do we belong? How do we belong? How do we belong to each other—and how do we belong to the world? Questions about "What is human?" include questions about how human beings differ from other animals, and the answer to this question has often been that human beings have a language that is qualitatively different from the languages of other animals. Language does not only make humans human, language also makes human beings able to connect to each other, to name and categorize the world. Languages contribute to a sense of belonging to other human beings and to the world, whether through speech or signed language. Communities create languages and language creates images of communities that eventually also are defined as societies or states.[1]

Traditionally, language has been confused with speech. Assertions like "language is at home in the audible, which, unlike the visible, is its natural medium of communication"[2] are not unusual, and witness first of all to a confusion of speech, sound, and language. Linguists studying signed languages have contributed to a revised understanding of human languages, and within linguistic fields speech is now considered one of the possible modalities of human languages. While the confusion of language and speech is no longer so substantial among linguists, there is still a long way to go before the presumed "natural" status of speech as the only true human language is deconstructed also within other scientific fields as well as with laymen.[3] Assertions of the "natural" status of speech thus provoke several questions. Why is the audible perceived as the natural form of communication? Is it just because a vast majority in the world communicates in audible languages? Or could there be something about the audible—the experience of sounds themselves—that causes such blur? What is so "natural" about speech, if it in fact is only one of the possible modalities of human languages?

In an attempt to answer these questions, I will take a step back and look at one property of speech. Speech has an attribute that is inherently a part of it—namely sound—that makes it different from sign languages. In my approach, I will not discuss the meanings of the particular sounds in languages, but rather look for the metaphysics of sound. With the lenses of a Deaf social anthropologist I ask: What is sound? Being an outsider in a hearing world, I am like other Deaf people "within hearing culture, but not of it."[4] My relationship to sounds is thus rather abstract. Through the process of listening, a hearing person most often hears things rather than sounds and "commit[s] what psychologists call the 'experience error,' which means that what we know to be in things themselves we immediately take as being in our consciousness of them. We make perception out of things perceived."[5] Deaf people may hear sounds, but rarely things, which means that we may perceive without making perceptions. According to Heidegger, "to hear a sound as sound was to hear badly."[6] This is a quotation that probably perfectly fits the experience of sound of quite a lot of deaf and hard-of-hearing people. Many deaf people do in fact have some experience with sounds. But deaf people's ways of "listening" are detached from the things that make the sounds; we are diverted from the sources of sound, so what some of us, unlike many hearing people, more easily can do is to "listen abstractly" to the few sounds some can hear. Hearing people are continuously and most often unavoidably and unconsciously interpreting the sounds they hear. The ability to abstract ourselves from the experience of sounds may give deaf and profoundly hard-of-hearing people a different perspective in the metaphysical study of sound.

In addition to the questions posed above, I will also take a look at how sounds and the experience of hearing sounds are described and explained through language. Also, I will discuss if sound itself (not only speech) has any implications for how human beings connect themselves, not only to each other but also to the world. Finally, like speech has had an enormous impact on the way language is studied, I will ask if *sound* plays a role in how human communities are constructed and studied.

I will seek some answers to these questions through three angles. The first goes through an exploration of descriptions of sound and use of metaphors of sound in language. Next, I will discuss how common life patterns of Deaf people reveal alternative ways of bonding and community building. Finally, I will round up with a discussion about the traditional view about what a community is, based on discussions of which fields social anthropologists have studied. Like studies of sign language have altered the understanding of what language is, studies of communities that establish connections through vision or other channels than the audible may challenge the understanding of what a community is.

Sound Is the Message

When people listen, they rarely hear sounds alone. Rather they hear the sources of the sound, and when they listen truly, they hear things, not sounds. They hear sea or the storm, not merely a roar; bells, not a ringing; an apple, not a falling; and the sensation of hearing does not stop at the sensation itself, but reaches out toward the source of the sound.[7] People do not listen to a sound without knowing how to "assimilate its place in relation to all other activity of the world, how to react to it, how to talk about it, how to know its relationship to other sounds."[8] The urge to interpret sounds is so strong that when the source of a sound remains unidentified, the sensation could be unsatisfying, disquieting. Unidentified sound "impels us to listen, to try to discover the material source of the sound, and we will not rest until we have succeeded in associating what we hear with something visible-tangible. In this way we perceive the entire audible world, as an adjunct to the world of visible and tangible things, as though wrapped around it."[9]

The notion of "wrapping" is interesting. It testifies to a comprehension of sound as a kind of metaphysical stuffing between the visible-tangible objects and the body. It is as if sound fills out the space between the seeing person and the visible and tangible things. While a person's spatialized gaze creates distance and confirms the presence of objects-in-the-world, sound, by contrast, penetrates the individual and creates a sense of communication and participation and reaches out to the source of the sound. Unlike light, the sound from the object is "a dimension of experience in and of itself."[10] There is no concept that stands to visual sensations like "sound" stands to audible sensations. Light makes things visible and helps sight to confirm the appearance of visible and tangible objects. The difference between what is seen and what is heard is not only about the physical or metaphysical properties of light and sound, but it is about the perceptual "principles that determine which categories of objects are placed in the foreground of sight and hearing respectively."[11] What Rée calls the *grammar or semantics of perceptual experience* is quite different to sight and hearing respectively. Except in the cases when one looks at the stars, at a blazing fire or the taillights of cars, one looks at the things that *light makes visible,* rather than at the light itself. Contrary to the grammar of seeing is the grammar of hearing; what one hears is always either sounds or sources of sound, not objects.[12] The very material property of sound is air waves, not just a mere reflection of the site of production of the sound. The sound is itself a relation, a connection between a source of sound and the ear; sound is a medium that itself is a message, or with McLuhan's famous statement: "The medium is the message."[13] With reference to Zuckerkandl,[14] Stoller writes about the effect of sound on bodies:

> the laws governing sound movements . . . have one thing in common: they are dynamic, referring to "states not objects, to relations between tensions, not to positions between, to tendencies, not to magnitudes." Taking this logical sequence one step further, "the forces that act in the tonal world manifest themselves *through* bodies but not upon bodies." In this sense, a tone or an incantation is not a conveyor of action, as Malinowski would have said; rather it *is* action.[15]

So when the audible is rendered the natural form of communication, it may not only be because a majority in the world communicates through audible languages. Rather, it may be because the sound itself is the message people hear, while they interpret the meaning of the messages in a process of listening. Confusing language with speech may thus be a consequence of the metaphysics of sound. The sound of the phonemes in language, not their words, is the message. The power is not in the words as carriers of referential meaning, but in the sounds of the words; *sound is the action.* Thus, a phenomenological glance at sound reveals that the sound *is* the message, not only the conveyor of the message. Sound is a noun, and it is a verb.

When one listens, one actually tries to interpret the messages of sound, and it is in the process of listening that sounds are given meaning. It is only in the process of listening that one is able to interpret these sounds, to assimilate their place in relation to all other activities of the world, evaluate them, know how to react to them and how to talk about them, and know their relationship to other sounds. Listening must be learned, and the interpretation and significance of various sounds are almost always a question of learned culture and social values added to the sound.[16] The process of listening, however, should not be confused with the embodied sensory experience of hearing sounds.

Sound in Language

Our observations and interpretations of the world are only made possible through the sensory experiences of the body. It is not possible to describe the world without being predisposed and biased—both mentally and bodily. The body itself is a condition and a premise in how the world is sensed, but as we grow and learn, culturally learned values also influence how we understand our sensations. George Lakoff and Mark Johnson show through various examples how the human body and our sensomotoric experiences influence the way we perceive, classify, and speak of the world.[17] Rather than clinging to the traditional folk view that the world makes systematic sense, and that we can gain knowledge about it through using our senses, they state that reason is fundamentally embodied, and that "categorization is therefore a consequence of how we are embodied. . . . Categorization is, for the most part, not a product of conscious, 'objective' reasoning. We categorize as we do because we have the brains and bodies we have and because we interact in the world the way we do."[18] Language, in turn, influences the ways we think, which eventually also have impacts on how we interpret perceptions. The concepts in language thus reflect embodied experiences, and Lakoff and Johnson reveal how language is a flourish of metaphors that directly or indirectly can be traced back to an embodied sensation or experience of a phenomenon.[19] Some of the examples they give of how primary metaphors are reflected in language are expressions like "Tomorrow is a *big* day," "The colors aren't quite the same, but they're *close*," "Prices are *high*," and "I *see* what you mean." These expressions are all using physical references to explain nontangible emotions or considerations. The latter expression, for example, is referring to the primary metaphor of "Seeing Is Knowing," where the primary experience is getting information through vision. The expressions are then used *as if* prices are *high*, and *as if* one actually can *see* what another person means.

Lakoff and Johnson mostly discuss metaphors based on visual or tactile senses. Sound metaphors are almost entirely overlooked in *Philosophy in the Flesh*,[20] and it could be asked why. It could be that if the sounds that are heard are identified with their sources, not as messages and experiences in and of themselves, the process of hearing may be confused with the process of listening. Meaning is given to the *things people hear*, not to the sounds themselves. The authors may actually have overlooked that how people *hear* before they listen contributes to the construction and categorization of the world. The book does not mention any primary metaphors referring to primary experiences of sounds, so there was a need to go to language itself to find these. Baffled and intrigued by the lack of sound metaphors in the otherwise interesting book, I started to search such metaphors in the languages by which I am surrounded. Being a native signer of Norwegian Sign Language and an everyday reader and writer of Norwegian, I first started my quest for metaphors of sound in the languages that were closest to me. Therefore, the discussion of sound metaphors in language will start with examples from Scandinavian and North European languages.

A most striking metaphor of sound in these languages is *høre sammen* (Norwegian), *höra tilsammans* (Swedish), *erbij horen* (Dutch), *zusammen gehören* (German), and *kuulua yhteen* (Finnish). The literal translation of all of these expressions would be *hear together* or *hear same*. Actually, they are widely used concepts that mean belong, connected or related to. Another word in Norwegian, with similar concepts in the other mentioned languages, is *tilhørighet,* in which the core is the word "hear." This is the concept for belonging or connectedness. Finding concepts for belonging that do not include the core "hear" invite us to considerable linguistic roundabouts in the mentioned languages. Since Norwegian, Swedish, Danish, German, and Dutch are related languages, it is interesting to register that Finnish, belonging to a different family of languages than the others, also uses the concept of "hear" to name *belonging.* In English, the relationship between hearing and belonging is not so explicit, but examples of similar notions of sound are not hard to find. Connectedness or belonging is expressed in sayings like *I am all ears* to announce attention, *he listened carefully* to underline seriousness or close attention. If one has not *heard from somebody* in a long time, it indicates that one has lost contact with this person. Also telephone producers Nokia and Sony Ericsson have mottos that underline connectivity or relationships. Nokia claims that they are "Connecting people," while Sony Ericsson helps to "Make yourself heard." Even though cell phones can send visual messages, the transmission of sounds must still be seen as the core feature of a telephone, mobile or not. The invention of the telephone was in fact a result of the work of Alexander Graham Bell, who intended to invent a machine that could help deaf people hear. Instead, he made hearing people able to connect through sounds also at a distance and reinforced the significance of sound in the communication between hearing people.

While metaphors of hearing seem to refer to senses of belonging or connectedness in the languages mentioned, *sound* is used as a metaphor in adjectives for phenomena and things that are conceived as firm, steady, or solid in English. Using sound as an adjective, as in a business being on *sound footing* or in *sound asleep,* gives connotations to the idea of something solid, which also is used in the sense of something tangible. It is as if the sound itself *is* sound, like in Zuckerkandl's notion of sound as a wrapping.[21] *Sound* is not only a noun and a verb; it is an adjective, too.

These expressions, and how sounds and hearing are used in these languages, confirm the descriptions of audible sensations others who have probed into the phenomenology of sound, like Zuckerkandl, Stoller, and Rée, try to give.[22] Metaphors of sound and hearing express that something or somebody is connected and fit the embodied experience of hearing people that sound is the message that connects them to each other. Sound *is* action, it penetrates the individual and creates a sense of communication and participation and reaches out to the source of the sound.[23] The sound is itself a relation, a connection between a source of sound and the ear; sound is a medium that itself is a message, a message that connects hearing people to each other and the world. When people *hear (the) same* or *hear together,* they sense that they belong to each other by sharing the same audible sensations. People who belong to each other hear the same or hear together and form communities where they hear the same languages, voices, noises, and music. They also see the same objects, but the sounds they *hear together* create a sense of connection to the things they see and to each other.

What people do, and what I have done so far in this text, is to describe sound *as if* it actually was sound and hearing that connected people to the world. The discourse that identifies sound *as if* it creates connections pervades our construction of self and world. The idea of sound as connective is an embodied concept that "makes use of the sensorimotor system of our brains. Much of conceptual inference is, therefore, sensorimotor inference."[24] Sensorimotor inferences leading to the belief that sound creates connectedness, based on the embodied experience of sound, do not invite questions—until deaf people, by their very existence, confront the world with the possibility of living without sounds and construct lives, connections, belonging, communication, and communities based on visuality and sight.

The Difference

From early onset, human lives are, among other things, about finding people with whom one can communicate. To deaf people, these people have rarely been found in the family or neighborhood. By far most deaf people are born into families in which they are different from their parents, and only a minority has Deaf parents. Traditionally, an early experience of many deaf people is a sense of difference from their families.[25] They communicate differently and perceive the world differently from the people who are supposed to be the closest—the family. The family members most often use their ability to hear the sounds around them to create connections with other people and to explain and relate to the world. A deaf person will use his or her ability to see to perceive the world and to create connections and relations. It is not the *lack of hearing* that foremost defines a deaf child's experience of the world, but the strong presence of sight, and next an experience of difference from the people that are supposed to be the closest, their parents.

A Deaf elderly woman's story about how she discovered that she was different may illustrate this point, and in particular also the way she tells this story. Her name is Kari, and her story is a kind of telling that is very often told among Deaf people—about the moment when they found out they were deaf or different from their family, if born into a hearing family. The story shows that deaf people with no or little experiences with sounds do not necessarily share the general ideas of sounds and the role sounds might play in connecting hearing people to the world. Kari's story of discovering her difference from her parents is from a visit to a hospital in the 1930s. Her mother had been encouraged to take her to the hospital when she realized that Kari did not give the expected response to her surroundings. Kari tells:

> When I was three, I traveled to the State Hospital with my mother. First, we took the bus to Kristiansand, and then we were traveling on a boat along the coast all the way to Oslo. We drove a taxi to the State Hospital. I was overwhelmed, and all the houses were so tall. I had

never seen such houses before. We walked inside. The ceilings were so high, and there were loads of pipes and cords under the roofs, and I wondered what all this was. Then we entered the doctor's office. He looked at me and he was nice. He told me to sit down at a high table, and used his hands to say that. And I climbed up. My mother was just crying, she cried and cried. She was sitting right in front of me, and we were facing each other. I looked around, but I could not see anything, the doctor had left. So I just sat there waiting.[26]

Kari certainly understood that something was wrong, but she did not know exactly what made her mother cry. But the mother's reaction was also Kari's first realization that something was wrong. She was the center between her mother and the doctor, and she somehow realized that her mother's sorrow had something to do with her. She might have been feeling that she was not like her mother wanted her to be. This story, which Kari used to introduce herself before an interview, can be understood as a story about the first experience of a basic difference between herself and her mother. But what this difference consisted of she did not realize until later. When she as a grown-up tells about the episode at the State Hospital, she also explains why she was "different." Without pausing, she continues, but now in a retrospective manner:

Later, I understood that the doctor had told my mother to just look at, not behind me, just right at me. Then he took a bell, because he was to test my hearing to see if I could hear or not. It was a huge bell, big and heavy. And I heard nothing. I just sat there waiting. And mom just cried and cried. After a while I turned around, and the bell was right beside me. I leapt into the air when I saw that big bell the doctor was swinging back and forth. I was wondering a lot about what this was.

She was using the perspective of a three-year-old child when telling about the journey and the first sight of the Hospital and the doctor, but in the retrospective explanation she takes the perspective of her mother. Using perspectives is an important grammatical element of telling stories or about episodes in sign languages. It gives important information about the people present in a story, and it is a way of adding texture and context. The episode at the Hospital is partly given meaning through the mother's perspective, as it was the mother who cried because Kari did not hear. Kari only understood something was wrong, without knowing why. When she says "And I heard nothing," this is a later interpretation of what happened when she was three. When she was a deaf toddler, she probably had no idea of hearing or sound. But when she as an adult woman tells this story, the story and the experience of difference have quite another context than when she was three, and she is now able to tell why her mother cried. But as this part of the story is told, it also indicates some kind of distance to the mother's reaction. The mother wailed over her daughter's hearing loss. The loss of hearing meant that she would not be able to communicate with or be connected to her daughter in the same way as she could communicate with and relate to Kari's siblings. To Kari however, the realization of difference—not the lack of hearing—was crucial to this story. This part of Kari's story about herself is about feeling *different*. She continues her story with a story of departure or transition. Kari tells about entering the deaf institute in Oslo just before World War II. She had to travel far away from her parents' home to get to the school.

I turned seven in June and I started first grade in the fall the same year. Dad came with me. We got there by boat, and dad gave me candy. When we arrived, we were met by a cheerful little heavy-set lady, Ms. Larsen, who became my first teacher. She was kind. She welcomed us, she gave me a hug. Held my hand, and then we entered the classroom. There were no students there at that moment. They were all outside. I think it was a break, or it was in the afternoon, I don't know. I held my father's hand the entire time they spoke together, and I was standing quiet, watching. I looked at the blackboard. There I found a white little thing and wondered what that was. I drew with it on the blackboard, I thought that was fun. There was already something written on it, but I was unable to understand what it was. All the time, I made sure that dad wouldn't leave me, I held his hand. Looked around, but always made sure that dad was sitting there. Then the teacher came and asked me to come with her. I understood some of it. She said "come and see something fun," partly with her hands, partly with her mouth. I came with her, and forgot about dad. I thought he'd sit and wait for me. So I came with the teacher into the bathroom. She asked me to come and look down in the toilet. I was wondering what it was. I had never seen a water toilet that one could flush. At home, we only had an outdoor toilet. Here, it was a toilet where one could pull a string, and I'd never seen anything like that before. I laughed and laughed and thought it was funny. The teacher asked me to come, and we returned to the classroom, but dad was gone. I yelled "dad, dad," screamed and shouted, ran around to different rooms, but dad was gone. He had left. It hurt. I cried and cried, I think I cried for 3–4 days before it became better. I asked for daddy all the time.

Sander writes that such a "parting" upon entering a Deaf boarding school was common, also for those starting school later than Kari did.[27] Many deaf children experienced a major breakup when they entered school, and this breakup takes on the character of a rite of passage as it is retold. Many of the children didn't have a language before they started school, and "the white years" is an expression that is used in Norwegian about the years prior to entering a school for the deaf. Without a tool (language) to think with, the memories from the first years of life are often vague. For many of the children, meeting other kids using sign language became their first encounter with a language they could learn spontaneously. Starting school thus becomes a transition from a life without language to a life where relationships built on linguistic communication with others is made possible. Starting school may also mark separation from the safe and familiar at home. The transition lasts for a brief period (for Kari, a few days), and the students then find themselves comfortable in school, finding a new kind of safety among their fellow pupils and with some of the staff.

> Some time went by, and things got better. Ms. Larsen was my teacher, but only for five years. She was the best teacher I've ever had.

Ms. Larsen, the teacher present when Kari's dad left, partially inherits the role that Kari's parents had, and Kari develops a close relation to her for the first years at the institute. Deaf people often experience a departure from home or the closest geographical surroundings in order to meet communication partners. Some experience a sense of belonging or sameness the first time they meet other signers, for example in school. Hence, the sense of belonging has, to many Deaf and hard-of-hearing people, been of translocal nature, like Kari's story also reveals. To meet other people with whom one can communicate freely and spontaneously, moving or traveling to another place, often a school with other sign language users, is the only solution for many Deaf people. Their lives are, from the moment they experience this belonging to people at distant places, translocal: they belong both at home and to the place where the school, and eventually later also where a smaller or larger Deaf community, is. In his doctoral dissertation, Breivik showed how many of his informants had life stories where translocal practices were crucial, and found "aspects of a strong translocal drive where identity conforming aspects were strongly connected to the reported praxis of communication with people that did not (regularly) live in their copresence."[28] Many had stories about travels away from the family, a quest for like-minded people at other places than where they were born. Several spent much time, effort, and money to travel to meeting places and events where many Deaf people meet. Some of the life stories were like travelogues, where the continuous traveling and meeting new people were crucial. Breivik also observed weak territorial anchorage in relation to present residences, neighborhoods, and biological families (and place of birth).[29] Rather, Deaf people make connections to and identification with people at distant places, and a Deaf stranger may feel like a closer acquaintance than the hearing neighbors next door. The Deaf community is characterized by its scattered translocality, where the members may live at a quite large geographical distance from each other. In its transitory and temporary meeting places, the communicative basis for constructing communities is put in the foreground. Many do not share an everyday life, and only meet occasionally: once a week, once a month, or once a year. Many confuse sharing a culture with sharing a place, and this may explain why people unfamiliar with Deaf communities have difficulties believing that Deaf people constitute a culture and make communities. There's no obvious "place" for Deaf Culture. There are no obvious places where sounds can be shared or *heard together.* By using "hearing" concepts of belonging through sounds, we are in danger of ignoring what is one of the basic features of the Deaf Culture: its meeting places are transitory and temporary, yet it exists in the everyday life of Deaf people. The embodied experience of belonging may thus be experienced differently by hearing and Deaf people respectively. To hearing people, part of their belonging is through hearing the same sounds as the people to whom they live close. A Deaf person might from an early age have a dislocated and another embodied experience of belonging, since Deaf people in fact do not hear the same as the hearing people surrounding them. The Deaf quest for belonging might be dislocated and not connected to a particular geographical site, but toward other sign language users or visual people. Deaf people, who live scattered, meet and continue to meet at long distances and scattered settlement. Meeting at temporary events like festivals, sports games, or national or transnational congresses eventually leads to a more intense realization of Deaf Culture and the value of (visual) communication. By this means, the events have consequences for the Deaf community far beyond the actual time span of the games themselves or the people who actually participate, and the networks of the Deaf community are transcended. The Deaf community could be perceived as a global community, which "is not a place, but a process."[30] The *centers* of this community move constantly, by the ever-shifting locations of the large transnational events like the biennial Deaf World Games and the quadrennial Deaf World Congresses. This also challenges the notion of a defined geographical place as the prime site for social life. Hearing people have of course also traveled, but they have had the ability to make ties at the place where they live, too. To Deaf people and the Deaf community, the traveling is necessary, and Deaf people meeting each other across long distances are the glue in the Deaf community. Deaf people learn from each other, and reinforce the Deaf ways and visual perspectives of life. The cross-national Deaf marriages are innumerable, and so are Deaf friendships across national borders and continents. Without traveling and the temporary meeting places, the Deaf community would not have been what it is like today.

Hearing people's quest for "integrating" or "including" Deaf people might be based in their auditive sense of belonging because this is their embodied way of making relations. Their attempts to "include" Deaf people and make Deaf people *hear same* too often results in oppression of the Deaf-embodied ways of perceiving, mapping, and learning about the world. At the same time, Deaf people's quests for belonging and equals might find a route away from those who *hear together,* and dislocated identifications are often a crucial part of "the Deaf experience."

Construction of Place, Space, and Communities in Social Anthropology

Social anthropology is one field that has been occupied with the study of human communities and ideas of spaces, places, and belonging. Data have traditionally been collected mainly through qualitative methods like participant observation during long-term fieldwork in localized groups or cultures. The "idea that 'a culture' is naturally the property of a spatially localized people and that the way to study such a culture is to go 'there' ('among the so and so') has long been part of the unremarked common sense of anthropological practice."[31] The traditional selection of fields to study seems to follow the belief that a group of people who belong to each other, a community or a village, are a group of people who *hear the same.* Sounds are traditionally local. The outreach of sounds (in the frequencies that can be heard by regular human ears) is rather restricted (provided a television, radio, telephone, or the like is not used) compared to the distances light can travel. Sounds are in this sense far more localized than light, and a condition for *hearing together* is thus physical proximity. But by sticking to a local audible context, which is traditionally facilitated by doing long-term fieldwork, certain observations and certain interpretations are channelled, and others are being blocked out.[32] Stoller calls for greater attention to the role of the senses in anthropology and asks, if "anthropologists are to produce knowledge, how can they ignore how their own sensual biases affect the information they produce?"[33] Participant observation cannot be extracted into two different entities—participation or observation. Participation and observation are a unity where observation in its very own sense is a participatory activity, since the body participates as a sensory being. Our observations are made possible through the sensory experiences of the body, and the sensory experiences are interpreted and given meaning in different ways. It is not possible to write anthropology without being predisposed and biased—both mentally and bodily. The discussions regarding ethnocentrism and cultural relativism have focused on the role of social and cultural conditions during fieldwork and interpretations. But that the body itself is a condition and a premise in the experiences made is rarely discussed, and perhaps even less—which role the senses play in our predisposed understandings of what a place, a field, or a community is.

In the wake of globalization, increased migration, and democratization of communication technologies, the need to loosen the ties to the traditions of long-term fieldwork in localized cultures is increasingly being discussed among social anthropologists. Greater mobility and increased long-distance interaction have weakened the dominance and "normality" of people as settled, bounded to places, and strongly patterned in terms of culture. Deaf people, as well as gypsies, migrants, refugees, gays, and lesbians, are some of the groups that contribute to a destabilization of the theoretical and empirical presumptions of regional territory of particular groups, because of their global presence and translocal spatial practices.[34] The perception of culture as local, audible practice is not sufficient to understand the lives and construction of human communities. How concepts like community, space, place, and belonging are constructed needs further investigation in order to better understand how human beings create communities.

A phonocentric emphasis on local, audible belongings as the "normal" human way to connect to each other may misguide both research and the researcher. Greater emphasis on shifting localities, translocal communities, and transitory meeting places, where audible communication is replaced with something else, whether electronic signals or sign language, may give new perspectives on belonging as an audible practice—and as visual and spatial practice.

Conclusion

If a community is confused with a group of people who *hear same*, this will limit the possible fields of anthropology and deteriorate the full picture of how human communities are constructed. As the confusion of speech and language has enormous consequences for the way we understand human thinking, the lack of awareness regarding the role of sound, both in speech and as such, has led to a belief that only people who live close enough to each other to hear the same sounds constitute true communities. In Western communities, at least, this has led to prejudices and discrimination toward groups of people who do not fulfill this criterion. Attempts to assimilate gypsies and make them settle at permanent places, attempts to integrate deaf children in local community schools to force them to use the audible language of their surroundings, and bans against homosexuality can all be read as consequences of the belief that the "natural" entity for a community, or a prerequisite to belong, is the defined localized, geographical place. Bauman suggests a definition of *metaphysical audism* as "the orientation that links human identity and being with language defined as speech."[35] I will add to this that metaphysical audism also could be "the orientation that defines human communities as groups of people who hear (the) same." In a world where Deaf people must be understood partly by their dislocated belongings and transnational traditions, defining communities as a group of people sharing the same sounds of a localized place is a contribution to a sedentary and spatially restricting version of audism.

Notes

1. Benedict Anderson, *Imagined Communities: Reflections on the Origin and Spread of Nationalism* (London: Verso, 1991).
2. Victor Zuckerkandl, *Man the Musician: Sound and Symbol,* vol. 2 (Princeton: Princeton University Press, 1973), 86–87.
3. H-Dirksen L. Bauman, "Audism: Exploring the Metaphysics of Oppression," *Journal of Deaf Studies and Deaf Education* 9, no. 2 (2004): 239–46.
4. Laura Lakshmi Fjord, "Images of Difference: Deaf and Hearing in the United States," *Anthropology and Humanism* 21 (1996): 60.
5. Maurice Merleau-Ponty, *The Phenomenology of Perception,* trans. Colin Smith (London: Routledge, 1962), 5.
6. Qtd. in Jonathan Rée, *I See a Voice: Deafness, Language and the Senses—A Philosophical History* (London: Metropolitan Books, 1999), 42.
7. Zuckerkandl, *Man the Musician.*
8. Carol Padden and Tom Humphries, *Deaf in America: Voices from a Culture* (Cambridge, Mass.: Harvard University Press, 1988), 23.
9. Zuckerkandl, *Man the Musician,* 86.
10. Paul Stoller, *The Taste of Ethnographic Things: The Senses in Anthropology* (Philadelphia: University of Pennsylvania Press, 1989), 112.
11. Rée, *I See a Voice,* 43.
12. Ibid.
13. Marshall McLuhan, *Mennesket og media* (Oslo: Pax Forlag A/S, 1997).
14. Victor Zuckerkandl, *Sound and Symbol: Music and the External World* (Princeton: Princeton University Press, 1956).
15. Stoller, *Taste of Ethnographic Things,* 120.
16. Steven Feld, *Sound and Sentiment* (Philadelphia: University of Pennsylvania Press, 1982). Stoller, *Taste of Ethnographic Things.*
17. George Lakoff and Mark Johnson, *Philosophy in the Flesh* (New York: Basic Books, 1999).
18. Ibid., 18.
19. Lakoff and Johnson, *Philosophy in the Flesh.*
20. Ibid.
21. Zuckerkandl, *Man the Musician.*
22. Zuckerkandl, *Sound and Symbol* and *Man the Musician.* Stoller, *Taste of Ethnographic Things.* Rée, *I See a Voice.*
23. Stoller, *Taste of Ethnographic Things.*
24. Lakoff and Johnson, *Philosophy in the Flesh,* 20.
25. Padden and Humphries, *Deaf in America.* Fjord, "Images of Difference," 55–69. Hilde Haualand, *I endringens tegn* [In the sign of change] (Oslo: Unipub forlag, 2002). Jan-Kåre Breivik, *Deaf Identities in the Making: Local Lives, Transnational Connections* (Washington D.C.: Gallaudet University Press, 2005).
26. This account (here and in following quotations) is from a personal interview conducted in January 2000, trans. Hilde Haualund. The name used here is not the interviewee's actual name.
27. Thorbjørn Sander, *Fra Christiania Døvstmme-institutt til Skådalen kompetansesenter* [From Christiania Deaf-Dumb Institute to Skådalen Resource Center] (Oslo: Skådalen kompetansesenter, 1998).

28. Jan-Kåre Breivik, "Doing Transnational Fieldwork: Methodological Challenges," in *Rome: A Temporary Deaf City,* ed. Jan-Kåre Breivik, Hilde Haualand, and Per Solvang (Bergen: Rokkan Working Paper, 2002), 10.

29. Breivik, *Deaf Identities in the Making.*

30. Manuel Castells, *The Information Age: Economy, Society and Culture* (Oxford: Blackwell, 1996), 417.

31. Akhil Gupta and James Ferguson, eds., *Culture, Power, Place: Explorations in Critical Anthropology* (Durham: Duke University Press, 1997), 3.

32. Breivik, *Deaf Identities in the Making.*

33. Stoller, *Taste of Ethnographic Things,* 7.

34. Breivik, *Deaf Identities in the Making.*

35. Bauman, "Audism: Exploring the Metaphysics of Oppression," 245.

PART III   *Language and Literacy*

7. On the Disconstruction of (Sign) Language in the Western Tradition: A Deaf Reading of Plato's Cratylus

H-DIRKSEN L. BAUMAN

> In the study of humanity there is a maine deficiencie, one Province not to have been visited, and that is Gesture.
>
> —John Bulwer, *Chirologia,* 1644

> Answer me this: If we hadn't a voice or a tongue, and wanted to express things to one another, wouldn't we try to make signs by moving our hands, head, and the rest of our body, just as dumb people do at present?
>
> —Socrates, in Plato's *Cratylus*

WE CANNOT HELP BUT WONDER what those deaf Greeks were talking about. Were they, like the eighteenth-century Parisian Deaf community described by Pierre Desloges, discussing matters of personal, political, and philosophical import?[1] Were they retelling scenes from the recent play by Sophocles or Aeschylus, gleaning what they could from the dramatic gestures of the actors? Or were they were wondering what that old man, Socrates, was always talking about. What about the language that brought these signers together—what was their particular Athenian brand of sign language like?[2] While this may seem like amusing speculation, such musing about the existence of a deaf signing community in the fifth century BC is buttressed by what we now know about sign languages and their communities. We now know that human language is not dependent upon the single modality of speech, but instead may manifest in other modes, especially through a visual channel.[3] It is not too much to imagine that in such centers of Western civilization as Athens, Rome, Constantinople, and later, Paris deaf people would have found each other and, in so doing, would have coaxed language to take on its manual modality. We also know that signing communities have evolved throughout the world as a result of a group's genetic propensity for deafness. Sightings of such communities have occurred in Martha's Vineyard; Henniker, New Hampshire; Yucatán Peninsula; Bali; and among a Bedouin tribe in Israel.[4] As Deaf leader George Veditz signed in 1913, "As long as we have deaf people on this earth, we will have signs."[5] Indeed, Veditz's claim has been validated by over four decades of historical and scientific research into sign languages and their communities that has shown us a very simple, paradigm-shifting fact: signed languages are not aberrations, nor mere supplements to speech; they take the form of one human language modality among others, equal to speech. In short: *to sign is human.*

Why did it take so long to discover this about ourselves? Speech has so thoroughly become the norm that it passes through us, often unnoticed. Is the dominance of speech and phonetic writing part of the human design? Clearly speech frees up the hands for work and allows us to communicate where we can't see—in the dark and from behind listeners.[6] Despite these advantages, the past four decades of linguistic and neurolinguistic research show that sign languages have their own advantages, such as their ability to convey precise visual, spatial, and kinetic information, coupled with the capacity to convey abstract concepts equal to that of speech.

Or is there, as Derrida contends throughout *Of Grammatology,* a metaphysical and political history that has privileged speech over other nonphonetic languages and communication systems? "The system of 'hearing (understanding)-oneself speak' through the phonic substance," Derrida writes, ". . . has necessarily dominated the history of the world during an entire epoch, and has even produced the idea of the world, the idea of world-origin."[7] An untold facet of the phonocentric orientation of our philosophical heritage has been the denigration of nonphonetic languages, which clearly includes sign languages of Deaf communities. While sign communities have never had to fight against the guns and words of imperial invaders, they have indeed been subject to a long campaign against them and their languages. Douglas Baynton has recounted in great detail the American campaign against sign language, where educators of the deaf denounced manual languages as "barbaric," "primitive," "proto-language," and "monkey-like gestures."[8] In the context of this historical inheritance, we can see the global campaign against signed languages that continues to be carried out in homes, schools, churches, hospitals, audiology clinics, and genetic counseling centers. Sign languages have historically been—and continue to be—targeted.[9]

As alarmist as this may seem, the repression of sign is mostly unintentional. Hearing people simply don't know any better. Why should they? The vast majority of the earth's 6.3 billion people are not even aware that they are "hearing." I, for one, did not realize I was hearing until age twenty-one. Only after I began working with Deaf people did I become "hearing." Unless we have an encounter with deafness and the Deaf world, why would we ever bother to consider an alternative to speech? We are, after all, the speaking animal. Clearly, there is no campaign to eradicate sign here, no malicious intent to deny a deaf child a visual language. Most people are simply unaware (nor do they even care) that to sign is human. Instead, to sign is strange, foreign, unimaginable.[10] Either way—intentional or unintentional—signed languages have historically been hidden from sight, overlooked for centuries.

It is this historical and metaphysical occlusion of sign that I refer to as a function of the *phonocentric blind spot.* Blind spots occur as a result of the tiny spot where the optic nerve attaches to the retina, leaving no space for light receptors to gather light to become vision; yet if we shift our perspective, what was previously hidden appears to our sight. Similarly, the human capacity to sign has been there all along, yet hidden from view. But once we shift our perspective away from the assumption that speech is the exclusive mode of language, this hidden dimension of the human language capacity comes into sight. Though signed languages have been eclipsed by the phonocentric blind spot, there have been numerous sightings of sign language throughout history, too numerous and varied in their messages to recount here in depth. Among the many sightings are those by Herodotus, Plato, Augustine, Montaigne, Leonardo da Vinci, Descartes, Rousseau, Diderot, and Condillac, all of whom have made observations about sign languages of Deaf communities prior to the founding of formalized deaf education in the last half of the eighteenth century.[11] Taken together, the perspectives on sign language reveal a complicated and contradictory history that has yet to be told. But there are clear patterns: sign language is often glorified as a more perfect and exact language than speech; yet it is more often seen as a primitive, proto-language incapable of conveying abstract thought. Either case is inaccurate. Those who have written and mused about manual languages have rarely known anything about those languages. While this may seem like a political statement rooted in Deaf identity politics, it is rather recognition that our historical ignorance of manual language has actually had a profound impact on the development of our modern notions of language, literacy, and literature. This construction of manual languages throughout our history might be better described as a *disconstruction* of (sign) language in the Western tradition—that is, of the particular constructions of language that have been evolved within a fundamental lack, resulting in, as O'Neill describes, "muddled conclusions" and "tangled webs of ideas."[12]

In the history of the disconstruction of speech = language, Plato's *Cratylus* occupies an important part. As one of the earliest and more significant treatises on language by the foundational father of Western philosophy, Plato's *Cratylus* searches for the nature of names and in so doing speculates on the language of the deaf as a viable alternative to speech. This brief sighting of sign has a more profound consequence than has yet to be explored by scholars on the *Cratylus*. In addition, Plato's sighting of sign has often been quoted in Deaf Studies publications but has yet to be more fully elaborated. By placing the sighting in context, the implications of signed languages suddenly become much greater and extend into how we have defined language in the West.

Cratylus (Or on the Correctness of Names)

The dialogue begins as Socrates joins an ongoing discussion between two men, Hermogenes and Cratylus, who are discussing the fundamental question of the dialogue: is there such a thing as a "correctness of a name, one that belongs to it by nature"?[13] Do names *(onama)* bear a natural relation to that to which they refer, or are they wholly conventional? Or, to modernize the terminology, are signifiers arbitrary, motivated, or the source of deconstructive play?

Hermogenes claims that "no one can persuade me that the correctness of names is determined by anything besides convention and agreement" while Cratylus contends that "a name that expresses a thing by being like it is in every way superior . . . to one that is given by chance."[14] The positions taken by Hermogenes and Cratylus form two poles of contrasting beliefs, around which discussions of language have revolved for centuries. As Thais Morgan explains, "the formation of linguistics as a discipline has involved a constant tug-of-war between resolute Hermogenists and equally determined

Cratylists, or between Saussurean conventionalists who would demotivate language and intuitive mimologists who would remotivate language in relation to material and emotional realities."[15] The *Cratylus* thus helps to launch one of the longest standing debates in the philosophy of language: just what *is* in a name, after all? Is there something *rosy* about the word "rose"? Or does a rose by another name smell as sweet? Or, as Gertrude Stein asks, is a rose is a rose is a rose is a rose?

For his part, Plato never definitively answers these questions.[16] Critics have long been debating Plato's position relative to the conventionalist or naturalist arguments. Several claim that Plato advocates a conventionalist view of names; others contend that Plato favors a naturalist thesis; and still others propose that the *Cratylus* is intentionally open-ended.[17] Such divergent and highly contested views reveal a high level of ambiguity, obscurity, and confusing logic in the *Cratylus*. Allan Silverman, for example, claims that the *Cratylus* "proceeds by misdirection" as it "concentrates our attention on misguided conceptions of how to understand 'correctness' of names. . . . That the dialogue works by misdirection is not, I think, a novel conclusion. Virtually all of the interpretations . . . agree that some parts of the discussion are to be ignored, especially the long etymological section"[18] (to be explained below). Though few claim that the *Cratylus* can be read as serious linguistic work, most concur that the issues at stake are of greater philosophical import than the correctness of this or that individual name. Rather, the dialogue is concerned more, as Silverman suggests, with "*naming in general*"—which is no small matter. Naming, as Michel Foucault recognizes in *The Order of Things,* was a central concern in classical discourse.

> One might say that it is the name that organizes all Classical discourse; to speak or to write is not to say things or to express oneself, it is not a matter of playing with language, it is to make one's way toward the sovereign act of nomination, to move, through language, towards the place where things and words are conjoined in their common essence, and which makes it possible to give them a name.[19]

While much of the *Cratylus* does seem like language play, it is most significantly a meditation on the very possibility of naming. The *Cratylus* is an unusual dialogue as it is a serious philosophical investigation of the conditions of semiosis, but the methodologies employed are, to quote Socrates himself, "outrageous and absurd."[20] Herein is a source of the contradictions in the *Cratylus:* on the one hand, we witness an earnest quest for the nature of names and being, and on the other, a potentially "outrageous and absurd" set of solutions regarding the correctness of names. In other words, the (Cratylean) Platonic Ideal of names is at odds with the reality of the (Hermogenist) nature of spoken names as we know it. The result is emblematic of Ynez O'Neill's "tangled web of ideas."

When we read through a Deaf theoretical lens, however, the causes of this contradiction are magnified and the implications on Western constructions of language made explicit. We see that Plato searches for an ideal language where names embody and reveal the nature of the referent, but he fails through absurd methodologies to show how spoken names actually are capable of such a natural relation. In short, Plato's ideal desire for a language of natural relation is at odds with the nature of spoken languages, where natural relation is difficult to detect. However, the ideal that Plato describes for language is actually much closer to the visual-spatial-kinetic properties of manual languages; it is almost as if Plato sensed that there was another medium for language and he groped for it—as one would a phantom limb. He sensed something there but couldn't quite grasp it. These claims will be explored during the course of a rereading of the *Cratylus*.

On the Nature of Names and the Names of Nature

Only a few exchanges into the dialogue, Socrates establishes the metaphysical framework in which the dialogue takes place. Before discussing the properties of names, he investigates the nature of the things to which names refer. "It is clear," Socrates observes, "that things have some fixed being or essence of their own. They are not in relation to us and are not made to fluctuate by how they appear to us. They are by themselves, in relation to their own being or essence, which is theirs by nature."[21] If a name is to be correct, then it must be correct in relation to a thing's nature, to its *being*. The same would hold true for actions. "An action's performance accords with the action's own nature, and not what we believe."[22] If we are given a tool that is designed for cutting, Socrates proposes, we would most likely use that tool in accord with the nature of the task at hand. "If we try to cut contrary to nature, however, we'll be in error and accomplish nothing."[23] Anyone who has tried to cut metal with asparagus would have to agree with this. If this is true of cutting, then what about *speaking* and *naming?*

> SOCRATES: Then will someone speak correctly if he speaks in whatever way he believes he should speak? Or isn't it rather the case that he will accomplish something and succeed in speaking if he says things in the natural way to say them, in the natural way for them to be said, and with the natural tool for saying them? But if he speaks in any other way he will be in error and accomplish nothing.
> HERMOGENES: I believe so.[24]

If words are like tools, then how do we know we have the right tool for the right job? There is a natural way to use a drill, but what is the natural way to name? "What do we do when we name?" Socrates asks.

> HERMOGENES: I don't know what to answer.
> SOCRATES: Don't we instruct each other, that is to say, divide things according to their natures?
> HERMOGENES: Certainly.
> SOCRATES: So just as a shuttle is a tool for dividing warp and woof, a name is a tool for giving instruction, that is to say, for dividing being.[25]

What does this mean, to divide being? Allan Silverman notes that "though the dialogue does allude to the principal conditions which any successful answer must satisfy, namely that a name must be capable of separating *(ovoia)* (dividing being) and be informative (giving instruction), it is left to the ingenuity of the reader to determine how these conditions relate to one another, what it would be to satisfy these conditions and how names could do so."[26] We may safely glean, though, that in order to be a natural and correct tool, a name must be able to instruct its users about the nature of the object to which it refers, and through this instruction, sort, categorize, and identify the particular object or action so that it may be separated out from everything else that *is*.

Fair enough, but the question remains as to how a name is to go about doing this. Here Socrates looks toward a naming agent—the "rule setter" or "name giver"—an Adam-like agent responsible for attaching names with their referents. How did he go about doing it? How do we know when a particular word stands in correct relation with a thing or an action's essence? What if the name giver made a mistake? How would we even know? For that matter, suppose the name giver could grasp the essence of, say, "tree" or "man" or "cutting"—how would he know what these essences *sounded* like? Perhaps the best case in point of a fundamental misnomer would be the case of *language*—based on the Latin *lingua*, or *tongue*, which is precisely the sort of renaming we hope to accomplish in this essay.

Socrates speculates that just as a "carpenter must embody in wood the type of shuttle naturally suited for each type of weaving . . . so mustn't a rule-setter also know how to *embody in sounds and syllables the name naturally suited to each thing?*"[27] In positing the name giver as a craftsman, the task cannot simply be arbitrary. Hence, "Cratylus is right in saying that *things have natural names,* and that not everyone is a craftsman of names, but *only someone who looks to the natural name of each thing and is able to put its form into letters and syllables.*"[28] As Socrates comes to this position concerning how one might go about fashioning the correct sound to a thing's nature, he launches into the long etymological section, testing word after word, proper name after name in search of the source of the correctness of names.

Search for the Correctness of Names

In the long etymological section, Socrates initiates a sort of absurdist dictionary of eponymical speculation. While there is no hard and fast methodology, there are some amusing possibilities. "Whereas etymology aims to trace words back to their historical origins according to laws of filiation," Thais Morgan writes, "eponymy allows for imaginative free play. Socrates—and a host of mimologists after him—analyzes words by adding, deleting, and/or substituting letters or syllables according to nonce rules of phonetic similarity and punning. As a result Socrates' eponymies initiate a potentially endless language game, limited only by the player's ingenuity."[29] Take, for example, the speculation on the etymology of *halios* or sun.

> If we use the Doric form of the name, I think matters will become clearer, for Dorians call the sun "*halios.*" So "*halios*" might accord with the fact that the sun collects *(halizein)* people together when it rises, or with the fact that it is always rolling *(aei heilein ion)* in its course around the earth, or with the fact that it seems to color *(poikillei)* the products of the earth, for "*poikillein*" means the same as "*aiolein*" ("to shift rapidly to and fro").[30]

Does such speculation shed any greater light on the sun *(halios)*? Which is it? Gathering or rolling or coloring? Perhaps it could be a little of this and a little of that. But what about the shifting rapidly to and fro? "Ultimately," Morgan writes, "*Cratylus* leaves us torn between philosophical doubts about language and the sheer fun of playing with words."[31] But if we are looking for the *correctness* of a name, it makes a difference *which* root gave rise to *halios*.

In this method, Socrates pursues the correctness of a name through investigating the names from which they derived; hence they are referred to as *derivative* names. While pursuit of a word's history often reveals instructive insights and metaphors, we soon find ourselves led into a giant tautology, a sort of house of mirrors where words refer to other words that refer to others and so on. Where does it stop?

Naming in the First Place

After an exhausting (and nearly exhaustive) search on the correctness of particular names, Socrates realizes that derivations can only go so far.

> SOCRATES: If someone asks about the terms from which a name is formed, and then about the ones from which those terms are formed, and keeps on doing this indefinitely, the answerer must finally give up. Mustn't he?
> HERMOGENES: That's my view at any rate.
> SOCRATES: At what point would he be right to stop? Wouldn't it be when he reaches the names that are as it were the elements of all the other statements and names? For if these are indeed elements, it cannot be right to suppose that *they* are composed out of other names. Consider "*agathos*" ("good"), for example; we said it is composed out of "*agaston*" ("admirable") and "*thoon*" ("fast"). And probably "*thoon*" is composed out of other names, and those out of still other ones. But if we ever get hold of a name that isn't composed out of other names, we'll be right to say that at last we've reached an element, which cannot any longer be carried back to other names.[32]

Socratic dialogue has followed the chain of signifiers into what is perhaps the original Gordian knot: *how is naming possible?* Here, Socrates makes a crucial distinction between *derivative* and *primary* names. Socrates contends that "there is only one kind of correctness in all names, primary as well as derivative, and that considered simply as names there is no difference between them."[33] However there *is* a difference yet to be explored: while derivative names are based on the correctness of primary names, we are not so sure what the correctness of primary names is based on. This question leads Socrates to the very limits of signification:

> SOCRATES: And if the primary names are indeed names, they must make the things that are as clear as possible to us. But how can they do this when they aren't based on other names?[34]

Indeed, this is the twenty thousand–drachma question: how do we get to "the place where things and words are conjoined in their common essence, and which makes it possible to give them a name"?[35] Nearly twenty-three centuries after Plato, Jean Jacques Rousseau came to a similar observation when he noted that "words would have been necessary to establish the use of words."[36] As Michael Corballis plainly asks, "How on earth could speech have evolved?" Indeed, "how *were* links formed between those arbitrary sounds we call words and the stuff of the real world—a real world made available to us largely through vision and touch, rather than through sound?" To which Corballis answers: "It seems almost *inevitable* that those links involved *gesture.*"[37]

Sighting Sign

We have finally arrived at a point where we can appreciate the relevant context in which Socrates' sighting of gestural language occurs—at the crucial moment where he ponders what is perhaps the most provocative question of the entire dialogue. Here is the question again, but this time in the context of what follows it.

> SOCRATES: And if the primary names are indeed names, they must make the things that are as clear as possible to us. But how can they do this when they aren't based on other names? Answer me this: If we hadn't a voice or a tongue, and wanted to express things to one another, wouldn't we try to make signs by moving our hands, head, and the rest of our body, just as dumb people do at present?
>
> HERMOGENES: What other choice would we have, Socrates?
>
> SOCRATES: So, if we wanted to express something light in weight or above us, I think we'd raise our hand towards the sky in imitation of the very nature of the thing. And if we wanted to express something heavy or below us, we'd move our hand towards the earth. And if we wanted to express a horse (or any other animal) galloping, you know that we'd make our bodies and our gestures as much like theirs as possible.
>
> HERMOGENES: I think we'd have to.[38]

Note the abrupt turn, leaving the unanswerable question hanging. Having followed the dialectical path into spoken names as long as it could take him Socrates glimpses the possibility of a completely human alternative to speech at work in the hands, heads, and bodies of Greek signers at the margins of Athenian society. Socrates seems here to have sensed the plasticity of language—had we no voice, language would find some other route. Such a realization could provide an answer to the question just asked. Sign, as will be discussed below, offers a model, a *way* for signs to bear a primary relation to the world.

Yet, this was not Socrates' intent. This brief sighting is like a quick flash of light into the phonocentric blind spot, illuminating sign for a moment, but quickly returning it to darkness. For in the dialogue following, we see that the discussion of deaf sign language was intended only to discuss the nature of imitation and speech, rather than as a valid mode of human language all its own:

> SOCRATES: Because the only way to express anything by means of our body is to have our body imitate whatever we want to express.
>
> HERMOGENES: Yes.
>
> SOCRATES: So, if we want to express a particular fact by using our voice, tongue, and mouth, we will succeed in doing so, if we succeed in imitating it by means of them?
>
> HERMOGENES: That must be right, I think.
>
> SOCRATES: It seems to follow that a name is a vocal imitation of what it imitates, and that someone who imitates something with his voice names what he imitates.

HERMOGENES: I think so.

SOCRATES: Well, I don't. *I don't think this is a fine thing to say at all.*

HERMOGENES: Why not?

SOCRATES: Because then we'd have to agree that those who imitate sheep, cocks, or other animals are naming the things they imitate.

HERMOGENES: That's true, we would.

SOCRATES: And do you think that's a fine conclusion?

HERMOGENES: No, I don't. But then what sort of imitation is a name, Socrates?[39]

While he has Hermogenes shaking his head "yes" throughout, agreeing to the correctness of signed names, Socrates takes an abrupt turn, noting that speech does not imitate as does the sign language of the deaf. Indeed, it is not a fine thing to say that speech is onomatopoeic, because, for the most part, it is not. Thus, by the time Hermogenes asks, "what sort of imitation is a name?" it is clear that the category of name has been fully inscribed as "spoken name." Plato securely locks in place the tongue and mouth as the exclusive organs of language—the default mode of human being, thus casting the hands, head, and rest of the body into another nonlinguistic realm.

At this point, we wish to break into this dialogue, as Bertold Brecht might do, to disrupt the drama and offer a new perspective. This philosophical aside offered 2,500 years later will take center stage for the following two sections.

Shedding Light into the Blind Spot: Sign as a "Natural" Language

Now suppose Socrates, Hermogenes, and Cratylus befriended those "dumb people" present in Athens. Suppose also that among these signers was a hearing person, say a child of deaf parents whose first language was an evolving Athenian Sign Language who could have interpreted between the signers and speakers. Socrates would undoubtedly have posed many questions. What would he have found? Perhaps he may have found what he was looking for all along—names that are "naturally suited to the thing," names that effectively "instruct and divide being" and even more importantly, he may have found the place in which name and word conjoin to make naming possible in the first place. He may also have come to realize that the occlusion of sign may have a hidden part in the contradiction between his ideal of motivated signifiers and the reality of arbitrary speech.

Socrates would have been pleased to find that his speculation on the signifying properties of sign is accurate. While it is impossible to know what the signs for "lightness," "heaviness," and "galloping horse" were in fifth-century BC Greece, a brief survey of sign languages indicates that signs do often embody the visual, spatial, and kinetic nature of a thing. Upward motion, for example, is an omnipresent movement in conveying *lightness* (Figures 7.1 and 7.2), just as Socrates assumes. And downward movement is a central feature in conveying *heaviness* (Figures 7.3 and 7.4). In a gravity-filled world, lightness may be logically conveyed through upward gestures and heaviness through downward gestures. These signs literally make sense as they take place in accord with every embodied experience of lightness and heaviness that cuts across cultural divides.

Figure 7.1. LIGHT.

Figure 7.2. LIGHT.

Figure 7.3. HEAVY.

Figure 7.4. HEAVY.

Despite the fact that each sign has different handshapes and locations, each engages in a movement that reveals a sort of primal embodiment of our body's being-in-the-world. In short, each name *instructs* or *reveals* an aspect of what it refers to.

In addition, the sign for HORSE GALLOPING (Figures 7.5, 7.6, 7.7, and 7.8) also embodies aspects of the object and action represented. The American Sign Language (ASL) sign HORSE derives from a horse's ear, and therefore embodies a degree of metonymical correctness. Further, the very motion of galloping is embodied in the sign GALLOPING as both handshapes (upside down Vs) convey the four legs of a horse, replete with bending of the finger-legs, galloping forward.

It must be emphasized at this point that these signs and sign language in general are not a species of mime or picture writing in the air. A nonsigner would not be able to automatically decode these signs. To be sure, no horse's ear flops directly forward as do the fingers in the sign, and certainly no horse could gallop with both sets of legs in unison; yet, due to the manual and neurological constraints of the language, front and hind handshapes move in tandem. Despite these discrepancies between sign and referent, there is little doubt that sign is far more rich in its ability to embody the world through motivated signifiers.[40] Isn't this, after all, what Socrates has been searching for when he

Figure 7.5. HORSE.

Figure 7.6. GALLOPING.

Figure 7.7. GALLOPING.

Figure 7.8. GALLOPING.

speaks of a name that stands in "natural relation"? As such, signs reveal something fundamental about the thing to which they refer, thus dividing their being accordingly.

In such a search for the correctness of names, iconicity becomes a valued commodity; but in the history of thought on language in the West, iconicity has most often been associated with primitive languages. Indeed, the long-standing prejudice against iconic dimensions of language has led many to assume that signed languages are not real languages. The history of disconstruction, which we are beginning to follow, may help to account for the disconstruction of the debate on the arbitrariness vs. the iconicity of the signifier. As Sarah Taub writes,

> Unfortunately, the intense prejudice against iconic forms led to prejudice against signed languages. People claimed for many years (some still do) on the basis of the iconic aspects of signed languages that they were merely mime, playacting imitations—not true languages at all, and incapable of expressing abstract concepts. This is wholly untrue, as linguists from Stokoe (1960) onward have shown. . . . Signed languages, created in space with the signer's body and perceived visually, have incredible potential for iconic expression of a broad range of basic conceptual structures (e.g. shapes, movements, locations, human actions), and this potential is fully realized.[41]

If Socrates had been searching for a means for language to operate "in accord with nature," he may have been better off by looking toward sign. Signed languages have a special advantage in the deployment of visual, spatial, and kinetic properties that may exist in a homological relationship with the visual, spatial, and kinetic properties of the real world. As a result of the correspondence of signs and the world, we may have an answer to the question Socrates posed directly before citing the sign language of the deaf Athenians: "What are primary names based on?" Which is to ask, where is the "place that makes names possible"?

Sign and the Origins of Language

A possible answer to Socrates' question can be found, some 2,400 years later, in Amos Kendall's address at the inauguration of the National Deaf-Mute College (later, Gallaudet University) in 1864:

> If the whole human family were destitute of the sense of hearing, they would yet be able to interchange ideas by signs. Indeed, the language of signs undoubtedly accompanied if it did not precede the language of sounds. . . . We read that Adam named the beasts and birds. But how could he give them names without first pointing them out by other means? How could a particular name be fixed upon a particular animal among so many species without some sign indicating to what animal it should thereafter be applied?[42]

An increasing body of literature now suggests that Adam or any of the rest of us would have to have gestured before we spoke. The theory of gestural origins was popularized during the late eighteenth century by French philosopher Etienne Bonnet de Condillac who originally posited the "*langage d'action*" as the original language that allowed for the initial connection between an object and its name. Both Jean Jacques Rousseau and Denis Diderot also explored the likelihood of the gestural origins of language, which subsequently became a central philosophical preoccupation of the French Enlightenment.[43] More recently Gordon Hewes, William Stokoe, David Armstrong, Sherman Wilcox, and Michael Corballis have all published various articles and books that put forward convincing theories as to the role of gesture in language development.[44] Michael Corballis writes "The growing recognition of signed languages as true languages with all of the expressiveness and generativity of spoken language, has provided a powerful boost to the idea that language originated as a gestural system, and may even have evolved to a fully grammatical system before being overtaken by speech."[45]

It was William Stokoe who first proved the fully grammatical nature of manual languages; he then turned his insight into questions of the origin of language. Stokoe notes that the modality of sign makes it a logical pathway for signification to occur:

> Visible language movements . . . can stand for things directly. Direct pointing, natural resemblance, and actions that replay other actions are effective in linking language signs to their meanings. This difference between spoken language signs and signed language signs takes the original idea forward—and backward as well. In its present form, the idea visualizes a signed language as the first language ever—in use as much as a million years ago.
>
> Human physiology supplies reasons for thinking that visible signs rather than speech first

expressed language. Human vision automatically sorts images and compares them for us. Working with vision and the perceptions it brings, human hands can point to things and imitate them. Furthermore, visible, manually produced signs with obvious meanings provided a context in which vocal sounds can carry meaning, simply by being produced at the same time as the gestural signs.[46]

How else could spoken words have become attached to particular objects? *This* is a tree, *those* are leaves, and *that* is a branch. Indeed, try speaking for a day without gesturing; try to pick out a particular piece of meat at the butcher or fish at the fish counter without pointing.

But more importantly, gesture points the way to a larger direction—toward the direction in which we all have become human—to the direction of language. It is perhaps in gesture and sign language then that we came to the "sovereign act of nomination, to the place where word and thing are conjoined in their common essence, which makes it possible to give things a name."[47]

It seems that Socrates was on the precipice of this insight when he asked the question about the source of primary names, and then switched to "Answer me this." This is a crucial moment in the history of disconstruction of sign language, when philosophy hung in the balance between speech and sign. But Socrates, Hermogenes, and Cratylus never befriended the deaf signers; they never seriously considered the signifying properties of sign in light of their discussion on naming. This sighting was short lived, as the flow of dialogue returns to an almost quixotic attempt at attaching sounds to things and actions.

The Return of the Phonocentric Blind Spot

Primary names are no different: correctness is still a function of corresponding. Socrates returns to speech as the source of imitation; only now in the case of primary names, Socrates looks toward the letters and syllables of sound to correspond with a thing's nature directly. If a sheep is not named "baaaa baaa" then how can sound correspond to a thing's nature? "Since an imitation of a thing's being or essence is made out of letters and syllables," Socrates responds, "wouldn't it be most correct for us to divide off the letters or elements first, just as those who set to work on speech rhythms first divide off the forces or powers of the letters or elements, then those of syllables, and only then investigate rhythms themselves?"[48] Socrates does provide a number of examples where a sound corresponds to the nature of a particular referent.

> SOCRATES: . . . the letter "r" seemed to the name-giver to be a beautiful tool for copying motion, at any rate he often uses it for this purpose. He first uses this letter to imitate motion in the names "*rhein*" ("flowing") and "*rhoe*" ("flow") themselves. Then in "*tromos*" ("trembling") and "*trechein*" ("running") and in such verbs as "*krouein*" ("striking") and so on. . . . He saw, I suppose, that the tongue was most agitated and least at rest in pronouncing this letter and that's probably why he used it in these names.[49]

In addition to the primal relation of "r" and motion, Socrates proposes that the name giver "observed that because the tongue glides most of all in pronouncing '*l*,' he uses it to produce a resemblance in '*oligisthanein*' ('glide') itself."[50] He was also partial to "o" to express roundness along with a host of other letters and correspondences.

But one must wonder, if "r" bears a natural relation to motion, is it used exclusively in motion words or can it arise in other words as well? What does it refer to then? For if "r" imitates the very nature of motion, why does it figure so prominently in words oppo-site of motion, as in the modern English "rest" and "relaxation." Sounds do indeed carry an emotive, evocative quality, which is foregrounded in poetic language. But if the ques-tion concerns the relation of a name to its *being*, Socrates' skewed methodology betrays the very limitation of speech. How can we be sure about the correct relation of sound and being given the multitude of languages that cannot even agree on onomatopoe-ias, such as the English "bow-wow" and the French "ouaoua." Further, one would think that the multiplicity of arbitrary words from other languages attached to the same idea would discount the ability of particular sounds to correspond to a thing's fixed essence. Anticipating the inevitable question concerning the multiplicity of signifiers across lan-guages, Socrates surmises,

> And if different rule-setters do not make each name out of the same syllables, we mustn't
> forget that different blacksmiths, who are making the same tool for the same type of work,
> don't all make it out of the same iron. But as long as they give it the same form—even if that
> form is embodied in different iron—the tool will be correct, whether it is made in Greece or
> abroad. Isn't that so?
> HERMOGENES: Certainly.[51]

While Hermogenes readily agrees, Socrates provides no further explanation as to how an enduring form could be constituted of radically different material.

Further testimony to the contradictory desire for a motivated language and the re-alities of speech is the haunting persistence of visual analogies used to describe the rela-tion of speech to the world. When describing his methodology of breaking down speech into letters and syllables to imitate a thing's essence, Socrates claims,

> It's just the same as it is with painters. When they want to produce a resemblance, they some-
> times use only purple, sometimes another color, and sometimes, for example, when they want
> to paint human flesh or something of that sort—they mix many colors, employing the par-
> ticular color, I suppose, that their particular subject demands. Similarly, we'll apply letters to
> things using one letter for one thing, when that's what seems to be required, or many letters
> together, to form what's called a syllable, or many syllables, combined to form names and
> verbs. From names and verbs, in turn, we shall finally construct something important, beauti-
> ful, and whole. And just as the painter painted an animal, so—by means of the craft of naming
> or rhetoric or whatever it is—we shall construct sentences.[52]

Through this analogy, Socrates hopes that we can *see* what he is talking about. But given the nature of vision and visual arts and languages, the abililty to represent is far greater than the ability of speech. Painting, as it appears throughout, is like the supplement to speech, filling in where it lacks, haunting its primacy.

Socrates does admit that "Perhaps it will seem absurd, Hermogenes, to think that

Figure 7.9. FLOW.   Figure 7.10. FLOW.   Figure 7.11. FLOW.

things become clear by being imitated in letters and syllables, but it is absolutely un-avoidable. For we have *nothing better* on which to base the truth of primary names."[53] So deeply buried in the phonocentric blind spot, sign language would not see the light of day in pursuit of the nature and origins of language. We now know that there *may be* something better on which to base the truth of primary names, as has been shown by the gestural theory of language origins. There is perhaps no better medium to represent motion than motion itself. Compare the phonemic constituents of the sign FLOW (Figures 7.9, 7.10, and 7.11) in comparison with the sound "R." This sign demonstrates how sign language offers a kinetic model of the larger world. Sign language instructs in very precise ways, so precise as to be infectious, where the body of the viewer engages in the revelation of meaning through the signer's body and facial expressions. As Merleau-Ponty writes, "The communication or comprehension of gestures comes about through the reciprocity of my intentions and the gestures of others, of my gestures and intentions discernible in the conduct of other people. It is as if the other person's intention inhabited my body and mine his."[54] As our bodies are intimately familiar with the worlds they inhabit, they are particularly adept at communicating a particular embodied experience—a linguistic reciprocity in signed languages that results in a sense of being in the presence of the event, object, or action cited.

Conclusion: The Legacy of Disconstruction

In light of the revelation that *to sign is human,* we may now reread the history of thought regarding language. In Plato's *Cratylus,* we can see a pattern emerge: a pronounced yearning and speculation for a "perfect language" in which names have a "natural relation" to the world. Umberto Eco's *Search for a Perfect Language* and Gerard Genette's *Mimologics* both document the ubiquity of the search for an alternative to conventional speech.[55] In an introductory essay to Genette's expansive *Mimologics* entitled "Invitation to a Voyage in Cratylusland," Thais Morgan writes, "Determining language's connection to the phenomenal world is an important enterprise because it bears upon the extent and accuracy of our knowledge about that world. At the same time, thinkers tend to use their imaginations quite freely when they discuss language, inventing clever—and sometimes ridiculous—explanations of how words imitate things."[56] In the *Cratylus,* we see a search for a perfect language and a grasping toward language's phantom limb—gesture. Yet we see that language is so fully bound to speech that there is fundamentally something "other" and strange about sign language.

Note the "we" in the passage where Socrates discusses the sign language of the deaf. "Suppose *we* hadn't a voice or a tongue." Here, this is very likely the first *hearing* "we" in philosophy. For this brief moment the boundary that holds the "we" in and the other out is drawn by the act of hearing and speaking. It would take centuries to find out that "those deaf people at present" have actually brought something present—the human capacity for sign language. It has taken this long to see that "those people" are actually a part of the "we." Particular sign languages indeed belong to the communities that have developed them, but the human capacity to sign belongs to us all, whether hearing or Deaf.

Notes

I wish to thank my students in DST 705, Sign and the Philosophy of Language, Fall 2005, for their discussion and comments on an earlier draft. David Armstrong also read and commented on an earlier draft. I assume all responsibility for the contents.

1. Pierre Desloges was the first deaf person known to have authored and published a book—in 1779—that defended the use of sign language against oralist educators. Of particular significance is Desloges's description of a signing Deaf community prior to formalized deaf education, begun by the Abbe de l'Epee. Desloges wrote that "there are congenitally deaf people, Parisian laborers, who are illiterate and who have never attended the abbe de l'Epee's lessons, who have been found so well instructed about their religion, simply by means of signs, that they have been judged worthy of admittance to the holy sacraments, even those of the eucharist and marriage. No event—in Paris, in France, or the four corners of the world—lies outside the scope of our discussion. We express ourselves on all subjects with as much order, precision and rapidity as if we enjoyed the faculty of speech and hearing." Pierre Desloges, "A Deaf Person's Observations about *An Elementary Course of Education for the Deaf*," in *Deaf Experience: Classics in Language and Education*, ed. Harlan Lane, trans. Franklin Philip (Cambridge, Mass.: Harvard University Press, 1984), 36.

2. Further speculation on the nature of ancient sign languages is prompted by the cinematic nature of manual languages. If manual languages tend to exhibit close up, distance shots, editing, and camera techniques, did the ancients tell cinematic narratives 2,500 years prior to the advent of moving images in film? Or to what extent have cinematic techniques influenced signed languages in the twentieth century? For further reading on the cinematic qualities of signed languages, see H-Dirksen L. Bauman, "Redesigning Literature: The Cinematic Poetics of American Sign Language Poetry," *Sign Language Studies* 4 (2003): 34–47, and Ben Bahan, "Face-to-Face Tradition in the American Deaf Community: Dynamics of the Teller, the Tale, and the Audience," in *Signing the Body Poetic: Essays in American Sign Language Literature*, ed. H-Dirksen L. Bauman, Jennifer Nelson, and Heidi Rose (Berkeley and Los Angeles: University of California Press, 2006), 21–50.

3. See L. A. Petitto, M. Katerelos, B. Levy, K. Gauna, K. Tétrault, and V. Ferraro, "Bilingual Signed and Spoken Language Acquisition from Birth: Implications for Mechanisms Underlying Bilingual Language Acquisition," *Journal of Child Language* 28 (2001): 453–96. See V. Penhune, R. Cismaru, R. Dorsaint-Pierre, L. A. Petitto, and R. Zatorre, "The Morphometry of Auditory Cortex in the Congenitally Deaf Measured Using MRI," *NeuroImage* 20 (2003): 1215–25.

4. For further discussion of Martha's Vineyard, see Nora Ellen Groce, *Everyone Here Spoke Sign Language: Hereditary Deafness on Martha's Vineyard* (Cambridge, Mass.: Harvard University Press, 1985) and Ben Bahan and Joan Cottle Poole Nash, "The Formation of Signing Communities," in *Deaf Studies IV Conference Proceedings: Visions of the Past—Visions of the Future* (Washington, D.C.: Gallaudet University College for Continuing Education, 1996), 1–26. For further discussion

of the signing community in Henniker, N.H., see Harlan Lane, Richard Pillard, and Mary French, "Origins of the American Deaf-World: Assimilating and Differentiating Societies and Their Relation to Genetic Patterning," in *Signs of Language Revisited: An Anthology to Honor Ursula Bellugi and Edward Klima,* ed. Karen Emmorey and Harlan Lane (Mahwah, N.J.: Lawrence Erlbaum Associates, 2000), 77–100. For further discussion of the signing community in the Yucatan Peninsula, see Robert E. Johnson, "Sign Language and the Concept of Deafness in a Traditional Yucatec Mayan Village," in *The Deaf Way: Perspectives from the International Conference on Deaf Culture,* ed. Carol Erting, Robert C. Johnson, Dorothy Smith, and Bruce D. Snider (Washington, D.C.: Gallaudet University Press, 1994), 102–9. For further discussion of the signing community in Bali, see Jan Branson and Don Miller, "Everyone Here Speaks Sign Language, Too: A Deaf Village in Bali, Indonesia," in *Multicultural Aspects of Sociolinguistics in Deaf Communities,* ed. Ceil Lucas (Washington, D.C.: Gallaudet University Press, 1996), 39–57. For further reading on the Al Sayidd Bedouin Sign Language, see Wendy Sandler, Irit Meir, Carol Padden, and Mark Aronoff, "The Emergence of Grammar: Systematic Structure in a New Language," *Proceedings of the National Academy of Sciences* 102, no. 7 (2005): 2661–65.

5. George W. Veditz, "The Preservation of the Sign Language," original version in *American Sign Language,* trans. Carol Padden and Eric Malzkuhn, reprinted in *Deaf World: A Historical Reader and Primary Sourcebook,* ed. Lois Bragg (New York: New York University Press, 2001), 83–85.

6. For further discussion on evolution of language with regard to sign language, see Michael Corballis, *Hand to Mouth: The Origins of Language* (Princeton: Princeton University Press, 2002).

7. Jacques Derrida, *Of Grammatology,* trans. Gayatri Spivak (Baltimore: Johns Hopkins University Press, 1976), 8.

8. Douglas Baynton, *Forbidden Signs: American Culture and the Campaign against Sign Language* (Chicago: University of Chicago Press, 1996).

9. For further discussion of the systemic nature of oppression of deaf persons, see Harlan Lane, *Mask of Benevolence: Disabling the Deaf Community* (New York: Alfred Knopf, 1992). While sign languages have been targeted, there is good cause to think that they will not, like so many other languages, experience language death. See Carol Padden, "Folk Explanation in Language Survival," in Bragg, *Deaf World,* 104–15.

10. For an excellent discussion about the fundamentally "strange" and foreign status of the Deaf world, see Tom Humphries, "Of Deaf-mutes, the *Strange,* and the Modern Deaf Self," in *Culturally Affirmative Psychotherapy with Deaf Persons,* ed. Neil S. Glickman and Michael Harvey (Hillsdale, N.J.: Lawrence Erlbaum Associates, 1996), 99–114.

11. For more on the intellectual history regarding perspectives on signed languages, see Jonathan Rée, *I See a Voice: Deafness, Language and the Senses—A Philosophical History* (London: Metropolitan Books, 1999); Jan Branson and Don Miller, *Damned for Their Difference: The Cultural Construction of Deaf People as Disabled* (Washington, D.C.: Gallaudet University Press, 2002); Sophia Rosenfeld, *A Revolution in Language: The Problem of Signs in Late Eighteenth-Century France* (Stanford: Stanford University Press, 2002).

12. Ynez Viole O'Neill, *Speech and Speech Disorders in Western Thought before 1600* (Westport, Conn.: Greenwood, 1980).

13. Plato, *Cratylus,* trans. C. D. C. Reeve (Indianapolis: Hackett, 1998), 1.

14. Ibid., 2 and 85.

15. Thais Morgan, "Invitation to a Voyage in Cratylusland," Introduction to Gerard Genette, *Mimologics,* trans. Thais Morgan (Lincoln: University of Nebraska Press, 1995), xlix–l.

16. It is Plato, not Socrates, that is the focus of discussion here, for the *Cratylus* is a later dialogue and hence primarily the work of Plato given voice through the character of Socrates. While the content of the *Cratylus* is clearly Plato's rather than Socrates' there has been considerable debate regarding the actual date of composition. For further inquiry, see J. V. Luce, "The Date of the *Cratylus,*" *American Journal of Philology* 85 (1964): 136–54, and M. M. Mackenzie, "Putting the *Cratylus* in its Place," *Classical Quarterly* 36, no. 1 (1986): 124–50.

17. Allan Silverman offers the following classification of readings of the *Cratylus,* with the caveat that this breakdown obscures the finer points made by all. Allan Silverman, "Plato's *Cratylus:* The Naming of Nature and the Nature of Naming," *Oxford Studies in Ancient Philosophy* 10 (1992): 25–71. Those who feel Plato advocates the naturalist thesis: G. Fine, "Plato on Naming," *Philosophical Quarterly* 27 (1977): 289–301; N. Kretzmann, "Plato on the Correctness of Names," *American Philosophical Quarterly* 8 (1971): 126–38; G. Anagnostopoulos, "Plato's *Cratylus:* The Two Theories of the Correctness of Names," *Review of Metaphysics* 25 (1971/72): 691–736; C. Kahn, "Language and Ontology in the *Cratylus,*" in *Exegesis and Argument,* ed. E. N. Lee, A. P. D. Mourelatos, and R. M. Rorty (Assen: Van Gorcum, 1973), 152–76. Those who contend that Plato sides with conventionalist arguments: R. Robinson, *Essays in Greek Philosophy* (Oxford: Oxford University Press, 1969); M. Schofield, "The Denouement of the *Cratylus,*" in *Language and Logos,* ed. M. Schoefield and M. Nussbaum (Cambridge: Cambridge University Press, 1982), 61–81. T. W. Bestor, "Plato's Semantics and Plato's *Cratylus,*" *Phronesis* 25 (1980): 306–30. Others feel that he advocates a bit of both, while J. Gold claims that he advocates neither, "The Ambiguity of 'Name' in Plato's *Cratylus,*" *Philosophical Studies* 34 (1978): 223–51. The fact that so many critics could arrive at opposite and highly contested views shows something of a tangled web of ideas throughout the *Cratylus.*

18. Silverman, "Plato's *Cratylus,*" 26–27.

19. Michel Foucault, *The Order of Things: An Archaeology of the Human Sciences* (New York: Vintage, 1973), 116–17.

20. Plato, *Cratylus,* 72.

21. Ibid., 5.

22. Ibid.

23. Ibid., 6.

24. Ibid.

25. Ibid., 10.

26. Silverman, "Plato's *Cratylus,*" 27.

27. Plato, *Cratylus,* 13. Emphasis mine.

28. Ibid., 15. Emphasis mine.

29. Morgan, "Invitation to a Voyage," xxiv.

30. Plato, *Cratylus,* 44–45.

31. Morgan, "Invitation to a Voyage," xxiv.

32. Plato, *Cratylus,* 66.

33. Ibid.

34. Ibid., 66–67.

35. Foucault, *Order of Things,* 116–17.

36. Rousseau quoted in Corballis, *Hand to Mouth,* 42.

37. Ibid., 43.

38. Plato, *Cratylus,* 67.

39. Ibid., 68. Emphasis mine.

40. For further reading on iconicity in American Sign Language, see Sarah Taub, *Language from the Body: Iconicity and Metaphor in American Sign Language* (Cambridge: Cambridge University Press, 2001), and Phyllis Wilcox, *Metaphor in American Sign Language* (Washington, D.C.: Gallaudet University Press, 2001).

41. Taub, Language from the Body, 3.

42. Quoted in David Armstrong, *Original Signs: Gesture, Sign and the Sources of Language* (Washington, D.C.: Gallaudet University Press, 1999), 16.

43. See Rosenfeld, *Revolution in Language.*

44. Gordon Hewes, "The Current Status of the Gestural Theory of Language Origin," in *Origins and Evolution of Language and Speech,* ed. H. B. Steklis, S. R. Harnad, and J. Lancaster (New York: Blackwell, 1976), 482–504. David Armstrong, William Stokoe, and Sherman Wilcox, *Gesture and the Nature of Language* (Cambridge: Cambridge University Press, 1995). William Stokoe, *Language in Hand: Why Sign Came before Speech* (Washington, D.C.: Gallaudet University Press, 2001).

45. Corballis, *Hand to Mouth,* 43.
46. Stokoe, *Language in Hand,* 11.
47. Foucault, *Order of Things,* 116–17.
48. Plato, *Cratylus,* 70.
49. Ibid., 73.
50. Ibid.
51. Ibid., 13.
52. Ibid., 70–71.
53. Ibid., 72. Emphasis mine.
54. Maurice Merleau-Ponty, *The Phenomenology of Perception,* trans. Colin Smith (London: Routledge, 1989), 185.
55. Umberto Eco, *The Search for a Perfect Language* (London: Blackwell, 1997). Genette, *Mimologics.*
56. Morgan, "Invitation to a Voyage," xxi.

8. *Turning Literacy Inside Out*

MARLON KUNTZE

UNDER CONVENTIONAL DEFINITIONS, the notion of sign language literacy is blatantly oxymoronic. However, I wish to argue that the problem exists with the conventional notion that literacy is about written language and also that limited understanding of literacy is problematic. An effort to contemplate how different acts of literacy may manifest themselves in different modes is necessary to further deepen understanding about literacy. A discussion about literacy in sign language or visual media is essential since conceptualization of literacy has been constrained largely by perceiving it in an audiocentric framework. While literacy is usually associated with language, it is nevertheless helpful to think about dimensions of literacy in visual media such as pictures, movies, cartoons, and art especially when attempting to document examples of literacy events in a nonwritten language like American Sign Language (ASL). Even though language and visual media are different in some of the ways meaning is constructed, a discussion on how complex meaning is constructed and conveyed by the visual mode is made illustrative by examining how it may take place in visual media and in ASL. In short, an attempt to transcend literacy as a phenomenon that pertains to skills in written language will help facilitate the discussion about some of the larger questions related to literacy.

The prominence of literacy surfaces in tandem with the growing indispensability of written language in society. So frequently has the association been made between literacy and written language that the term "literacy" has come, in the minds of many people, to simply mean the ability to read and write. After all, according to the etymology of the term, "literacy" comes from a Latin word meaning "marked with letters." Anyone familiar with the skills of reading comprehension knows that there are two major components of reading comprehension. The first one, "literal"—also coming from the same Latin root—means to comprehend words and sentences at face value. The second one involves cognitive aspects of the ability to read and write, for example, making inferences, predicting, or using decontextualized language, and this essay concerns this second component.

The stance that literacy concerns written language, however, has the unfortunate effect of limiting the scope and depth of the discussion. The importance to be attributed to literacy should concern the quality or state of being literate. One is said to be literate when he or she is "educated and knowledgeable." In the context of a modern Western model of learning, it may seem counterintuitive that one can be educated and knowledgeable without having read extensively. However, it is important to seriously question the convention that it is only through skills in reading and writing that one may come to be literate. To truly understand these issues, we need to deconstruct literacy in a quest to lay bare its essence. In deconstructing literacy, it is paramount that we look at the cognitive skills needed for facilitative reading and writing and the cognitive benefits that come from the habit of reading and writing and see if similar cognitive skills and benefits are evident in other modes of communication. Only when our understanding of literacy is sufficiently dissociated from written language and we see it as being more grounded in the cognitive domain can we begin to look at the cognitive abilities and their development that are part and parcel of the development of literacy skills. It is then that we can ask questions about alternative approaches that can bring about the kind of cognitive transformation and abilities that are fostered by the process of learning to read and write.

If we are to have a meaningful discussion about the manifestations of literacy skills in different domains such as visual media or sign language, we need to move beyond the popular understanding of the term. For example, we cannot begin to formulate a theoretically sound approach to supporting literacy development of children who use ASL given the narrow definition of literacy as a matter of learning to read and write. Research on the literacy development of deaf students has been largely constrained by theories of how children who can hear learn written language, and it is often about making an association between written language and spoken language. Because deaf children do not have access to spoken language, research on them based on a model that comes from a different population is not without the risk of making interpretations that inadvertently foster mistaken notions about deaf children's abilities and needs. Deaf children's difficulty with reading and writing is often interpreted to be a direct result of not having phonological knowledge of English.[1] We have to start thinking about literacy in a new and revolutionary way if we are to have a meaningful discourse on literacy development of those whose primary language is different in one way or another from the language on which the written language is based. The primary language of those populations may not exist in a written mode, or they, for one reason or another, may not have access to the spoken language on which the written language is based, for example, the Japanese children learning written English as an L2 without having access to an English-speaking community nor having learned spoken English first.

Furthermore, the discussion about literacy in a nonwritten language like ASL is important as it can delve into the heart of literacy and portraying literacy in a radically new way. One interesting area related to ASL literacy concerns the meaning of text. It is an opportunity to push for the definition of text that extends beyond writing. Text should rather be seen as content that is recorded and left "suspended" in time. There are things we can do with language and content that is recorded and displayed in front of us that is not possible in any other way.

Analogic and Digital Symbols in Human Communication

The range of communicative tools available to humans extends from one that is fully analogically based, such as pantomime or drawing, to one that is fully digitally based, like writing. Most of them fall between those two poles and combine both analogic and digital means of representing meaning, and they vary in how much of each is utilized. Analogically based communication attempts to imitate reality by re-creating it in some ways while digitally based communication uses arbitrary symbols such as words whose meanings have been conventionally agreed upon. In making utterances more animated, a speaker would add to words analogically based information such as gesticulating or making more liberal use of intonations. So one way the use of language varies is through the extent to which analogically based information is incorporated. As for films, while images are the chief means of conveying meaning, they almost invariably do incorporate language. Films vary—from those that are "action packed" in which less language is used to those whose unfolding of the plot depends more on dialogues. In the traditional way languages are studied, little attention is paid to the analogic component of communication; however the emerging studies of cospeech gesture are increasingly suggesting that gestures are an important part of human communication.[2] Crosslinguistic studies, especially those of non-Western languages, have yielded evidence that the grammar of those languages is more intertwined with gestures than what is seen in Western languages.[3]

An important difference between spoken language and written language lies in the fact that the conventions of writing do not present language in the way language is used in speaking. Written language has no devices for conveying analogically based meanings such as intonations, gestures, and facial expressions. Writing has to compensate, albeit in a limited way, by utilizing more words and punctuation symbols. In essence, writing is more digital than speaking is and that is one of the important reasons why communication in written mode is difficult and challenging.

Linguistics based on Western languages, especially language in written form, has largely been the filter through which the description of ASL grammar has been developed. Furthermore, it was done during the time there was a strong motivation to prove to a skeptical world that ASL was in fact a language, and as a result effort was made, probably a little obliquely, to show that ASL was indeed like any spoken language that traditionally has been portrayed as digital. Unfortunately it has resulted in some blind spots in our understanding of how ASL works. There are structures of ASL such as classifiers that linguists are now beginning to understand as digitally based symbols being used as analogic devices for describing gradiency in verbs of motion, in verbs of location, and in appearances and shapes of objects.[4] In the past, there was understandably a strong ideological resistance to any discussion that may lead to a view that ASL incorporates analogic structures because of the historical stigmatization that ASL was nothing more than "gestures." Now with the linguistic study of ASL having matured and ASL already established in the annals of linguistics, interest is increasing in how ASL exploits analogic means of representing reality and weaves together analogic and digital modes of representation.

The extent of gradiency possible in analogic representation exceeds the extent that is possible in digital representation. For example, in facial expressions, meaning conveyed in a smile may be that the smiling person is happy. There are gradient ways of smiling to show different degrees of happiness, that is, a little happy, somewhat happy, quite happy, or very happy. At the same time there are different ways of smiling, each with a meaning such as being satirical, sadistic, or painfully polite or trying to restrain joy or to conceal disgust. Furthermore, each meaning of smiling has its range of gradiency. Adding an analogic symbol such as an intonation to a word helps infuse gradiency in the meaning of the word. For example, by uttering the word "long" in different ways, the meaning of the word is modified to convey the gradiency of "long-ness" (e.g., a little long, somewhat long, quite long, very long, or too long). Analogic means of meaning representation constitute a prominent component of the linguistic structure of ASL. More incorporation of analogic means of communicating is evident in ASL and other signed languages than in auditorially based languages. The greater combinatory possibilities of digital and analogic modes of representation give a language like ASL some characteristics not found in spoken languages.

Inference-Making Skills

One of the goals of literacy development is the development of higher-order thinking and reasoning skills such as making an inference that involves making use of existing knowledge or identifying relevant pieces of information to help arrive at meaning that is not in the content on the literal level. I want to discuss the act of inference making when processing content not only in writing but also in other modes such as speaking, signing, acting, or drawing. Briefly stated, the process of making an inference involves going beyond what is explicitly expressed in order to arrive at what is implied. What is expressed on the literal level ("meaning at face value") is often not the full message. The assumption is often that the person or audience the message is intended for has the necessary background information and/or reasoning ability to help arrive at the implied meaning. Sometimes the necessary contextual information is provided in the content, and the expectation is that the reader/listener would be able to identify these pieces of information to help contextualize the content.

Sometimes information understood at the literal level may, at the first blush, seem adequate. However, a skilled reader may see that there is more to the message than what is evident at the surface or that something is amiss on the surface. Having skills to make inferences does help one see if an inference has to be made and how to do it. In the following passage the language and details are relatively sparse; however by making inferences the reader can "create" more details in his/her mind and get more complex meaning:

> A man gave $10.00 to the woman behind the ticket window and got $4.00 back. A woman with the man gave him $3.00, but the man refused to take it. Once inside, she proceeded to buy him a large bag of popcorn.

The passage just states a series of events: a man paying and getting change, a woman trying to give him money and buying popcorn. The reader may stop here with an acknowledgment of these events. However, if the reader wonders where, when, or why these events take place, the only way to get answers to those questions is by making inferences. By thinking where one would buy popcorn and pay at a ticket window, the best guess is that it most likely takes place at the movie theater. One can connect the dots from when the woman offers three dollars to the man, is refused, and then buys popcorn. It is reasonable to infer that she buys the man popcorn because she is trying to pay for her share of the cost of going to the movies. If one knows how expensive it is to go to the movies nowadays, the fact that it is three dollars per person in the passage would make one pause and wonder. By using background information, one can conclude that this event probably did not happen recently.

Whether the same content is expressed in written language or in a different language such as ASL or in a different mode like film, the act of inference making will be necessary if one is to achieve a richer interpretation of the content. The particulars of the inferences to make may more likely vary for each. While some commonalities exist in how meaning may be inferred, the variance among them may be due to the extent and the manner to which analogic representation is utilized. In ASL, analogic representations such as changing facial expressions or eye gaze would be obligatory. As typical in ASL narratives, the narrator would tell the story through the "voices" of the characters. In so doing, a skilled narrator would show the facial expressions, eye gazes, and occasionally body movements of the characters. The narration would have included a series of changing facial expressions and eye gazes of the woman that begins when she attempts to reimburse the man for the ticket. They would change to show the woman's reaction when her offer is refused and again when the woman decides to pay her share by buying the man popcorn. The additional information provided by such analogic means doubtlessly facilitates the act of inference making that is needed for interpreting why the woman buys popcorn. However, written English has an advantage that ASL does not. Content in written English is permanent; the reader can reread a passage while thinking of the intended meaning and trying to make inferences. ASL is evanescent, and the interlocutor has to memorize the details while thinking about their meaning. The cognitive requirements for arriving at a richer interpretation of the passage will be qualitatively different in some particular ways for each language, but in other particular ways, such as inferring that the event probably took place some time in the past, it is virtually similar for each language.

A comic strip or film provides more analogic information than ASL does. When the same content is portrayed in a film, it would be obvious that the couple is going to the movies. At least there will be more details in a film on how the couple interacts with each other as one attempts to reimburse the other and is refused. Some of the same inference-making activities will still be required, such as understanding why the woman buys the man popcorn. One can also infer from the way the couple looks, their clothing and hair styles, that paying three dollars was how much it cost to see a movie in the past.

Visual Literacy

Visual literacy is often thought of only as the ability to recognize and understand ideas conveyed through visible actions or images; however, many of the same cognitive skills required for comprehending content in writing are also required for complete comprehension of ideas presented through visual media. Richard Sinatra defines visual literacy as the ability to actively reconstruct past experiences with incoming visual information to obtain meaning.[5] In a quest to develop a definition of visual literacy, attempts have been made to describe the characteristics of a visually literate person. One such example is that a visually literate person is someone who can "discriminate and interpret visible actions, objects, and symbols, natural or man-made."[6]

A comic strip is a good example of largely nonlinguistically based content for which considerable inference making is often required to ensure a fuller comprehension. While comic strips are often a combination of images and words, they may come without any captions. Even without captions and even in cases where meaning at the "literal level" seems initially adequate, a full understanding of those wordless comic strips is often not possible without first making inferences. In a Calvin and Hobbes comic strip, Calvin is shown in the first frame walking past his mother, who is not paying attention to him. In the second and third frames, she looks up and then she walks up the stairs. In the final frame, we see Calvin building a snowman in one of the rooms and his mother covering her eyes.[7] The reader can stop at that level of reading, thinking it funny that Calvin would try to build a snowman in the house. The reader may also cringe, feeling sorry for the mother. However, there is a lot more to the strip that is left unsaid, and what remains unsaid becomes obvious only after the reader attempts to interpret the fourth frame through the prism of information provided in the first three frames. As in a well-crafted piece of poetry, the cartoonist is sparse in detail and those details are carefully chosen. Full comprehension of what the cartoonist tries to convey hinges on the reader being able to make a full sense of each detail. In the second frame, Calvin's mother suddenly looks up. The reader needs to infer why the mother looked up. The first frame shows Calvin being fully clothed for cold weather. The third frame shows the mother going upstairs. These pieces of information should lead the reader to infer that Calvin being fully clothed for cold weather and going upstairs is what probably caught his mother's attention. We are able to make this inference because we know that when one is clothed for cold weather, it means going outdoors. Staying indoors and going upstairs is the opposite outcome. Familiarity with the Calvin and Hobbes comic strip will provide the reader with additional information about the kind of child Calvin is. When the reader uses that background information, it is possible to make an inference that if the circumstances prompted Calvin's mother to stop what she was doing to check on Calvin, it meant Calvin must be up to something. The reader will know that it may be something that his mother dreads. So his mother must have known something is up that she cannot ignore or leave unchecked. We can make several more inferences from the information provided in the fourth frame. The room is likely Calvin's; the mother covers her eyes because she is upset. The reader familiar with the Calvin and Hobbes comic strips would be able to infer from the look on Calvin's face that he seems baffled why his mother is upset. Understanding the punch line of the comic strip is not possible until the reader makes an inference that Calvin is likely thinking that he has followed the rule that if he is to play in snow, he needs to dress warmly. That is exactly what he is doing. He is at a loss as to why his mother is upset and what in the world could be wrong with what he is doing this time around.

ASL Literacy

Signed languages, being visually based, have more latitude in employing analogic symbols than spoken languages do. In ASL poetry and narratives, the use of analogic representation is more heightened than in colloquial ASL. A more liberal use of classifiers, facial expressions, role shift (direct speech), changing perspectives, and changing body postures is found in literary productions of ASL. In fact it is "arranged more like edited film."[8] Bauman proposes that the lexicon of film techniques should be used to discuss or critique ASL poetics.[9] He pointed out that in making a film a collaboration among individuals is required, but the craft of ASL poetry is done by a single author who "is a screenwriter who composes the linguistic text; the cameraperson who arranges the visual-spatial composition of individual shots; the editor, who decides how to organize the various shots; the actor, who embodies the characters and images; and finally, the director who unites all these interconnected aspects into a single text."[10] Content expressed analogically, however, has a higher likelihood of being ambiguous in meaning than content expressed digitally. For example, the lexical item "happy" is more explicit in meaning than a smile is. The meaning of a person's smile in a portrait, for example, is not always obvious. Only when the picture is put in some context would one then have a basis for making an inference related to the person's smile. In ASL narrative, if the protagonist is to smile, the narrator will most likely smile. The meaning of a smile in a drawing, a picture, or a narrative may be disambiguated by making an inference on the basis of the context. In a narrative the narrator may either tell why the protagonist is smiling or leave it unexplained for the interlocutor to figure out on the basis of the details provided in the narrative. In a well-crafted narrative, judicious decisions have been made on the level of details to provide in the narrative that would give the interlocutor just enough context to make an inference about the protagonist's smile. Maximal and efficient use of analogic representations in ASL utterances and making sure there is just enough information in the context to enable the interlocutor to make the needed inferences is the mark of a high level of ASL skills. Only sign masters have a command for the kind of language often found in ASL poetics.

A literary piece of ASL called "Uncoding the Ethics" is a good example of an abundant use of analogic devices.[11] The storyteller conveys a lot of facial expressions, different eye gazes, and gestures of the protagonist and other characters in the story. The narrative is a parody on the Code of Ethics to which professional interpreters are bound to adhere. It is a story of how an interpreter defies the code by manipulating the conversation between a deaf man and his hearing aggressor for a personal gain. The story begins with a deaf man who sees his hearing neighbor burying a bag of what appears to be money. The deaf man finds the manner by which the neighbor buries the money very ineffectual, so he decides to help, unbeknownst to the neighbor, by putting it somewhere else in a more concealed way. Later the hearing neighbor finds the money gone. Seeing footprints leading to the deaf man's house, the neighbor knows who the culprit was. He brings out his gun but stops short as he realizes he is not able to communicate with the deaf man. He solves the problem by calling in an interpreter. In the conversation that ensues between the agitated hearing neighbor and the deaf man who tries, but with limited success, to be helpful, the interpreter collects valuable information from the deaf man and in the end tells the hearing neighbor that the deaf man would not reveal where the money is. Then the narrator, role-playing the interpreter, grimaces and wiggles a finger into her ear as if in response to a loud noise. Then she slowly smiles with a sly arch of her eyebrow. The punch line of the story is conveyed through purely analogic means. It is done using only pantomime and facial expressions. The inferences that the audience can make that the interpreter wiggled her finger into her ear because there was a loud noise and that the noise was from the neighbor's gun will become a basis for an inference that the deaf man was shot dead. The next inference to make on why the interpreter was smiling, by interpreting it as a result of being now thirty thousand dollars richer, helps affirm an earlier inference that the deaf man is dead.

The extent of incorporating analogic representations in literary pieces of ASL is a chief reason why they are noted for their vividness and ease of visualization. While analogically based information helps make the content increasingly accessible on the literal level, the intended meaning or message nevertheless can be still complex and is often not made explicit. One will thus need to exert effort to think deeply about what is said in order to determine what is meant. Thinking deeply about the content has the effect of triggering the act of making inferences.

Text and Literacy

Text is commonly defined as content that is shaped and thus preserved through writing. However, I would argue that the term should be understood more broadly, to mean content that has been linguistically recorded in one way or another. There are things we can do with content that is permanent that would be more difficult with content that is evanescent and disappears as soon as it is uttered. Content that is written on paper or recorded on a tape allows one to step back and deliberate the manner by which the content is organized and how language is crafted to convey it. Text provides a means for content, as well as the language it is in, to become separate from the speaker and becomes an object for the speaker to look at, to think about, and to critique. When preparing a text for communicating to an unseen audience, the author needs to deliberate what to say and how to say it by thinking about what the audience may already know and what additional information it may need in order to make sense of the content as intended by the author. The ability to see the content and language in a detached way helps the author on several fronts: to clarify the ideas being communicated, to include the necessary background information, and to reflect on how the content is being linguistically packaged in a quest to get the content across to the target audience in an effective way. The ability to do it is a mark of literacy whether it is in writing, signing, or speaking as well as drawing a comic strip or making a movie.

The process of rephrasing language and refining ideas when developing a text often leads to a denser as well as more eloquent use of language. Text exposes the reader to the kind of language not commonly encountered elsewhere. Literacy is promoted when others have an opportunity for exposure to language that has been thoughtfully and carefully crafted and to consume content whose development of complexity takes place through using text as a tool. The permanence of language in text also enables one to digest content at his/her pace, which is important for maximizing comprehension of the content. The elimination of time constraints in processing language when it is in text is what helps enable one to process language at a higher level of complexity or unfamiliarity than when it has to be handled online. Text is something that can be read/viewed repeatedly, and such an activity fosters the act of reflection and the development of critical thinking.

The cognitive benefits traditionally associated with written language are arguably also available when working with spoken language on an audiotape or with sign language on a videotape. The benefits accrue more from the means of working with language in text. Working with ASL text is a recent phenomenon that has been propelled by the wide availability of videotaping technology. It is providing a means to facilitate the act of crafting and critiquing not only the literary work of ASL but also the language used to convey intellectual content through ASL. The electronic publication of intellectual, narrative, or informative content in ASL is on the rise on the Internet.[12] The proliferation of content in ASL text and the growing access to it will provide an important avenue for promoting literacy development through ASL.

On Being Literate

One of the conclusions one can make based on this essay is that in an extreme case it is entirely possible for one to become literate without ever having read a sentence. As a matter of fact, there was an account of a young man who was so dyslexic that reading a sentence was painful for him.[13] His collegiate application was turned down everywhere because of "poor grades and low board scores." He had a chance to go to Claremont College as a special student. There he managed to pass all his classes and got an A+ in his Senior Seminar without ever having read a book or written a paper. His friends read books for him and he would dictate his papers to a friend who would type them in rough draft. He would edit his paper while his friend read each page out loud. It would be incorrect to call this young man illiterate. As far as his ability to process the content and to organize his thoughts, he is highly literate.

An important objective of literacy development is the development of skills to think about information and to respond to it thoughtfully. Literacy is less about the skills to access information. Learning to read is about learning how to access information through print. When one begins to read, it means he/she begins to access one of the means of becoming literate. However, the actual process of becoming literate depends on whether one gets to be cognitively engaged with the content. Because books are a depository of knowledge, ideas, and viewpoints accumulated over time, they will always be the most important and powerful means of literacy development. At the same time, books should not be thought of as the sole means. We have seen, in the case of the dyslexic student discussed above, how he became literate by accessing books through oral means. Actually if he has access to all the content he needs for college through spoken language in a recorded form and if he can submit his work on an audiotape instead of paper, he would not have to depend on his friends to read his books aloud and to type for him. In fact it is entirely conceivable to conjecture a society that builds its knowledge, ideas, and viewpoints by recording them in spoken language and creating libraries full of audiotapes. Such a society, in theory, should not be less literate. On the contrary, because content is more accessible in spoken language than in written language it is plausible to argue that the literacy level in such a society can possibly exceed that in a written society.

One of the important questions that this essay also attempts to hint at is whether literate skills acquired through one mode are the same as those acquired through another mode. It is an important question to pursue especially if we want to think about literacy development through multiple means. However, for now it seems reasonable to speculate that they are the same at least to the extent that they concern specific cognitive processes that are similar crossmodally. If it is true, it means that at least some literacy skills acquired through one mode are transferable to another mode. That question has a lot of implications related to the issue of ease of access to the content. It seems reasonable to argue that there may be an advantage from a developmental perspective to utilize a mode that provides the best access to content as a starting point for literacy development while skills for accessing content through other modes are being developed. For example, an opportunity to develop skills in making inferences through comic strips or ASL narratives may give a child a headstart in literacy development while the child develops skills to access content in written English. It could be that we are making literacy development artificially difficult for many children by conjecturing it as a process that takes place only through the written domain.

In Summation

One way to delve deeper into the heart of literacy is to test the boundaries within which the discourse about it is currently confined. An investigation to understand literacy in ASL, which is not only nonwritten but also visually based, is an opportunity to achieve a more global understanding of literacy, as it allows us to move beyond the traditional associations between literacy and written language. An investigation to understand literacy in visual media that are largely nonlinguistic but visually based like ASL is an opportunity to move beyond the traditional association between literacy and language. A discussion about literacy as it cut across different modes of communication is important for the effort to understand literacy in a more encompassing way.

Various tools of communication may share some of the same literacy skills, but some of those skills may be particular to a given modality or to a given mix of analogic and digital representations of meaning. Literacy concerns a kind of dimension in communication that is a product of various cognitive processes such as logical reasoning about the content and planning on how to get it across to others. Cognitive requirements and procedures for planning may vary to some extent across different modes of communication. For example, the lack of analogic information in written language may contribute to its difficulty as a medium for communication and visualizing information. The cognitive engagement required for visualizing content presented in written form constitutes one kind of literacy skills. In public speaking, the lack of interaction with the audience means not getting the kind of feedback we normally use for modifying content "online" as it is being communicated in a quest of getting the message across. To compensate for the lack of feedback, the lecturer will necessarily have to plan ahead. In planning ahead the lecturer has to judge the background information the audience may have and use that judgment to determine what pieces of information to include in the speech. In the case of crafting a work of literature in ASL, one has to walk the fine line of permissible ambiguity that results from increasing the visual-spatial-kinetic dimensions. Gee argued that literacy concerns skills with communication that are outside the sphere of everyday interpersonal communication.[14] Colloquial discourse is more spontaneous while communication that is outside the sphere of everyday interpersonal communication, such as academic discourse and poetics, requires planning.

The level of discussion on literacy should reflect the nature of literacy as a complex subject. We should try to understand how it may manifest in various modes of human communication. It requires us to understand the commonalities and differences across sign language, written language, and visual media. Keeping the scope of discussion limited will keep deeper issues of literacy obfuscated.

Notes

1. Charles Perfetti and Rebecca Sandak, "Reading Optimally Builds on Spoken Language: Implications for Deaf Readers," *Journal of Deaf Studies and Deaf Education* 5, no. 1 (2000): 32–50, argue that phonological knowledge is essential for learning and using written language.

2. For recent work on cospeech gesture, see a collection edited by David McNeill, *Language and Gesture* (Cambridge: Cambridge University Press, 2000).

3. Some work on cospeech gesture attempts to investigate the interaction between gesture and grammar. See work done by Susan Duncan, "Grammatical Form and 'Thinking-for-Speaking' in Mandarin Chinese and English: An Analysis Based on Speech-Accompanying Gestures" (PhD diss., University of Chicago, 1996), and Nick Enfield in both "Demonstratives in Space and Interaction: Data from Lao Speakers and Implications for Semantic Analysis," *Linguistic Society of America* 79, no. 1 (2003): 82–117, and "Producing and Editing Diagrams Using Co-Speech Gesture: Spatializing Nonspatial Relations in Explanations of Kinship in Laos," *Anthropology of Visual Communication* 13, no. 1 (2003): 7–50. For other related work, check J. Blake, E. Olshansky, G. Vitale, and S. Macdonald, "Are Communicative Gestures the Substrate of Language?" *Evolution of Communication: An International Multidisciplinary Journal* 1, no. 2 (1997): 261–82.

4. See Karen Emmorey, ed., *Perspectives on Classifier Constructions in Sign Languages* (Mahwah, N.J.: Lawrence Erlbaum Associates, 2003) for a collection of linguistic and psycholinguistic discussions on classifier constructions; the volume contains a few chapters that focus on the role of gesture in classifier constructions. Also see Scott Liddel, *Grammar, Gesture, and Meaning in American Sign Language* (Cambridge: Cambridge University Press, 2005) for a discussion on how grammar and gesture are integrated in ASL in meaning construction. Liddel suggests that the conventional concept of "language" has been much too narrow and that a more comprehensive look at vocally produced languages will reveal the same integration of gestural, gradient, and symbolic elements.

5. Richard Sinatra, *Visual Literacy Connections to Thinking, Reading and Writing* (Springfield, Ill.: Charles C. Thomas, 1986).

6. An attempt to define visual literacy was probably first attempted by John Debes in "Some Foundations for Visual Literacy," *Audiovisual Instruction* 13 (1968): 961–64, in which his definition incorporates three key components of visual literacy as skills to discriminate and interpret; create; and

comprehend and enjoy. For additional sources on the discussion and definition of visual literacy by Debes, see "The Loom of Visual Literacy," *Audiovisual Instruction* 14 (1969): 25–27, as well as Roger Fransecky and John Debes, *Visual Literacy: A Way to Learn—A Way to Teach* (Washington, D.C.: Association for Educational Communication and Technology, 1972). A discussion on the need to redefine literacy to encompass visual thinking is provided by C. Hedley, W. E. Hedley, and A. Baratta, whose chapter "Visual Thinking" appears in *Literacy: A Redefinition,* ed. N. Ellsworth, C. Hedley, and A. Baratta (Hillsdale, N.J.: Lawrence Erlbaum Associates, 1994), 109–26.

7. Bill Watterson, *The Complete Calvin and Hobbes* (Riverside, N.J.: Andrews McMeel, 2005).

8. An observation made by William Stokoe about the cinematic properties of ASL was quoted by Oliver Sacks, *Seeing Voices: A Journey into the World of the Deaf* (New York: HarperCollins, 1990), 90.

9. Dirksen Bauman first mentioned an analogy between films and ASL poetics in "Line/Shot/Montage: Cinematic Techniques in ASL Poetry," in *Deaf Studies VI Conference Proceedings: Making the Connection* (Washington, D.C.: College for Continuing Education, Gallaudet University, 1999), 137–49. Dirksen's discussion on the analogy was further refined in "Redesigning Literature: The Cinematic Poetics of American Sign Language Poetry," *Sign Language Studies* 4 (2003): 34–47.

10. Ibid., 37.

11. "Uncoding the Ethics," narrated by Freda Norma, is a part of the collection of literary work of *ASL in Signing Treasures: Excerpts from Signing Naturally Videos* by Ella Mae Lentz et al. (San Diego: DawnSignPress, 1996).

12. Patick Boudreault gave a presentation at the Revolutions in Sign Language Studies conference (Gallaudet University, Washington, D.C., March 22–24, 2006) on how technology is now unleashing new opportunities to create and publish content in ASL on topics ranging from journalism to academic discussion. For a different but related discussion on how language differs when it is spoken as opposed to written, see Khoarow Jahandarie, *Spoken and Written Discourse: A Multidisciplinary Perspective* (Stamford, Conn.: Ablex, 1999).

13. Barry Sanders, a professor at Claremont College, gave an account of a dyslexic student he knew from several of his classes. See *A Is for Ox: The Collapse of Literacy and the Rise of Violence in an Electronic Age* (New York: Vintage, 1995).

14. James Gee argues that the traditional definition of literacy is too constrained and maintains that literacy is about skills with language that are outside the scope of everyday use of language. He attempts to define literacy on the level of discourse and by discourse he means "a socially accepted association among ways of using language, of thinking, and of acting that can be used to identify oneself as a member of a socially meaningful group or 'social network.'" A community may come into being because of a common language or because of shared interest and knowledge such as a scientific community. For more information on his attempt to define literacy, see "What Is Literacy," in *Language and Linguistics in Context: Readings and Applications for Teachers,* ed. Harriet Luria, Deborah Seymour, and Trudy Smoke (Mahwah, N.J.: Lawrence Erlbaum Associates, 2006), 257.

9. *Critical Pedagogy and ASL Videobooks*

LAWRENCE FLEISCHER

IN *PEDAGOGY OF THE OPPRESSED*, Paulo Freire illustrates how he empowered the Brazilian peasants to learn not only to read the words, but also to read the world.[1] Freire presented the role of *conscientizacao*, a process that caused the peasants to become more critically conscious of their surroundings and to take necessary steps for improving their lot. Simply stated, Freire wanted the peasants to find out the causes, through reasoning, for their oppressed condition. Through the peasants' emancipatory literacy, they were able to examine the power structures of the dominant society and sought some solutions to lessen, if not eliminate, their oppressed condition.

The Freirian notion of critical pedagogy is applicable to educational settings in which the dominant culture utilizes its power to dominate and control students who come from the nondominant cultures. Included in this scenario is the perpetuation of language domination on students of nondominant cultures in which they are silenced by their beliefs that their language is inferior to Standard English.

In many schools, deaf children are forced to accept the institutionalized practices that discourage them from using American Sign Language (ASL) in its truest form. Some educators of the deaf believe that ASL will impede deaf students' progress with English, thus slowing down their linguistic and intellectual development associated with the mastery of the English language. They do not realize that they disempower deaf learners from generating a powerful mechanism in themselves for their literacy development. Deaf education's uncritical pedagogy results in depressing the academic achievement of the majority of deaf students. The educational successes of deaf students are few and far between.

This essay is presented as a case study in which you note that a hearing educator's values and beliefs are deeply ingrained in determining education practices for deaf learners, and even dominate language policies in the ASL Videobooks project.

Before I make further comments on the important connection between ASL Videobooks and critical pedagogy, I would like to explain briefly the ASL Videobooks project. ASL Videobooks is a project funded by the State of California in hopes of promoting literacy in deaf students through storytelling in ASL. The Office of Clearinghouse for Specialized Media and Technology under the auspices of the Department of Education coordinates the project with the California School for the Deaf, Riverside (CSDR). The State of California has spent approximately $300,000 through CSDR for the production of three hundred ASL Videobooks thus far. CSDR has state-of-the-art media equipment to produce the tapes. There is no charge for use of the production facilities at CSDR. According to the Director, Office of Clearinghouse for Specialized Media and Technology, the school "transcribed, directed, edited, captioned, added voice, added music, and provided the masters to my office for duplication and distribution." All funds, approximately $1,000 on each tape, were expended mainly for the personnel cost.

ASL Videobooks are, conceptually speaking, an excellent resource for literacy development in deaf children. They deserve to enjoy "listening" to stories as much as hearing children do. Storytelling plays an important part in increasing children's language and cognitive power. The early success in language learning and cognitive development through storytelling has led to a positive impact on many children for their educational development by means of knowledge expansion. The idea of how ASL Videobooks could benefit deaf children with respect to building knowledge through the stories they watch presents an important parallel to how hearing children often benefit from storytelling.

This essay specifically addresses the domino effect, falling down from either direction—right to left or left to right—between critical pedagogy and ASL Videobooks. In between is critical literacy, which takes one "deeper into more complex understandings of the word and world" through the use of a language.[2] The breakdown in critical pedagogy affects critical literacy, which ultimately makes ASL Videobooks impractical, if not useless, for use. Conversely, ASL Videobooks, if not properly developed, will carry no value for critical literacy and ultimately no effect on critical pedagogy. The important part in critical pedagogy is new knowledge continually obtained in order to advance one's cognitive domain. If one fails to obtain new knowledge, there is no change in one's cognitive growth.

The Power of Knowledge

"Knowledge is power" is a phrase often echoed in American minds. Gaining knowledge is the bedrock of education in which knowledge is sought, discovered, and shared through the interaction between teachers and students. Needless to say, knowledge as one obtains it in American society is of crucial significance simply because it is largely constructed within the principle of American meritocracy. Thus, American people are individually judged on merits based on "knowledge" they obtain and contribute. Seeking merit is one of the major obstacles for Deaf individuals in their search of the American dream. Why do Deaf people feel that way? Critical pedagogy for deaf learners is often not properly implemented. We have seen that many measures of educational and economic success indicate that deaf individuals, when they become adults, do poorly in comparison with hearing individuals. Why is this the case?

There is no mystique as to why there exists the merit gap between hearing and Deaf people. There's no doubt that Deaf individuals have been victimized by the constant siege of audism. Many Deaf individuals were often told that they did not do well in school and interpreted their prospects for the future as decidedly bleak. The miseducation of Deaf people for many years unwittingly caused by audism has embarrassed some hearing people and enraged Deaf leaders. Political "activism" might be necessitated to improve the lot of Deaf people with respect to education through the proper application of critical pedagogy.

To make it more difficult, deaf people rarely spoke out for their rights to demand what they knew to be the best way in terms of critical pedagogy. We were silenced for a long time and let things pass by to appease the "worldly knowledge" of hearing educators for their decision making and to save ourselves from further embarrassment. Deaf people themselves did not have enough respect in the abilities of deaf learners for educational achievement. In addition, they blamed both deafness and Deaf cultural disadvantage, not even the legacy of audism, for their educational failures and deficiencies. To counter these problems of their hesitancy to speak out, deaf learners must be empowered during the early part of their lives through critical pedagogy.

The Importance of Critical Pedagogy and ASL

Joan Wink defined critical pedagogy as "a process that enables teachers and learners to join together in asking fundamental questions about knowledge, justice and equity in their own classroom, school, family, and community."[3] What she does emphasize is that critical pedagogy is a very important human idea for teaching and learning for the purpose of empowering the learner in every possible way. Joan Wink proposed that the theoretical base of any educational practice must be continually examined by educators if they want to transform their classrooms into learning environments that are conducive to the real needs of their students. Through the spirit of critical pedagogy, students are given the opportunity to develop their abilities to the fullest, to understand critically their lives, and to seek ways on how to engage in the world. Critical pedagogy cannot be relegated to a fixed system because it would lead to the weakening of human spirits.

Fundamental to critical pedagogy for deaf learners is that educators of the deaf must understand the powerful relationship between culture and language and its dynamics relating to the development of critically thinking and socially active deaf individuals. The failure to change what is believed to work better for deaf learners prevents the cultivation of empowerment and intellectual development for those deaf students. As a result, deaf learners are marginalized and are doomed to "captivity."

In order to help deaf learners be "free from captivity," the current system of deaf education, we must first and foremost look at ASL. Without ASL, we permit ourselves to be languished in the tragically flawed educational system. The demand for respect toward Deaf thinking on ASL must first and foremost be recognized if critical pedagogy for deaf learners is to happen in deaf education. The general understanding that hearing people process language aurally while deaf people process language visually must also take place first before we could put critical pedagogy on the right track. It's also important to note that, by strengthening the deaf "critical pedagogy," the difference does not make Deaf people less human than hearing people. It's a blessing to see that more people accept signed languages as part of today's human languages and understand that, while there are some differences between signed and spoken languages, the main purpose is the same and very human; that is, to communicate with others.

Should a positive attitude toward ASL pervade American Society, we would probably see many Deaf people with fluency in both languages, ASL and English. From
there, they are able to enjoy both cultural and linguistic richness in both the hearing
and Deaf worlds.

The Potential Contributions of ASL Videobooks to Deaf Learners

The "language arts" materials in ASL specifically designed for deaf learners are scarce
and in desperate need of further development. Since English has been established as
the primary language of instruction in the United States, the plethora of K–12 materials in English language makes it possible for hearing children to enjoy language arts as
a part of building the knowledge base during the early grades. There is a dearth of ASL
materials for deaf children, who do not have the same opportunities for exposure to
build the knowledge base during their early years of schooling. To reduce a big imbal-
ance between hearing and deaf learners, ASL Videobooks appeared to offer a good solution to the aforementioned problems. The concept behind the ASL Videobooks was
perfect, I thought, until I saw some tapes of the ASL Videobooks; then it turned out to be
a major disappointment for me.

While I expressed my disappointment over the ASL Videobooks, I was consciously
aware of sociopolitical trends in education of the deaf that have slowly changed, affecting this project. The mastery of the English language for deaf students continues to be
the primary, nearly obsessive, goal in deaf education settings. Even though educators
of the deaf have begun to see the value in ASL and included ASL as part of the language
policies in their schools, they didn't have a full grasp of what ASL is as a language. Their
support for the inclusion of ASL in schools is definitely in the right direction. Deaf children learning through ASL are more likely to enhance their possibilities for intrinsic
motivation to learn and, as a result, acquire new knowledge. Thus, I took initiative in
writing a letter, with a stance of both sensitivity and frankness, to the Office of Clearinghouse for Specialized Media and Technology under the Department of Education in
the State of California. Below are the exchanges of communication, with some contents
removed, in chronological order that are relevant to the concerns and hopes I have for
the ASL Videobooks.

Addressed to the Director of Clearinghouse for Specialized Media
and Technology from Lawrence Fleischer

This letter is to applaud the endeavor, in which your office has worked in partnership
with the California School for the Deaf, Riverside, for making the ASL Videobooks possible and available to many of us for use with Deaf children. I have every reason to believe that such a concept of the ASL Videobooks is of paramount importance to Deaf
children's education. I thought that the idea for having Deaf students signing different
stories is really magnificent.

However, I want to share a major concern I have pertaining to the ASL Videobooks.
My comments are limited to what I have seen in about twenty different stories that Deaf

children signed. The signing patterns they produced are obviously in the form of literal translation from English to ASL. The literal translation as rendered/displayed by Deaf signers in these tapes came to me, a native user of ASL, nonsensical to the point that it has little communication value as far as ASL is concerned. By translating sign-for-word, their "ASL" signing appears unnatural to the eyes of ASL users.

Mildred Larson in her book *Meaning-based Translation: A Guide to Cross-Language Equivalence* stresses the importance in avoiding literalisms in translation work. She emphasizes that "the translator's goal should be to reproduce in the receptor language (ASL in this case) a text which communicates the same message as the source language (English) but using the natural grammatical and lexical choices of the receptor language." She calls it "idiomatic translation."[4]

I am sorry that I had to bring to your attention the concern I have for the ASL Videobooks that have been produced so far. I remain hopeful that the project will continue with a major shift in translation work; that is, from literal translation that produces nonsense to idiomatic translation that produces much sense.

Addressed to Lawrence Fleischer
from the Director of Clearinghouse for Specialized Media and Technology

Thanks for your letter dated March 21 concerning CSMT's library of ASL Videobooks. It's great that you are interested in our effort to improve access to the general curriculum for students who are Deaf. We believe the videos help students glean more meaning from literature adopted by the State Board of Education.

Addressed to the Director of Clearinghouse for Specialized Media
and Technology from Lawrence Fleischer

First of all, they must enjoy the story being told. Second, they must understand the purposes behind the story: plot, character, etc. Third, they pass on their knowledge of the story and read, with excitement, the English text of that story. I strongly believe that full understanding of a story as delivered in one language generates enthusiasm, excitement, and energy in students for learning the other language. Unfortunately, I haven't yet seen one story from the ASL Videobooks that stirs and hold[s] my interest in watching the story from the beginning to the end. I suspect that there is another major problem (in addition to utilizing rather heavily the English syntax when signing a story) as to why the storytelling in the tapes I saw was not appealing. Mostly, it is because of monotone, unsegmented signing that appears unnatural to the eyes of ASL users. In this manner, prosodic features such as proper rhythm, tempo, stress, interest, intonation in ASL are missing.

I recognize that translation work is not always easy for languages including signed languages. Per your suggestion, I am willing to do translation work from English to ASL on selected stories. You can pick two stories appropriately fitting for each age group: 3–4 years old, 5–6 years old, 7–8 years old. I will try my best to complete them by October 1st.

To me, ASL Videobooks is one of the best things that has happened to Deaf Education. It is also a worthy investment for our deaf children today and tomorrow. We need to make it right and better. Indeed, it will require our hard work ahead!

Many thanks for your willingness to have discussions with me about the ASL Videobooks.

Addressed to Lawrence Fleischer
from the Director of Clearinghouse for Specialized Media and Technology

Thanks for your letter dated June 6, 2002 regarding CSMT's ASL Videobooks. I am very pleased that you are willing to transcribe stories for the CSMT. I will send you several children's literature books in the near future.

Addressed to the Director of Clearinghouse for Specialized Media
and Technology from Lawrence Fleischer

Last month I had a good talk with Peter Wolf, a Deaf filmmaker, about the ASL Videobooks. He had the opportunity to see some samples of the tapes (spreading over the four years). We both agreed strongly that the multiple stimuli on the screen appearing simultaneously—signing, captioning, and background scenes—are too confounding to the eyes of a deaf person. Peter and I brainstormed some ideas for the ASL Videobooks if you plan to resume funding for additional stories. With the ideas proposed below, we believe you could make it better and more "user friendly" too:

1. The program should have a host and several deaf youngsters sitting in a semi-circle.
2. The host should give a brief summary of the story (to a viewer) before showing the background scenes of a story in sequence without any person signing on the screen and even without captioning. It is a kind of a walk-through for the viewer to visualize the scenes prior to "reading" a story in ASL.
3. A signer tells a story in its entirety with the solid color of the background wall behind the signer (no background scenes drawn from a book). More importantly, he/she doesn't have to follow the text in English from the book. A signer simply carries out the meaning from the source language (English) and delivers in the natural form of the receptor language (ASL) to ASL viewers.
4. The English text of a story should be limited to "rolling up" slowly from the beginning to the end without the presence of a storyteller and without the background scenes. The host can prepare the viewers for the reading of a story in English before the text rolls up.
5. The host and deaf youngsters can have group discussions including a "question & answer" session on the story being told—covering some points about scenes, ASL, and English.

The ideas that Peter and I suggested above are rather simple. Effective planning is all you need to make it a reality. It might be more costly to produce a tape for each story but the investment for the ASL Videobooks in this kind of arrangement will return many times by greater use of the tapes, both in class and out of class.

Further dialogue on this matter is very much welcome.

E-mail Correspondence between Lawrence Fleischer and the Director of Clearinghouse for Specialized Media and Technology, December 18, 2002

FROM LAWRENCE FLEISCHER TO THE DIRECTOR

Just to let you know that I just sent you a package with a videotape inside. In that tape, you will find five or six signers (all but one are second language users of ASL) telling the stories as listed below:

> "Arthur Meets the President"
> "The School Mural"
> "How to Make an Apple Pie"
> "The Old Barn"
> "A Summer Job"

FROM THE DIRECTOR TO LAWRENCE FLEISCHER

Thanks for your letter and your e-mail. I look forward to seeing your transcriptions of the books. I'm sure we'll find the videos very informative. I seriously doubt that we'll be producing any new ASL VideoBook titles this year due to staff reductions and the budget crises. When we are in a position to produce new videos, I'll certainly let you know.

We are always interested in how information is organized (in this case children's literature), how information is processed, and how differences arise when languages are transcribed. Failure to capture conceptual distinctions is always a risk in the art of translation. Teaching English requires the use of grammatical structures and word forms and it is indeed instinctive for educators to do so. CSMT's goal is to provide a tool which teachers can use to help students capture content of the story using ASL and simultaneously stir interest in reading the print book. I believe we are accomplishing that goal.

I am interested in the similarities, differences, styles, and expressions of meaning when representing English in ASL and ASL in English. There are aspects of English that have literal meaning in ASL and there are aspects of English that should be communicated idiomatically in ASL. The art of transcription is clearly the issue and thank goodness we are far removed from the literal translation of "butterfly." . . . smile. I am afraid that there may be a tendency to consider English and ASL as inherently independent when we need to weave them together to benefit children who are Deaf and who need to develop the ability to read and write English effectively in a world that demands these skills.

I would like to make the following proposal . . .

I think it would be terrific if one of your students did an independent study. I would provide three short children's literature books and the student would transcribe the books into ASL. The student would then be videotaped telling the story based on his/her transcription. Naturally, a home video would suffice . . . no special effects, no captions, no voice. If the transcription were blessed by you and your staff, we could use the videos as study guides in the future. What do you think?

Addressed to the Director of Clearinghouse for Specialized Media and Technology from Lawrence Fleischer

I would like to reiterate how much I appreciated the endeavor you have made toward the ASL Videobooks project. Needless to say, the plethora of K–12 English curriculum packages which outline well-planned language arts programs and activities beginning in the early grades offers hearing students excellent learning materials for not only the development and refinement of English, but also growth in conceptual understanding of the world. Deaf children should also have the opportunities in their exposure to language arts in ASL for the same purpose as hearing children. ASL videobooks, if properly developed, could make a significant contribution to the field of deaf education. We, however, need to work together in order to see that deaf students avoid falling into the pit of meaningless lessons through watching these so-called ASL tapes.

As a native user of ASL, I must say with much frankness that deaf students signing in the tapes that I have viewed so far don't look like ASL. I understand your desire in seeing that deaf learners gain the mastery of English through ASL storytelling by weaving together both languages as much as possible without disrupting conceptual distinctions. I do share the same belief with you that deaf youngsters can make good progress in English from ASL but ASL initially must come out to them crisply and crystal clear.

E-mail Correspondence from the Director of Clearinghouse for Specialized Media and Technology to Lawrence Fleischer, January 3, 2003

Thanks for your holiday greetings and the videotape of your CSU Northridge students.

Your students are skilled in the tradition of theatrical interpretation and show a lot of talent as ASL interpreters for the performing arts. I believe all have the ability to render an author's meaning through such artistic performances.

Thanks too for your interest in augmenting our ASL VideoBook formula. However, I believe your ideas could be best implemented as a new project. As valuable and entertaining as traditional storytelling methods are to students, it does not meet our current objective. Our intent is to transfer an author's content and meaning in a format that will achieve a balance between the original, printed, English version and an ASL transcription. A major task is to convey the book's meaning to students who are Deaf while simultaneously stimulating their interest in reading and understanding the print version of the book. The connection/relationship between the print book, closed captions, speech, and the ASL transcription must be available, though optional, for each audience.

Should the CSMT embark on a new ASL project, I will certainly contact you. If you would like to see copies of the books produced by CSDR's high school students this year, let me know. I'll be happy to send them to you.

Concluding Remarks with a Question

The best I can say about ASL Videobooks is that it needs to be "fixed up" to provide meaningful experiences for deaf learners. It will require a considerable amount of time and energy to make it right. In other words, no change in ASL Videobooks means that we permit deaf learners to fall into the pit of meaningless lessons in ASL language art activities. If we make no mention of such deficiencies in ASL Videobooks to educators of the deaf, they might say: "We have tried everything, even in ASL. Better skip the ASL part because it is found not to benefit literacy development in deaf children. Look at the lack of results we were getting from ASL Videobooks. We better stop investing in them because it is too costly." As I have earlier argued, I do see the enormous potential of ASL Videobooks for it can cultivate deaf learners to build up the power of knowledge. In turn, they become not only critical thinkers but also good communicators in both languages, ASL and English. They can also become competitors in the workplace on the basis of merit. This leads us to ask: In the name of critical pedagogy, should we prevent the domino of ASL Videobooks from falling down?

Notes

1. Paulo Freire, *Pedagogy of the Oppressed* (New York: Continuum, 1997).
2. Joan Wink, *Critical Pedagogy: Notes from the Real World* (New York: Longman, 2000), 55.
3. Ibid., 71.
4. Mildred Larson, *Meaning-based Translation: A Guide to Cross-Language Equivalence* (Lanham, Md.: University Press of America, 1984), 17.

PART IV   *Places and Borders*

10. The Decline of Deaf Clubs in the United States: A Treatise on the Problem of Place

CAROL PADDEN

THERE ARE VERY FEW "PLACES" Deaf people can call their own. For most of their history in the United States, they have occupied spaces built by others and largely controlled by others. Schools for deaf children are a prime example: from the time the first schools for the deaf were built in the early part of the nineteenth century, spaces were designed and organized exclusively for deaf children by their teachers and benefactors, but rarely if ever by Deaf people themselves. Records from some of the first deaf schools included discussions among their boards of directors about how to organize the lives of deaf children into built spaces.[1] Identified first by deafness, deaf children were typically further organized within these schools on other dimensions as well: gender, race (until as late as 1978), and educational method.[2]

Outside of deaf schools and within their local communities, Deaf people had some opportunity to organize their own spaces. Most notable are the associations they organized throughout the United States, beginning almost at the same time as the new deaf schools.[3] These associations and the social clubs they supported provided the foundation for the enormously popular Deaf clubs of the 1940s and the 1950s. Many of these clubs were successful enough that they could buy their own buildings, or acquire long-term leases to accommodate their growing membership. As these clubs became more permanent in the sense of brick-and-mortar places, Deaf people designed and controlled what activities took place within their walls. But after a period of rapidly expanding membership, Deaf clubs suddenly reversed their pattern and began a steep decline to where there are now very few such clubs left in the United States. Of the few that still remain, their membership is very small and very elderly.

William Leach in his book *Country of Exiles* worries that there are new social and economic forces that are leading to the disappearance of "place" in the United States—city centers, community parks, and other places where Americans can gather and meet on a regular basis.[4] Leach argues that American civic life crucially depends on brick-and-mortar buildings, town-spaces, and other physically real spaces where people can meet face-to-face and interact. The much-heralded modern "spaces"—on the Internet, in bars, and other "imagined spaces"—are poor substitutions because they are too temporary and too tenuous to serve the same functions as more physically stable places. If we continue to lose traditional places, Leach argues that we may find ourselves facing large-scale disengagement and social apathy.

Deaf clubs are a case study in the "problem of place" in American life. For most of their history, Deaf clubs were places where Deaf people could meet face-to-face and conduct social business with one another, but as with a number of American social organizations, many have since closed or declined. As we trace back their recent history, we can see a trajectory of change, of a rapid expansion followed by an almost equally rapid decline. What does the history of Deaf clubs tell us about the future of the Deaf community in the United States and, more generally, about the future of "place" in American life?

At their height of popularity, Deaf clubs could be found in nearly all major cities in the United States. Ohio in the 1940s had at least one Deaf club in each of its cities, not only in Akron, where many Deaf men and women found employment in the rubber tire industry during World War II, but also in the cities of Toledo, Cincinnati, Columbus, Cleveland, Warren, and Dayton. New York City had at least twelve different Deaf clubs spread out throughout the boroughs. The Union League was the largest and most popular, open through the week and every weekend night.[5] Some clubs in the city were organized around sports teams: the Naismith Club in Brooklyn (named after the inventor of basketball) often played against the District of Columbia Club for the Deaf, where my father played for a few years after he graduated from Gallaudet in 1945. Formed in opposition to the larger Union League and other sign language clubs, there were oral-only clubs whose membership was made up of oralists, or those who previously attended oral schools where sign language was prohibited, like the Laro Club ("oral" spelled backwards) and the Merry-Go-Rounders.

The clubs were also segregated by race and ethnicity; the black Deaf club in Cincinnati was separate from the white Deaf club, as were clubs in the rest of Ohio and throughout the country. The Lincoln Club, a black Deaf club in Chicago, had a powerful basketball team. The Imperials Club in New York City, also for black Deaf members, didn't have a fixed location; instead meetings were held in a member's home in Harlem.[6] The Hebrew Association of the Deaf (HAD) had two clubs, one in Manhattan and another in Brooklyn, both organized for Deaf Jewish members. Bernard Bragg, the well-known Deaf actor, frequently attended the clubs in the shadow of his father, Wolf Bragg, who as director and producer staged signed plays under the auspices of the HAD.[7]

The few Deaf clubs that remain open today are mostly in the Midwest and the South. There is reportedly a club still remaining in Rochester, N.Y., where the local Deaf community says it is working hard to maintain the club and its traditions. One man reported that while visiting the Akron Club he had discovered he was the youngest person there—at age sixty-eight. In the major cities, New York, Washington, D.C., Los Angeles, or San Francisco, there are no clubs left.

Deaf clubs in Europe have experienced decline as well, but not as dramatically. Most clubs in Finland are still operating, but as in the United States, they are increasingly populated by the older generation, with involvement of younger Deaf people more sporadic and fleeting. In southern Europe, Deaf clubs still maintain a strong presence in Spain and Italy, for example. In Spain, the Deaf clubs form the network of the community's political structure. Each province in Spain, from Galicia to Catalonia and in the capital city of Madrid, sends representatives from their clubs to the national organization. In the United States, there was once a similar structure that formed the basis of the state organizations and the national associations. Until the 1970s, the National Association of the Deaf and the National Fraternal Society of the Deaf drew its leaders from among club presidents: Fred Schreiber began his career as a community leader at the District of Columbia Club for the Deaf, and then moved up to become executive secretary of the National Association of the Deaf, a post he held for many years.

The Deaf clubs of the World War II years were very much brick-and-mortar places: many clubs aspired to own their own buildings in order to have complete management of the activities within their walls. Income from selling alcohol and hosting card games, lotteries, and other forms of entertainment went toward the maintenance of club activities and their buildings. At their height, the largest Deaf clubs could count on steady attendance several days a week if not daily, and a steady income from money-making activities. At special events, their halls were teeming with members, many visiting from other cities in the country. Clubs were places of respite where Deaf people could find companionship away from the loneliness of the workplace where many Deaf people worked alone.

The decline of Deaf clubs is usually told as a story about the effects of technology. As new technologies began to be used in the community, Deaf people shifted their interest inward to the domestic sphere. Instead of partaking in Deaf club entertainment, Deaf people began staying at home more, preferring instead the entertainment of the close-captioned television or the captioned film. Or the text telephone is blamed, because Deaf people no longer needed to meet at the club to make arrangements for future events; they could simply call one another on the telephone.

However, the timing of the introduction of these technologies does not match the pattern of the clubs' decline. For example, captioned television did not become widely available until after 1978, a time when many clubs had already begun their steep decline. Text telephone machines grew slowly during this period: in 1968, there were only five hundred machines in use increasing to just seven thousand worldwide by 1974. In 1988, after many clubs had already closed, the number of machines reached five hundred thousand.[8] It is often argued that the closing of clubs led to a sharp increase in use of these technologies, as Deaf people turned to devices to carry out what had previously been done face-to-face. But the types of convenient technologies that are popular among Deaf people today for reaching friends and communicating with them—pagers, e-mail, voice relay—all were developed within the last five years, long after most clubs had already closed.

We have argued elsewhere that factors other than new technologies played a role in the decline of Deaf clubs.[9] Deaf people's economic and work lives changed prior to the Second World War, and changed again following the war. When viewed historically, factors that contributed to the clubs' popularity in the first place in the years leading up to the Second World War ironically contributed to their demise as well in the years after.

The types of jobs that Deaf people had during the first part of the twentieth century were artisan-type jobs, where they worked in small shops doing specialized work. With the rise of industrial capacity during the Second World War and the great demand for factory-type labor, Deaf people found they could work in factories and large plants and earn more than they did before.[10] Deaf men and women left their homes and relocated where there was likely to be work: Akron, Los Angeles, New York, and Baltimore.

The Akron Club for the Deaf was hugely popular in the war years, open seven days a week, twenty-four hours a day to accommodate Deaf workers ending their shifts at Goodyear Aircraft. GAC, as it was called by its Deaf workers, was built to assemble in record time the fighter planes and other forms of transportation that were needed to support America abroad. In 1941, Goodyear Aircraft sent out a nationwide call for workers and hired men and women in large numbers, including Deaf people. If the person appeared reasonably able-bodied, they were hired, despite having no experience at all in the building of aircraft or in manufacturing operations. GAC was a typical World War II factory, designed to accommodate large groups of untrained workers, toiling long hours at specific tasks, managed by a small layer of highly skilled managers. John Bradley, a resident of Kent, Ohio, remembers that his parents heard from friends in New Jersey that Goodyear was hiring Deaf people and offering a decent wage, so they moved the family there. His father got a job as a riveter though he had no previous experience in the trade. His mother did assembly of small parts in another part of the factory. He remembers barely literate Deaf people being hired at GAC, but it didn't matter as there were so many jobs to be filled, including packing boxes and moving goods from one part of the operation to another. Buchanan estimates the number of Deaf people employed in Akron defense industries as approaching one thousand. The local club became a place to go after finishing one's shift, to unwind from the long hours of work. There were so many new Deaf people in the city, a virtual population boom, that the club became a good place to meet friends and for young Deaf men and women to seek out possible marriage partners.

The membership of the Union League and the Chicago Club for the Deaf were driven by a different trade—men and women who were members of the ITU, the International Typographical Union, and made good income as printers. Friday nights at the club offered regular poker for printers who picked up their paychecks earlier that day. My grandfather, David Padden, was a staunch ITU man and a frequent habitué of the Chicago Club for the Deaf's poker games. Those wanting something other than poker games could find regular entertainment at the club. Home films of the Los Angeles Club for the Deaf in the 1940s show crowds of men and women drinking and socializing in the club halls. Deaf performances of all kinds appeared regularly in these films, from beauty pageants to skits, including objectionable blackface performances and men dressed in drag doing vaudeville. For family fare, there were picnics held in city parks.

When my father was offered a position at Gallaudet, my grandfather told him that the real money was not in teaching, but in printing. Printers could count on steady work and good job security, and if they wanted, they could work in almost any town. The privilege of being an ITU member is that they could work at any union shop in the country. If they had a yen for travel, they could move from shop to shop, substituting for regular members and earning as much as they needed. My father eventually took the job at Gallaudet, but he held on to his union membership, registering as NAT or "not at trade" status so he could work part-time on weekends at the *Washington Post*.

Club treasuries were supported by membership dues and admission for visiting nonmembers. More income came from poker games, selling food and drink, and the occasional raffle drive. Some clubs earned enough income to buy their own buildings, as did the Akron Club and Thompson Hall in St. Paul, Minnesota. Each club had a president and a management structure, from the treasurer to the person who worked behind the bar selling drinks.

At the height of these clubs' popularity, they excluded black Deaf men and women from membership. This was active segregation in the Deaf community, carried over from a long history of separate schools for black and white deaf children in the southern states. A deep divide in job opportunities for black and white Deaf workers contributed as well. GAC did not hire many black workers; instead black Deaf workers migrating to Ohio found employment in the World Publishing Company, which printed Bibles. These workers would later open the Cincinnati Charter Club, a club for black Deaf men and women.

As the war ended, and GAC shut down production, a few Deaf workers at GAC found jobs making tires at the restructured factories of Goodyear or Firestone, but there were never as many jobs as there were during the war. In the decades to follow, Deaf workers moved into other occupations. Printing remained a good occupation until the 1970s when "cold type" and computerized forms of reproduction began to make inroads in the newspaper industry. The Government Printing Office, the *Washington Post,* and the *Washington Evening Star* were among the largest employers of Deaf printers in the Washington, D.C., area. As the printing industry changed and "hot" linotype machines were replaced by computers, the numbers of workers in those industries began to decline. ITU lost its grip on the industry, and union membership dwindled. It is during this time that Deaf people once again moved into different kinds of work, away from the traditional "solitary trades" that characterized much of Deaf people's work lives in the 1940s and 1950s to professional and government-type jobs. The federal government expanded during the 1960s, offering more programs, and they began hiring a new workforce: women, minorities—and Deaf people. Deaf people found employment in the professional sector, as civil servants, teachers, rehabilitation counselors, and in other types of advocacy jobs.

In a book about the explosive rise in purchases of home videocassette recorders, Mark Levy finds that videotape players were available in the mid-1960s, albeit expensive and difficult to operate, but few homes had them.[11] It was not until the late 1970s that home videocassette recorders became popular. Levy argues that the rapid growth in the technology coincided with a mass employment pattern shifting away from manufacturing jobs to service jobs. As workers found themselves required to accommodate employers' demands for "flex-time," and no longer following a predictable work schedule, workers were shifted off the normal network viewing schedule. They began to buy videocassette recorders in order to record programs for viewing at another time. (The other major use for videocassette recorders, rental of home videos, came later, once the technology was well established in the home.) According to Levy, the public did not suddenly discover that videocassette recorders were a good technology to own; rather they sought out the technology in order to satisfy changed circumstances in their lives. The technology was not popular in the 1960s, not because it was not expertly designed, but because the practical benefits of the technology did not become apparent until later.

I argue along similar lines about the rise of communication technology in the Deaf community. In another paper I wrote some years ago, I described the impact of the professionalization of deaf education and the introduction of middle-class, professional-type work to the Deaf community.[12] By the early 1970s, many Deaf printers and factory workers made the transition to professional life, as did my father and a number of his friends. My father joined the faculty at Gallaudet in 1945, and for a number of years after he occasionally worked as a printer on weekends at the *Washington Post* for extra income. He stopped in 1960 as his salary increased. Fred Schreiber was a printer at the *Washington Evening Star* before he became executive secretary of the National Association of the Deaf.

As Deaf men and women moved to the professional class, the working class became less broad, and became divided between those who joined the professional class and those who remained in the trades. The split affected membership in clubs as well, as the professional class moved on to other kinds of associations. Instead of Deaf clubs, professional associations became popular: for teachers of the deaf, rehabilitation counselors, sign language teachers, and mental health professionals. New organizations recognizing gender, race, and ethnicity formed a different social dimension, moving from the local to the national level: the Black Deaf Advocates, the National Asian Deaf Congress, the Deaf Latino Conference, the Jewish Deaf Congress, and Deaf Women United. Now, some thirty years after Deaf clubs declined, the community no longer divides itself between rival basketball clubs, oralists and manualists, or the Hebrew Associations of Manhattan and Brooklyn; instead the principal dimensions are class, ethnicity, gender, and race. The Deaf club, designed for older kinds of social affiliations, did not seem able to accommodate the new social realities. For reasons that may have to do with how closely Deaf clubs were linked to local working-class life, either in Akron or in New York City, Deaf clubs didn't change for the new social reality; instead they declined.

It could be argued that Deaf clubs metamorphosed into the Deaf advocacy centers that sprang into existence in the 1980s in large urban centers like Los Angeles and San Francisco. Funded by local and state agencies, these advocacy centers, including the Greater Los Angeles Association of the Deaf (GLAD) and Deaf Counseling, Advocacy and Referral Agency (DCARA), are decidedly more political than the Deaf clubs ever were. While Deaf clubs were largely self-funded, from membership dues, raffles, and food service, Deaf advocacy organizations lobbied for funding from the state to support direct services to Deaf clients: for interpreting, counseling, and job training. The ambitions of advocacy organizations have always been larger and more socially conscious than Deaf clubs ever were, but what advocacy organizations do not always provide is free unstructured social space.

Deaf clubs were first and foremost places to congregate, to meet after work on weekday and weekend nights. Deaf clubs organized cultural entertainment: skits, beauty pageants, storytelling, and other forms of narrative. Advocacy organizations can have a cultural agenda, but it is planned and infrequent. Deaf clubs invited drop-ins from anywhere around the country, even the world, but advocacy organizations are professional spaces first and foremost, and social spaces secondarily. Instead of selling beer on weekend nights, these organizations have bookstores and sell educational materials about Deaf people, their sign language, and their culture.

We remain romantic about Deaf clubs because they seem more like real "places" compared to the more fluid and porous meeting places that exist today in the United States. In San Diego, young Deaf people meet at a local coffee house every Friday, borrowing a corner of the commercial space for social interaction. In other towns, shopping malls attract Deaf youth, but by the time they find a regular place to meet, security officers ask them to keep moving to avoid loitering. There seems to be no dedicated "place" for impromptu social gatherings. The Deaf clubs of the 1940s and 1950s met in buildings that were rented or owned by Deaf people. They had budgets, though small, but there was autonomy and entrepreneurship (and sometimes a little embezzling, as in Bernard Bragg and Eugene Bergman's fictional Deaf club in their play *Tales from a Clubroom*).[13] Much of the popular American Sign Language (ASL) literature that can be found in sign language books—fingerspelled alphabet stories, popular narratives, even styles of performance—can be traced back to Deaf club performances.

Leach's worries notwithstanding, American Deaf clubs were places for a certain kind of time and economy, and that era has passed. Deaf clubs were fiercely segregated spaces, such that few white Deaf people today remember or know very little, if anything, about black Deaf clubs in their cities, even as they mourn the passing of their favorite Deaf clubs. The clubs of the 1940s and 1950s mapped onto a social dimension that is changed today; instead of oralists and manualists, black and white, athletes and nonathletes, poker players and entertainers, we have black Deaf advocates and Latino Deaf advocates, Deaf academics and mental health professionals, interpreter program trainers and ASL teachers. These identities exist along dimensions of civil rights, citizenship, and professions, which are very much of the twenty-first century.[14] It may be that the new "places," such as advocacy organizations, are more fluid and porous because they are more accommodating of these different social dimensions. A few advocacy groups have built their own centers; for example, GLAD recently opened a home office built with donated funds, returning perhaps to the brick-and-mortar ambitions of older Deaf clubs, although with a different social mission.

The story about American Deaf clubs is often told as a story about technology and how it rendered social spaces irrelevant, as Deaf people found new and efficient means of carrying out social interaction. But in this case, the timing of a particular technology, the captioned television or the text telephone, did not take place *before* social change; instead the technology was adopted *after* their social lives had changed, and after Deaf people realized that their social circumstances were ideal for a new technology. The story about American Deaf clubs should be told as a narrative about how Deaf people's work lives changed, and how their relationships with each other changed, introducing new tensions of class, race, gender, and ethnicity, in the end rendering the Deaf club irrelevant to the new social realities. Now if one visits one of the few remaining Deaf clubs, it feels as if traveling back in time: the elderly sitting in meeting halls, playing cards perhaps, and gossiping about friends. Whatever "place" is, it cannot be about resurrecting the old, but must be about reinnovating and regenerating new kinds of spaces. From her study of a church in Los Angeles with a Deaf congregation, Rayman finds that the Deaf members shared a remarkable tolerance for temporary and borrowed spaces.[15] The hearing members, on the other hand, became distressed when the space began to fluctuate during a period of relocation, and many left the church. Rayman argues that Deaf people in the United States are accustomed to "instabilities of place" because of their particular history in this country. As her fieldwork with the congregation neared an end, the church's fortunes shifted, and a new permanent space was located for the two congregations to share. Given even a tolerance for temporary spaces, Deaf people eventually do seek to make their spaces more physically permanent.

Returning to the question that opened this essay: does the disappearance of Deaf clubs signal a different future—perhaps a declining one—for the Deaf community? It is too soon to tell, or maybe Deaf clubs aren't the right kind of evidence of decline of a community. They were designed for a certain time and type of workforce that has long passed. They rose in popularity because they suited the structure of the factory work-day—the isolation Deaf people experienced while working in a factory and their need for social gathering at the end of the workday. When Deaf people moved into different kinds of jobs, Deaf clubs no longer suited their lives, and they began their long decline. In their place are other kinds of associations, more fluid in their locations but not entirely. What we need to understand is how in the midst of change, communities rebuild and redesign their spaces.

Notes

1. H. Van Allen, *A Brief History of the Pennsylvania Institution for the Deaf and Dumb* (Mt. Airy, Penn.: Board of Directors of the Pennsylvania Institution for the Deaf and Dumb, 1893).
2. Carol Padden and Tom Humphries, *Inside Deaf Culture* (Cambridge, Mass.: Harvard University Press, 2005).
3. John Van Cleve and Barry Crouch, *A Place of Their Own: Creating the Deaf Community in America* (Washington, D.C.: Gallaudet University Press, 1989). Jack Gannon, *Deaf Heritage: A Narrative History of Deaf America* (Silver Spring, Md.: National Association of the Deaf, 1981).
4. William Leach, *Country of Exiles: The Destruction of Place in American Life* (New York: Pantheon, 1999).
5. *The Silent Worker,* Advertisement, July 1953, 21.
6. Ernest Hairston and Linwood Smith, *Black and Deaf in America: Are We That Different?* (Silver Spring, Md.: TJ Publishers, 1983).
7. Bernard Bragg and Eugene Bergman, *Lessons in Laughter: The Autobiography of a Deaf Actor* (Washington, D.C.: Gallaudet University Press, 1989).
8. Bill Graham, *One Thing Led to the Next: The Real History of TTYs* (Evanston, Ill.: Mosquito Publishing, 1988).
9. Carol Padden, "Folk Explanation in Language Survival," in *Collective Remembering,* ed. D. Middleton (Los Angeles: Sage, 1990), 190–202. Also Padden and Humphries, *Inside Deaf Culture.*
10. Robert M. Buchanan, *Illusions of Equality: Deaf Americans in School and Factory, 1850–1950* (Washington, D.C.: Gallaudet University Press, 1999).
11. Mark R. Levy, *The VCR Age: Home Video and Mass Communication* (Newbury Park, Calif.: Sage, 1989).
12. Padden, "Folk Explanation."
13. Bernard Bragg and Eugene Bergman, *Tales from a Clubroom* (Washington, D.C.: Gallaudet University Press, 1981).
14. Michael Schudson, *The Good Citizen: A History of American Civic Life* (New York: Martin Kessler, 1998).
15. J. Rayman, "Enacting Culture: Dynamic Tensions within a Deaf Congregation" (PhD diss., Department of Communication, University of California, San Diego, La Jolla, 2004).

11. *Think-Between: A Deaf Studies Commonplace Book*

BRENDA JO BRUEGGEMANN

> Perspective, as its inventor remarked, is a beautiful thing.
> —George Eliot [Mary Ann Evans], *Daniel Deronda*

FOR SOME TIME NOW I have been imagining a theory of "betweenity," especially as it exists in Deaf Culture, identity, and language. And because I teach a great deal in the larger umbrella of "Disability Studies" these days, I have also been thinking about the expansion of that deaf-betweenity to "disability" more largely. (Of course, I've also then been thinking about the way that deafness itself occupies an interesting "betweenity" in relationship to disability identity.) In any case—whether deaf, disabled, or between—I'm finding that I'm generally more interested in the hot dog rather than the bun, the creme filling in the oreo (which, if you've noticed, has been changing a lot lately) rather than just the twinned chocolate sandwich cookies on the outside. Give me a hyphen any day. To be sure, the words on either side of the hyphen are interesting, too; but what is happening in that hyphen—the moment of magic artistry there in that half-dash—is what really catches my eye.

Between "Deaf" and "deaf" (or, The Names We Call Ourselves)

In disability culture and studies, as well as in Deaf Culture and Studies, we often get back to—or maybe, yes, we also get forward to—discussions about what we do and don't want to be called. Deaf Culture, in particular, has been around the block with this discussion for a long, long time. I offer three exhibits for consideration:

EXHIBIT A:

From the University of Brighton, UK, http://staffcentral.brighton.ac.uk/clt/disability/Deaf.htm:

> Note on terminology:
> The term "Deaf" (with a capital D) is the preferred usage of some people who are either born profoundly deaf or who become deaf at a very early age and who regard themselves as belonging to the Deaf community. Like people in many communities, those within the Deaf community are bound together by a feeling of identifying with other Deaf people. People in the Deaf community share, amongst other things, a sense of Deaf pride, traditions, values, lifestyles, humour, folklore, art, theatre, as well as a rich common language.

EXHIBIT B:

From a copyedited essay (on interpreters) that I received back from the university press editors:

> I do not understand the distinctions between use of upper and lower-case D for deafness? Please clarify for my own knowledge and for the general scope of this book.

EXHIBIT C:

From Gina Oliva, author of *Alone in the Mainstream: A Deaf Woman Remembers Public Schools,* the first book in the new "Deaf Lives" series of autobiography, biography, and documentary at Gallaudet University Press that I edit.[1] This is a memo Gina sent to me after the copyeditors asked her to double-check and "clarify" her use of Deaf/deaf in the manuscript:

> Subject: deaf vs. Deaf
> To: brueggemann.1@osu.edu
> Hi Brenda . . . I took a look at Padden and Humphries and decided it made sense to use Deaf when referring to adults in the Deaf community. If they are oral deaf, I will call them deaf. As for children, I would stick with deaf and hard of hearing children (lower case). This means that the "big D" will appear much in my book, as I say "Deaf adults this" and "Deaf adults that" a lot. I also say "deaf and hard of hearing children" a lot.
> Then I looked at "Journey into the Deaf-World" (Lane, Hoffmeister, Bahan) and see that they advocate using Deaf for any child who is deaf and couldn't access info without assistance. Hmmmmm. . . . Do you have any opinion about this???? I checked some other books. . . . Wrigley uses Deaf predominantly. Preston does not. I have others I can check . . . but my guess is there is little consensus about this.

As these exhibits illustrate, where we draw the line in relationships between "deaf" and "Deaf" is a question of common placement.

In Deaf Studies we can explore, and perhaps even expand upon, the definitions of the terms of d/Deaf operations—subtracting, adding, dividing, and multiplying the possibilities—for the key naming terms like "deaf," "Deaf," "hard-of-hearing," "late deafened," "hearing-impaired," "has hearing loss," "think-hearing," and my mother's personal favorite for me, "has selective hearing." But we can also move further out in the concentric circles by studying, for example, the mapping and meaning of mental proficiency labels alongside audiometric ones and noting their in-common categorizations—"moderate," "severe," "profound." Interestingly enough, these IQ labels parallel those assigned to hearing loss by medical practitioners—and both sets of terms came onto the diagnostic screen in our culture at about the same time. Moreover, if you simply rotate the axes of the two bell curves created by either the IQ or audiometric charts as they plot out "normal," "moderate," "severe," and "profound" you would find them folding neatly right on top of each other. Is this parallel only circumstance or do the angles between these two medical charts make more meaning in their overlay and intersections?

For one way to further explore this curious commonplace, we might consider that in the Nazi's national socialist regime during the early 1940s, people with disabilities in psychiatric institutions throughout the German Reich became subject to "euthanasia" at the hands of their own doctors and nurses. In what became known as the T-4 program during 1941–42, at least 270,273 patients from these institutions were transported to seven designated institutions and here, at these seven killing centers—usually immediately upon transport arrival—they were killed in gas chambers that became the experimental locations of "the Final Solution" targeted at Jewish people a few years later. Before the T-4 program, in the 1930s, many of these patients/people were also sterilized. After the T-4 program officially ended in 1942 an estimated additional one hundred thousand "patients" in these institutions may have died as victims of what is now called the "wild euthanasia" period when patients were administered drug overdoses or starved to death "unofficially." My point in telling these troubling facts is that at this time, as well as other times both past and present, people who were deaf in Germany (*taubstumme*—deaf and dumb) were often as not collapsed in diagnoses of other mental disabilities as well. I have looked at remaining records from one of these killing centers (which is still, eerily enough, a fully functioning psychiatric institution even today) as well as some records from the T-4 program housed in the German federal archives *(Bundesarchiv)* and I have, for myself, seen this conflation written on the records of several patients.

My point is that in the commonplace book of "deafness" things are not always clearly or singularly defined, designated, determined as "just," or "pure," or "only" deafness. And however much some deaf people may want to resist being labeled as "disabled," the fact remains that they *are* often labeled as such and that these labels—in all cases—are not always accurate though they may be, as it were, with consequences. Certainly deaf people should want to resist the easy conflation of their "condition" with others that coexist in degrees of "moderate," "severe," and "profound"—realizing the violence that can be (and has been) done with such an overlay. Yet also, just as certainly, I would suggest that to resist and distance one's self-identity and group identity from those whose condition has been deemed (for better or worse, for right or wrong) affiliated with hearing loss, would also be, in essence, to do further violence to those others with whom "authorities" have placed us (deaf people) in categorical similarity. Who—or what—are deaf people so afraid of when they resist placement in the commonplace of "disability"?

This unnamed fear also has us (and them) working (hard, very hard) to *contrast* "deaf" and "Deaf." The originary location of the Deaf/deaf divide dates around 1972, purportedly from coined usage in a seminal Deaf Studies essay by James Woodward, *How You Gonna Get to Heaven If You Can't Talk to Jesus? On Depathologizing Deafness.*[2] Thus, the definitional divide has been around for over thirty years. Yet aside from its usage in presses and publications long familiar with the commonplaces of "deafness," it must commonly still be footnoted in an academic text in order to explain, yet once again, what the distinctions between Big D "Deafness" and little d "deafness" are. Even when the distinctions are used, they are most often used, interestingly enough, in direct relation to each other; one is just as likely to see "d/Deaf" or "D/deaf" written as one is to see just "Deaf" or even "deaf" standing alone in a text that has set up this distinction. Thus, the divisional/definitional terms of "Deaf" and (or versus) "deaf" more often than not come in tandem as d/Deaf. As such, they are twinned—doppelgangers. *Mirror mirror on the wall* . . . they whisper and sign back and forth to each other.

The twinning of d/Deaf is perhaps safer that way since often, when pressed, it will be hard to determine at any one moment in a text whether the Big D "cultural/linguistic" arena is where we are or if we are just in the small d "audiological/medical" space. And what if we are in both places at the same time? The long-standing and footnoting practice of establishing some kind of border patrol between these terms tries to define and differentiate—apples here, oranges there—but more often than not the aliens still wind up looking very much like the natives. And perhaps it is really an avocado that is wanted, anyway? In most cases, for example, deaf students can't enroll in a state residential institution—long deemed the center of American Deaf Culture and the sanctuary for American Sign Language (ASL), and thus, a common place for Big D cultural/linguistic Deafness—without offering an audiogram and first being able to claim their little d deafness. Until just 2002 and the establishment of Gallaudet University's new HUG program (Hearing UnderGraduates), you could not get into the world's only liberal arts college for deaf and hard-of-hearing students without proof of (flawed) audiogram: you had to be *deaf* in order to go there and engage in the particular Gallaudet cultural practices that might also then mark you as *Deaf.*

Yet when the question is often posed about the differences between "deaf" and "Deaf"—as it was by a recent editor I worked with (see Exhibit B above) and, really, by almost every editor I've ever had in twenty years of writing about, in, from, around deafness[3]—most often the answer given is either "language—the use of ASL" or even more simple (yet complex), "attitude." And suddenly, there you are again, in another dark and thick forest without a working compass: "What kind of attitude?" you have to wonder. And what levels and types and uses of signed communication?

And what does it mean, anyway, to locate the choice position within the capital D? Is this not also an assault and an oppression—a dominance of one way of thinking (epistemology) and being (ontology) over another? This think-between space between "deaf" and "Deaf" is a rock and a hard place for Deaf Studies. I wonder what happens if we squeeze (more) in there? What if we don't "draw the line" on, around, through, or under where someone is (and isn't) "culturally deaf" or not? What if we stop footnoting and explaining (and educating "them" again and again and again, as we have for almost thirty years now) what we've learned to chant from almost rote memorization when we endeavor, once again, to explain the "difference" between little d and Big D deafness? But "they" never seem to hear a word of any of this, and so we go on footnoting and explaining and educating about the distinctions between "Deaf" and "deaf." If a (deaf) tree falls in the (hearing) forest, does anyone then really "hear" it?

Can we create a new geometry, a new space for "deaf" (and thus "Deaf" as well) to be in and for those trees to fall in? To answer such questions might be to enter more into questions of perspective. How, for example, might we follow both the dynamic flow and static stance of terms like "deaf," while along the way working also to understand our culture's long-standing cure-based obsessions with definitive causes and effects where deafness matters? What were—and are—the circumstances that create "deaf" or "Deaf" to begin with (and in continuance)? Whose testimony counts—and when and where and why and how—when it comes to authorizing d/Deaf identity or the "condition" of "deafness"?

What I am suggesting with these questions is that we might begin in Deaf Studies to push beyond the mere recitation of the "d/Deaf" pledge in our footnotes and to explore, instead, all the rhetorical situations that arise from the d/D distinctions, that bring the distinctions to bear, and that, most importantly, keep shifting them like an identity kaleidoscope in our own hands.

The (Deaf) Cyborg Space

Within the deaf kaleidoscope is the fragmented but also contained—and beautiful—image of the ever-shifting deaf cyborg. The seamed and seeming boundaries between "cure" and "control" in constructing the deaf cyborg body is a potent commonplace, especially for late twentieth- and early twenty-first-century Deaf Studies. Obviously, this seamed space might be illustrated in the controversy over cochlear implants and the deaf cyborg who, borrowing on cultural critic Donna Haraway's terms, becomes the "hybrid of machine and organism," the creation of "a creature of social reality as well as a creature of fiction" that has already "change[d] what counts as [deaf people's] experience in the late twentieth century."[4]

What Haraway's cyborg myth foretells is that deaf people and the Deaf world won't likely disappear, implanted as alien others. This is instead likely to be a tale of "transgressed boundaries, potent fusions," as Haraway's cyborg myth suggests: the boundaries might change, but the fusion will likely remain potent. At Gallaudet University, for example, they have begun counting the numbers of their students who arrive now with cochlear implants, and for each of the past four years that they have been counting, the number virtually doubles itself each year. In effect, the cochlear implant seems to be squaring itself as the technology advances and the next generation of young deaf and hard-of-hearing people comes of counting age. Even at Kendall School, the demonstration elementary school on the Gallaudet campus, education about the implant (for those who have them as well as for those who don't) takes the form of several children's books and a Barbie-like doll, "C.I. Joe" (who also happens to be African American). Even at hearing-dominated state universities like my own (Ohio State University), the cochlear implant makes headlines as one of the major Friday feature stories in the campus newspaper—and this at a university that records only two students with cochlear implants (among the fifty-four thousand enrolled here).

In Deaf Studies we might begin to rethink the potent fusions in the boundaries created by cochlear implants—between then (the past) and now (the present), as well as between now (the present) and then (the future). Tough, opportunistic, interesting, and sometimes even beautiful things grow in the cracks of structures seemingly well established and impenetrable; the cochlear implant cyborg might just be such a crack-dweller. It will take far more than an implant to make deaf identity (whatever it might be) go away. Like dandelions on the hearing lawn, deaf people greet the cultivated green

with sunny color and tenacious bearing season after season, generation upon generation. Hearing aids have never pulled the rug entirely out from under deafness; eugenicists couldn't either (although they are tugging very hard again); and oral-focused educators mostly just continue to sweep things under the rug so the house looks very tidy
on the surface.

This is not to suggest that we should not worry. We should. We need only glance over
our shoulders at the specter of those doctors during the Nazi era who had themselves
(and important others) convinced that living a life with a disability was a life simply
not worth living. Under such a conviction, these doctors killed over 270,000 of those
lives deemed "unworthy" in gas chambers (as well as through nurse-administered drug
overdoses or even through "simple" starvation) in a program they termed "Euthanasia."
Deaf people were one of the eight categories of people targeted for these "mercy deaths"
in the T-4 program of 1941–42, as well as being common victims of the sterilizations
that occurred for a decade before the T-4 "Euthanasia" program. Those Nazi doctors
also thought they were "improving" the lives of their patients and they developed chill-
ing technologies (the gas chambers) to efficiently carry out those "improvements." The
smoke rising in thick acrimonious billows day and night from the psychiatric institute
set up on the hill over the sleepy little village of Hadamar, Germany, during 1941–42 (as
but one example captured with disturbing clarity in several photos of the time) makes
at least one thing very clear: where there is smoke, there is fire.

Still, while we look for the fire, we should also be critically careful not to let cochlear
implants create a smoke screen that hides other strong magic at work. Even the technology in hearing aids, FM systems, real-time captioning, video conferencing, instant messaging, the Internet, and e-mail matters in the cyborg mix here. If you have been to Gallaudet University lately you would likely notice how electronic pagers (instant e-mail)
have radically changed "the Deaf gaze." These days when you walk across the campus
of the world's only liberal arts university for deaf and hard-of-hearing students, you are
just as likely—perhaps even more likely—to see an individual deaf student with head
bent and thumbs flying at her pager as she walks from place to place as you are to see
the older scene of two students signing with hands high above their head, "shouting" at
each other from across Kendall Green, the oval grassy area at the center of Gallaudet's
campus.

Do these pagers and other devices of instant communication really connect—or
disconnect—deaf people? What distortions and/or enhancements are aided by "the
electronic eye" extension of the Deaf gaze in these instances? What might be the form
of the SEE sign for extended pager gazing? And why are such devices, when used to aid
the deafened ear, commonly referred to as "assistive" or "adaptive" technologies when,
after all, technology/ies are—by the very nature of the definition of the term—assistive and adaptive to begin with? Why is it, for example, that a Blackberry in the hands
of a hearing person suddenly sheds its adaptive or assistive skin and becomes instead
just another device to fill up one's airport or driving time or to conduct one's business
incessantly?

With questions like these—as well as attempts and critical discussions about
them—Deaf Studies would be attending to the rhetorical relationships between our

technologies and our identity. In essence, we would be investigating the shape and substance of purpose, intention, motivation, and communication that such small but strong technology has in refiguring "the Deaf gaze," in changing deaf people's status as "people of the eyes." We would be considering the dynamic or static perspectives that these technologies—as "adaptive technologies" or "assistive technologies"—play in not just our (deaf) lives but in hearing lives too, as well as the relationships and lives between those spaces. Deaf Studies would do well to gaze here.

Lingering in the (Un)Common Space of Language

Deaf people and their uses of signed (or even/additionally/predominately oral) languages offer a rich commonplace site for the study of how language inherently oppresses, standardizes, and yet also resists—all at the same time—whatever it comes in contact with and even, too, whatever it makes for and of itself. Language duplicates, replicates, reinforces itself (so that, as George Bernard Shaw wrote in "Maxims for Revolutionists," "no man fully capable of his own language ever masters another"),[5] yet language also resists its own pure replication and dominance. This is not to signify that deaf people have no respect for their sign language (or their multiple other forms of language), but only to suggest that language is always refiguring its own space just as it makes that space operate much like a kaleidoscope—where elements and perspectives may often shift but the whole and its contents really remain the same. Thus, to aim for some sort of standardization of (a/the) language is only, in effect, to assure that it is awfully (and awesomely) darn slippery to begin with; sooner or later something or someone comes along and bumps the kaleidoscope—a little or a lot—and a new image (still with the same basic contents) appears. Perspectives shift.

Such shifting also happens to represent the slippery business of rhetoric where the communication triangle and its emphasized angles are always in changing relationships to each other. Aristotle's entire second book of the *Rhetoric* emphasizes this contextually dependent shifting as he attempts to categorize and consider all the kinds of audience a rhetor might be dealing with and how those audiences might react to given kinds of subjects presented in certain kinds of ways.[6] "Discovering all the available means of persuasion," which was how Aristotle defined the art of rhetoric, becomes much like the number of combinations one can view in the elements contained in a kaleidoscope.

In this space of ever-unfolding possibilities, Deaf Studies (which is, often as not, associated with the study and teaching of sign languages) could consider the way that sign languages are themselves reaching for, lurching toward, grasping at, and pushing against standardization. And this is not uncommon. Language is only a tool—and an often inadequate one—for ever trying to get at or toward or even around "the truth." Dictionaries and attempts to "capture" or standardize any language also operate under such perspective-oriented prevailing paradigms. Yet dictionaries are definitely needed—if for no other reason than to record the revolutionary and rhetorical shifts that language can make. "Hold still, we're going to do your portrait," writes French feminist theorist Hélène Cixous about the rhetorical act of representation, "so that you can begin looking like it right away."[7] In Deaf Studies we should be focusing on the portrait-doing involved in developing and publishing any kind of sign language. No scholar has yet, for example, to undertake a serious study of even the earliest representations of hand alphabets or sign systems published. To be sure, these early printed representations can often be found in history/ies written about deaf people and their use of sign languages. But they are more often than not simply gestured toward and not ever (yet) analyzed in terms of what their shifting representations might mean and say "at large" for language systems or even in comparison with each other as commonplace sign systems.

We might also then look backwards (yet still forwards) to the commonplaces of a sign language's (near) disappearance or considerable reconfiguration. For an example of its reconfiguration, there are sites such as seventeenth-century English educator and rhetorician John Bulwer's adaptation of signs, gestures, body configurations, and facial expressions in his classical and seminal rhetorical-elocutionary treatises, *Chirologia* and *Chironomia*.[8] Bulwer is credited for founding the "elocutionary movement" in the history of rhetoric with his elaborately detailed descriptions (and prescriptions) of what the hands, body, and face could do in the act and art of persuasion in his two treatises on "the art of the hand." We now also know that he was one of the earliest English deaf educators and even more significantly, we now also know that he had a deaf daughter whose name happened to be *Chirolea*. Yet Bulwer himself never credits any "language of gestures" he might have acquired from these two deaf sites in his life that would, most likely, have had a significant influence on his ability to create these two rhetorical treatises to begin with.

We could also contemplate, for example, the changing shape of sign language in places like rural Nebraska now that the state residential institution for deaf students has been closed. How does the lack of such an important site for developing and sharing language among deaf and hard-of-hearing children who are more often than not isolated and singular in their deafness change the face of American Sign Language overall? Or too, we might explore more about how deaf people negotiated sign language in Germany during the Nazi regime when they were not only targets of forced sterilization but also the potential victims of the T-4 "Euthanasia" program of 1941–42. How did deaf people sign when their lives likely depended on not marking themselves as deaf in any way? And after World War II, what happened to deaf ways—their schools, clubs, workplaces, and shared language—between East and West Germany? Further, how have (or haven't) German signs "reunified" since the wall fell in 1989? We would also want to look forward to the development of "new" sign languages in developing or "third world" countries or in places like reunified Germany or, even, say across the city of Berlin where not so long ago four nations occupied the city limits. What can we learn about standardization and the values of language—any language—from these developments?

And finally, we would also do well to look across the plains of the present, to squint our eyes in the startling sunlight of American Sign Language's immense popularity on high school and college campuses where it is now taught (usually as a "foreign" language requirement). While the Deaf world frets over the loss of Deaf Culture and identity at the hands of geneticists, cochlear implant surgeons, and hearing parents (to name but a few of the largest threats), the truth of another matter is that on campuses where it is offered, no language except Spanish enrolls better than ASL right now. In Summer

2003, the Modern Language Association's new report on college foreign language offerings marked ASL courses in higher education as up a remarkable 432 percent in the
past five years.[9] (The next closest increase figure was Arabic at 94 percent.) This put ASL
officially in the fifth-place seat for "most commonly taught language in college." Yet, if
we were also to factor in that the other four languages ahead of ASL in this survey are
likely taught at each and every college where foreign language is offered—and that ASL
is still very much a lesser-taught language that is, in fact, still rarely taught at most colleges—the popularity of ASL probably outstrips the four languages that place ahead
of it. In fact, demand almost never matches supply in the case of ASL instruction since
qualified ASL instructors at the high school and university certification level are as rare,
say, as oceanfront property in Kansas.

How is this massively popular instruction changing the face—and shape—of ASL?[10]
And what should be the "perspective" of Deaf Studies on these issues when, ironically,
more and more deaf/hard-of-hearing children are "mainstreamed" and implanted and
often kept away from sign language while their hearing peers flock to ASL classes? What
interesting rhetoric is at work on the two sides of this single language-learning coin?
Who profits from such a great increase in ASL instruction? The wise owl of Deaf Studies
should be forming this "who?" on its own lips and hands.

Writing (and) Deafness

The wise owl should also ponder writing. As a form of expression typically (and too
often) considered oppositional for modern deaf people, what in fact might writing (typically an English-ed act) have in common with signing? How might writing extend signing—and how too, might signing extend writing? Jacques Derrida has raised this question "at hand":

> When we say that writing *extends* the field and the powers of locutionary or gestural com-
> munication, are we not presupposing a kind of *homogeneous* space of communication? The
> range of the voice or of gesture appears to encounter a factual limit here, an empirical bound-
> ary of space and of time; and writing, within the same time, within the same space, manages
> to loosen the limits, to open the *same field* to a much greater range.[11]

In Deaf Studies I think we have some remarkable and rich work still left to do, philo-
sophically and practically, in the space between writing and signing. Not only can we
perhaps de-Derrida Derrida himself in expanding the philosophical space between
writing and signing, but we can, just as importantly, work to find better ways to translate
and transliterate what happens in the space between English and ASL. This multiper-
spective orientation would be especially important for both deaf and hearing students
who are struggling to enter that between space.

It will be most fruitful to do this practical and philosophical "perspectival" work
not from the center of English studies (where it has already been tried and yet never
true) but rather from the center (and margins) of Deaf Studies. When Deaf Studies starts
thinking about how to translate, transliterate, and teach in the space between English

and ASL, for example, we are likely to become all the more able "to loosen the limits, to open the *same field* to a much greater range," as Derrida has suggested. Why leave it up to English departments and deaf education and (socio)linguistics? These three sites, in particular, have long skewed the center and arranged themselves as the triangle of matters associated with "deaf language and literacy instruction."[12] Why keep the location of locution always already there? Certainly, English Studies and Deaf Education and scientific linguistic study have things to offer the study of signed languages—and they should continue to do so. But how much longer must we continue to look for the keys to the uses and power of signed languages for deaf people under the brighter lamps of these more dominant (and better funded) areas of the academy just because the light is there when, in fact, we know the keys are in a less well-lighted place a few steps back or around the next corner?

Let Deaf Studies take up the questions often left to the long legacy of Western philosophy—from Plato to Derrida and back again: What difference does writing make? Do feminist theories about "writing the body" (Cixous, for example) apply to and invigorate, or further erase, deaf people and their way of performing literacy? If writing is a performance (as the latest theoretical rage proclaims)—and sign language is also performative—do these two have even more in common than we have yet begun to explore? Is deafness the hiccup—the errant locution in the location—of the all-too-standardized connections between reading and writing that are chanted in our educational history? Deaf Studies might attend to asking and exploring a question that one professor of philosophy at my own university recently titled his own campus lecture with (even though he did not have sign languages in mind)—"how can language change your hearing?"

Let us begin, now even more than ever, to answer that question from within Deaf Studies. Not only should we begin, for example, to critically engage the construction of "deaf lives" from these other fields, but we should also (and this is very important) be encouraging the creation, production, and reception of deaf lives through such channels as biography, autobiography, and documentary. As I revised an earlier version of this essay from a café in Berlin, Germany, I was reminded, you see, that I am deaf in any and all languages and cultures; the German language does not, in essence, seem to change my hearing.

"How can language change your hearing?" Indeed, that is no small question. It is also not an unfamiliar question since "deaf education" has been around the block with it at least several times over. What if we also began to ask more about how it is that "deaf ways" can actually be used as a method and means of changing even dominant Western classroom and pedagogical practices? And what if we just stopped rehearsing the already well-articulated history of deaf education in the United States? What if instead we asked, for example, what this history (of "deaf education") shows us about *all* of Western education? As Margret Winzer has challenged us in her excellent history of special education, we might think more of how deaf education ripples in the larger pond:

> The way that children are trained and schooled is a crucial demonstration of the way that they are perceived and treated in a given society. . . . Discovering who was taught, and when

and how, is related far more to the social, political, legislative, economic, and religious forces at work in a society than it is to the unique social and educational needs of disabled persons. At the same time, this history mirrors our progress toward appreciating the basic humanity of all people.[13]

Deaf education did not—and does not—occur in a socioeconomic-historical vacuum. We can get so hung up on A. G. Bell and his legacy, for example, that we forget to answer the other incoming calls about the interplay of speech, education, and "normalcy" as this tangled braid brought us into the twentieth century.

Think-Eye

Where I fit in and can answer the calls I've proposed myself for Deaf Studies is also about all the calls I probably cannot answer but still yearn to engage in or make. Some days I am so energized by all the possibilities of Deaf Studies that I am exploding. Other days, I am so daunted by all the possibilities that I am imploding.

I come to Deaf Studies as a "hard-of-hearing" (the only term my family could use) girl from the extremely rural region of western Kansas; there are still less than twenty-five people per square mile in Greeley County, Kansas. I come as someone who didn't even know what sign language or, say, Gallaudet University was (let alone a single sign or the idea of "deaf education") until the age of twenty-nine. I come as the granddaughter of a deaf woman (although she was called hard-of-hearing too) and the inheritor and carrier and engenderer of a complicated string of hearing loss and kidney "abnormalities" in my family. I come with two children (one has the kidney abnormalities) who perhaps understand my "deafness" in ways that my own parents didn't and in ways, too, that I myself still don't. (They are perhaps more "deaf" than me, I've written elsewhere.)[14]

I come always wanting to fit in. Yet I also come always wanting to ask questions and not fit in. I arrive doubly hyphenated (hard-of-hearing), with a lot going on in those multiple hyphenated between spaces. I come, I suppose, thinking between—thinking in another kind of between space between think-deaf and think-hearing: think-eye. For the deaf space is a visual space, an "eye" space—and also too, an I-space. We still have a lot to learn from each "I" and from each "eye." Perspective (the "eye") really matters; the personal (the "I") experience really matters as well. This little between space can be, in fact, rather expansive. It is a space of potent possibilities, contained and yet kaleidoscopic in its perspectives. As late nineteenth-century English novelist George Eliot (Mary Ann Evans) knew, as she was writing a novel named for a male protagonist and using a male pseudonym herself, perspective is a beautiful thing.

There are so many ways to bump and see the same pieces again, but now all arranged differently. In keeping our eyes out for deaf commonplaces while also admiring the ever-shifting capabilities of perspectives (in both our "eyes" and our "I's") and attending to the value of being *between* worlds, words, languages, cultures even as we can be contained in either one, the sites and sights of Deaf Studies promise us ever enchanted explorations.

Notes

I owe a great debt to several colleagues for their roles in making this essay happen. First, and most significantly, Dirksen Bauman not only helped instigate—and inspire—the ideas here when he invited me to be a part of the Summer 2002 Deaf Studies Think Tank, but he gently harassed me into writing an introductory "personal statement" for the Think Tank that became, in essence, the genesis of this essay's content. Later, as we continued to hold vibrant electronic and face-to-face conversations about my ideas and examples under development, he further influenced not only the content but also the form of this essay. In a sense, I think of this piece as a collaboration with Dirksen. Colleagues Cathy Kudlick (California State–Davis) and Jim Ferris (University of Wisconsin) also came to play a part in the production of this piece as the three of us shared a kind of trialogue performance in a session called simply (but profoundly) "Between" at the 2004 Society for Disability Studies meeting in St. Louis. When they helped me further expand the signing and body space to create a six-armed insect, I knew then that after nearly two years of tinkering with this essay I had finally reached the (between) place where I not only felt comfortable but now actually *wanted* to put the ideas in print.

1. Gina Oliva, *Alone in the Mainstream: A Deaf Woman Remembers Public Schools* (Washington, D.C.: Gallaudet University Press, 2004).

2. James Woodward, *How You Gonna Get to Heaven If You Can't Talk to Jesus: On Depathologizing Deafness* (Silver Spring, Md.: T.J. Publishers, 1982).

3. Here you can now imagine a Big D if you want, but for now, I'm going to just let one term stand and use "deaf" or "deafness" (little d) to represent both the "deaf" and "Deaf" positions since, as I have been arguing, no one really seems to completely understand the differences and distinctions between the two terms to begin with.

4. Donna Haraway, "A Cyborg Manifesto: Science, Technology, and Socialist-Feminism in the Late Twentieth Century," in *Simians, Cyborgs and Women: The Reinvention of Nature* (New York: Routledge, 1991), 149 (brackets mine).

5. George Bernard Shaw, "Maxims for Revolutionists," in *Man and Superman: A Comedy and Philosophy* (New York: Penguin, 2000), 254.

6. Aristotle, *On Rhetoric: A Theory of Civic Discourse,* trans. George A. Kennedy (New York: Oxford University Press, 1991).

7. Hélène Cixous, "From *The Laugh of the Medusa,*" in *The Rhetorical Tradition: Readings from Classical Times to the Present,* ed. Patricia Bizzell and Bruce Herzberg (Boston: Bedford, 1990), 1244.

8. John Bulwer, *Chirologia; or, The naturall language of the hand . . .* (1652; repr., New York: AMS Press, 1975).

9. Elizabeth B. Welles, "Foreign Language Enrollments in United States Institutions of Higher Education, Fall 2002," *ADFL Bulletin* 35, nos. 2–3 (2004): 7–26 (http://www.adfl.org/resources/enrollments.pdf).

10. These issues over American Sign Language in the academy and its relationship to "foreign language" instruction were the subject of a three-session "Presidential Forum" at the 2004 Modern Language Association Annual Convention in Philadelphia, Penn.

11. Jacques Derrida, "Signature, Event, Context," in *Margins of Philosophy,* trans. Alan Bass (Chicago: University of Chicago Press, 1982), 311.

12. For more discussion on the consequences of the lack of contextually and culturally based approaches to scholarship in "deaf language and literacy," see the introduction to Brenda Jo Brueggemann, ed., *Literacy and Deaf People: Cultural and Contextual Perspectives* (Washington, D.C.: Gallaudet University Press, 2004).

13. Margret Winzer, *The History of Special Education: From Isolation to Integration* (Washington, D.C.: Gallaudet University Press, 1993), xi.

14. Brenda Brueggemann, "Are You Deaf or Hearing?" in *Lend Me Your Ear: Rhetorical Constructions of Deafness* (Washington, D.C.: Gallaudet University Press, 1999), 237–60.

12. Border Crossings by Hearing Children of Deaf Parents: The Lost History of Codas

ROBERT HOFFMEISTER

> The role of Deaf Studies has great potential in contributing to Border Theory/Studies. We should explore issues of border within the Deaf experience/World. There are tremendous implications for study and finding a "lost history."
>
> —Brenda Brueggemann, 2002

In this chapter I will discuss the lives of Hearing children of Deaf parents (HCDP) and attempt to relate their lives to the idea of living on the "border."[1] Border is a concept recently developed by examining the lives of minority groups in the United States and their handling of two cultures.[2] The concept of borderlands comes to mind when we discuss the Deaf world and many of the issues that are internal and external to it.

The following descriptions of borders are pertinent to the discussion of the Deaf world and how they and their children live. Since this chapter deals with Hearing children of Deaf parents, the border becomes a dissection of both the hearing and the Deaf worlds. I submit that the borderlands consist of the following conditions. We might think of them as contained within a Venn diagram, where they are not exclusive of each other but have overlapping and separate components.[3] We will have to deal with the following descriptions and their conceptual constructs.

Physical Borders; Real Borders: continents, oceans, islands, shorelines, rivers. Included in physical borders could be the connotation extended to the body, a physical demarcation, such as "hearing" or "not hearing," as a border process. This is similar to constructed borders: for a specific purpose, that is, the idea that there is a thing called "amount of hearing" and whether it is a real category.

Political Borders; Legal: nations, states, nation-states, towns, cities, etc. Here we enter divisions of greater societies that include minority groups. Ironically, the Deaf are a minority group in the Hearing society and HCDP is a subgroup of the Deaf world. However is it a subgroup within the Hearing world?

Social Borders: Here the idea of border becomes vague and ill defined. The Hearing society does not really believe that the Deaf constitute a social group. This definition of a social border is only on the Deaf side of the border. The advent of Deaf Studies as an academic endeavor has begun to expand the understanding of Deaf as a cultural concept much like the concepts of black, white, "Hispanic," Jewish, etc. However, all of these cultural terms have complicated definitions known only to the subgroups within their borders, a process that will directly relate to the discussion of HCDP in this chapter.

Psychological borders: In the understanding of psychological borders, the academy in higher education and medicine become the holders of the concepts. The idea of "normal" vs. "abnormal" and what these terms mean in relation to individuals and groups is the substance of great debate. But this debate appears to only be on the side of the border where the academy resides. In most cases, the academy, because it is also invested in the political and physical borders of the body, is not interested in examining its meanings within the borders of each group that might be delineated by the social borders.[4]

As can be seen above, "The idea of the 'border' or 'borderlands' has also been expanded to include nearly every psychic or geographic space about which one can thematize problems of boundary or limit."[5] This then provides us the opportunity to look at the borders that the Deaf world is involved within and then examine a single group within those borders.

I will first begin by trying to place the HCDP inside the border process by trying to explain the extent of their relationship to the Deaf world. Then I will try to expand the border processes and move into particular border ideas such as *home, language,* and *family.* Within each of these areas I will try to offer some of my own observations and those of others. Since this area is relatively scant of information, much of what I write is my own and I am fully responsible for its content and how other writers are interpreted.

Who and Where Are the Hearing Children of Deaf Parents?

Hearing children of Deaf parents are typically the succeeding generation in the Deaf world. When Deaf people marry they typically have hearing children. It is almost the reverse of the Hearing parents of Deaf children situation. Ninety percent (or more) of Deaf children are born to Hearing, whereas it is probably true that 90 percent of children born in Deaf families are hearing. The irony extends when we later look at language and find that more than 60 percent of the HCDPs are exposed to a signed language and may become fluent in that language.[6] Recently, the HCDP has become known as a Coda,[7] a child of Deaf adults. This is the term that is now common among HCDP and Deaf people in general; hence it will be used from now on in this essay to address HCDP.

What do we know about Codas? We know very little, so much of this is from my observations and my own life. The data on Codas are abstracted from keynote presentations, autobiographical books, one research-based text, Preston's *Mother Father Deaf,* and information from the Coda conferences, the official CODA publications, and my notes. My life may be a unique experience, but I doubt it.

Where Are the Codas?

Why has it been so difficult to open up and talk about our lives? Deaf people generally feel free to talk about their lives with all the negatives and positives that go along with it. Why is it so difficult for Codas to say what they feel and talk about who they are in Deaf or Hearing groups? As a Coda I can talk to Deaf people freely about their lives and some parts of my life, but there seems to be a real psychological border that I cannot cross to talk with Hearing people about my life as a Coda. There are a small number of areas that I will not cross into when in discussions with Deaf people, but I don't think there are any areas of reserve among Deaf people and Codas on topics of the Deaf. This is beginning to change.

Codas grow up in a Deaf family; not all Codas grow up in the Deaf world. This is an important distinction. Many Codas do grow up in the Deaf world, exposed to many other Deaf adults, Deaf clubs, Deaf meetings, etc. However, many Codas also grow up separated from this exposure. But all Codas grow up in two worlds, the Deaf world of their families and the Hearing world. Every Coda leads two lives: one as Coda and one as a hearing person. They may chose to only live one life, but all of them have two. The Coda life in most cases is not visible. Hence we share the invisibility of the Deaf in the world.

Outside of the Deaf world, I can talk about the hearing person but not the Coda life. Codas continue to be on the border when they are in contact with the Deaf world. Since we don't know much about Codas, I am not sure they are border people when they escape.

"One Generation Thick"

If there are two million Deaf people[8] and half are adults, then we could estimate that half of the adult population of the Deaf are married yielding a potential of 250,000 families. If we estimate an average of two children per family we extrapolate that there are about 500,000 Codas in any one generation. One generation is all that there will be since most Codas will have hearing children of their own. This process is typical in bicultural immigrant families.[9] It typically takes three generations to become fully acculturated. In the Deaf world for many Codas it is completed in one generation. Here the idea of One Generation Thick (OGT) was conceived.[10] The Hearing children of Deaf adults are removed from the Deaf world after one generation because the culture and the language are not passed on from parent to child. I believe that because we are OGT, we are not interesting to look at since we assimilate into the Hearing world so rapidly. A possible reason for this is that it's easier to assimilate into the Hearing culture.

Codas are not easily identifiable and therefore are not visible within either culture. They are clearly not visible to Hearing people, but within the Deaf world they are a known entity because of family ties. What happens to these Codas when they become adults and cross the border into the Hearing world permanently? There are no demographics available on Codas and there are only about five hundred to six hundred Codas that are associated with the CODA organization or on its mailing lists. Where do they go and why do they disappear?

The closer one lives to the border the more aware one is of its consequences and its meanings. If one lives deep in the culture, far away from any "reminders" that there is a border that has been created, the less the border issues appear. Creation of a border is to create demarcations, designations, separations, or examples of differences. Since the border signifies this process, the further one is removed from the border the less one has to deal with border issues.

Take the case of the first, second, and third generations of immigrant children. The first generation must live literally on the border; they must learn to deal with two cultures, two languages, two sets of rules, behaviors, etc. The second generation is distanced from the border but still has maximal contact through the extended family. Most likely the second generation will deal with two cultures but it will be filtered through parents who are the first generation. The second generation will have contact with the two languages but will probably only learn one fluently and might have a passing knowledge of the other. The rules the second generation lives by will be the rules of the dominant culture, and they will only be aware of the nondominant cultural rules. By the third generation, the border issues are far removed and are either only a memory or something one must "learn" about. The third generation consists of acculturated and assimilated descendants.

Typically, the firstborn male Coda will learn the language of the family. Many, for various reasons we will explore later, do not acquire the language well, whereas the firstborn female Codas often will become fluent. The rest of the siblings may learn the language but not always to fluency. Or if there is a large separation in age between siblings then more Codas will acquire greater proficiency. In addition, the background of the Deaf parents and their attitudes toward ASL or a signed language also dictate fluency levels and skill within the culture/family.

First- and secondborn females clearly dominate the group of fluent signers and knowledge holders of the culture within the Coda population. However, in the United States and most countries the issue of gender also becomes a border. The border issues of gender interact with the Deaf border issues to make the process of assimilation into the culture, access to power, and control of one's life more complicated.

An excellent example of this is that the interpreting field is dominated by females. In the United States both cultures appear to view the female as the one in the "server role" in the family. The Coda female may well internalize the larger cultural roles of helplessness, nonaggressive personality, and subservient attitude. All the beneficial values that maintain the borders of each culture will perpetuate the helping idea and become inculcated into interpreting values. The result of females becoming good signers is dealt with in a later section on interpreting.

Internal Borders

Can you have borders within borderlands? Is that the place for Codas? Negotiating borders for Deaf people is complicated because national heritage does not accurately imply their roots. Borders for Deaf people are established based on contact between people who are like them and people who are different from them. We are culturally and physically surrounded by borders since borders can be political, physical, and psychological. As the title of the film *Passport without a Country* suggests, Codas are subject to amorphous borders. This documentary is important in that it clearly places Codas in between cultures. We live on the border or we seek to move as far from the border as possible. There are these burning questions of not only where we belong, but what is our identity. Are Codas Deaf and Hearing; that is, are they bicultural?

The distinction between Deaf and Hearing people appears to be a well-defined process within the Deaf world. However, it is not necessarily so in the Hearing world. The use of the terms Deaf and Hearing implies a clear border. In my growing up there were Deaf and there were Hearing; rarely did the two mix or were they confused as to whom the terms applied. These boundaries are often clear to Codas but remain unclear to others.

In fact for me, since I lived on the campus of a school for the Deaf, it was very clear who the Hearing people were as there was a real border. The street physically bordered our house and the school. When I crossed the street it was clear that I was moving into the Hearing side of the border. Most Codas did not have this clear a physical dividing line, but if one considers the door to your house the border, this clearly holds for all Codas,[11] since once you enter the house you are now in a world constructed and controlled by Deaf parents. Once you left the house you knew that you had to "become" Hearing in all ways.

Who Are Codas?

It is possible that the contribution Codas can make is to help clarify the definition of culturally Deaf or the word "deaf." By investigating the question of whether Codas are deaf or hearing we become clearer on what it means to be Deaf. The binary relationship we have established by the terms Deaf and Hearing must be depolarized. Codas present a problem to that binary relationship. If we continue to maintain this binary split, understanding our many borders becomes more difficult. If we are able to remove this idea of a binary relationship between "hearing" and "deaf," we may arrive at some useful discussion as to membership and transmission of the culture. What is important to recognize is that to understand who the Coda is requires a change in definitions in both the Hearing and Deaf cultural demarcations. Essentially, it's not only hearing loss. It consists of many other things. Because of the attitudes, misconceptions, and lack of real knowledge in the Hearing world, Deaf Culture is the only culture in the world where the definitions of who belongs are so confusing. Hence, a Coda would do better to escape all this confusion and move as far from the Deaf/Hearing border as possible.

To begin with, having a hearing loss is one of the significant factors in membership of the Deaf community. This fact creates an interesting dichotomy. Hearing loss is avoided as a major factor because it begs the question as to whether a disability underlies the definition of who is "Deaf." If Codas are not to be viewed as members of the Deaf world the problem is exacerbated. A really interesting question is that if Codas are a subgroup within the Deaf world should we adopt an ethnic model for Codas? This would mean that Codas would be viewed as integral members of the Deaf community and would be seen as one of the carrier groups of the culture across generations.

"To claim that Codas are not part of the Deaf World is puzzling to me. What could be stronger than the parental bond? How can we not be part of you, Deaf people? We are of you."[12] Davis's questions pose significant issues. There is some reality to the issue of who can claim to use the label "Deaf" in that some Codas are "Deafer" than most Deaf people.

Can Codas Be Considered Deaf?

"If Deaf is characterized by a 'condition,' a 'pathology,' then no. But if it is exclusively a cultural distinction, characterized by experience and language, then surely Codas can be at least partially 'Deaf.'"[13] Todd Czubek's comments lead us to look at some questions and try to frame some answers that will create further discussion. Who are Codas and where is our center?

It is clear that Codas do not have a hearing loss. Hence, hearing loss by itself may not be the distinguishing characteristic of the Deaf world. Hearing children of parents who have a hearing loss are viewed as "Codas." In this chapter I will refer to these parents as Deaf. However, Deaf must be understood in the cultural terminology on the Deaf side of the border. Deaf is someone who identifies as Deaf. The issue of hearing loss is not an absolute with regard to who is "Deaf." We all know that "Deaf" as a cultural term includes people whose hearing loss can be very slight, what the Hearing might refer to as Hard of Hearing (HoH). Many of these people have decided as an identity process to stop using their voice when interacting with the Hearing. However, we all know that sometimes, a Deaf person who is capable of speaking will use their voice if they feel it is necessary. Hence, "hearing loss" and "voice" are not necessary conditions for someone to be considered Deaf. There are many Codas who do not use their voice on the Deaf side of the border. They will use their voice on the Hearing side of the border. This situation is equivalent to the HoH above.

From Whom Do Codas Learn?

In the case of language acquisition there are simple and complicated processes for Codas. In the case of the parents who use a signed language, the firstborn Coda typically learns this language, especially if they are female. If there is enough time between the second- and firstborn (say four years or more), the secondborn Coda will learn sign language. If the secondborn is a female, they will learn to sign no matter the time distance between first- and secondborn. One of the first paradoxes we will encounter begins here. Many of the Deaf parents of Codas have Hearing parents themselves. As a result, many of these Deaf parents have learned to sign either from other Deaf children when they were young or from adults (hearing or Deaf) who were their teachers and their language models.[14] This issue is not an insignificant one, in that most of these Deaf parents, due to the educational system's lack of cohesion, have learned an inadequate version of American Sign Language (ASL). As a result they graduate from school with an impoverished knowledge of both ASL and English.[15] In terms of language acquisition, we now know that in the case of Deaf children of Deaf parents (DCDP) whose Deaf parents are not fluent ASL users, the DCDP will operate on the signed language input and make it a more fluent language. There is no reason not to believe that the same situation happens with Codas. This suggests that the first generation of Coda signers will be the first generation of fluent ASL users. For the Deaf world, the use of a signed language is one of the criteria for membership in Deaf Culture.

When Do People Become Deaf?

With regard to use of a signed language in the community, another factor is the idea of those Deaf persons who join the Deaf world later in their lives. For the Hearing side of the border the meaning of "to become Deaf" has to do with the date of acquiring a hearing loss. There is a great deal of nomenclature on this issue, as a number of terms and definitions garner a large amount of print to discuss this idea.[16] For the Deaf world, "to become Deaf" does not relate to when hearing loss occurs in a person's life but to when they learned to accept and use a signed language. There are many people who have acquired a hearing loss but are not members of the Deaf world. These people are distinguished from those who have decided to learn a signed language and join the Deaf world. This is a conscious identity issue. However, with respect to Codas, since we are born into the Deaf world, it is not a conscious decision to join the Deaf world but to separate and be excluded from it.

Given the above discussion, as children more Codas are fluent in a signed language than the majority of the Deaf world. Some maintain their fluency throughout adulthood; some lose their fluency as they separate and become more full-time members of the Hearing world and, in effect, remove themselves from the Deaf world.

What distinguishes Codas from their peers in the Deaf world is the exposure and use of spoken English. All Codas (with very few exceptions) become fluent in the spoken language of the Hearing community in which their parents reside (spoken English in my case).

Many Codas initially think they are Deaf. It is not uncommon to hear stories of Codas who did not realize there were Hearing people out there, who did nothing but use their voice. However, by the time a Coda learns to interact with others, the Hearing world is clearly evident. Most Codas are bilingual by the time they are three to five years of age. Given the Hearing world's fear of the effects of hearing loss, there is typically great effort by the Hearing extended family to ensure that the Coda offspring will learn to talk. Codas who are able to use a signed language[17] and who use a spoken language are in fact the true bilinguals of the Deaf world, even in comparison with DCDP who learn English very well. Although the DCDP's English will be excellent, it will not always be fluent. Another irony may be that the Coda who is fluent in ASL and English more resembles the person who has lost their hearing later (after age six) and learns ASL fluently.[18]

Acculturation

If a culture is passed down from parents to children then Codas learn Deaf Culture from birth. In addition Codas also learn Hearing culture. Hearing culture is mostly learned from the extended family, or in some cases from older siblings when there are large age differences between children in the family. Aside from the transmission of language, Codas learn many of the beliefs, mores, and values of the Deaf world. It is through this process that Codas also learn about the Hearing world and the conflict that the Hearing world presents to both Deaf and Codas. To the Deaf the Hearing world is dangerous, one of which to be suspicious and aware. Hearing people exhibit an igno-rance of the Deaf way of life and one must be careful when crossing the border and in-teracting with the Hearing. In addition, the Hearing who are professionals are to be en-countered with extreme caution. Those Hearing professionals who "know" about the Deaf are the most dangerous. For it is through them that the Deaf have learned about the Hearing world. Deaf people grow up in schools and learn the values of the Hearing world that are in essence founded on the fact that to be Deaf is negative and therefore the closer you can be to acting Hearing is a positive. This belief is the antithesis of the Deaf world, and Codas learn this at a very young age. In fact, it takes Codas a great deal of time to understand that even though they are "hearing" they are not included in the reference to "Hearing" people by Deaf people. This issue, itself, deserves a great deal of discussion but will not be expanded upon here. However, suffice it to acknowledge that when Deaf people discuss their problems with Hearing people and Codas are present, this can cause a real identity crisis. Codas have been able to solve this crisis on their own, since it is unique to the Deaf/Hearing worlds and is probably the major issue of sitting on the border.[19]

An interesting result of growing up in a Deaf family is that for Codas the iden-tity issue is a psychological division having no physical demarcation. So in essence we must borrow our parents' physical condition as part of our own identity process. Then we must go through great effort to understand this issue and separate ourselves from our Deaf sides. It is probably this reason that drives so many Codas into fully par-ticipating in the Hearing world and keeping the Deaf world at arm's length (no pun intended).

Who Can Pass as Deaf?

There are two more issues that cause Codas to have an unclear definition as to who they are. In many situations, for those Codas who sign, they are often mistaken for being Deaf. Typically, this is by those Deaf people who have Hearing parents. Some Codas are even able to fool those who are highly fluent users of ASL as in the DCDP. Codas are adept at code switching and adjusting their signing to the requirements of the inter-action levels. It is for this reason that many Codas are mistakenly thought of as Deaf.[20] This ability to move in the Deaf world, understand how it operates, and function as a Deaf person demonstrates that many Codas are actually more culturally Deaf than many Deaf people.

All of this results in raising the issue of identity formation. How does the Coda become a fully integrated person, capable of functioning in both worlds but under-standing what place we inhabit? Clearly, one avenue is to escape totally into the Hear-ing world and ignore or even reject the Deaf world. This process can clearly instill that the border is truly a border and does not need to be crossed except under very special conditions. To obtain a better picture of Codas and the process of identity in adult-hood, the reader is referred to an excellent documentary entitled *A Passport without a Country*.[21]

Hearing versus Deaf

How does the Coda handle the dilemma suggested above? Since there are two lives in the border process, what actually might happen when many Codas cross the border into the Deaf World is that they become Deaf. That is, they begin to sign and many turn off their voice (unless members of their hearing family are present; more about this later in this chapter), ignore any of the noises or talking around them, and enter into conversations with different groups of Deaf people. If there are introductions to be made, these are conducted under Deaf cultural rules. If I meet someone new it is important that they know where I came from, in my case that I grew up in a school for the Deaf, which one, and where my parents grew up, where they currently live, and with what schools they were associated.

However, even after being integrated into the Deaf group, a Coda will still be considered Hearing. When I enter or function within the Hearing world, I must attempt to put aside all of the Deaf behaviors, attitudes, and beliefs in order to participate smoothly. For example, it is not important where you came from or where you lived when you are introduced to someone new. This creates a conflict, in that this shallow introduction suggests that the hearing person is not really interested in you; they are only doing this as a courtesy. For me, it has been hard to function in new Hearing groups because I am not really aware of how to expand the conversation with a new person. If I ask where they are from and about their family, it could be taken as too personal an inquiry.

When I meet hearing people I initially avoid telling them I have Deaf parents. This prevents much confusion and extended explanation. Since the Hearing world has been socialized to view the Deaf as a problem group, the conversation always ends up with preconceived standard questions. How did you learn to talk? Do you use a sign language? Do your parents talk? Etc. It is interesting to note that many Codas have developed this strategy because they are always tired of explaining their parents to the world.[22]

Alternatively, when I would meet Deaf people they would see me as a Coda, an automatic ally but not part of the Deaf world. When I meet hearing people who find out I am a Coda they would not label me as a Coda, but they would also see me as an ally of the Deaf world and not a member of the Hearing world. We end up being uncategorized. No other cultural group goes through this process except maybe children of Gays and Lesbians.[23] It doesn't matter which side of the border you are on, you are not "one of them."

As Codas we meet different types of Hearing people who are able to create inner conflict. For most of us, the average Hearing person poses no threat other than asking some questions from ignorance. On the other hand, there is a subgroup of Hearing people who are professionals whether in the field of hearing loss or in fields with which we may come in contact. For example, members of two professional groups cause great disharmony for Codas: medical professionals and educational professionals, two groups whose goals are to "help" people live better in the world. The medical people are typically encountered in two ways. First, for every Coda they are encountered when our parents enter the hospital. It is here that all of us must return to the Deaf side of the world. The ignorance displayed by the medical professionals about Deaf people is rampant. One of the major themes of stories told by Codas has to do with how to handle the medicine man and the hospital setting. The conflict that ensues is undeniably the greatest for Codas. It is probably here that the attitude about the Hearing world is solidified in the Coda psyche.

As one example, I have been put in the position of interpreting for one of my parents while they were in the emergency room. My father was on a gurney, both hands were tied to the gurney, and compresses were covering his eyes. The doctor was yelling at him to stop fighting, even after my repeated attempts to explain that he was Deaf and couldn't hear. What the doctor mistook for "fighting" the restraints was my father finger-spelling "A-M I D-E-A-D" because with the compresses over his eyes, his hands tied, and some drug that was injected to partially paralyze him, he was unable to figure out where he was. After I removed the compresses and was able to converse with him, he quieted down. However, the doctor continued to yell at my father "to stay awake." There was much more to this incident, but this gives you the flavor of the scene. In another example, a Coda arrived at the hospital and the father had been preparing a meal for his sick spouse but was sitting in the waiting area at the request of the nurses. It happened that the spouse had died earlier, and the doctors and nurses felt it best to wait for the Coda to arrive to tell the husband/father. These actions demonstrate that medical personnel treat Deaf people as children with little respect and that they do not believe Deaf people are able to function as competent adults. Many times when Codas return to the border, they are put in the position of interpreting for their parents in times of extreme stress, which serves to drive them even further from the border. Many of these kinds of stories are known within the culture.

Another group consists of Hearing educators who are supposed to be knowledge-able about the Deaf, especially if these educators are in the oral educational field, which is becoming more pertinent given the cochlear implants of today. It is not uncommon for educators to have instilled in many Deaf people that the use of ASL is very negative. And these professionals promote the myth that those people who use ASL are illiterate and unschooled. If you use a signed language you will never be a fully functioning person. Many parents of Codas have internalized these beliefs/myths, even though they may be fluent users of American Sign Language. As a result some Deaf parents may not sign to their Coda children. These Coda children will grow up without a means of really communicating with their own parents, somewhat the reverse of the Deaf child in the Hearing family where the Hearing parents do not learn to sign.[24] This inability to sign is a major issue when Codas get together. Those Codas who do not sign may feel that they are not part of either the Deaf world or the Coda world, and don't know how they feel about the Hearing world. It is probably another reason to escape far from the border. The further away the less inner conflict encountered.

Identity and Belief Systems

In his Coda memoir, Lennard Davis writes,

> I knew my mother was loving and devoted, working hard at a low paying job to earn the necessities of life. I knew my father was a gifted artist and capable writer. He wrote a column for

the national Deaf magazine and authored plays that he and his friends performed at the Deaf Club. I also knew, when I looked at the pile of old *New York Times* issues in the closet, that headlines were blazoned with my father's name for having been a world-class race-walker, all the while working as a sewing machine operator in a sweatshop.[25]

I am amazed at the resiliency and strength of identity that Codas achieve given the tension and conflict that enters their life at times when identity formation and individuation occurs. Codas are immersed in the Hearing world view of Deaf people and find conflict in that view when looking at their own parents, as the quote from Davis above attests. As another example, a Coda student arrived at the university as a freshman who could not believe a Deaf person was getting his PhD at a major university. In addition, this Coda could not believe that this same Deaf person was going to be their professor and advisor for four years. Yet this same student came from four generations of Deaf people. The internalization of what Deaf people are developed out of experience. This Coda witnessed his own family as having a great deal of struggle with the Hearing world. It appeared that the solutions to the struggles were always solved by contacting the Hearing member of the family. This is not atypical of young Codas. In growing up, we do not know who is right in their view of Deaf people. Many Codas continue to believe that their parents are less capable than other people and that it is a direct result of their being Deaf. Our knowledge of the world is derived from a very small sample, and as children of Deaf parents, we learn early the false belief that the Hearing know what is best. It is always important to give deference to Hearing people, a belief that Deaf people learned in their educational programs, and consequently this myth has been passed on to us.

Codas as Hearing: Acculturation and Identity

The "cultural" acceptance of one group or another clearly is defined by the acceptance and access allowed by the power/dominant group. It is at "the edge of culture"[26] that the problems of Coda and Deaf culture have faced the "border wall." Codas are able to easily move across or between the two populations. This is parallel to those Deaf people who speak well and constitute the "bridge" Deaf members of the community. Many of the Deaf leaders are from this membership group within the Deaf community. Deaf leaders also come under the archetype of the "Gallaudet Deaf," a distinction made by members within the Deaf community. This ability to travel easily across the border engenders suspicion and mistrust because those Deaf who cannot traverse the border easily do not have the same access to the information, purpose, or control of this border-crossing process. Hence, divisions within the Deaf world are created. Codas are viewed within these divisions and are suspect as to their purpose when residing on either side of the border. When the Coda resides in the Hearing sector of the border the issues become, what does the Coda say about the Deaf, about the Deaf community, about their Deaf parents, about their Deaf parents' friends, etc. As a result Codas are looked upon with a wary eye especially if they are in the business of the Deaf (i.e., teacher, social worker, etc.).

How does a child growing up in a Deaf household and living in a Hearing neighborhood come to understand and to resolve the tremendous conflicts about their parents and themselves to which they are exposed? At very young ages, Codas are exposed to attitudes around language and around their parents as follows:

SIDE OF BORDER	BELIEF
Deaf	Hearing is bad.
Hearing	Deaf is bad.
Deaf	ASL is good.
Hearing	ASL is bad.
Deaf	ASL is broken English.
Hearing	Broken English is bad.
Deaf	English is bad.
Hearing	Literacy is good.
Deaf	Can't read or write.
Hearing	Deaf are illiterate.
Deaf	ASL and English are *both* languages of the Deaf world.
Hearing	Bilingualism is bad.

The above issues can be referred to as border control issues. These are the issues that inflame the two cultures and that carry misunderstanding, illogical beliefs, pain, and suffering within families and across generations. These border issues create the greatest conflict. As young children Codas learn that English is supreme, to the point that many Deaf parents do not want to sign with their children for fear it will interfere with their English development. There is no research to support this in the history of the Deaf in the world. In fact, in contrast, those Codas who grow up in a signing environment do not lack English skills in comparison to the general population. It is possible the interpreting process may support the learning of both languages to fluency. Since interpreting requires one to move from one language to another, it is critical to know what the meanings are in both languages.

The greatest conflicts in the development of a Coda reside around the issues of language and education, issues clearly controlled by the Hearing side of the border. It is in this process of control over the language issue that the development and feeling of powerlessness occurs in both Codas and their parents. Language is the train that carries the culture across the community and from one family to another. It is also the train wreck that prevents intergenerational interaction when the grandparents are Hearing.

The real irony is that ASL is thought to be bad by the Hearing and yet it is the main process with which many of us communicate with our parents and our parents' friends. For those Codas who do not sign, many feel they have been cheated, cheated by some unknown group called the "Hearing." Many Codas who do not sign may not have had an in-depth conversation with their parents for most of their life.

Finally, how does a youngster listen to the countless stories and statements that imply a "hate the Hearing" attitude by many Deaf people? Codas are subjected to these statements by their parents, sometimes direct, sometimes incidental, and it becomes a confusing mess, when we know that we are "Hearing." As children, we probably don't recognize the conflict immediately, but as we get older, it becomes very clear that "Hearing" people are the enemy. One of the most complicated situations Codas face is understanding that the term Hearing does not apply to us. But we learn very late about this. A real problem is that we listen to our parents and their friends complain about those "Hearing" people, and then we look at ourselves, and we are Hearing. Our parents then turn around and call us Hearing. This is difficult to rectify in our lives. It sometimes drives us away from the community.

How does one rectify these confusing, alienating, and opposing views? What type of personality is developed in which the parent is viewed as the child who is unable to communicate and the child has all the communication tools at their disposal? How is a child to grow into adolescence and eventually adulthood and come to terms with all this conflict?

The young Coda becomes initially stigmatized in the Hearing world and has no way to obtain quick answers or explanations for what is happening. As a result some outcomes are predictable, such as many Codas become shy at first and some stay shy in the Hearing world. Some Codas become peacemakers to reconcile both the internal and external conflicts.[27] If you can solve the external conflicts then maybe you can reduce the internal conflict that has built up for so long.

Some Codas solve the internal conflict by "running away," metaphorically speaking. Most remove themselves physically from the Deaf world. And for those who escape, the death of both parents is the final border crossing for most Codas, since most of them are not in the Deaf business. Once our parents die, there is no need to continue the association with Deaf people. Since most Deaf people have hearing children and hearing grandchildren, the connection with the Deaf is truly only "one generation thick."

The border walls become thick at this juncture because of the two views of our parents: Deaf parents are capable versus Deaf parents are not capable. It is here that some of the most complicated identity processes occur. For example, when we are in the midst of a Deaf conversation or interacting with our parents over some event that occurred on the Hearing side of the border, the phrase "It's hearing people's fault" pops up in our presence. We know we can hear but are we part of the "hearing" as referenced in these attacks? In addition, we are subjected to countless interactions where Hearing people make negative references to our parents. The terms "dummy," "dumb," "illiterate," and "stupid" are bandied about over the time of our development. It is no wonder that we rebel in adolescence or become passive as adults and for the most part escape this constant conflict that becomes our cultural heritage. We learn at a young age that Hearing people do not understand our parents, and our parents do not understand them. We learn that the Deaf club is a place where Deaf people are treated as people with all the positives and negatives associated with the treatment of equals. We learn that as we grow we will be expected to "leave" the community. In fact, we are groomed for it. As adults there is no official membership for Codas in any of the Deaf organizations, the cultural events, or the social processes. There is no shaping us to assist in shaping the future for better or worse. There is no process for Codas to learn how to access power in the Deaf world.

This results in feelings of powerlessness to shape our lives.[28] In the hearing world, hearing parents are invested in shaping the lives of their children so that they can access, learn, and participate in the culture as adults. Hearing people learn about the mechanisms through which you can access power. Now clearly all power is not accessible by everyone, but there is the myth that "anyone can be president" in the Hearing world. There is no such myth in the Deaf world for Codas. You can only be what the Deaf world dictates you can be. There is no role for Codas in the Deaf world other than the border-riding interpreter.

Access to shaping the consequences of skill acquisition and learning in the Deaf world is in the Hearing world as, for example, in two areas: education and law. In education, the decisions or policies are made by hearing people (even including disabled people but not Deaf people) and these policies eventually influence the Deaf world. What Codas learn from these policies is just how powerless our parents are and by extension how powerless we really are. The myth of democracy says that the majority rules, and if you are a minority, it is extremely hard to get a majority vote. In the case of Deaf people, they are a minority within a minority (the "disabled" population). To the point, mainstreaming as a policy is a Hearing world creation. It heavily impacts on the Deaf world and splits the Deaf adult population into those who use ASL and those who don't. In fact, the identity confusion of our parents is the direct result of the Hearing world's treatment of Deaf children in the education field. As adults, Codas become confronted with an identity crisis. Codas have more access to this policy-making process because they are Hearing. Yet, Codas who do not and are not embraced by the Deaf world as adults see themselves as Hearing people. As adults many Codas bring with them all the inaccurate and unfounded beliefs of the Hearing world since there is no mechanism for them to believe or learn otherwise. As a result Codas have the potential of being in a unique position, but the history of Codas suggests they see themselves as part of the Hearing world not the Deaf world.

As an example when the two worlds collide, when Coda superintendents of schools for the Deaf and Coda program directors and Coda principals in regular school settings have an opportunity to mix at meetings and conferences the border issue becomes pronounced. These professional Codas function in the Hearing world even though they are in schools for the Deaf, which are supposedly viewed as part of the Deaf world (another myth).[29] In reality schools for the Deaf are part and parcel of the Hearing world except when the business of education has been completed for the day. It just so happens that the Deaf world is encased as a minority group inside the school for the Deaf. Deaf adults run the school after hours; Hearing adults run the school during the academic time and Hearing adults make policy, raise funds, etc. Hence the Hearing run the school as part of the Hearing world from a hearing perspective. Coda professionals bring all their baggage to the operation of the school. And in most cases, this baggage if full of the internalized Hearing views of their parents and what they have learned along the way. These include the use of ASL is bad, Deaf opinions are one-sided and narrow, there are many options that should be available to parents, to learn to talk is very important, the average Deaf person will never really learn to read, etc. All of these views result in the continuation of our Deaf parents not being able to obtain a good education, not feeling as participants in their lives, growing up without any control over their own destiny, etc. The cycle continues. Yes, there are some superintendents who hire the Deaf, who look to the Deaf for advice; however, when it comes to academics the Hearing policy reverts to the Hearing world. This Hearing control of attitudes and beliefs is passed on to Codas. So in essence if one wishes to become a leader and participate in the power structure, Codas must adopt the Hearing world views. Becoming Hearing in the cultural and political sense is easier for developing a personality and belief system because it reduces a great number of conflicts.

Border Talk: Language, Communication, and Signing

"I saw the intelligent and lively side of my parents and their friends at the Deaf Club. I knew that my father and mother were capable of subtle communication, and that sign language was as adequate, capacious, and poetic as any language. I could tell my parents almost anything that any other kid in the Bronx could tell his or her parents."[30]

The Deaf say they are not disabled and do not want the same things that the general disabled population want. However, the Deaf want captions, interpreters, TTY access, relay, etc. Are not these accommodations similar to what the general disabled population wants? For a Coda this paradox is difficult to understand as a person growing up and extremely difficult to explain to others. Hence, many Codas get into a defensive posture defending the Deaf perspective without having a strong supporting rationale behind it.

If we did identify as "Deaf" are we required to experience the same discrimination, trauma, and prejudice as our parents and other Deaf people? In fact, many times we do receive the same treatment as our parents and as our parents' friends. It can best be seen in the interpreting situation.

Many times as children and young adults we are exposed to extremely prejudicial comments about the Deaf. Sometimes the comments are not always obvious but subtle, and since we are not trained to be professional interpreters it is very difficult to know what to do. Many times discriminatory comments arise out of the situations where the interpreter is misconstrued to be part of the Deaf person and is not there on behalf of the Hearing person. There is no place a Coda can go to get advice on how to handle this type of discrimination. As a result I believe that Codas develop either of the following two types of strategies to handle their own inner conflict.

The first strategy is to develop into a peacemaker, which borders on the passive side of the spectrum, while others may develop into what has been called the freedom fighter.[31] In truth, there is some of each of these components in all Codas. Many Codas in an attempt to avoid conflict keep to themselves any negatives from both sides of the border. Hence, we become repositories of the rampant discrimination and prejudice of both populations with no outlet that would provide some type of resolution to this conflict. Here is where the attempt at therapeutic intervention is thwarted. As cauldrons of information about both groups, yet not belonging to either one, where does one go to relieve the pressure when the cauldron is full? If you go to the Hearing therapist, you must process the information about the Hearing through Hearing minds in that you must see the Coda's information based on the norm of the Hearing. How do you discuss the positive nature of having Deaf parents from the Hearing point of view? No matter what a therapist may say, there is an underlying foundational belief that to be Deaf is bad or negative. This is a psychological and cultural fact. You can't just dismiss it and say let's talk about you, or whatever therapeutic exchange is made. And vice versa with the Deaf. It is another place one cannot go because there is no rationale on the Hearing side for how we think. Ironically, it is much easier on the Deaf side since there is more awareness and knowledge about the Hearing world and its ways. Hence, it is more comfortable for a Coda to be with Deaf people who unofficially accept Codas as transient members. The Coda is a mirror of both cultures.

Power of Interpreting

Initially, interpreting is translating what Hearing people say to your parents and vice versa. All Codas begin this process at a young age. Some Codas continue to interpret for their whole lives; all Codas interpret for their parents until their parents die. The interpreting process carries with it great power and sometimes great confusion.

At a very young age in the interpreting situations you learn about the power you have. You learn about the attitudes of the Deaf and Hearing toward each other as explained above. Mostly you learn that you are in almost absolute control of the communication process. The interpreter controls:

1. Who speaks when. The initiation, timing, and length of time of the interaction.
2. What language will be used. The language choice is typically decided during the interaction and is determined by the level of the participants. However, the Coda interpreter has free reign as to the language process of the event. The tone of voice, the level of the register, and the emotional level are controlled via the language used.
3. What will actually be "said" between the Deaf and Hearing participants. The Coda interpreter has control over the translation process and content. It is clear that the interpreter can make either party look good, appear knowledgeable, competent, and in control or vice versa.

For example, there is a major border issue as to how one handles the type of interpreting situation below, probably encountered by all Coda interpreters.

If Dad is upset during an interaction and says, "Tell the clerk he is a jerk!" young Coda interpreters are more likely to respond as follows: "My father thinks you are not correct." Or some may go it straight the first time and tell them what their father has said. Typically, this will only happen once. An excellent example of this situation is provided by Bonnie Kraft on the videotape *Tomorrow Dad Will Still Be Deaf.*[32] It is during these situations that the young Coda hears the side comments reflecting the attitudes of both sides. It is here that the idea that the Deaf hate the Hearing and that the Hearing think the Deaf are stupid, incompetent, and "dumb" is reinforced. In addition, in many interpreting situations young Codas learn that hearing adults treat you as the adult and your parent as the child. All of these situations must be handled and incorporated into the Coda's psyche. Given this process, it is a tribute that most Codas are able to function well as adults.[33]

In addition to the power of the interpreting process, the young Coda has to contend with the fact that the interpreter is really not supposed to be part of the conversation between the Deaf person and the Hearing person. The idea of the interpreter being the nonperson in the interaction has a significant psychological bearing on how to handle each side of the border. It is more through acquired skill than actual training that many Codas have become good interpreters. However, it is also true that Codas who obtain interpreter training will be better interpreters. But those who become interpreters as adults, whom we would call Hearing interpreters, face these issues as adults and not as children. Hence the skills and strategies that one may need to deal with these types of psychological events are much more mature. In addition, the Hearing interpreter does not have the emotional stake in an interpreting event since they never have to interpret for their parents.

A final example of the complexity of interpreting as a Coda, and another paradox that must be understood, is that many Deaf people do not like to have Codas as interpreters. It is possible this has stemmed from the Coda as interpreter who has access to the most private of private things and access to the community, access to what might be called the underbelly of the community, thereby posing a threat to the confidentiality of the situation. There is a double problem with this: the Deaf want Coda interpreters but don't trust them, but they request them because there is a greater distrust of the Hearing interpreters. This creates all kinds of tension between the Deaf, the Coda as interpreter, and the Hearing interpreters. These are only a few examples of the many conflicting processes created when crossing the border. The psychological toll this has on young Codas who do not fully understand how to deal with these types of situations could be the major reason why most Codas are missing from the Deaf side of the border.

Family

There are differences in Coda family makeup just as there are in the world at large. Some Codas have large Deaf contingents, that is, grandparents who are Deaf and aunts, uncles, brothers, and sisters or any combination who may be Deaf. However, the most common situation is that there are no Deaf people in their family other than their parents. This family dynamic mirrors the situation of Deaf people, our parents included, where in the typical Hearing family with a Deaf child, the Deaf child tends to be the only Deaf person in the family. I am able to present only my family. There is not very much research or literature on Deaf families unless they have Deaf children. There are some memoirs beginning to surface that provide some poignant and realistic descriptions of Deaf families with hearing children.[34] There are some papers that present a discussion of family.[35]

My family is not the typical Deaf family. Both of my parents were college-educated Deaf people although my mother never completed her college education. My parents were teachers of Deaf children and were very active in both grassroots functions and the non-grassroots activities. My parents were very active in the national and local athletic associations of the Deaf and the local Deaf clubs, and at the same time they were involved in the International Catholic Deaf Association, National Association of the Deaf, state government committees, and other leadership areas that wanted to both set policy for Deaf people and manage the community to maintain its future. In essence, they were Deaf leaders.

What does it mean to be part of a family? In the Deaf world the term family has a different meaning depending on which side of the border you are on. The idea of a nuclear family is probably more appropriate in meaning on the Deaf side of the border and the idea of an extended family is more in line with the meaning on the Hearing side of the border. That is, Deaf families tend to be removed from the Hearing extended family. Hearing families tend to have more contact and interaction with extended family members. Clearly, the issues surrounding communication create a border within families.

The Notion of the Extended Family as "Family" on the Hearing Side of the Border

In my extended family my father had thirteen siblings that survived and my mother had four siblings. This is a total of seventeen siblings, all of whom were Hearing, and not one of them could use sign language or in my lifetime has made the effort to learn to sign. Only one sibling on my mom's side learned to fingerspell. Ironically the spouses (one of my uncles) or children (one of my cousins) of my father's family learned to sign and/or fingerspell. If there was to be any meaningful communication the burden fell to my sister and I to interpret within the extended family.

Typically during the interpreting situation my father's and mother's sisters would tell me that it was my job to take care of them. When my extended family members would refer to my parents they would use the phrase "poor Bet and Alfred." This was a favorite reference that was used for as long as I can remember. There was a constant suggestion that I was to take care of my parents and that they were viewed as less than capable adults. This message created a huge psychological border between me and my extended family, a border that I find difficult to cross even into my adult years. The interactions with my extended family allowed me to develop a clearer understanding of what the terms Hearing and Deaf meant depending on what side of the border they were used.

The Idea of the Nuclear Family

In addition to my parents being relatively untypical in the Deaf world, my growing up was also not typical of most Codas. For the majority of my life at home I was raised in a school for the Deaf, which is a different experience than many Codas have. We actually lived on the border of the Deaf and Hearing communities (I do not use Deaf world here as the school for the Deaf was more a part of the Hearing world for me) as we lived in a house that was on a town street but also was within the boundaries of the Deaf school campus.

Life at our home was very Deaf. Deaf people, other than my parents, would often be there at night. There were no lights connected to doorbells, hence the house was never locked. Deaf people would just let themselves in. We had a large kitchen in the house, and many times there would be five to six Deaf people in the kitchen. During these times there would be discussions and many times complaining about the Deaf school, the Hearing people who worked there, etc. Deaf people gathered at my home because my father was a leader and a teacher at the school. The irony of this is that my extended family did not see my father as a leader.

Both of my parents used ASL, with my mother much more fluent than my father (who lost his hearing at sixteen and became Deaf when he learned to sign at Gallaudet when he was eighteen). As a result both my sister and I learned to sign when we were very young children, much like how the typical hearing child learns the language of their home. In my case, my fluency in ASL is much less than my sister's who took over the interpreting role when I left home.

Many Codas do not learn how to sign very well. Many Deaf parents have grown up in oral programs and learned to sign in the dormitories from other Deaf people, not from the adults in their environment such as the teachers in the schools. In addition, Deaf parents have been told ASL is bad and will hinder the development of English, so they don't sign with their kids. Many Codas may not have the skills to have an in-depth conversation with their parents: this mirrors the Deaf children of Hearing parents who are unable to sign until they meet other Deaf children or enter the Deaf world as adults. As a result some Codas are able understand their parents but can't understand their parents' friends. Both groups grow up angry and resentful toward their parents. Our Deaf parents become estranged from their Hearing parents and Codas become estranged from their Deaf parents mostly centered around the issue of learning American Sign Language.

Coda identity within the family can be seen from different perspectives. In one instance, the issuing of names can become a border issue. Names are important parts of identity for people. In the family the membership issue of who is Deaf and who is Hearing becomes established by how one is referred to.

The title "Coda" claims ownership to something not acknowledged in the past by our families. The term has only been in existence for about twenty years. It was coined by Millie Brother, the founder of the CODA organization in 1982. As a result Codas have been meeting and many issues are seen as patterns within our families. One pattern is the creation and use of name signs for Hearing children of Deaf parents as a true border issue.

For example, in the Deaf community many of the older Codas began our identities with:

Son of _____ (in my case Hoffy or Betty)
Daughter of _____ (Hoffy or Betty).

There were no name signs for me or my sister. Our names were short enough to be finger-spelled. However, I do not recall any of my parents' friends referring to me as "B-O-B"; it was always Hoffy's son. I did not receive a name sign until I was an adult. My father's name sign was an "H" handshape at the shoulder; I was given the name sign with an "H" handshape in contact with the crook of the arm. When my father died, some of my parents' friends raised my name sign to his location. Later, Marie Philip assigned a name sign to me when I arrived in Boston. This is a "B to H" handshape at the shoulder. It is this name sign that has been used for the past twenty-six years. I didn't even know that my mom had a name sign in the community until I was an adult. The awarding of name signs to Codas is an unexplored area. I am meeting many Codas whose parents have given them name signs and they have used them their whole lives. This could be a generational issue or an issue of stratification within the Deaf world. That is, could the non-college-educated Deaf parent be more prone to create name signs for their children? This could also be an identity issue within the community. Names could be construed as membership tags and the Deaf World still has not figured out where Codas reside.

Adult Families: Relationships with Spouses

Mirror of the Deaf world: most Codas marry non-Codas. This is literally the opposite of the Deaf world. It is at this stage in a Coda's life that the borders become very well defined and begin to harden (suggesting that the border will be difficult to traverse easily). The relationship with a spouse may have a range of internal processes, from being accomplished easily to handling the situation with great repression of emotions and affiliation.

Typically spouses of Codas will not have had any contact with Deaf people in their lives. As with all interactions between the borders, the issue of communication process will underlie the relationship. Many spouses will attempt to learn to sign. This has both good and bad implications. In many cases the level of skill will result in parents not really being understood, and the spouse is not really understood by parents. This issue is then dealt with through a politeness process. Each interlocutor knows they are not understood but lets it go. Many times the Coda is responsible for explaining what took place but at another time. Spouses then gain a false sense of accomplishment and become more confident so that when the fall arrives, the harder it will be. It is usually at its critical point when the phrase "I know/understand your parents and your situation" appears. In many ways this is similar to the professional who learns to sign.[36] Many professionals who learn to sign because of the acceptance and effort to understand the conversation by Deaf people have an overblown sense of their signing skills.

The case where the spouse doesn't learn to sign can create real problems for Codas. Once again the Coda is forced into an interpreter role explaining both the content of the message, the reason for the interaction, and the cultural meanings behind the messages to both the parents and the spouse.[37] Hence, the Coda can be cornered into a defensive role, and all the childhood skills come into play to make sure there is no friction. The stakes are very high, higher than the interactions with Hearing people outside the family, since it's one's marriage and immediate family that are the players not the Hearing outsiders.

A common example encountered by Codas is when Deaf parents sign: "What's wrong with your husband/wife? He/she doesn't like us" or "I don't understand what he/she signed, please explain what they said." The Coda is then in a double bind: if they encourage their spouse to learn to sign problems will occur, and if they don't there are still problems. It's a lose-lose situation. However, most Codas work very hard to solve the issues of communication with their Deaf parents and their spouses.

Another example is the misreading of facial expressions that is very common when the borders are crossed, especially in a marriage situation. Research indicates that Deaf people are no better at reading Hearing facial expressions than Hearing people.[38] In fact, in my experience, the problem in misreading facial expressions is more prone to be on the Hearing side of the border. Hearing people are more prone to misread the Deaf person's facial message. Since facial expression can be emotional and syntactic in the Deaf world but is only emotional in the Hearing world, Deaf people have more experience in reading faces.

A number of defensive strategies are entertained to accommodate the situation. Soon the Coda begins visiting their Deaf parents alone, or frequent visits become a rarity. Many of the strategies we used in growing up will be implemented at this time. It is much easier to be in groups (family) when all the members are Hearing or Deaf. If there is a mix of Deaf and Hearing then the Coda's role and identity within the group becomes a problem. The Coda becomes the "interpreter" in the family, not the son or daughter(-in-law). As a result Codas begin to restrict their contact with Deaf people in general, and then restrict our interactions with our Deaf parents to the relay or the TTY. Prior to the TTY there was just avoidance of contact with our Deaf parents or with Deaf people in general. In my generation, these strategies can be recognized when we find ourselves spending more time with the Hearing grandparents.

An easy and common solution to avoid all this is to move far away from both sets of grandparents. Schedule visits once or twice a year. This can slowly build up conflict within either spouse. Hearing spouses can become resentful because there might be a lessening of contact with their parents. The conflict may be lessened these days by the technological revolution. TTYs, videophones, and relay access are common now, and most Deaf people have or use them. However, many Deaf members of the older generation are not fully comfortable with TTYs, e-mail, or instant messaging. These are the next generation's tools. It is probably subtle at first, as the Coda may or may not recognize that they are unconsciously entering into these types of patterns. But when recognition occurs resentment may begin to build in Codas.

The underlying issue is that a Hearing spouse can never really know and understand. They can sympathize, empathize, and support, but understanding how interactions with their Deaf parents are intended to be resolved may not be possible. This is not to say that relationships between Codas and their spouses are always going to be a problem. Many Codas have developed excellent survival skills that they can then implement to function fully on the Hearing side of the border.

In the case of Hearing grandchildren the border becomes a wall, and the wall is in many cases difficult to climb over. Again that issue with signed language reappears. Most Codas do not teach their children how to sign. Most Coda grandchildren have a superficial or fleeting relationship with their Deaf grandparents. It could be compared to the benevolent Hearing person attempting to interact with the Deaf. The grandchildren are able to interact, but there is no depth to the interaction unless the Coda parent interprets, explains, and leads. It is here that the idea of a one generation thick process is at work. The number of grandchildren who are able to sign well enough to interact at more than a superficial basis is very small. The cycle continues and the fluency at using ASL reduces with each succeeding generation.

As a result of these processes we end up developing "border management" strategies.

This is very much an extension of childhood behaviors. Avoidance of the problems, keeping a lid on feelings, moving away from one's Deaf self, repressing emotions are all strategies Codas implement to maintain relationships with the Hearing and the Deaf worlds.

The CODA Organization

The Coda conference is like "coming home."[39] However, it is important to clearly distinguish the difference between "home" and "family." In the Hearing world coming home is coming home to the family in which you grew up and from whom you learned all your values and in which you feel full membership. In the case of Codas, family is where you grew up and learned all your values, but membership issues are clearly faced in this process. Crossing the border to family means visiting the Deaf world, not entering as a member. It is for this reason that I think the CODA organization has become such a strong and respected phenomenon. Although the CODA organization meets annually and only attracts three hundred or so Codas, the impact of the group can be seen in the Deaf world. The term "Coda" is now within the vocabulary of all Deaf people, Codas have established an identity as a group, and Coda has become a symbol for a subcultural movement. As a result of the CODA Organization, the leadership in the Deaf world is now discussing where Codas fit, not only nationally but internationally.

Unlike other cultural or subcultural groups, Codas had to claim and stake out the definitional territory of children of Deaf adults and our heritage on our own, where typically cultural identity and heritage is passed on from parent to child. When this identity was claimed and an organization begun, the Deaf initially viewed us with misgivings. When CODA was established as an organization, there was the perception that Codas were dissatisfied with the homes in which they grew up. It is interesting to see how much of a parallel process the Coda annual meeting has with many of the Deaf clubs we all participated in as children. I will address two issues that I think have great import and that represent the Coda crossing the border to the Deaf world. The Coda meeting represents the Deaf world side of the border. As children we were viewed as having a place in the Deaf world; as adults we have been excluded from participation in its internal structures and politics. I will address the issues of closed meetings and the myth of Deaf voice.

Closed Meetings

The annual meeting of the CODA Organization is open only to Codas who are at least eighteen years old. There has been a considerable uproar about this issue by both the Deaf and the Hearing. It seems that Coda-only meetings have engendered suspicion and distrust on both sides of the border. This should not be confusing when you realize that Codas have grown up in the Deaf world, their values are the same, their behaviors are the same, and many of their issues are the same. They have learned these values from their parents. Codas have learned that the Hearing do not understand, and Codas are always explaining themselves to others. Interpreting all the time for the Hearing members of our families is many times a burden. We are constantly stressed by the knowledge of both cultures (one open, one closed) and this results in the constant weight of responsibility (always on guard defending Deaf people to the Hearing and vice versa).

These are issues germane to Codas and to the Deaf world.[40] Deaf people have "closed" meetings yet many cannot see the parallel with Coda meetings. One issue could be projection. Since the Deaf have closed meetings and many meetings are to figure out what to do about the Hearing, many Deaf think that the Coda meetings are to complain about the Deaf and, closer to home, to complain about our parents. As in any group, there is always an issue or two to complain about, but this is not the purpose or the portrayal of a Coda conference. Ironically, it is a celebration of our parents, their resiliency, their fortitude in the face of constant persecution, and how these attributes have been handed down to us. The CODA meeting is a celebration of the many skills and talents that all of us seem to hold in a hidden part of our psyches. The meeting presents talents of Codas across a range that continues to astound me. I have seen musical talents equal to many of the professionals in our world to storytellers whose ASL fluency is equal to some of the most respected professionals (some compare to Garrison Keillor) to those who present intellectual workshops on issues germane to our lives and the history of Deaf people, which includes Codas and Deaf Culture.[41] The range of talent, knowledge, and intellect is displayed for the group to see and for the individual to gain the respect they deserve.

The annual CODA meeting functions as the place for a "home." At CODA meetings, the bottom line is that it is safe to say what you feel and that this will be understood without great explanation and creating cultural conflicts.

A Border Myth: Deaf Voice, the Myth of Silence, and the Deaf

The second issue that needs to be addressed is the meaning of Deaf voices and the myth of silence in Deaf families. Re-creating the sound of how your Mom or Dad called you home is one of the most shocking borders to cross upon entering the CODA meetings. Many of us did this in private with siblings[42] but never in a wider group and rarely as adults.

The Deaf club was a cacophony of sounds that we encountered as children. These sounds were normal and natural and in some cases lovingly warm. These sounds of home helped put meaning to "place" in Coda lives. The irony is that as a child, I never laughed at the sounds of the Deaf community. But when I crossed the threshold into the Hearing side of the border these sounds became stigmatized, they were viewed as awful, vulgar, horrible. The inability of the Deaf person (our parents) to speak well or even clearly is the central problem of all Deaf people as far as the Hearing world is concerned. These sounds are the sounds of our families.

The most humorous and loving feelings are felt when stories are told that include Deaf voices. Many stories revolve around the attempts to call us home for dinner or whenever our parents needed us. We all knew who was calling (so did all the neighborhood kids), and the joke was to see how fast you could get home to quell the "noise."

For me one of most striking border issues is that of using Deaf voice. It allows me to be a real person again, no facades, no false fronts, no covering of who I am; it allows me to be full and genuine. As kids we were probably appalled and embarrassed when our parents attempted to call us or talk to us in front of our friends. Yet as adults, these sounds have come to mean so much, especially in those Codas whose parents have died.

The sounds and the voices are much like the accented sounds that many children of immigrant parents heard. These accents and the warm remembrances that these voices bring back probably cover more than the instantaneous and embarassing moments of our childhood. These voices bring back the smells, the sights, the feelings of our child-hood; they bring back security and signal the complete crossing of the border. This is not an issue that we make fun of but honor and respect.

Yet, even with these feelings, Deaf voice has engendered one of the longest and most extensive discussions within CODA. Codas who are not part of the CODA Organization and many in the organization still discuss it at length.

Deaf voice has evolved into what has been called "Coda talk." "Coda talk" is the met-alinguistic and metacognitive awareness of the border. It is possible that this may be the true pidgin of the Deaf world. For example, we use English in a pidgin process in the production of ORANGE EYES; ORANGE is the handshape change for the sign ORANGE in ASL.[43] This handshape change is moved to the location of the eyes thus resulting in ORANGE EYES translating into being "shocked." ASL is the base language providing the structure and the semantics and English provides the vocabulary, almost the opposite of signed English where English provides the structure and the semantics and ASL pro-vides the vocabulary.

Coda voice is the different sounds of home, something with which only Codas can identify. Our Deaf parents cannot relate to this, yet it is directly derived from them. Only Codas can cross this border.

Reflections

To my knowledge there are no stories told by the Deaf that include Codas. Does that mean we are members of the community and just ignored? Codas are not mentioned in any of the texts that talk about the "Deaf," deafness, Deaf community, Deaf Culture, etc. In other words we are invisible to those who study the culture, yet we are a significant part of the population, much like how black people were ignored in the history books of the past.

The Deaf have an idea of home, be it a residential school, a Deaf community, a Deaf club, etc. Codas have found the concept of home to be elusive. It turns out, I think, that our concept of home is the house and the family we construct ourselves. The video *A Passport without a Country* clearly demonstrates that we are searching for a space, a place to locate our lives. It is possible that the CODA Annual Conference has established this place for us and for our lives. There has never been any place a Coda can go in order to understand these situations. This is why we are survivors. We have done all this grow-ing up, essentially on our own. We can all be proud of this. We have accomplished lives with and without the support of the Deaf or the Hearing.

It is my hope that this chapter will open up discussions about the topics covered and illuminate them so that we can move toward a fuller understanding of Codas, who they are, how they got there, and what it means to have a home, a place, and a family. It is clear that every generation of Codas faces both negative and positive differences in their lives. However, the common denominator is that we all have Deaf parents and must cross the Deaf and Hearing borders constantly during our lifetimes. The more we discuss the issues, the easier it will be to cross the borders and expand our understanding of all the lives that are part of the Deaf world.

Notes

I would like to thank all the members of the Deaf Studies Think Tank who so generously shared their ideas with me about Codas. I want to thank Todd Czubek and Rachel Mayberry for their helpful critique. Though they are Codas they bring to the table different backgrounds. I want to thank Aurora Wilber for her help in keeping me on track to complete this manuscript. Most of all, I wish to thank Gertrude R. Schafer, as a Coda and my wife, for her support and willingness to read this over and discuss its points at length. In the end all of this work is my responsibility. To my parents Alfred and Betty (Mary Elizabeth) for without them, who would I be? Part of the title was coined by Brenda Brueggemann.

1. I use the capitalized convention of *Deaf* for all Deaf people who identify themselves as being Deaf, which makes them a member of the culture. I capitalize Hearing because this is the cultural contrast group. We have not explored the meaning of Hearing very much in the literature. Since I use it as identifying a cultural group it needs to have the H capitalized. This chapter is about Codas who do not have a hearing loss; however, I would not include them as part of the Hearing.

2. Scott Michaelsen and David Johnson, *Border Theory: The Limits of Cultural Politics* (Minneapolis: University of Minnesota Press, 1997).

3. Robert Hoffmeister, "Using Words: Maintaining Borders and the Marginalization of the Deaf" (unpublished working paper, Deaf Studies Think Tank, Washington, D.C., July 2002).

4. Ibid.

5. Michaelsen and Johnson, *Border Theory*, 1.

6. Paul Preston, *Mother Father Deaf: Living between Sound and Silence* (Cambridge, Mass.: Harvard University Press, 1994).

7. "Coda" refers to the individual HCDP whereas "CODA" refers to the organization.

8. Jerome Schein and Marcus Delk, *The Deaf Population in the United States* (Silver Springs, Md.: National Association of the Deaf, 1974).

9. Bonnie Kraft, "Faith and Adversity" (lecture, Lesley College, Cambridge, Mass., 1991).

10. OGT: I write a column for the CODA, Int. quarterly newsletter called *One Generation Thick* (OGT). We are OGT because most Codas are Hearing. Probably 90 percent of all children of Deaf people are hearing. And Coda children tend to be Hearing. Codas grow up and marry hearing people, have hearing kids, and lose the connection to the Deaf community; therefore, I am the last link to the Deaf community.

11. Benjamin Bahan, "Upon the Formation of a Visual Variety of the Human Race," this volume, describes the image of "doors" for Deaf people. A door could be a border demarcation between two worlds.

12. Lennard Davis, Transcripts, Deaf Studies Think Tank discussion (Deaf Studies Think Tank, Washington, D.C., July 2002).

13. Todd Czubek, personal communication with the author, 2003.

14. Harlan Lane, Robert Hoffmeister, and Ben Bahan, *A Journey into the Deaf-World* (San Diego: DawnSignPress, 1996).

15. R. Mayberry, E. Lock, and H. Kazmi, "Linguistic Ability and Early Language Exposure," *Nature* 417, no. 6884 (May 2, 2002), 38.

16. The whole discussion over the terms prelingual, postlingual, adventiously, and HoH in the education and speech and hearing literature demonstrates the lack of examination of what Deaf means on the Deaf side of the border.

17. If Singleton is correct this language is ASL; see J. L. Singleton, "Restructuring of Language from Impoverished Input: Evidence for Linguistic Compensation" (PhD diss., University of Illinois Urbana–Champaign, 1989).

18. See C. Chamberlain and R. Mayberry, "ASL Syntactic and Narrative Comprehension in Good and Poor Readers: Bilingual-Bimodal Evidence for the Linguistic Basis of Reading," unpublished manuscript, University of California, San Diego, 2006, for a discussion of who scores high on ASL and English tests; also P. Boudreault and R. Mayberry, "Grammatical Processing in American Sign Language: Age of First Language Acquisition Effects in Relation to Syntactic Structure," *Language and Cognitive Processes,* 2005: online.

19. This issue could be compared with how Mexicans and Puerto Ricans who grow up in the United States must deal with the issue of terminology with respect to "Anglos" and all the problems their parents have with "Anglos." However, a major difference is that the Mexican or Puerto Rican offspring is never considered to be an Anglo, except when they as adults become assimilated into the white society (see Michaelsen and Johnson, *Border Theory*).

20. Robert Hoffmeister and C. Shettle, "Adaptations in Communication Made by Deaf Signers to Different Audiences," ed. Robert Hoffmeister and James Gee, special edition on ASL, *Discourse Processes: A Multidisciplinary Journal* 7 (1984), 259–74.

21. *Passport without a Country,* producer C. Davie, 2002, is available from the CODA Organization's Web site: http://www.coda-international.org.

22. Preston, *Mother Father Deaf.*

23. It has been suggested to me that a comparison with children of interracial marriages might have a great deal in common with the Coda's quest for identity (Trudy Schafer, personal communication, 2000).

24. Lane, Hoffmeister, and Bahan, *Journey into the Deaf-World.*

25. Lennard Davis, *My Sense of Silence: Memoirs of a Childhood with Deafness* (Urbana: University of Illinois Press, 2000), 148.

26. Tom Bull, *On the Edge of Deaf Culture* (Alexandria, Va.: Deaf Family Research Press, 1998).

27. Robert Hoffmeister and M. Harvey, "Is There a Psychology of the Hearing," in *Culturally Affirmative Psychotherapy with Deaf Persons,* ed. Neil S. Glickman and M. Harvey (Mahwan, N.J.: Lawrence Erlbaum Associates, 1996), 73–98.

28. H. Schlesinger, "Effects of Powerlessness on Dialogue and Development: Disability, Poverty, and the Human Condition," in *Psychosocial Interventions with Sensorially Disabled Persons,* ed. B. Heller, L. Flohr, and L. Zegans (New York: Grune & Stratton, 1987), 1–27.

29. Donald Moores, *Educating the Deaf: Principles and Practices* (Boston: Houghton-Mifflin, 2001) points out the change in education placements from 80 percent in Deaf Schools and 20 percent in Hearing schools in the 1960s to 20 percent in Deaf Schools and 80 percent in Hearing schools for this generation of future Deaf adults.

30. Davis, *My Sense of Silence,* 148.

31. Hoffmeister and Harvey, "Is There a Psychology of the Hearing."

32. Bonnie Kraft, *Tomorow Dad Will Still Be Deaf & Other Stories,* videotape (San Diego: DawnSignPress. 1997).

33. Preston, *Mother Father Deaf.*

34. R. Miller, *Deaf Hearing Boy* (Washington, D.C.: Gallaudet University Press, 2004).

35. Jenny Singleton and M. Title, "Deaf Parents and Their Hearing Children," *Journal of Deaf Studies and Deaf Education* 5, no. 3 (2000): 221–36.

36. See Hoffmeister and Harvey, "Is There a Psychology of the Hearing."

37. D. Tannen, *That's Not What I Meant! How Conversational Style Makes or Breaks Relationships* (New York: Ballantine, 1986).

38. J. Reilly, M. McIntyre, and H. Seago, "Differential Expression of Emotion in American Sign Language," *Sign Language Studies* 75 (1991): 113–28.

39. Preston, *Mother Father Deaf*, 234.

40. See Lane, Hoffmeister, and Bahan, *Journey into the Deaf-World;* Lois Bragg, ed., *Deaf World: A Historical Reader and Primary Sourcebook* (New York: New York University Press, 2001).

41. Donna Ryan and John Schuchman, eds., *Deaf People in Hitler's Europe* (Washington, D.C.: Gallaudet University Press, 2002). A. Topliff, "Deaf Culture for Codas" (lecture, Annual CODA International Conference, Denver, Colorado, 2000).

42. See Davis, *My Sense of Silence.*

43. M. Bishop, "ORANGE-EYES: The Amazing Story of Coda-Talk," unpublished manuscript (Washington, D.C.: Gallaudet University, 2003).

PART V　*Intersections and Identities*

13. Dysconscious Audism: A Theoretical Proposition

GENIE GERTZ

Dysconscious Racism and Dysconscious Audism

IN JOYCE KING'S WORK on dysconscious racism, she shares her interpretation of how her university students perceived the meaning of racial inequity. She claims that her students exhibited uncritical ways of thinking about racial inequity: they did not think of the underlying causes of racism and, more importantly, possible solutions to racism. To think critically is to explore, analyze, and evaluate thoroughly the conditions caused by racism. Why did a certain situation happen and how can it be improved or modified? Instead, her students accepted and perpetuated "certain culturally sanctioned assumptions, myths and beliefs." King discovered that students had "impaired consciousness" of what racism means due to their limited understanding and experience.[1]

King then defines dysconscious racism as a form of racism that implicitly accepts dominant white norms and privileges. She emphasizes that it is not the absence of consciousness but rather impaired consciousness that engendered this term. When challenged to think critically, we must question the ideology of racial inequity and be able to identify and criticize it objectively. The students did not recognize that structural inequity is linked to racial inequity as a form of exploitation. King's students were aware of the racial issues, racial inequity, and racial prejudice. However, they lacked the depth of ethical judgment connected to formulating some rationale for inequity. King realized that their thinking was impaired when analyzing racial ideology. King builds a framework for us to recognize dysconscious racism where an analysis can be developed of how clearly people understand the consciousness of minority groups.

Some Deaf people do experience an impaired consciousness the same way students experienced it in King's study. Some Deaf people, though they resist being assimilated into the dominant culture, still incorporate some antithetical values from the dominant culture. In this manner, these Deaf individuals experience an impaired consciousness: a phenomenon for which I coined the term "dysconscious audism." This is a new concept and I have created this phrase based on Joyce King's work on dysconscious racism.

With the term "dysconscious audism," I describe a phenomenon that is defined as a form of audism that tacitly accepts dominant hearing norms and privileges. It is not the absence of consciousness but an impaired consciousness or distorted way of thinking about Deaf consciousness. "Dysconscious audism" adheres to the ideology that hearing society, because it is dominant, is more appropriate than the Deaf society. Such Deaf people can be characterized as not having fully developed Deaf consciousness connected to the Deaf identity, and they may still feel the need to assimilate into the mainstream culture.

Dr. Rachel Stone and California School for the Deaf, Riverside: Audism and Dysconscious Audism

In the year 2000, California School for the Deaf, Riverside (CSDR) selected Dr. Rachel Stone as the superintendent.[2] She became the first Deaf and female to head the school. Less than two years after the appointment, Dr. Stone was dismissed, likely for her strong views of Deaf bilingualism and biculturalism on educating Deaf students. She also emphasized the importance of bilingualism for the students—with equal importance placed on both English and American Sign Language (ASL). Her priority was student success, as she saw no reason that the deaf could not receive quality education. Dr. Stone believed that effective pedagogical approaches specifically appropriate for Deaf students would make all the difference in their academic success, which up to this point had not been progressing sufficiently. Dr. Stone's desire for an effective bilingual-bicultural environment was simply oppressed by administrators, teachers, and parents who espoused traditional hearingcentric education for the CSDR students and wanted to see that system remain status quo. Quite a few Deaf staff along with some hearing individuals did take a position in support of Dr. Stone and fought valiantly on her behalf. However, a sizable number of Deaf teachers, administrators, and parents who supported her philosophical stance stood helplessly in the ouster of Dr. Stone as CSDR Superintendent.[3]

The unwillingness to accept Dr. Stone's leadership and vision for a Deaf bilingualism and bicultural education at CSDR reveals the hidden power of oppression; namely, audism. It has a strong bearing on the hearing supremacy in educating deaf learners, even in a Deaf school setting like CSDR. While the term audism is not yet inserted in dictionaries, an in-depth treatise on audism can be obtained by reading Dirksen Bauman's article "Audism: Exploring the Metaphysics of Oppression."[4] His article will strive to further define the term as well. Some CSDR members were clearly audists in their overthrow of Dr. Stone. As for those Deaf administrators, teachers, and parents who took no action to aid Dr. Stone, even though they supported her goals for CSDR, why did they do nothing for her? The term dysconscious audism might provide some explanation for their lack of action in taking a strong stand for her and indirectly for themselves. This article will both introduce the concept of dysconscious audism, as well as present a theoretical proposition of it. Further examples will best illustrate the important features of dysconsious audism and its strong connection to audism.

Deaf Education Agenda Controlled by Hearing Educators

Now more than ever, I see so many issues at hand, especially with the larger society due to its lack of understanding about Deaf language, heritage, and culture. The true benefits of education escape most Deaf individuals because a large majority of hearing educators controls the "deaf education" agenda, which is laden with misconceptions.

To make matters worse, even as more effective means of educating Deaf individuals are demonstrated, Deaf language and culture are still not receiving widespread acceptance in the classroom.[5]

Hearing educators' main focus is on the stigma that Deaf individuals need to be "fixed" to correct their hearing and speaking deficiencies. More often than not, this further perpetuates society's larger view of Deaf people as inferior and subhuman and who need to be "rehabilitated" into being like hearing individuals for the sole purpose of assimilating them into mainstream American society.[6]

Basically, this is a classic example of ethnocentrism. However, it does not mean that hearing educators who are comfortable subscribing to Deaf bilingualism/biculturalism cannot be our allies. At present, the system of educating deaf individuals is failing to meet their educational and societal needs. There is a very common pattern among Deaf individuals who are kept away from effective visual language and a rich cultural heritage. As a result, many of them proceed through school life without a sense of direction. To properly educate and motivate Deaf individuals in life, we must see that, first and foremost, they are treated as human beings and are empowered with a natural language and rich cultural heritage.

Let's look at the story of Dr. Stone's ouster at CSDR once again. Were CSDR Deaf people's perceptions of their experience shifting away from Deaf empowerment toward the hearing dominant majority? They might have unwittingly accepted the changing values in the Deaf community to "please" the hearing world. Do Deaf people, generally speaking, experience the loss of their Deaf empowerment? Is the loss of their Deaf center creating Deaf individuals who view the Deaf world differently? Without Deaf empowerment, the Deaf consciousness is affected, becomes chaotic, and brings nothing to the world from Deaf people but a strange version of hearing people. The voice from Deaf-empowered individuals is critical to creating a just society of Deaf people.

Deaf Consciousness toward Audism

In order to explore the impact of audism on the lives of Deaf individuals, I conducted an ethnographic study that included eight Deaf adults of Deaf parents who were selected for the study to validate the existence of oppression on Deaf people.[7] They shared their experiences as members of the Deaf community. They have had Deaf Culture, American Sign Language, and other features that made being Deaf a positive experience. At the same time, they faced the negative experiences of oppression. Oppression has continually and, in most cases, surreptitiously been interwoven into the lives of Deaf people, including their own life encounters that are layered with audism.

The oppression of Deaf people appears to be omnipresent and everlasting. Some of the eight Deaf adults of Deaf parents experienced firsthand the prohibition of the use of sign language because they were told that sign language would ruin their chance for succeeding in American society. Some witnessed hearing people's devaluation of Deaf people's attempts to build up their Deaf identity. Some valued a strong Deaf identity to counteract their indoctrination about the superiority of hearing people's language, identity, education, and community/culture. They expressed the awareness of hearing people who tried to recast Deaf people into the image of hearing people, but as lesser citizens in the hearing world. Some of them noted that hearing educators reported the deficiencies of Deaf learners in order to justify and validate themselves as worthy individuals or as acknowledged experts on the education of so-called helpless Deaf individuals. As a consequence, the hearing populace supported the hearing educators' plan of action in educating deaf children. Some saw that hearing people discredited Deaf people's yearning for their own community and culture. Even the history of Deaf community/culture had no meaning to such hearing people. All they wanted to do was erase Deaf Culture and history. In the name of their expertise on deafness, these hearing people felt obligated to eliminate deafness, by any means, as well as Deaf people whom they thought brought an embarrassment to the society.[8]

Below are the examples of situations as described by each to illustrate the different forms of oppression that are structural rather than individual, often happening in relationships between hearing and Deaf groups. Alan commented about the oralists from the Alexander Graham Bell Organization who tried to put a stop to sign language being promoted in public through an NBC television show. Bonnie encountered a hearing woman working at a school for the deaf who could not sign at all. The school for the deaf was ready to dismiss Bonnie because she took a position challenging to the nonsigning woman. Carl related the frustrations of his father, who was a top-notch printer but never received a bonus for his excellence at work while his hearing counterparts who showed less commitment to work received the bonuses. When Felicia was a young girl, she saw her deaf classmates beaming with pride for being rewarded for good speech while she was slapped by her teachers for signing. As an adult, Felicia looked back to that scene and cringed at the overemphasis on speech and underemphasis on real education. Edward reported that there were no history books on Deaf people when he was growing up. Debbie made a choice to attend a regular university with the provision of support services to Deaf students. At one time, she wanted to drop out of the university due to her frustration over dealing with incompetent interpreters who made her feel more isolated from her professors and fellow classmates by interfering with direct communication. As a native signer of ASL, Glenn found SimCom (an abbreviated term of Simultaneous Communication, which refers to the simultaneous use of signing and speaking) to be an obstacle to him in terms of undermining his comprehension of what was being said. Yet SimCom continued on no matter how many Deaf individuals held it to be an abomination. Helen mentioned a hearing-oriented media report that glowed with praise for former Miss America Heather Whitestone's decision to get a cochlear implant. In that case, Helen argued, the media had no clue as to why the Deaf world did not applaud Whitestone in the way the hearing world did.

The thoughts and feelings as expressed by the eight Deaf persons in the above paragraph necessitate the attention to the term audism. These stories confirmed the existence of a deep-layered shroud of audism. Because of the prevalence of audist practices, both conscious and unconscious, Deaf people are oppressed in many ways. See Figure 13.1 for effects of audism on Deaf individuals. Presently, there is still a sizable group of Deaf people who would be categorized as "dysconscious audists" because they haven't developed their own Deaf consciousness and identity to the fullest. Generally

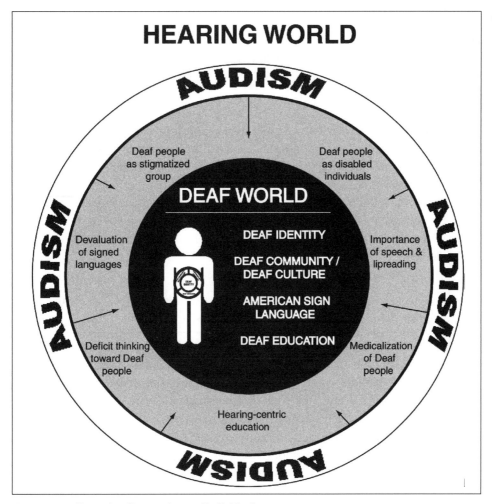

Figure 13.1. Effects of audism on the Deaf individual.

their Deaf consciousness is distorted to varying degrees. Dysconscious audistic Deaf people unwittingly help to continue the kind of victimized thinking that they are responsible for their failure. Such thinking enables hearing people to continue pathologizing Deaf people.

The marked difference between "unconscious" and "dysconscious" when used with the word audism is that the word unconscious implies that the person is completely unaware whereas the word dysconscious implies that the person does have an inkling of his or her consciousness but does not yet realize it is impaired. Some Deaf individuals choose to do nothing about it or to take a "so be it" attitude. In this manner, it is not that they are completely unaware of the issues; it's just their decision on how to live with them.

With the "dysconscious audism" framework in mind, the weakening of Deaf identity associates with the lack of Deaf consciousness within the present context and the impact of hegemonic forces. Hearing people's obsession over the cure of deafness contributes significantly to the weakening of Deaf people's identity. When the Deaf person's identity is distorted, they cannot fully understand their own behavior. A large number of Deaf individuals are not even aware that they possess, to varying degrees, these kinds of audistic behaviors and attitudes. The critical features of dysconscious audism are the following:

- Dysconscious audism disempowers Deaf people from becoming liberated.
- Dysconscious audism disables Deaf people from expressing Deaf cultural pride.
- Dysconscious audism intimidates Deaf people and limits their promotion of the Deaf perspective.
- Dysconscious audism hinders Deaf people from attaining quality education.
- Dysconscious audism denies Deaf people full acceptance of ASL.
- Dysconscious audism weakens Deaf people in the development of their Deaf identity.

Responses to Two Selected Topics by the Eight Deaf Adults of Deaf Parents in Quest of Understanding Dysconscious Audism

The eight Deaf adults of Deaf parents had been raised in the Deaf world since birth and, in the early years of their lives, knew the other side of the world known as the hearing world. They had been told stories about hearing people during their formative years by their Deaf parents. They had made their own personal observations of hearing people from some distance, and they had had real-life interactions with hearing people. These all influenced the impressions, attitudes, judgments, beliefs, etc. that they had about hearing people and the hearing world.

This section focuses on Deaf adults of Deaf parents and their slices of reactions to two topics that affect the Deaf community. The educational experiences and socialization they had in school added an important dimension to their present outlook at today's Deaf world. While they are all Deaf individuals with an affiliation to the Deaf world and the fluency of American Sign Language, each one represented is unique. Moreover, no two Deaf families are alike. These individuals covered a span of the three generations of Deaf individuals in which their life histories illustrated the changes in America in its societal treatment of Deaf people over fifty years. Most of them were either second- or third-generation Deaf individuals. Only one of them was a fourth-generation Deaf individual. Almost all of them attended residential schools for the deaf. Their philosophical stances and views on deafness, language, and culture were not identical, yet they offered many similarities. Their sharing of their views has contributed vital information to the reader about what the lives of Deaf people coming from Deaf parents might look like. Figure 13.2 provides the backgrounds of the eight Deaf adults of Deaf parents in five areas: age, Deaf generation, school attended, undergraduate college attended, and whether or not the parents were college educated.

SIMULTANEOUS COMMUNICATION

A limited number of people are particularly skilled at talking and signing at the same time, but many other people are really not able to do it. They try to talk and sign at

Informant	Age	Deaf generation	School attended	Undergraduate college attended	College-educated parents
Alan	early 70s	second	deaf school	Gallaudet University	no
Bonnie	late 40s	third	deaf school	Gallaudet University	no
Carl	mid-50s	third	deaf school	Gallaudet University	no
Debbie	early 40s	second	deaf school	hearing university	no
Edward	early 40s	second	deaf school	Gallaudet University	no
Felicia	early 40s	third	deaf school	Gallaudet University	no
Glenn	early 30s	second	deaf school	Gallaudet University	no
Helen	late 20s	fourth	hearing school	Gallaudet University	yes

Figure 13.2. Backgrounds of informants.

the same time and nothing clear comes out. As a result of using SimCom, many signs are dropped out. The sign also deteriorates significantly in its quality and intelligibility. Often, many Deaf people can't understand what people are saying, and they have to work so much harder to try and receive the message. When people speak English, the ASL becomes unintelligible. SimCom is an incomprehensible mix of two different modalities.[9] "I would rather see somebody explaining or speaking their piece by using American Sign Language or English," Felicia said, to emphasize that point. "They don't mix well." She could tell the difference when one used SimCom.

> I can tell if somebody is using their voice at the same time with signs, and once a hearing person, or even a Deaf person for that matter, starts to use speech, I will bust them right on the spot: "Are you talking while you're signing?"

"If it's clear enough, that's fine," Alan said. He accepted SimCom. If it becomes very muddled, and a lot of signs get dropped, then he is not in support of it. He has written a book on the topic of communication and an article on talking and signing at the same time. "If I had a choice [to communicate with] a person who was fluent in talking and signing simultaneously and somebody who was fluent just in sign," Alan said, "I would choose the person fluent in sign."

"For certain purposes and functions, I think SimCom is fine," Bonnie said. She accepted the use of SimCom. "It goes back again to the importance of open communication." Why must one say, "You can't do that," if it can work out satisfactorily? In this particular situation, should communication be forfeited because we are not allowed to use a resource that could possibly help us communicate? In her mind, restrictions of this type are not justified. "Why not, whatever helps."

What results often in SimCom is the utterances come out in English word order. It's due to the fact that the person is not able to speak English words using ASL syntax. "It just doesn't make sense to me when the speech skews the message in ASL," Glenn said succinctly.

Helen explained her "Dr. Jekyll and Mr. Hyde" communication split:

> I do admit that when I sign, I mouth. Sometimes I mouth the shapes of words and sometimes I don't. What's odd is that when I'm at my workplace, I will definitely sign and mouth simultaneously. At home, I use full ASL and do not mouth any words.

It is reasonable to suspect that the settings influence the language that she uses. "If I'm in a restaurant or bar, I use ASL but still may switch to SimCom. It depends on who's present and my desire to make myself clear." She didn't want any misunderstandings to occur. Helen does not support using speech and signing at the same time because she is keenly aware that it is the sign language that suffers in the end. The mouth movement or the English production with SimCom, she felt, "is obviously for the hearing person." The quality of the sign language is degraded when SimCom becomes the primary source of communication. The message delivered through SimCom becomes unclear. "It's hard to understand. I don't want that," she concluded.

Most often, the intended meaning of your comment is lost when using SimCom. One is so focused on speaking and using sign at the same time that it is not ASL anymore, and it makes signing a lot less intelligible. "Many times I get lost when people speak and sign at the same time. I don't understand what they are saying," the informant Debbie admitted. She added that she has, in the past, requested dropping the "speech" modality when she failed to grasp the message via SimCom. "When I tell them to drop the speech part and just sign, it becomes crystal clear. It's the dual modality that is very confusing and usually ineffective."

People who are bilingual often face that dilemma, as Edward explained in his own struggle:

> I would say that I support it. I mean, I do that sometimes with my use of language. Saying that I support it puts me in a position that I'm either against it or support it. I don't want to say either way.

He acknowledged the fact that when one is signing and speaking at the same time, one's skills, the clarity, and the way that one expresses those languages diminish. "If you are using one language, then you can use that language to its fullest. It's most clear and in-depth," Edward admitted.

The language issue with deaf children addresses the fact that the acquisition of a first language is very important. By trying to teach ASL and English, SimCom confuses deaf children further because, when some people sign and speak at the same time, they are ultimately doing neither correctly.

Carl told his older brother, who is proficient in using SimCom: "You don't have to do that. Who are you trying to impress? You should just use sign language and let the interpreter speak for you." His brother's motivation to use SimCom was his lack of trust in the interpreters. "He is one of the rare people who can do it, but there aren't many who can," Carl said of his brother's SimCom. "Of course, he does sign a little more English in SimCom than if he were using ASL only."

SimCom doesn't work because ASL and English are two completely different languages. The underlying mechanism of SimCom requires the "speaking" part that imposes on Deaf people to use English, often for the convenience of hearing people. In this sense, SimCom disempowers Deaf people from using ASL to the full extent and consequently weakens them in development of their Deaf identity. Some of the eight Deaf adults of Deaf parents were opposed vehemently to the use of SimCom for valid reasons. Yet the others who have accepted SimCom by allowing its existence reveal the dynamics of dysconscious audism because they thought of nothing in SimCom that affected Deaf people in everyday communication.

THE DEAF STUDIES CURRICULUM

The focus of the "Deaf" agenda would hold the idea that Deaf children are not to be perceived as disabled but as linguistically and culturally identified individuals. It is important that Deaf students interact with other Deaf individuals (youths and adults) early in their school career to take advantage of a critical period in language and social development. As a matter of fact, interaction with other Deaf people on just a social level does make a huge impact on their development and is a top priority; the earlier the better. Later, Deaf students would tap into Deaf Studies courses to further enrich their lives (e.g., Deaf History, Deaf Literature, Issues in the Deaf Community).

Alan elaborated on his list of reasons for why it is important to incorporate Deaf Studies in schools:

> There's one simple reason: for Deaf pride. It means including in the curriculum "Deaf people who have succeeded"; where Deaf people are from; sign language; and all other aspects of our heritage. All of that is important for the Deaf child. Deaf Studies in schools for the Deaf help in the identity formation of Deaf children.

Yet Alan expressed his fear about the overemphasis on the Deaf part as he felt that they have to get on with life and school. "Deaf is part of their experience, understanding of who they are as a Deaf person. But I don't want to overemphasize it," Alan said, in a cautionary manner. "Deaf power builds negative feelings inside of the children against the hearing world. I saw that happen. I find that very dangerous." He stated that the oppression swings from one extreme to the other. For this very reason, Alan was not in favor of Deaf Studies curricula and continued on to say: "It's okay to be Deaf. It's okay. And Deafness is a way of life for these people, but it can be a nuisance and an inconvenience."

Felicia claimed it is very important to establish a Deaf Studies curriculum. It's about their own history, their culture, and their heritage. The curriculum allows them to make strong connections to their life experience and build self-pride. Many ethnic groups promoted their awareness by establishing things like Black Pride Week or Chicano Heritage Month. They also created textbooks about their history and heritage. Their goals were to help children develop self-esteem and an understanding of their heritage. "Deaf children are not exposed to that and have difficulties in developing a Deaf identity." To reduce their feelings of inferiority, she felt that a Deaf Studies curriculum is what they really need. Felicia suggested this approach:

> You can incorporate different subject matters into the Deaf Studies curriculum. You can teach Deaf Studies even through math. When they learn about percentages in math class, you can

raise a question about the percentage of Deaf people attending a residential school as compared with a mainstream program and how to calculate that.

One could talk about the different events that happened in the Deaf world throughout
history. Deaf students could do research papers with the application of their own Deaf
experience. Felicia was well prepared to summarize the importance of the Deaf Studies
curricula.

Bonnie said that she could see the benefits of a Deaf Studies curriculum and the
positive impact that it would have on Deaf learners by "helping Deaf children understand their own identity and accept themselves." She also felt that they could access
their Deaf heritage through a Deaf Studies curriculum. In turn, it might help hearing
people not only recognize them as a minority group but also accept them as people.
"It's an education for hearing people and Deaf people alike," Bonnie said, firmly and af-
firmatively. "It's the purpose of learning, and it facilitates that."

"They can learn about Deaf culture and figure out who they are," Glenn said. He
took the position that a Deaf Studies curriculum is important. "They analyze the world
around them and where they stand based on knowing who they are and having that
identity." One's sense of strength and sense of self allows him or her to better handle different situations. He observed that some students who have not had a strong identity or
a foundation tend to have a hard time dealing with Deaf issues and become frustrated.
Much later, after they have struggled with them, they realize it's not just a Deaf-hearing
issue. It might have been about other things that had to do with communication in the
home when they were children. They could not figure these things out for themselves.
They thought it was something that went wrong because of their deafness. In reality,
they were not having a complete understanding of who they were as Deaf people until
much later in life. "If a Deaf Studies curriculum was incorporated into these schools,"
Glenn said, stressing that it would attribute positively to Deaf people, "they would experience less agitation against hearing people." He added that the preservation of Deaf
Culture and Deaf community is a very important step for passing Deaf-related information on to younger generations: "If they don't receive the information as younger children, they miss out until much later as Deaf adults." This kind of cycle happens so often
with many Deaf people. "It would benefit everyone a lot if they started early," Glenn said
emphatically.

"I think it's very important! I wish that my Deaf daughter had exposure to a Deaf
Studies curriculum in her school," Helen said rather plaintively. "She doesn't, so I teach
it at home." She tells her stories relating to Deaf history. For example, Helen related a
story about a Deaf architect who designed many beautiful buildings and graduated
from Gallaudet. She took her to see plays conducted in sign language. Helen incorporated Deaf Studies in her home environment for her daughter. "It's not just about exposure for her to community events but I also support and affirm my daughter's Deaf
identity," she concluded.

For Black History month, Martin Luther King Day is celebrated so that children who
are of African American descent can take pride in the fact that there are people from history who, like them, are black and are acclaimed and honored. "The black experience
for black children is akin to the Deaf experience for Deaf children," Debbie summarized

poignantly. "They need to know about their history, their culture, and their people. I would say that a Deaf Studies curriculum would definitely be a valuable inclusion in schools."

"[Deaf Studies] should be paramount for all d/Deaf people of varying degrees of hearing loss," Edward said as one thought, but then he turned and assumed a different position. "To just inundate a hard-of-hearing person with ASL would be inappropriate." He suggested another approach, "We need to look at them individually and design a program for them so later on they will be able to discuss all aspects of Deaf Studies and Deaf culture." In the final outcome, they would know what their preferences and choices would be. Deaf people generally did not know anything about their own deafness, which led to the establishment of Deaf Studies, with the hope of helping them become more aware of their Deaf experience. "It is very, very important," was Edward's answer. He said, with deeper consideration, that the residential schools have had Deaf Studies since the early to mid-1800s. It was more of a natural occurrence through conversations and interactions, but it was never introduced formally into the classroom. By having Deaf role models around these schools, Deaf schools, so to speak, already had Deaf Studies programs. When Edward talked about Deaf Studies for residential schools, mainstream programs, Gallaudet University, a public university, he emphasized the fact that Deaf Studies differs from one venue to another. If you take away Deaf Studies from a person, Edward indicated that he would consider it a crime, because an education in Deaf Studies could make a difference for Deaf people. "Language and culture go hand in hand," was his closing remark.

Deaf Studies, Carl strongly believed, "will encourage deaf children to accept themselves as Deaf people, to develop a Deaf identity, to understand what ASL means, and to appreciate Deaf role models." Many deaf children did not have these understandings. They might think they are the only deaf person out there. "That's wrong. They need to know Deaf people can do anything. We have Deaf doctors, we have Deaf engineers, and so on. There are many choices. There are no limitations," Carl said, beaming with positive assertion.

Through the Deaf Studies curriculum, Deaf individuals begin to internalize who they are and accept themselves as Deaf people. In addition, they will develop a greater sense of pride in themselves and their culture, thus taking a more active part in society and serving as role models for the generations to follow. By utilizing a cultural perspective rather than a disability model, Deaf communities can, if properly promoted, increase their political influence in the bureaucracy and legislation affecting Deaf people.

Any Deaf individual who does not support the incorporation of a Deaf Studies curriculum in Deaf educational settings may be labeled as a dysconscious audist because an act of opposing the Deaf Studies curriculum limits Deaf individuals from expanding the Deaf perspectives.

This section has provided some insights into the views of the eight Deaf adults of Deaf parents on two topics of discussion: Simultaneous Communication and the Deaf Studies Curriculum. The similarities and differences in the responses of the eight Deaf adults of Deaf parents were noted. In many ways, their responses were kaleidoscopic. In the broadest sense, the personal views they expressed were related to and shaped by the formation of their Deaf consciousness. Not all eight individuals had a strong stance in their Deafcentricity, even though all of them possessed some degree of a Deaf identity that had roots in their familial upbringings. All of them were fluent in the use of American Sign Language, yet some supportive of SimCom as a primary means of communication in the Deaf community.

Some were not comfortable with the importance of a Deaf Studies school curriculum for fear that it might cultivate in deaf children a rebellious attitude toward hearing people, while the others cherished it in hopes of helping deaf children increase their Deaf consciousness (and confidence) in order to become active participants in rightfully seeking their place in the world. Deaf Studies recognizes the existence of Deaf Culture and, to varying degrees, accepts it as an important aspect of socialization to strengthen the process of linguistic and cultural development. Their actions, beliefs, views, and perceptions toward the centrality of Deaf identity, along with American Sign Language, differed in some respects.

Deaf adults of Deaf parents who are college educated, knowledgeable about the Deaf World, and leaders in their endeavors supposedly comprise the most "progressive" group of the Deaf population. They function as Deaf bilingual-bicultural individuals who accept the realities of coexisting with hearing people. The weakening of their Deaf identities was present in some of them even though all of them continued to see themselves as big D Deaf, fluent users of ASL, and members of American Deaf Culture. Under the constant siege of audism, some of them, even with their clear thinking on their Deaf experience and their positive Deaf upbringing, had a weakened resistance to audism. This was demonstrated by their acceptance of audistic-generated practices. More often than not, they did not realize that they had internalized audist values and that these values had altered their perception. Such effects on the Deaf consciousness, in which they accept dominant hearing norms and privileges, may be best described as dysconscious audism.

Critical Pieces of Evidence for the Existence of Dysconscious Audism

The constant pressure of audism on the Deaf world brought out the salient features of dysconscious audism in some of the Deaf adults of Deaf parents. Figure 13.3 visually demonstrates the weakening of Deaf identity through the siege of audism. The critical pieces of evidence for the existence of dysconscious audism emerged in the interviews with the eight Deaf adults of Deaf parents. From the full study, following are some examples of dysconscious audism as depicted in their responses to questions on the cause of dysconscious audism.

Dysconscious audism disempowers Deaf people from becoming liberated.
- Lack of full support for Deaf Studies programs
- Lack of full support for ASL
- Acceptance of a cure for deafness

Dysconscious audism disables Deaf people from expressing Deaf cultural pride.
- Danger of offending hearing people
- Belief that heavy participation in the Deaf community is limiting
- The value of Deaf Studies courses being questioned

Dysconscious audism intimidates Deaf people and limits their promotion of the Deaf perspective.
- Fear of challenging hearing people's authority
- Denial of the impact of audism on the individual
- Lack of full support for Deafcentric curricula

Dysconscious audism hinders Deaf people from attaining quality education.
- Support for communication methods favored by hearing people
- Acceptance of English-based signing system
- Obsession with the idea of English mastery as a critical foundation for education

Dysconscious audism denies Deaf people full acceptance of ASL.
- Belief in the paramount importance of English
- Support of Simultaneous Communication
- Tolerance for different choices of communication methods with Deaf individuals

Dysconscious audism weakens Deaf people in the development of their Deaf identity.
- Acceptance of the term "hearing-impaired"
- Lack of resistance to the label "disability"
- Avoidance of fighting back against audism

Few hearing people understand what it means to truly be Deaf. To have a Deaf identity is equivalent to achieving a status of human being in the fullest sense. The weakening of the Deaf identity often causes them to feel like lesser human beings and to become more alien to the hearing world as well. It is ironic that deaf people who are shaped into "hearing people" are often less connected to the hearing world because they become marginalized in that society as well. Discrimination against Deaf people tends to increase when Deaf people are perceived in the medical model of deafness. The cultural model of deafness, on the other hand, defines Deaf people as contributing members of American society; educates Deaf people to be fully cognizant of the deep meanings of their rich Deaf Culture; creates a better environment for Deaf people to live in; and transforms their voices from silence to vibrancy, even with the full blast of audism working against them.

Being raised by Deaf parents, their lives are structured at a very early age on the positive possibilities of their future, a very sharp contrast to the often negative message passed down to d/Deaf children raised by hearing parents, who echo the sentiments of

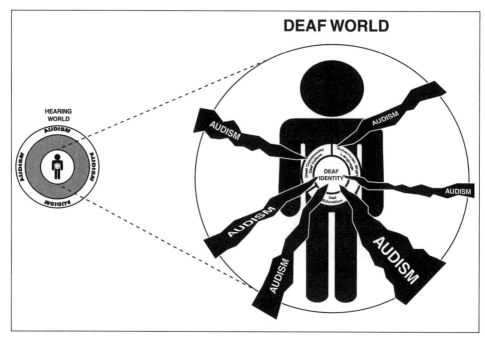

Figure 13.3. The weakening of Deaf Identity: dysconscious audism.

the larger hearing society. Unlike the barrier d/Deaf children of hearing parents experience at home, Deaf children of Deaf parents experience accessible communication at the earliest stage. The lives of successful Deaf adults of Deaf parents could unlock some of the mysteries associated with raising d/Deaf children by providing hearing people with greater insights and perspectives on issues related to Deaf identity, language, community/culture, and education. Needless to say, language, culture, and identity are interconnected and important to a person's existence. It is even more important to Deaf people's existence because they grow up and experience the larger society in a minority role.

The theorizing of dysconscious audism has stressed the importance of understanding the oppression, barriers, and discrimination that are caused by audism. An important link between audism and dysconscious audism can be traced to the power of hearing people over Deaf people in the domains of education, medicine, law, and the media. When Deaf people get a chance to deal with those issues within the aforementioned domains, they often find themselves brushed aside because they do not have the power and do not even share with hearing people the same language and culture of power. These factors have serious implications for the Deaf community, especially when the imposition on Deaf people of hearing people's discriminatory views intensifies and manifests into action, such as with cochlear implants. From a greater awareness of dysconscious audism, an increasing power of Deaf discourse could result. A greater Deaf consciousness and stronger stance taken by Deaf people may ensue and influence the Deaf-hearing dialogue. Deaf people must be clear on their values and positions before they initiate dialogue with hearing people on Deaf matters.

Arden Neisser, a hearing woman with no prior knowledge of the Deaf world, Deaf people, and deafness, made a journey into Deaf America in the early 1980s for several years before writing a book, *The Other Side of Silence: Sign Language and the Deaf Community in America.* In the Prologue section of her book, she states with both eloquence and magnificence her thoughts about Deaf people:

> Although the deaf live in a world without sound, it is the same world we all inhabit. To the problems of living in the environment they bring the full range of human resourcefulness, intelligence, and ingenuity. They have created for themselves a language that is not only comparable to all the world's great languages, but is perfectly adapted to their lives and needs. They do not speculate long about the nature of sound, or the mechanics of normal hearing. No living creature organizes its behavior around something it doesn't have. The deaf perceive the world through skilled and practiced eyes; language is at their fingertips.[10]

The life stories and thoughts of the eight Deaf adults of Deaf parents would have been lost if they had not been willing to participate in "culture talking."[11] Their openness about their "cultural" upbringings revealed the richness of their Deaf experiences. Their voices came alive and broadened our understanding of their lived experiences as Deaf adults of Deaf parents. In return, they had time to reflect on their understanding of "Who am I?" Too often, Deaf life stories are not recorded or considered important by the hearing world. As a result, it is nearly impossible to penetrate and positively influence the educational system in which educational planning for deaf children could better be implemented if these life stories were considered. These eight Deaf adults of Deaf parents may understandably not be indicative of all Deaf adults of Deaf parents. Still, they have not only supplied but also illuminated vital information regarding the lives and perspectives of Deaf adults of Deaf parents in today's world.

In conclusion, the full recognition of the Deaf identity is a vital step for making real changes to see that Deaf people are treated as human beings and as first-class citizens of the societies in which they live. The affirmation of the Deaf identity enables Deaf people to gain confidence in challenging audist practices. Deaf identity, Deaf community/Deaf Culture, ASL, and Deafcentric education must be respected and affirmed. To prevent exposing Deaf people to hearing ethnocentric attitudes, hearing people must be conscious of their past action. In order to combat audism, hearing people need to reach out to Deaf adults for the development of a partnership before navigating further into the Deaf world. The eight Deaf adults of Deaf parents must be profoundly thanked for their courage to share everything they could for this humankind. What they have done is provide a map with which to better understand the Deaf experience, one that was drawn up with their own burgeoning consciousness of the effects of dysconscious audism.

Notes

1. Joyce King, "Dysconscious Racism: The Cultural Politics of Critiquing Ideology and Identity," in *Critical White Studies: Looking Behind the Mirror,* ed. Richard Delegado and Jean Stefancic (Philadelphia: Temple University Press, 1998), 128–32.
2. World Around You, interview with Rachel Stone, "A 'Lucky One' Remembers," September 2005, http://clerccenter.gallaudet.edu/WorldAroundYou/mar-apr2000/interviews.html.
3. These various Web sites have been collected into a single site, which may be accessed at http://

www.deafnotes.com. Deafnotes, "Unfair Firing of California School for the Deaf-Riverside Super-intendent" (June 2001), http://www.deafnotes.com/bb/ubb/Forum3/HTML/000085.html.

4. H-Dirksen L. Bauman, "Audism: Exploring the Metaphysics of Oppression," *Journal of Deaf Studies and Deaf Education* 9, no. 2 (2004): 239–46.

5. Douglas Baynton, *Forbidden Signs: American Culture and the Campaign against Sign Language* (Chicago: University of Chicago Press, 1996); Paddy Ladd, *Understanding Deaf Culture: In Search of Deafhood* (Clevedon, UK: Multilingual Matters, 2003); Harlan Lane, Robert Hoffmeister, and Benjamin Bahan, *A Journey into the Deaf-World* (San Diego: DawnSignPress, 1996); Owen Wrigley, *The Politics of Deafness* (Washington, D.C.: Gallaudet University Press, 1996).

6. Edna Levine, *The Psychology of Deafness: Techniques of Appraisal for Rehabilitation* (New York: Columbia University Press, 1960); Harlan Lane, *The Mask of Benevolence: Disabling the Deaf Community* (San Diego: DawnSignPress, 1999).

7. Eugenie Nicole Gertz, "Dysconscious Audism and Critical Deaf Studies: Deaf Crit's Analysis of Unconscious Internalization of Hegemony within the Deaf Community" (PhD diss., University of California, Los Angeles, 2003). This is also the source for following quotations from the eight adult Deaf children of Deaf parents.

8. Katherine Jankowski, *Deaf Empowerment: Emergence, Struggle, and Rhetoric* (Washington, D.C.: Gallaudet University Press, 1997); Lane, *Mask of Benevolence.*

9. Gloria Marmor and Laura Petitto, "Simultaneous Communication in the Classroom: How Well Is English Grammar Represented?" *Sign Language Studies* 23 (1979): 99–136; Charlotte Baker, "How Does 'Sim-Com' Fit into a Bilingual Approach to Education?" in *Proceedings of the Second National Symposium on Sign Language Research and Teaching,* ed. Frank Caccamise and Doin Hicks (Silver Spring, Md.: National Association of the Deaf, 1980), 13–26; Charlotte Baker-Shenk, "Sociolinguistics: Simultaneous Communication," in *Gallaudet Encyclopedia of Deaf People and Deafness,* vol. 3, *S-Z Index,* ed. John. V. van Cleve (New York: McGraw-Hill, 1987), 176–79.

10. Arden Neisser, *The Other Side of Silence: Sign Language and the Deaf Community in America* (New York: Alfred A. Knopf, 1983), 5.

11. The term "culture talking" is elaborated by Tom Humphries in this volume.

14. *The Burden of Racism and Audism*

LINDSAY DUNN

THIS CHAPTER will attempt to raise issues in the form of a debate about culture, social justice, and identity. It is based partly on conversations with hearing and Deaf friends and is intended to raise critical and controversial dialogues on the twin conditions of race and audism that are heavy burdens on Deaf people of color in general and black Deaf people in particular.

The author is a Deaf black South African who is married to a hearing African American; they have three South African–American children who are hearing. The author grew up in a multicultural and multilingual environment in both rural and township areas of South Africa. He became deaf from spinal meningitis at age eleven and acquired sign language skills at age thirteen (Irish Sign Language used at the Dominican School for the Deaf in Cape Town, which he attended for five years).[1] He learned American Sign Language (ASL) at twenty-one when he enrolled at Gallaudet University.

The antagonist in the dialogue is a white hearing male (WHM).

WHM: You know, the pharmaceutical industry has made great strides in introducing various new products over the years with great potential to alleviate social problems.

LD: Absolutely, I most certainly concur. Hopefully there will be a cure for cancer and the global HIV/AIDS epidemic in my lifetime.

WHM: Yes, but I am referring to the potential benefits of melanin, hair strengtheners, and even hair dying products.

LD: Oh, I see. But I am not sure I understand where this is leading to.

WHM: Well, actually since you and I have been in conflict over our views regarding the status of black people and minorities in this country as well as the status of deaf and disabled people, I have given great thought about the possibilities of medicine and technology as possible solutions to social problems.

LD: You are definitely kidding. Right?

WHM: Well, actually no. I would assume you would agree with me. Don't you?

LD: Please elaborate; I think I am losing you here.

WHM: I mean, let's look at it this way: it is definitely an advantage to be a normal hearing white person in society today, wouldn't you agree?

LD: Meaning that is a disadvantage to be black and deaf, is that what you mean?

WHM: Absolutely my friend; so you get the gist of my thinking?

LD: Actually, the isms, racism and audism, appear to be the first words entering my mind right now and frankly I hope I am exaggerating.

WHM: Oh come on, won't you agree that your children would live a more satisfying life if you had them looking white and don't you think that deaf children would integrate more easily and comfortably in society if they were implanted with cochlear implants from the time they were diagnosed as being deaf?

LD: No.

Perplexed, my friend shook his head and looked at me in consternation.

WHM: But my friend, affirmative action, multiculturalism, diversity, Deaf Culture, and all that bunk is really nothing but political correctness and such fads are just temporary attempts to penetrate the conscience of the dominant race. Frankly, I think you are abusing your children if you deny them this opportunity to become normal white children.

LD: Abusing my children by raising them as black children in America? Are you also suggesting parents who raise deaf children are abusing their children by allowing them to use sign language as their primary mode of communication and rejecting cochlear implants?

WHM: Absolutely. For one thing, there is no real hope for black folks and other minorities to ever gain equality in American society. It is just the way this society is designed. From the very beginning the idea was for this to be a white-dominated society and nonwhites were basically always going to be "guests" invited to serve at the beck and call of white superiors. It is just the reality of things. Just look at labor statistics and you find black and disabled people have high unemployment rates; just look at academic scores whether SAT, LSAT, GMAT, or whatever, and white students consistently rank well above black students. It is a fact that prime neighborhoods will always be the domain of the privileged white majority, and wealth will most certainly remain concentrated within this ethnic group wherever they are in the world. I mean I am sure you have read Charles Murray's *The Bell Curve*[2] haven't you? While I agree with the black Republican J. C. Watts[3] who noted that affirmative action programs were one of a very few legal tools available to black folks that gave black folks a chance to squeeze inside the door of opportunity, the reality is that these doors will shut down. I envision the same fate for the Americans with Disabilities Act. Disabled people are a burden on society and demand too much in terms of resources and only remind society of imperfections we must eliminate in order to create a perfect world. Don't you agree that the recent mapping of the genetic code is a major scientific breakthrough? I am absolutely ecstatic as I ponder the medical possibilities.

LD: You mean such as cloning and its potential to eliminate black people and people with disabilities?

WHM: Well, since there is no benefit for being either, I certainly believe cloning offers society the best potential for eliminating burdensome conditions.

LD: Burdensome conditions? I have read Murray but have you read Bahan, Hoffmeister, and Lane's *A Journey into the Deaf-World?*[4]

I was reminded of a discussion at the National Conference on Race and Ethnicity (NCORE) conference in 2003 where Dr. Francis Kendall gave a workshop on "Being an Ally as a Person with White Privilege: This is Not Just About Being Friends."[5] Dr. Kendall pointed out that: "we (white people) have been given unearned privileges that affect

each of our lives every minute of every day." The effect of these privileges brings nothing but bliss to the holder and nothing but misery for those who are not so privileged. It
is the law of the haves and have-nots and it is necessary for this equilibrium to be maintained at all costs. So why would I deprive my children of melanin, hair strengtheners,
and perhaps an eye implant to make their eyes blue? Why would I not want my children
to enjoy this unearned privileged existence?

WHM: Surely you cannot force your children into a "pseudo Black Culture." Assimilation into mainstream America and into the majority (white) culture was the only way
black people could be liberated from the bondage of their race.

LD: Wait a minute. The world was already quite familiar with examples of cultural
genocide and eugenics.

WHM: That my friend is a fat load of bunk. If the Jews had assimilated into German
society and behaved like Germans rather than Jews with their own separate places of
worship, communities, and business, there would never have been a Holocaust. They
would have assimilated and become German.

LD: Are you aware you are teetering on rather precarious grounds with this insinua-
tion? For one thing, the majority of people in this world is neither white nor speaks English as their first language and therefore, since white people are a global minority, there
is the possibility that the nonwhite majority will eventually determine the minority's
fate. I hope you are not suggesting that Hitler's solution was rational and that majority
cultures ought to use the same methods to eradicate minority cultures. After all, that
would be tantamount to you suggesting that this be an option for the world's nonwhite
majority to solve the "problem" of the Caucasian minority.

WHM: Your argument has merit; however, because of the intellectual superiority of
the white race, power was vested in this minority white race for reasons you and I could
not possibly fathom and therefore it was necessary to colonize or better yet, eradicate
the nonwhite threat to protect white liberty, wealth, and the pursuit of happiness. The
superior ability to harness the power of destructive violence will maintain white dominance for as long as the white race exists.

LD: So are you suggesting that your race is one that acknowledges its propensity to
dominate over others forcefully with the weapons of violence, destruction, propaganda,
colonization, and other "tools" usually associated with those you refer to as uncivilized?
Is this not terrorism and therefore does it not imply that your race is no better than
"terrorists"?

WHM: Actually no, I have never looked at this issue as uncivilized nor as a form of
terror. It is merely dominance by the superior. I guess civilization and terrorism are relative concepts. Whoever has power is free to define them according to their whim.

I shook my head in disbelief at such a response.

LD: So given that you believe that the majority values must dominate, you would
find it justifiable for the biomedical and biotechnology industries to seek solutions to
remove disabled people from society? Is that right?

WHM: I most definitely believe that this will create a more harmonious society.
Cochlear implant technology was only the beginning, and biotechnology will eventually
eradicate imperfections in human beings. I believe that one day, even homosexuality

will be eradicated from society. After all, how does such deviant behavior benefit a heterogeneous society? The fields of psychology are going to be obsolete as genetic engineering would ensure perfect children would be born in a world where it was possible to design a nation that was uniform in its uniformity—blond, blue-eyed, rose cheeked, heterosexual, with IQs that embodied the superiority of their whiteness and physical prowess that would render the accomplishments of today's athletes nothing more than puny in comparison. This is simply human progress and as long as humanity possesses the capacity to invent, create, and genetically modify any living organism, there is no limit to what humans will ultimately achieve.

LD: But wouldn't this scientific industry exhibited by human beings ultimately demand subservient uniformity, or will human diversity in all its awesome variety be lost as a vital ingredient in this mystery we call human life?

I certainly could not concur with my friend on any of his points. Then I pondered the "burden of my race" and somehow I did not wish to be, and could not imagine myself being, anyone other than the black deaf male that I am proud to be. Although I was born hearing, I have lived the majority of my life as a deaf person, and yet I do not consider myself imperfect or inferior in any way to my friend. In regards to my deafness, I consider myself unique in that I am able to see the world without the nuisance of "noise" or the false security of a privilege not earned but granted solely by being born into a certain race. I see myself as a contribution to this gorgeous human mosaic that makes our world vibrant and stimulating. However, it is a heavy burden to be a pawn in a chess game where physicians attempt to make a cyborg out of me. I am rather tired of being a pawn in this game in which someone else gets the satisfaction of manipulating my life in order to savor the delight of power over me simply because of my race and inability to hear.

Charles Mills, in his book *The Racial Contract* states that "white misunderstanding, misrepresentation, evasion, and self-deception on matters related to race are among the most pervasive mental phenomena of the past few hundred years, a cognitive and moral economy psychically required for conquest, colonization, and enslavement. And these phenomena are in no way accidental, but prescribed by the terms of the Racial Contract, which requires a certain schedule of structured blindness, and opacities in order to establish and maintain white polity."[6]

Thinking about such a powerful assessment of those who are conditioned to colonize, conquer, and enslave, I pondered my own state of mind and my position in a society where I was already handicapped by being a black male in a society that fears my kind like the plague. According to a Justice Policy Institute publication, *Reducing Disproportionate Minority Imprisonment,* black youth represent a disproportionate number in our prison system. The Justice Policy Institute states that "The number of black men in jail or prison has grown fivefold in the past 20 years, to the point where more black men are behind bars than are enrolled in colleges or universities."[7] The study also noted that "the increase in the black male prison population coincides with the prison construction boom that began in 1980. At that time, three times more black men were enrolled in institutions of higher learning than behind bars."

What does this imply? That our young black males are better off in prison than in college? That society is safer with the black man in confinement? That whiteness must be protected from this threat to liberty, wealth, and the pursuit of happiness? Is this not the same colonizing, enslaving, and conquering tendency that historically permeates Western history? (I shook my head in disgust at this thought.) I did not think melanin or cochlear implants were a justifiable response to deafness just as Hitler's idea of the "Final Solution" was unpalatable to every decent human being anywhere on earth. My race was obviously a major disadvantage in a society that sees me more as a threat than as an equal member of society.

WHM: My friend, as difficult as it is to acknowledge that your race is a burden on you and presumably on society that fears your ilk, your deafness does not offer an opportunity to lighten this burden but rather, I believe it further hinders your ability to integrate and assimilate into privileged society. Let's take, for instance, the fact that deaf people in general read at the 3.8 grade level. In a society that demands advanced literacy and numeracy skills in order to survive in a rapidly expanding technology-based society, what are your chances of living a decent life? Surely you must give great consideration to the alternatives that science offers. Deaf education has failed and only offers the misguided idea of a "pseudo deaf cultural identity" just as the failure of multicultural-based education for black children has only lead to a misguided pseudo black culture that is steeped in anti-Western historical and cultural thought. Neither prepares you for the realities of modern society.

LD: Wait a minute; I am not sure I understand what you are implying here. Are you suggesting that deaf education, and education of black children in particular, is the problem?

WHM: Absolutely.

LD: In other words, you are implying that auditory-based, Eurocentric education would be most appropriate in enabling deaf and black people to better integrate into society.

WHM: As an alternative to eradicating the twin conditions, yes, I would suggest that as the most viable alternative. The oral method after all, has afforded deaf people better access to the hearing world.

LD: Are you implying that sign language is a hindrance to the effective education of deaf children? And that we ought to adopt the oral method?

WHM: It definitely has some advantages in that it is auditory/verbal-based and therefore affords deaf children the same quality education as hearing nonsigners. Don't you agree?

LD: I am not an expert in linguistics but I am rather certain that education via one's native language is preferable to education in a foreign language. Could you imagine yourself, an American English user, going through college using German or French in all your subjects? Wouldn't that be difficult for you and isn't that similar to a deaf person using the oral method rather than his/her native sign language?

WHM: Well, fortunately I never had to deal with that hypothetical question; after all this is an *English*-speaking nation and I hope it will always remain so. After all, English is the political, social, economic, and scientific language of our modern global society.

LD: That is not necessarily the case in the rest of the world. In my native South Africa, the average South African spoke three to seven languages and it was also common among Europeans to speak English, French, and Spanish and perhaps even German.

Obviously multilingualism is possible among human beings; why is it a problem for Americans to be comfortable communicating in other languages? Many Americans speak Spanish, French, and other indigenous Asian, European, and African languages, so why would it be a problem for them to also learn sign language?

WHM: But sign language is *not* auditory based and therefore cannot constitute the academic or scientific definition of a language.

LD: Are you familiar with the work of Dr. William Stokoe, Dr. Ursula Bellugi, Dr. Carol Padden, or Dr. Harlan Lane?

WHM: No! But I can imagine that they are all simply attempting to justify the existence of a "Deaf Culture" and to do that, it is necessary to prove that this language of signs is evidence of the existence of the culture; correct?

LD: So what then is it about this language of signs that actually allows us to understand a signed or sign-interpreted reading of Shakespeare, Virginia Woolf, Frantz Fanon, Toni Morrison, Paulo Freire, James Baldwin, Amy Tan, Harlan Lane, and Oliver Sacks? What then is it about this language of sign that allows us to enjoy a theatrical performance that is either sign-interpreted or performed by skilled performers in ASL? If this language of sign makes this possible, why is it not accepted as equal? After all, the end objective being to understand the dialogue and therefore the story being told is ultimately achieved in both mediums. How can one be accepted as a language and the other not if the end result is the same? Didn't humans communicate nonverbally by means of gestures prior to developing verbal communication systems unique to their ethnocultural enclaves?

My friend hesitated a bit and seemed a bit confused.

WHM: You mean deaf people can follow *Othello* in sign language? But why would they be interested in theater? After all, theatrical performances place heavy emphasis on sound.

LD: Actually one of my favorite activities during summer is going to the Carter Barron Amphitheater in Washington, D.C., or a "Shakespeare in the Park" play in Central Park, New York City, which often either have ASL-using actors or are sign interpreted.

WHM: I don't mean to sound rude or ignorant, but I really have never seen black deaf folks at any theatrical performance I have ever attended—do you folks really go to dramatic events?

LD: Well, actually, I thought Phylicia Rashad's recent performance in *A Raisin in the Sun*[8] on Broadway was superlative. But I think Phyllis Frelich's performances are classics. After all, she is a native signer and, like Rashad, an award-winning actress also.

He was now genuinely perplexed. His brow furrowed in deep contemplation.

According to his reasoning, deaf people are technically, functionally illiterate and on top of that, being a black male, statistically I should either be in jail or dead, not enjoying cultural activities that are normally the domain of the "cultured white elite." It was inconceivable. Furthermore, I do not even have a cochlear implant or hearing aids so how could I possibly even understand cultural events that demand hearing? It was obvious that my friend had little understanding about language and culture.

> All communication is culturally bound. The very means of communicating (writing, the use of a telephone, person-to-person interaction) are affected by unwritten cultural rules and, in turn, influence how we learn. One of the greatest sources of miscommunication among people who are culturally different from one another is communication style.[9]

However, despite my admiration for Phylicia Rashad and enjoyment of sign-interpreted performances, I still would rather attend a naturally signed performance than an interpreted one. Our language is vibrant and expressive and, in a sense, enables us to enjoy visual performance mediums in a dynamic manner.

Identity Development Theories

Although there is much work already done on ASL and Deaf Culture, there is much needed to be done to explore the phenomenon of identity development among deaf people. This is especially essential in light of the fact that much research and literature on deafness has been from a Eurocentric perspective and mainly based on the Euro-American experience. Neil Glickman has done an outstanding job of developing a Deaf Identity Development Scale (DIDS),[10] which is based on the work of Dr. Janet Helms and others. It is often necessary to look at the parallels with the African American experience to understand the experience of Deaf people in a culture that oppresses those different from the majority.

We like to think of our visual language as expressive, dynamic, emotionally intense, and demonstrative just like black folks view their use of the English language. A sign-interpreted performance featuring well-trained sign language interpreters enables us to derive intense satisfaction from visual arts performances. My encounter with my protagonist suggests that cultural and social experiences apparently made it more likely that our perspectives would differ.

Janet Helms was concerned with the dominant bias in counseling psychology, which focused on the pathology of blacks. Helms found "from the experience of her White colleagues that their relationships with people of color were so rarefied that they resembled those who experience culture shock when visiting or living in another country."[11] This appears to describe my protagonist's response to my arguments that deaf people are in fact normal, intelligent human beings who enjoyed the same pleasures he assumed were beyond us, especially black deaf people, given our race and deafness. It further reminded me of the many stories black deaf folks have of their encounters with white deaf people in situations such as Deaf clubs or organization events where the black deaf person is perhaps the only person of color in the room or one of a few. The most recurring comment is "I am so happy to see you here. I hope you can bring more of your people to come here next time." I usually ask "Why?" and the answer invariably suggests that it is my responsibility to promote their event within the black Deaf community as if I am some official representative rather than just an individual accompanying my white friends to a Deaf club for the very same reasons my friends are attending. It's as if I am some foreigner and the people here are unsure as to how to respond to my presence at their establishment. Helms's model on black identity development is based on four stages: preencounter, encounter, immersion/emersion, and internalization.

In my particular experience where I became deafened at age eleven and had no prior encounter with deaf people, my preencounter experience was one of apprehension, confusion, and fear of a possible world without sound. When I first encountered deaf people at the Dominican School for the Deaf in Cape Town, South Africa, apprehension was replaced with awe, excitement, and determination to master this language that would free me from this new world I was entering. My attitudes to hearing people changed somewhat in that my dependence was reduced and my internalized assumptions of hearing people, which were similar to my assumptions of white people based on my experience being born into a segregated nation, changed drastically. The Irish Sign Language, which was used at my school, afforded me an opportunity to engage in dialogues regarding racism and audism and how these twin vices affect my life.

My subsequent immersion into this world and new consciousness was almost parallel with the Black Consciousness Movement of my generation, which culminated in our rejection of the perceived inferiority of black people as a race. I was now rejecting this perceived inferiority of myself as a deaf person. I went on to attend a hearing high school without interpreters or note-taking support and did exceptionally well because my consciousness was changed and I no longer saw myself as deficient in comparison to my hearing peers. Rather than internalizing negative stereotypes of my experiences under a brutal apartheid regime and an ignorant hearing world, I found liberation and hope that there was a very important place for me in this world. I was beginning to reclaim my humanity, and this was absolutely liberating.

Those of us who are socialized into Deaf Culture through sign language and early interaction with adult members of the Deaf community tend to have a comfortable sense of ourselves as Deaf people. In families where sign language is used early in our life, we have a social environment where our deafness is not perceived as a disabling condition but rather in a similar manner as black people perceive peers who use Ebonics, or native speakers of languages other than English. We participate in cultural activities within the Deaf community, and this in turn leads to our having a greater sense of our cultural self. We are therefore more likely to have a strong sense of awareness of audism and are more likely to respond in the same way people of color respond to oppression. It is no accident therefore that the four student leaders during the Deaf President Now movement were children of Deaf adults and the group of young Deaf men who organized behind the scenes were also mostly children of Deaf adults save for only one. They were socialized into the culture from an early age and were therefore comfortable with their self-concept as normal Deaf individuals and members of a vibrant community.

On the other hand, there are those who reject the concept of a Deaf Culture and a community. They insist that deaf people can be assimilated into the dominant culture's concept of "normal." Rather than acknowledge the validity of sign language as a natural and normal form of communication equal to verbal language, we have proponents of the oral method whose premise is that Deaf people can be taught to speak intelligibly regardless of their degree of hearing loss. I believe this is possible among those with sufficient hearing ability that they are able to make sense of verbal utterances. This conflict regarding the best educational methods for deaf and hard-of-hearing people has continued for over a hundred years and there are very few signs that this debate is reaching a conclusion. Proponents of inclusion believe that every disabled child should be receiving the same education in the same environment as nondisabled students. While there are conflicts in regards to the definition of disabled within the general disability community and the Deaf/hard-of-hearing community, deaf and hard-of-hearing children are the ones victimized by political sparring among various groups. It is often difficult for disability activists to fathom the reality that deaf people are extremely disadvantaged in environments designed for audio-based learning except in the case of those who have sufficient hearing to manage to some degree. However, there are those who have enough hearing to manage in a one-on-one social environment and can also utilize sign language interpreters for larger group encounters.

Mainstreaming assumes that deaf students must interact with "normal" hearing kids and therefore adapt the values of the "normal" society. Jean Kim refers to Sue and Sue whose model, she suggests, presents what is essentially a personality typology in their description of the Asian American identity development process.[12] The three-part model consists of traditionalist, marginal, and the bicultural. According to their theory, the traditionalist places family first and has strong traditional Chinese cultural values. These may encounter conflicts when majority cultures are perceived to conflict with these traditionalist values. In the second example, the marginal person attempts to mainstream and adapt/assimilate into mainstream culture. This person finds it necessary to earn acceptance from the majority culture and often experiences conflict when they find that they are not equally or fully accepted by the majority regardless of their academic, economic, or social successes. The third part of this model is the bicultural where the traditional values are integrated into the realities of the majority culture. The latter apparently finds a middle ground that fully accepts their ethnic/racial identity while acknowledging the majority culture without attempting to become assimilated into it at the expense of their traditional values.

The black community has a similar experience and history that is well represented with caricatures of so-called Uncle Toms who discover that they are not immune to the same fate as others of their race. We also have those exemplified by the Black Power Movement who attempted to do a complete makeover of their identity. Rather than shiny straightened hair, they let it grow into Afros of all sizes, declined skin lighteners, took up African names, and rejected the "Colored" or "Negro" classification for the terms "Black," "Afro-American," and the present "African American." Then there also are those "tweeners" who value the traditionalist ways of their race and yet are not intimidated by the requirements of successful coexistence in a majority white society. They are able to adapt and move effortlessly between multiple cultures.

The Deaf world has its own examples of these experiences. We have the traditionalists who are invariably referred to as the Big D. These are folks that Padden and Humphries, Bahan, Lane, and Hoffmeister, and others refer to as people who are from Deaf families and attended Deaf schools, and as Kannapell suggests, membership within this group requires not only ASL skills, but shared values, beliefs, and experiences.[13] Members of this group tend to have a strong sense of identity as Deaf members of society and do not consider themselves disabled but rather refer to themselves as a cultural-linguistic minority. We also have people who have a negative self-image attributed to their deafness and often feel isolated and inferior. They grow up believing that they must become "hearing" in order to assimilate into society. They reduce contact with other deaf people or behave as if they are "not like them" and, because they have had cochlear implants and speech training, are more "hearing-like" than "them," and therefore should be afforded more privileges in society. This conflict is at the root of the Deaf community's struggle to gain legitimacy in society's eyes. Since a greater number of people with hearing loss are able to "pass," it is often assumed that they are therefore evidence that deafness is a condition that can be fixed.

However, like the "marginals" in Sue and Sue's model, they are also vulnerable to rejection by normal hearing people and experience conflicts in their self-identity. After all, skin lighteners and hair straighteners did benefit many dark-skinned and nappy-haired black people but did not exempt them from experiencing racial discrimination.

In the black community we have what is known as the "brown bag standard" that was used to determine if a black person was light enough to enroll at certain schools, and even a few Historically Black Colleges and Universities (HBCU) at one time used this standard. Ms. Julia Pitt, my longtime assistant in the Office of the President at Gallaudet University and a native of Washington, D.C., told me that she failed the "brown bag test" and could not attend one of the finest public high schools for blacks in the 1960s and was too "black" to be admitted to Howard University. Spike Lee illuminated this problem in his movie *School Daze.*[14] I believe that human deficiencies are the major cause of intolerance and that it was the simple desire to usurp power over others that was the fundamental barrier to peace and brotherhood within our communities and in the global community we are destined to share. Blackness cannot be a problem in itself. Why else would white men, brothers to be exact, kill each other simply for the right to own this human who was black? What was it that even a great American President would love this thing that is black and father children from her? And yet racism has survived centuries and persists to this day. Deafness in itself does not threaten humanity in any manner, and yet it is perceived as a social stigma for reasons that cannot be logically or scientifically justified.

However, I began to consider what might cause us to feel secure or insecure and looked up literature that addressed identity development for insights. Sonia Nieto in her book *The Light in Their Eyes* begins chapter three with this excerpt attributed to Mary Kalantzis, Bill Cope, and Diana Slade from their book *Minority Languages:*

> [We] are not simply bearers of cultures, languages, and histories, with a duty to reproduce them. We are the products of linguistic-cultural circumstances, actors with a capacity to resynthesize what we have been socialized into and to solve new and emerging problems of existence; we are not duty-bound to conserve ancestral characteristics which are not structurally useful. We are both socially determined and creators of human futures.[15]

I thought this aptly described the current attempts to legitimize Deaf Studies. We are, after all, a linguistic-cultural community and we do have the capacity to resynthesize what we have been socialized into believing is our status in society. What then was it that caused us to see differently from the majority that has for many years attempted to describe us? Hardiman and Jackson's Racial Identity Development Theory model suggests that there are five stages, which are as follows:

- Naïve/No Consciousness: unaware of the rewards and sanctions associated with membership in a racial group and with breaking the rules of one's racial group.
- Passive/Active Acceptance: person unaware of own outlook, then when person becomes aware, moves into Active Acceptance where person is conscious of biases and perpetuation of racial stratification occurs.
- Resistance: in this stage person focuses on understanding and resisting the existence of racism and its manifestations (begins to question the status quo).
- Redefinition: redefining own racial group's history and culture.
- Internalization: occurs when people look to internalize a new sense of racial identity not based on or in reaction to the assumptions and functions of racism.[16]

Could this model be used to discuss identity development in deaf children? I believe it is possible. Wing and Rifkin suggest that we all look at the world through the lens of one of the stages of identity development.[17] A hearing person with little or no experience or knowledge about deafness is probably very likely to begin with the Naïve stage; then when he/she begins to understand a little more, they may develop a sense of superiority and perhaps assume that a deaf person's inability to hear automatically suggests that deaf people are inferior to those who can hear. However, interaction and more understanding about deaf people awakens a sense of resistance to prejudice against deaf people, and this hearing person may begin to question assumptions. With a greater sense of understanding of the biases that deaf and hard-of-hearing people endure, this hearing person may begin the redefinition process whereby they may realize a need to review society's assumptions. William Stokoe and Harlan Lane might be useful examples. Stokoe is known to be a poor sign language user and yet it was his breakthrough research on sign language that basically forced a rewrite of old assumptions about sign languages. Dr. Harlan Lane has published powerful treatises in defense of Deaf people and their culture and yet he is a hearing scholar who initially had little knowledge of deafness until his exposure to deafness through his research in sociopsychology led to his redefining hearing views of deafness in his powerful book *When the Mind Hears*.

While the attempts to remove deaf people from the mosaic of humanity will continue to exist, there will also be resistance to these attempts. The Deaf community is resilient and has survived Alexander Graham Bell's eugenicist movement and many other attempts that both preceded and followed Bell. As a resident of a democratic nation, I also concur that individuals have a democratic right to choose a cochlear implant or any other scientific option that may be available in order to become part of the hearing majority. However, I should also have the right to choose my mode of receiving information, which is basically the function of hearing. A child with a cochlear implant will receive it auditorily through artificial means while I could receive the same information through a sign language interpreter or in text form. A child with a cochlear implant would also, like a hearing child, be required to acquire knowledge through the institutions of family, school, and community. The same holds true for a black child and a deaf child. A black child would face barriers due to his/her race while a deaf child would face barriers due to his/her inability to hear. The condition of blackness and deafness per se should not be rationale for unequal treatment or the denial of options available in a democratic society.

WHM: Black teachers are ill prepared to provide decent education for black children.

LD: Oh! Really? Why would this be so? I would like to remind you that until just a decade or two ago, black superintendents of school districts were rather rare and many black people believe that this was by no accident but an intentional effort by states and federal agencies to handicap the black community's ability to offer top notch education for fear that it would contradict commonly held notions of black intellectual inferiority. The arguments of Thurgood Marshall's legal team in their Supreme Court argument in Brown vs. Topeka Board of Education convinced the court that America had two educational systems "separate and unequal." In regards to deliberately offering false assumptions of black inferiority that have been used for social engineering purposes, let me point you in the direction of the "pseudo-scientific" research done in the controversial publication *The Bell Curve*,[18] which implied that there is scientific evidence that black people had intellectual deficiencies that were genetic. While white conservatives eagerly embraced the proclamations in this book, history has offered numerous examples that simply contradict the basic assumptions Herrnstein and Murray offer.

WHM: If you are referring to the content of J. A Rogers's book, *The World's Great Men of Color*,[19] that is revisionist bunk. Cleopatra was Macedonian for one thing and the Egyptian Pharaohs were of North African stock and not black sub-Saharan.

LD: Whether Cleopatra or the Pharaohs you are referring to were sub-Saharan Africans or not is moot because it still does not make them Caucasian and therefore the title is indeed valid. Dr. Henry Louise "Skip" Gates, of Harvard University, in a partnership including Microsoft, embarked on a historical journey to Africa to produce and narrate the documentary *The Africans,* and what he found and learned absolutely debunks the misinformation black people have been given for years.

WHM: So what are you suggesting?

LD: I am suggesting that black people were deliberately miseducated. I am suggesting that there was fear of the black person's intelligence when white slavers forbid black people from reading and writing and those African slaves who were found to be literate had their tongues and hands dismembered. I am suggesting that this was because the notion of a Negro who was intellectually superior to the slaver definitely terrorized the slaver to the point of barbaric responses to this fear. I am also suggesting that even colonialism, evil as it was, is a good example of the debunking of this intellectual inferiority myth. How? British boarding schools that offered top-notch education to even the poorest Africans produced Africans who went on to receive advanced education in the finest European universities. How could this be possible given that this education is offered in a language foreign to the native African who has to master his master's tongue before conquering his master's science? I am therefore suggesting that fear of the truth has paralyzed oppressive classes throughout history and encouraged these oppressors to invent artificial social structures intended to preserve a lie.

WHM: Okay . . . but deaf people? Surely you must concede that it is impossible to expect them to be educable.

LD: Again, let me suggest you consider the implications of sending your children to a Chinese high school that does not offer English as a medium of instruction. What will be your children's chances of earning superior grades in such a school? Do you believe that your children would master the language sufficiently to ace the SATs and gain entrance to Harvard? Let's be realistic. Now suppose a deaf child was socialized in an environment where ASL was his/her first language and this child grew up in an environment that provided bilingual cues (English and ASL). This child is able to express thoughts, communicate desires, and receive responses in a language he/she understands; would it be difficult to imagine that this child would possess normal language skills? The ability to learn to read is not dependent on the ability to hear or speak. It is dependent on the ability to comprehend vocabulary and grammar of a particular language, and that happens within the socialization environment (home and school). Attempting to force oralism on a child that can neither hear nor speak is the equivalent of sending your child into a language environment where the child is simply unable ever to articulate the sounds or comprehend the language. Would this make this child genetically inferior or would this simply imply that this child is placed in the wrong environment? By the way, there are already quite an impressive number of deaf graduates of Harvard University and several other Ivy League schools.

WHM: Hhmmmmmmm. Interesting point. Wait a minute, you mean deaf students have graduated from Ivy League schools including Harvard?

LD: I am sure you will enjoy verifying this with phone calls to Ivy League schools. Have fun.

The Power to Determine Our Destiny Is in the Hands of Others

I believe that if we provide top-notch early childhood, elementary, and high school education for *all* deaf children (regardless of their race and degree of hearing loss) in an environment where the children's intellect is challenged from birth to completion of their undergraduate education, we would probably see results that would indeed disprove this myth that deafness has any connection to intelligence. Corbett and Jensema reported that the vast majority of teachers of the deaf are white and hearing,[20] so if these white and hearing educators are responsible for our children and they are members of a superior race, shouldn't we expect them to attain superior results with our children? Why is this not happening? What if black people and deaf people had full control of their schools on all levels? What if they had the necessary funding to ensure that their facilities adequately meet the academic expectations of local and state education boards? Are we so blinded by a "blame the victim" mentality that we refuse to consider the systemic factors necessary for a community to advance? I believe people, regardless of race and disability, simply wish to be given a chance to learn, work, and live in peace. In order to seek answers to these questions, I needed to understand this phenomenon of institutionalized oppression. It is widely understood that "isms" are a product of the desire to have power over others.

Lisa Delpit describing the culture of power suggests that

- Issues of power are enacted in classrooms.
- There are codes or rules for participating in power; that is, there is a "culture of power."
- The rules of the culture of power are a reflection of the roles of those who have the power.
- If you are not already a participant in the culture of power, being told explicitly the rules of that culture makes acquiring power easier.
- Those with power are frequently least aware of—or least willing to ac- knowledge—its existence. Those with less power are often most aware of its existence.[21]

I believe that deaf people, like black people, are victims of this culture of power from the day they step inside a school room where the educators are different from learners. It cannot therefore be presumed that a deaf child or a black child can enter a classroom with a white hearing teacher on equal terms as a hearing child or a black child since they are more likely to not have access to these codes or rules that determine participation in the culture of power. Since those who own this power are likely also to be least aware of it, there is little likelihood that it would be checked and, hopefully with greater con- sciousness, redefined.

My friend thought about this a while and conceded that there was merit in this perception. "Life demands constant change and yet human nature constantly resists change," he stated with what I thought was incredible foresight. It appeared this debate was indeed enlightening to him as much as it was to me, and I felt confident that there would be brighter days to look forward to in this world. Hopefully I had changed his ini- tial perspectives (even if some were meant to engage me in a controversial argument) sufficiently for him to become a much stronger ally in our constant struggle to over- come racism and audism. Of course it was not lost on me that it also applied both ways. Deaf and hearing people must continue to revisit our own beliefs and constantly rede- fine them as we gain more knowledge and understanding about the human condition in its many diverse forms. There are, among us Deaf people, those afraid of the rapid changes in society, which we feel are changing the way we live. We feel the frustration of closing schools for the deaf and closing of Deaf clubs. However, we sometimes take for granted that technology is also narrowing the gap in other ways. We do indeed find visible examples of extraordinary progress such as the growing number of Deaf people holding PhDs, law degrees, and even medical degrees. Deaf people in the fast-growing Information Technology sector often say that technology has removed barriers in their workplace, and the only barriers are those who harbor bigoted attitudes to those differ- ent from themselves.

Kendall suggests that antibias/racism work is integral to good education for *all* children. Derman-Sparks defines antibias as:

> an active/activist approach to challenging prejudice, stereotyping, bias, and the "isms." In a society in which institutional structures create and maintain sexism, racism, and handicappism, it is not sufficient to be non-biased. . . . Nor is it sufficient to be an observer. It is necessary for each individual to actively intervene, to challenge and counter the personal and institutional behaviors that perpetuate oppression.[22]

Conclusion

In conclusion, I would like to suggest that we continue this dialogue on racism and audism. Deaf intellectuals have for some time recognized that the liberation struggles of various minority groups parallel their own struggle for equity. Despite laws such as Section 504 of the Rehabilitation Act of 1972 and the Americans with Disabilities Act (ADA) of 1989, deaf people are far from achieving equality in society, with current challenges to affirmative action under the strange logic that it constitutes "reverse discrimination" when its sole objective is to legally ensure that *qualified* women (of all races), people of color, and people with disabilities (of all races) are afforded equal opportunities to enroll in schools that would otherwise refuse their admission or to jobs that would otherwise not be offered them because of their race, gender, or disability. The goals or numerical targets that an institution or workplace sets up are being attacked as "quotas" when it is acceptable for policy makers to use statistical numbers for making policy decisions. It seems hypocritical that laws that were written barely thirty years ago and intended to remedy injustices that were enacted legally over a few centuries are suddenly considered unconstitutional because it is perceived that a certain group of people are going to have to reduce their privileges and power. There ought to be enough at the dinner table to feed everyone who has a seat. ADA is also under attack and the pending confirmation of an anti-ADA Justice for the First Circuit is perceived as threatening the civil liberties of disabled people. As a black Deaf person, I have this strange feeling of having bars sprouting up all around me, and it is very uncomfortable. Racism and audism, like all isms, cause great pain, anguish, and injustice, and we must do whatever is necessary to fight this threat to human dignity.

Notes

1. From the time they arrived in South Africa the Irish Dominican Sisters undertook the teaching of the deaf. Mother Dympna Kinsella, who had considerable experience teaching the deaf in Ireland at the School for the Deaf in Cabra, Dublin, was the main driving force behind establishing South Africa's first school for the deaf. Bishop Grimley, vicar apostolic at the Cape, gave the project his support, and when the school opened in 1863 it was named after him. The Grimley School for the Deaf did more than provide a religious and academic education for deaf children in Cape Town. It also served as an example to the authorities, showing them what could be done for handicapped children. All schools subsequently founded for the deaf took inspiration from this source. Since then the Grimley School has moved from Cape Town city centre to Hout Bay. Two other schools were also opened: the Dominican School for the Deaf in Wittebome (1937) and Hammanskraal

School for the Deaf (1962). See http://www.nationalarchives.ie/search/index.php?browse=true& category=19&subcategory=148&offset=60&browseresults=true and http://www.stmarysdeafgirls. ie/s2_history.html.

2. Richard Herrnstein and Charles Murray, *The Bell Curve* (New York: Free Press, 1994).

3. J. C. Watts, "J. C. Watts Goes Home to Oklahoma," *Journal of Blacks in Higher Education* (Autumn 2002: 34.

4. Harlan Lane, Robert Hoffmeister, and Ben Bahan, *A Journey into the Deaf-World* (San Diego: DawnSignPress, 1996).

5. The author has attended the National Conference on Race and Ethnicity the past eleven years and attended a number of Dr. Kendall's Institutes and workshops on White Privilege: http://www. ncore.ou.edu.

6. Charles W. Mills, *The Racial Contract* (Ithaca: Cornell University Press, 1997), 19.

7. V. Schiraldi and J. Ziedenberg, *Reducing Disproportionate Minority Confinement: The Multnomah County, Oregon Success Story and its Implications*, 2002, http://www.justicepolicy.org/downloads/ MultnomahSuccessStory.pdf.

8. See http://www.raisinonbroadway.com/about.html.

9. Francis Kendall, *Diversity in the Classroom* (New York: Teachers College Press, 1996).

10. Neil Glickman, "Deaf Identity Development: Construction and Validation of a Theoretical Model" (PhD diss., University of Massachusetts, 1993).

11. Janet Helms, *Black and White Racial Identity: Theory Research, and Practice* (Westport, Conn.: Greenwood Press, 1990), 16.

12. Jean Kim, "Asian American Identity Development Theory," in *New Perspectives on Racial Identity Theory,* ed. Charmaine Wijeyesinghe and Bailey W. Jackson (New York: New York University Press, 2001), 111. D. W. Sue and D. Sue, *Counseling the Culturally Diverse: Theory and Practice* (Hoboken: John Wiley & Sons, 1971).

13. Barbara Kannapell, "Inside the Deaf Community," in *American Deaf Culture: An Anthology,* ed. Sherman Wilcox (Silver Spring, Md.: Linstok Press, 1989), 22–28.

14. *School Daze* was a social documentary movie by the African American director Spike Lee. The movie was about the internal conflicts black people deal with based on skin tone and fraternity and sorority affiliation among other issues that are debated within the black community and that cause intergroup tensions.

15. Sonia Nieto, *The Light in Their Eyes* (New York: Teachers College Press, 1999). The quote is from Mary Kalantzis, Bill Cope, and Diana Slade, *Minority Languages and Dominant Culture: Issues of Education, Assessment and Social Equity* (London: Falmer Press, 1989), 47.

16. Rita Hardiman and Baily Jackson, "Conceptual Foundations for Social Justice Courses," in *Readings for Diversity and Social Justice,* ed. M. Adams, W. J. Blumenfeld, R. Castaneda, H. W. Hackman, M. L. Peters, and X. Zuniga (New York: Routledge, 2000), 23–29.

17. L. Wing and J. Rifkin, "Racial Identity Development and the Mediation of Conflicts," in Wijeyesinghe and Jackson, *New Perspectives on Racial Identity Development Theory,* 189.

18. Herrnstein and Murray, *The Bell Curve.*

19. J. A. Rogers, *The World's Great Men of Color* (New York: Touchstone, 1996).

20. E. Corbett and C. Jensema, *Teachers of the Deaf* (Washington D.C.: Gallaudet College Press, 1981).

21. Lisa Delpit, "The Silenced Dialogue: Power and Pedagogy in Educating Other Peoples's Children," *Harvard Educational Review* 58, no. 3 (1988): 282.

22. L. Derman-Sparks and C. Brunson-Phillips, *Teaching/Learning Anti Racism* (New York: Teachers College Press, 1997).

15. Where Is Deaf HERstory?

ARLENE BLUMENTHAL KELLY

ONE OF THE MOST EFFECTIVE WAYS in which dominant groups maintain their power is by depriving the people they dominate of the knowledge of their own history.[1] This is well understood by Frantz Fanon, a leader of the Algerian resistance against the French in the 1950s, who wrote in his *Wretched of the Earth* that "colonialism is not satisfied with merely holding a people in its grip . . . but by a kind of perverted logic, it turns to the past of an oppressed people, and distorts, disfigures, and destroys it."[2] Members of oppressed communities are frequently deprived from appreciating their own historical experiences and the glory of the actions of their own people. Because of this lack of appreciation, the colonized are kept powerless. Instead this glory should come alive to those living in the present and future in order to reduce the dominance of the others.

Women have long understood this deprivation. In 1404, Christine de Pizan, chronicler of great women, wrote to bring her readers "out of the ignorance which so blinds your own intellect."[3] Philosophers also have long trivialized women. Christine de Pizan suggested that women who did not know their history were like a field without a defense.[4] On the other hand, knowing their historical experiences allowed women to become like a strongly constructed city wall.[5]

In the mid-nineteenth century, American women began to archive their history. Most notable was Elizabeth Cady Stanton and Susan B. Anthony's six volumes of *History of Woman Suffrage* completed in 1881.[6] Meant to be an arsenal of facts for the next generation of scholars, these volumes were unfortunately largely ignored. In 1933, historian Mary Beard wrote that an accurate understanding of the past required an analysis of women's experiences and this analysis needed to be conducted with as much attention as historians devote to the experience of men.[7]

Five decades later, historian Gerda Lerner suggested four stages in writing women's history, each stage more complex than the last. The first stage is known as "compensation history" in which historians seek stories about women who succeeded in their actions. Examples are Amelia Earhart, the solo airplane pilot in the 1930s demonstrating courage, and Zora Neale Hurston, an African American folklorist who brought life to independent black women. The next stage is "contribution history" in which women's contributions to topics, issues, and themes of the day are described. For example, the women behind Jane Addams's Hull House project in Chicago aided in promoting Progressive reforms of the day. The third stage of writing women's history moves to understanding what actually happened, thus prompting us to rewrite our own history. For example, we were taught in schools to believe that American slaves were given adequate diets when in truth, male slaves were better fed than their female counterparts even if the women were pregnant. This rewriting process forces a new perspective on social relations between the sexes. Finally, the fourth stage challenges Women's Studies scholars to see gender as a social construction where people apply new meanings to their historical experiences and live on the basis of these constructions.

This essay then challenges us to ponder how Deaf Studies can benefit from the history of the field of Women's Studies. It is interesting to note that both fields emerged after a sense of historical consciousness was engendered. While women have been long aware of their "less than equal" position in society as exemplified by the 1848 Woman's Suffrage convention in Seneca Falls, New York, it was not until 1960 that the field of Women's Studies began in San Diego.[8] Likewise, while Deaf people have been long aware of their own historical experiences, it was not until 1965 when William C. Stokoe, Dorothy S. Casterline, and Carl Croneberg proclaimed American Sign Language (ASL) as a bona fide language that a new sense of awareness emerged.[9] Understanding the intricacies within ASL brought forth pride in their own language. This awareness and pride allowed a new insight into the Deaf historical experience, leading to a heightened sense of consciousness among Deaf people. The field of Deaf Studies eventually emerged.[10] But a plethora of questions remains to challenge both this field and its scholars. They may be answered by exploring the feminist standpoint and epistemology and methodology. Will this yet new awareness remove the longstanding oversight of the Deaf female experience in the field of Deaf Studies? What about removing dominance, also known as audism, still so prevalent?

The Feminist Standpoint

The field of Women's Studies has been concerned with both methodology and epistemology since its inception. Debates were plentiful. One of the debates led to a key point known as the feminist standpoint. Feminist theorist Nancy C. M. Hartsock offered that this standpoint, while not simply an interested or informed position, posits a duality of levels of reality reflecting the relations of humans among each other and with the natural world.[11] Consciousness plays a major role in developing a standpoint. Having knowledge produces awareness. For example, in 1848 Marx and Engels published a treatise in which they proposed equality across various social classes.[12] Differences in wealth and property should not, they argued, separate people. Instead, people of all social stations in life should be treated equally. This concept of equality across class was later understood as Marxism. Picking up on this Marxist thread, Hartsock develops the feminist and women standpoints, which are invariably presented in introductory Women's Studies courses:

> The "feminist standpoint" is a self-conscious perspective on self and society that arises out of a class (or gender) grouping's critical awareness of itself and its location in relation to the system it lives in. The "women's standpoint" is that the perspective arises out of a class's or gender's received and unanalyzed engagement with its material environment, as seen through the worldview of the dominant group.[13]

This suggests that when women analyze their position in the society, in the world, they become aware of their existence as an oppressed population. This consciousness, or awareness, allows them to explore their historical experiences of oppression. They see how and by whom they were and are discriminated against. Due to these enlightened women's position within the sexual division of labor and sexist oppression, they then have greater insights as researchers of other women.[14] These women then assume a feminist standpoint. They see through a different lens in rewriting women's history. On the other hand, there are women who, by virtue of not knowing their own history, do not realize that they are being oppressed or discriminated against. They accept their lot, thus assuming the women's standpoint as described by Hartsock.

The feminist standpoint is further characterized by philosopher of science Sandra Harding.[15] She argues that objectivity is maximized not by *excluding* social factors from the production of knowledge—as the Western scientific method has purported to do—but precisely by "starting" the process of inquiry from an *explicitly social* location: the lived experience of those persons who have traditionally been excluded from knowledge production (for example, women).[16] By exploring women's experiences as a starting point, rather than as a foundation, standpoint epistemology seeks to produce a more *generally* useful body of knowledge.

Like most women, or more specifically feminists, many Deaf people assume duality in their lives. As both women and Deaf people live and study and work within the mainstream culture, both groups also possess a certain sense of affinity amongst themselves, a sense of survivorship, to succeed in life. While socioeconomic status and ethnic backgrounds in each of the two cultures vary tremendously, there is a common group identity.[17] For women, their commonality is tied to their gender. For Deaf people, the commonality lies in language rather than in the inability to hear. For example, most Deaf people prefer the company of their Deaf friends over their own hearing blood relatives on account of communication accessibility.[18]

Another dual experience shared between these two groups is a history of social discrimination based on presumptions held by the mainstream society, such as lower intellectual skills.[19] Inability to perform on the job, as imagined by the mainstream society, was also seen as an obstacle for both women and Deaf people. For example, the female informants in my ethnographic research remembered being dismissed from their places of employment or being denied a salary raise simply because they were Deaf, not because they were women.[20] Personally, while working as a backroom clerk at the Tucson Public Library, I was passed over for promotion to the front desk clerking several times. According to the interviewers, this happened because of my inability to use the telephone. Thus being deaf was an obstacle for my promotional opportunities.

The Deaf standpoint may need to be established and defined in order to answer research questions in the field of Deaf Studies. One of the primary concerns is a body of knowledge of and a sense of understanding about Deaf history. Does this knowledge exist for many Deaf people? If so, how is this achieved? In schools? From watching storytellers? How do these storytellers know Deaf history? Can we begin to say that the Deaf standpoint is a perspective on self and society that arises out of a minority language grouping's critical awareness of itself, of its language, of its history, and in relation to the system in which it lives? And in contrast, is the deaf standpoint a perspective based on unanalyzed passivity? Is having a standpoint truly essential? We may, however, want to explore aspects of Deaf epistemologies before establishing and defining the Deaf woman standpoint. What constitutes the duality of being Deaf and female? It then becomes useful to look at epistemology and methodology, which can assist with our exploration here. Additionally, the field of Deaf Studies should also be concerned with the production of accountable Deaf knowledge.

Epistemology and Methodology

Hartsock urges the study of epistemology and methodology in order to establish a standpoint.[21] In addition, Sandra Harding, as cited in Liz Stanley's "Methodology Matters," suggests that epistemology is concerned with investigating and presenting facts away from other social influences such as masculine assumptions and ways of working.[22] Social scientists Norman Denzin and Yvonna Lincoln define epistemology as a way of exploring *how we know* the world, and the relationship between the inquirer and the known.[23] In general, it is a subdiscipline of philosophy concerned with the validation of knowledge.[24] For example, in cultural anthropology, epistemology helps justify factual knowledge gleaned from fieldwork, historical reconstruction, and comparative studies on human cultures. In short, epistemology allows us to look at knowledge and how much power it can engender for those being researched.

Methodology, on the other hand, focuses on *how we gain* knowledge about the world.[25] It is more concerned with goals and procedures of inquiring and gaining knowledge.[26] In other words, it is a path to achieve an understanding of goals. British sociologist Liz Stanley encourages asking questions such as "what makes an idea 'feminist' or not?" "how can the field be taken more seriously within the academy?" "why is 'gender' a concept so difficult to understand?" and "why are some ideas feminist, and others not feminist?" Methodology then becomes important because it enables asking questions and answering these questions.[27] Methodology also enables the production of a body of knowledge. Methodology deals with knowledge rather than opinions and feelings.[28] For example, it determines how our research should proceed and what the goals of inquiry are. Method implies systematization of procedure leading to the goal of clarity.[29] Selecting a method to answer epistemological questions can defamiliarize the anthropologist of the culture being studied. Instead a new lens, or a new perspective, develops.

Epistemological and methodological concerns are common in social and behavioral sciences, and the humanities. Ethnography is a popular methodology in cultural anthropology. Participation and observation, interviews and fieldnotes play crucial roles in gaining knowledge about other cultures. Often reflexive, these lead the researcher to understand her own culture as well as allowing an introspective look at the researcher as she explores the researched. Both the researcher and researched become informed of issues revealed in the process. Being informed can further enlighten the society at large. On the other hand, in sociology, symbolic interactionism links meanings to social positions or problems, explores how people negotiate their social positions in the activities of daily production, views the society in terms of processes rather than structures, and sees how people carve out areas of autonomy.[30] Women's Studies scholars often prefer ethnography as one of the methodologies.

How do epistemology and methodology work for the field of Deaf Studies? How do these two create a standpoint? This field is interdisciplinary in nature, embracing but not limited to linguistics, history, sociology, anthropology, and literature. Each of the mentioned disciplines has its own epistemology and methodology, or at least a specific focus. Thus, what is epistemology for Deaf Studies? What about methodology? Can this field adopt one? Or should it be as flexible as its interdisciplinary nature? Should Deaf Studies scholars adopt whichever method fits their specific needs? How important are epistemology and methodology for this field? If so, for whom? How about a Deaf, or a Deaf woman, standpoint? Do we need to develop a Deaf standpoint before we can proceed with a Deaf woman standpoint?

In addition, we need to address how the role of the Institutional Research Board (IRB) at most institutions of higher education can either hinder or boost the field of Deaf Studies. The sole purpose of the IRB is to protect both the researcher and the researched, and that is commendable. Yet we need to explore how their procedures are formulated. Traditionally, most IRB-approved research is not geared to cultural research. Examples are psychology and audiology, to name a few. While historians and sociologists are often required to submit to IRB regulations, the questions in IRB application forms ask about possible harmful consequences to the subject(s). Why aren't IRB concerns more cultural? Perhaps it is time for a paradigm shift in this arena so that we can begin to have a Deaf epistemology and Deaf methodology, thus a Deaf (and Deaf woman) standpoint. Yet I have one more area of concern—omission of Deaf people in historical texts—that needs attention.

Marginalization in Historical Texts

Rarely do we find mention of Deaf people, specifically Deaf women, in generic history texts. We need to now look at how marginalized people are overlooked in such texts. Black Studies scholar Maulana Karenga says that "History is the struggle and record of humans in the process of humanizing the world, i.e., shaping it in their own image and interests."[31] Historically, members of minority groups are overlooked in mainstream historical texts. Karenga says that society often imposes limitations on the defense and development of human life at various historical points.[32] Typically the historical approach includes dredging up old records; providing objective, not interpretive, descriptions of events and/or persons; and overlooking the catalyst(s) behind events. There are tendencies not to have a personal contact(s) with the biographee, and to focus on the "white male," excluding members of diverse cultures. Thus because history tends to be written by men of wealth and leisure, the historical approach is usually from "the white gaze," for example, imposing the white subjectivity on the history of African Americans.[33]

Most American history texts discuss slavery from the white male perspective, or lens. Rarely do these texts reveal exactly how life was for the slaves. Oftentimes, slaves are presented as passive domicile servants living in harmony with their white owners. We do not read about their hunger, their hardships, their being at the mercy of the slave owners. In time, Black Americans, inspired by the civil rights movement in the 1960s, sought to bring their own images and interests to their history.

Likewise, the role of women is given minimal attention in most historical texts. They are often regulated to the background, in the roles of daughters, sisters, wives, or mothers. Their names often appear as an afterthought. Rarely do we know about their lives. Archival holdings of many famous women are often listed under their husbands' names. In the early 1970s, two Women's Studies professors, Sherna Gluck and Daphne Patai, were frustrated by the glaring absence of women in generic historical texts and began to record using the oral history methodology. The research in the field of Women's Studies then became "research by, for and with women."[34] This new consciousness brought forth an explosion of literature on women.

But not all was rosy even then. Women's history focused on the Caucasian population. Classism was clearly at work here then. Feminists Audre Lorde, bell hooks, Angela Davis, and Patricia Hill Collins, however, lamented the absence of their black sisters in this field of Women's Studies, historically and theoretically.[35] Their laments, presented in lectures and essays, moved some women including Carol Berkin and Leslie Horowitz, Linda Kerber and Sharon De Hart, and Sandra Opdycke to write inclusive historical accounts.[36] It would be fair to also say that such inclusiveness is not always evident even in the twenty-first century. For example, cultural historian Marilyn Yalom failed to include Asian and African women in her research on wives.[37]

How can the role of historical studies help with the development of epistemology and methodology? As mentioned earlier, there is a dearth of mention of Deaf people in history texts. But for Deaf women, the dearth is even greater. Come to think of this: have you ever encountered Deaf people in history texts? I have not, not in mainstream academic historical textbooks. Unless you can prove me wrong. But seriously, there have been many famous people who were deaf and made significant contributions to the society: music composer Ludwig van Beethoven (1770–1827), Texan spy Erastus Deaf Smith (1787–1837), sociologist Harriet Martineau (1802–76), inventor Thomas Alva Edison (1847–1931), astronomer Annie Jump Cannon (1863–1941), anthropologist Ruth Fulton Benedict (1887–1948), Girl Scout founder Juliette Gordon Low (1860–1927), to name a few. They were not exactly members of the Deaf community, but they were audiologically deaf. For example, Benedict, a classmate and colleague and possibly lover of Margaret Mead, studied various Native American tribes and taught at Columbia University. Oftentimes, their being deaf is not even mentioned.

How about other significant Deaf people: educator Laurent Clerc (1785–1869), poet John Carlin (1813–91), writer Laura Redden Searing (1840–1923), professional baseball player William Hoy (1862–1961), publisher Robert Palmetto McGregor (1849–1926), activist Fred Schreiber (1901–85), among many others? These were culturally Deaf people who, at one time in their lives, attended state residential schools for the Deaf and made significant social contributions. For example, Searing, a former student at the Missouri School for the Deaf, was sent to cover Washington, D.C., during the Civil War, and interviewed and befriended many politicians including President Abraham Lincoln and General Ulysses S. Grant.

Can the field of Deaf Studies benefit from the insights raised by Lorde, hooks, Davis, and Collins? What can we begin to do about this absence of Deaf people in history texts? Whose responsibility is it? What do we do about it? What do we need to do to convince the mainstream academic society that many Deaf people merit a mention in such texts? Furthermore, what is the standpoint epistemology, if any, for the study of Deaf women? If we do know these standpoints, how do these overlap (or not)? We now explore the challenges posed by the omission of Deaf women in historical texts and materials.

Deaf HERstory?

When I began to teach the Deaf Women's Studies course in 1997, I already knew of the great dearth of reading materials by, about, and for Deaf women. But I took up this challenge, not for myself but for students to become aware of this omission. What I had found in the way of reading materials barely scratched the surface, in comparison with the wealth of materials available in Women's Studies. Ingenuity was the name of this game. It then became illogical to require my students to purchase several books when we would read just one chapter from each book. For the first two course offerings, I compiled some articles from journals and books into a notebook and placed them on reserve in the university library. Unfortunately, most of these readings were outdated.

In addition to this challenge was the fact that oftentimes most of the students were rarely knowledgeable about Women's History. This compelled me to focus the first month of the course with an overview on Women's History, starting with the 1848 Seneca Falls Convention. We ended this unit with a tour of the Sewall-Belmont House, which was the headquarters of Alice Paul's National Woman's Party.[38] Having done this, we moved to explore the social role of Deaf women. Again this required creativity on account of scant sources. For the last two course offerings, a new addition made to the Deaf Women's Studies curriculum, the students were required to select a book written either by or about a Deaf woman, review it, and discuss it in class. Their reviews were then showcased in a book display case at the university library, encouraging the students to want to read other books as reviewed by their peers.

To date, there is only one book about the history of Deaf American women by two Deaf women.[39] While I do praise this effort, this is a less than satisfactory attempt because it is an archival work listing Deaf women with data such as birth/death dates, achievements, and anecdotes. It sorely lacks a theoretical framework. A more recent development had emerged from Canada, which again is an archival listing with personal anecdotes.[40]

In 2001, upon invitation to Kentucky's Gallaudet University Alumni Association chapter's annual Gallaudet/Clerc Day celebration, I was asked to speak about Thomas H. Gallaudet and Laurent Clerc. Instead I decided to shift the focus to six influential Deaf women of the nineteenth century, those who lived during the Gallaudet/Clerc era. However, I faced many obstacles in preparing my presentation about Alice Cogswell (1805–30), Eliza Boardman Clerc (1792–1880), Sophia Fowler Gallaudet (1798–1877), Alto Lowman (1869–1912), May Martin (1869–1908), and Agatha Tiegel Hanson (1873–1959). I was already well aware that there are very scant historical documents on Alice prior to her graduation from the Connecticut Asylum for the Education and

Instruction of Deaf and Dumb Persons (CAEIDDP) and none between her graduation and early death. All we know of Alice is her childhood, her few years at the Asylum, and her early death. Nothing is known of her six years after graduation.[41] In addition, there are no photographs of Alice, but a silhouette that has appeared in many texts. Furthermore, we do not know much about Mrs. Cogswell, Alice's mother, who is relegated to the background.

In developing this presentation, I realized that I was guilty of an archival compilation of birth and death dates, and one or two lines of achievements. Most of the information came from Holcomb and Wood's *Deaf Women*. In an attempt to improve the presentation, I went to the Gallaudet University Archives to seek more information about these six women's achievements. Along with the three archivists there, we could find only their obituaries. Not much was said about their achievements beyond being students. For example, Elizabeth and Sophia were mentioned among the earliest students at CAEIPPD. Additionally, the three archivists and I already knew that in 1890 May Martin suggested that Gallaudet University establish a student-run newspaper known as *The Buff and Blue*. Although her brainstorm, she was not selected as the editor-in-chief. Instead a man was chosen. This factual information was not even in the May Martin file, but in the *Buff and Blue* file.

Because of such scantiness in this presentation, I fleshed it out with the history of the 1887 admittance of women to the college. This first group of women included Ella F. Black (Indiana), Georgianna Elliott (Illinois),[42] Anna L. Kurtz (Indiana), Hattie A. Leffler (Pennsylvania), Alto May Lowman (Maryland), and Margaret Ellen Rudd (Nebraska). Again, the archivists and I dug into files, coming up somewhat empty-handed except that Lowman was honored as the first female graduate of the college.[43] Nevertheless, the presentation was quite a hit in Kentucky, prompting the audience into thinking about their Deaf foremothers who may have made social achievements or contributions. I also hope that there has been some action since, perhaps in the way of school or class projects, searching the Kentucky School for the Deaf library and archives, as well as interviewing their Deaf retired employees and graduates.

Few other published works about Deaf women tend to focus on the management of motherhood in terms of language acquisition.[44] These pieces emerged from research projects studying how Deaf mothers, regardless of the hearing status of their offspring, can be linguistic and cultural role models for hearing parents with deaf infants. For example, my 1995 chapter described how a Deaf mother used fingerspelling with her daughter from five weeks old to four years old.[45] Other journal articles and dissertations about Deaf women address educational, employment, and social issues.[46] In addition, it is interesting to note that only three authors mentioned in this endnote are Deaf themselves: Kelly, Jauregui, and Singleton.

While there are several dissertations with Deaf women at their centerpieces, there are only two known ethnographic dissertations that explore directly the meaning of the term "gender" among Deaf women.[47] Both Doe and I set out to interview a small pool of Deaf women to learn how they construct the social meaning of gendered terms such as "gender," "sex," "feminism," and "patriarchy." Doe's informants were Canadians who attended Deaf residential schools. My ASL teacher-informants had various educational experiences, ranging from being the only Deaf student in a public school to attending an oral program to having lived their entire childhood in a state residential school. One of the commonalities among all of my informants was graduating from Gallaudet College.[48] Yet, and in spite of the eight years' gap in Doe's and my works and the distant locations of research, we both reached the same conclusion: "gender," "sex," "feminism," and "patriarchy" were not actively part of their vocabularies. Does this linguistic omission indicate a lack of historical knowledge? In addition, both groups of women identified themselves primarily as Deaf persons rather than Deaf women.

Additionally, not only are Deaf women or Deaf people often overlooked in mainstream publications, but literature about them also tends to be "degendered." That is, Deaf women are rarely given significant space. Pedagogical research in the education of deaf children rarely separates the sexes. We do not know, for example, if there are different learning strategies for deaf girls and boys, whereas we do know this difference from research conducted on hearing adolescents.[49] It would be interesting if researchers would take upon themselves to explore if there are any significant differences between deaf girls and deaf boys. In spite of its attention to issues of marginalization and oppression by the dominant hearing culture, the field of Deaf Studies has yet to include the study of the Deaf female experience.

New Directions?

The Deaf women's view of themselves as Deaf persons rather than as Deaf women leads me to wonder if the serious absence of Deaf women, or even Deaf people, in generic historical texts is responsible for this perception. Had they been aware of achievements made by other Deaf women, especially in the late nineteenth century, would they have a different self-perception? How do we bring forth this awareness?

With apologies to my colleagues Lane, Hoffmeister, and Bahan who coauthored together, I profess much disappointment that their 1996 *Journey into the Deaf-World* has only one paragraph on page 162 discussing Deaf women. Historians Van Cleve and Crouch have written a widely read and popular historical account of the development of the American Deaf community.[50] I have yet to meet a Deaf Studies scholar who has not read this text. Still, this text was written from a hearing white male perspective. More recently is Wayne Coffey, which is indeed a fascinating read, however, written by a hearing white man.[51] As I look at my own bookshelves at home, I find so few books written by culturally Deaf women: Padden, Holcomb and Wood, Jankowski, Brueggemann.[52] Most Deaf-related historical texts on my shelves are written by hearing men: Battison, Winefield, Schuchman, Sacks, Schein, Lane, Preston, Baynton, Wrigley, Armstrong, Stokoe, among other books that focus on Deaf Culture as well.[53] Some of the ASL teacher-informants interviewed for my dissertation also lamented the high number of hearing people writing our histories.

In teaching the Deaf Women's Studies course, I am always faced with the dilemma of a lack of substantial reading materials on Deaf women. How do we improve this sorry lacking state of literature on the Deaf female body? One idea is to encourage Deaf women to donate, or will, their written materials, photographs, and artwork, especially journals, to the Gallaudet University Archives or their state residential school for the Deaf. This would encourage young Deaf Studies scholars to research and to publish to expand the repertoire of historical texts to be available to future generations to come.

Furthermore, curricula for most of the Introduction to Deaf Studies and Deaf Culture courses seem to be based on a white male construction. An exploration of current materials shows a glaring omission of the Deaf female experience. Not only is that missing, but also the diversity within the Deaf community, such as Black people, Hispanics, Asians, Gay/Lesbians, Native Americans, and now women. Why this omission? In other words, why should white hearing people, or men, care about us? Write about us? Include us in historical texts? How have the others been writing about us? Why are they doing that? What new directions should we undertake, to encourage the inclusion of the Deaf female experience, the Deaf experience even, in generic historical texts?

In writing this essay, I realize that I posed more questions than answers. But then I hope these questions bring forth more food for thought for you.

Notes

1. Linda K. Kerber and Jane Sherron De Hart, *Women's America* (New York: Oxford University Press, 2000), 3.
2. Frantz Fanon, *The Wretched of the Earth*, translated by C. Farrington (New York: Grove Press, 1963), 170.
3. G. Lerner, "Placing Women in History: Definitions and Challenges," *Feminist Studies* 5, no. 14 (1975): 6.
4. Christine de Pizan, *The Book of the City of Ladies* (1404), trans. by Earl Jeffrey Richards (New York: Persea, 1982).
5. Lerner, "Placing Women in History," 8.
6. Elizabeth Cady Stanton and Susan B. Anthony, *History of Woman Suffrage*, 6 vols. (New York: self-published by S. B. Anthony, 1881).
7. Kerber and De Hart, *Women's America*, 4.
8. While the beginnings of the women's movement in America can be traced to 1848 when Stanton and Anthony organized the first Woman's Rights convention in Seneca Falls, it took over a century for Women's Studies to emerge. Women began to reconsider their social roles during the Vietnam War era. Student radicals then organized "teach-ins," rallies, and marches and closed down college campuses. Women were active participants in these activities; however, many felt dismissed by their male compatriots: Sandra Opdycke, *The Routledge Historical Atlas of Women in America* (New York: Routledge, 2000). Women typed and filed while men made public statements; women offered suggestions and men made policy; women cooked and cleaned antiwar offices. The women's movement and Women's Studies then emerged first in San Diego in 1970, setting the stage for a new paradigm in cultural studies programs: B. Luebke and M. E. Reilly, *Women's Studies Graduates: The First Generation* (New York: Teachers College Press, 1997).
9. William C. Stokoe, Carl G. Croneberg, and Dorothy S. Casterline, *A Dictionary of American Sign Language on Linguistic Principles* (Washington, D.C.: Gallaudet College Press, 1965).
10. For the history of the Deaf Studies field, see Charles N. Katz, "A Comparative Analysis of Deaf, Women, and Black Studies," *Deaf Studies IV Conference Proceedings: Visions of the Past – Visions of the Future* (Washington, D.C.: Gallaudet University College for Continuing Education, 1996), 133–48; Arlene Blumenthal Kelly, "A Brief History on the Field of Deaf Studies," *Disability Studies Quarterly* 18, no. 2 (1998): 118–24.
11. Nancy Hartsock, "The Feminist Standpoint: Developing the Ground for a Specifically Feminist

Historical Materialism," in *Discovering Reality: Feminist Perspectives on Epistemology, Metaphysics, Methodology, and Philosophy of Science,* ed. Sandra Harding and Merrill Hintikka (Boston: D. Reidel, 1983), 283–310.

12. Karl Marx and Friedrich Engels, *Manifesto of the Communist Party* (New York: International Press, 1948). It is interesting to note that the first woman convention in Seneca Falls was held in 1848, the same year that the Manifesto of the Communist Party appeared. Note that the Manifesto came out in 1848, but it was not for another one hundred years that it became available in English.

13. Nancy Hartsock, *The Feminist Standpoint Revisited and Other Essays* (Boulder: Westview Press, 1998), 285–88.

14. Diane L. Wolf, "Situating Feminist Dilemmas in Fieldwork," in *Feminist Dilemmas in Fieldwork* (Boulder: Westview Press, 1996), 13.

15. Sandra Harding, *Whose Science? Whose Knowledge? Thinking from Women's Lives* (Ithaca: Cornell University Press, 1991).

16. E. Hirsch and G. A. Olson, "Starting from Marginalized Lives: A Conversation with Sandra Harding," *JAC* 15, no. 2 (1995): http://www.jac.gsu.edu (site now discontinued; last accessed June 13, 2006).

17. Ila Parasnis, ed., *Cultural and Language Diversity and the Deaf Experience* (Cambridge: Cambridge University Press, 1998), 13.

18. This phenomenon is discussed in various texts but not limited to the following: Carol Padden and Tom Humphries, *Deaf in America: Voices from a Culture* (Cambridge, Mass.: Harvard University Press, 1988); Parasnis, *Cultural and Language Diversity and the Deaf Experience;* Harlan Lane, Robert Hoffmeister, and Ben Bahan, *A Journey into the Deaf-World* (San Diego: DawnSignPress, 1996); Arlene Blumenthal Kelly, "How Deaf Women Construct Teaching, Language and Culture, and Gender: An Ethnographic Study of ASL Teachers" (PhD diss., American Studies, University of Maryland, College Park, 2001).

19. Parasnis, *Cultural and Language Diversity and the Deaf Experience,* 13.

20. Kelly, "How Deaf Women Construct Teaching, Language and Culture, and Gender," 254–56.

21. Hartsock, *Feminist Standpoint Revisited.*

22. Liz Stanley, "Methodology Matters!" in *Introducing Women's Studies,* ed. Victoria Robinson and Diane Richardson (New York: New York University Press, 1997), 209.

23. Norman Denzin and Yvonna Lincoln, *Handbook of Qualitative Research* (Thousand Oaks, Calif.: Sage, 1994), 99.

24. Thomas Schweizer, "Epistemology: The Nature and Validation of Anthropological Knowledge," in *Handbook of Methods in Cultural Anthropology,* ed. H. Russell Bernard (Walnut Creek, Calif.: Alta-Mira Press, 1998), 39.

25. Denzin and Lincoln, *Handbook of Qualitative Research,* 99.

26. Schweizer, "Epistemology," 40.

27. Stanley, "Methodology Matters!" 198.

28. Ibid.

29. J. Fernandez and M. Herzfeld, "In Search of Meaningful Methods," in Bernard, *Handbook of Methods in Cultural Anthropology,* 93.

30. Sherryl Kleinman, Barbara Stenross, and Martha McMahon, "Privileging Fieldwork over Interviews: Consequences for Identity and Practice," *Symbolic Interaction* 17, no. 1 (1994): 40.

31. Maulana Karenga, *Introduction to Black Studies* (Los Angeles: University of Sankore Press, 1993), 70.

32. Ibid., 71.

33. G. Lipsitz, "Listening to Learn and Learning to Listen: Popular Culture, Cultural Theory, and American Studies," *American Quarterly* 42 (1990): 615–36.

34. Sherna Gluck and Daphne Patai, *Women's Words: The Feminist Practice of Oral History* (New York: Routledge, 1991), 1.

35. Their issues were raised in the following works: Audre Lorde, "The Master's Tools Will Never

Dismantle the Master's House," in *Sister Outsider: Essays and Speeches* (Freedom, Calif.: Crossing Press, 1984), 110–13; bell hooks, *Feminism Is for Everybody: Passionate Politics* (Cambridge: South End Press, 2000); Angela Davis, *Women, Race and Class* (New York: Random House, 1981); Patricia Hill Collins, "The Social Construction of Black Feminist Thought," *Signs: Journal of Women in Culture and Society* 14, no. 4 (1989): 745–73.

36. Carol Berkin and Leslie Horowitz, *Women's Voices, Women's Lives: Documents in Early American History* (Boston: Northeastern University Press, 1998); Kerber and De Hart, *Women's America;* Opdycke, *Routledge Historical Atlas of Women in America.*

37. Marilyn Yalom, *A History of the Wife* (New York: Harper Collins, 2001).

38. Alice Paul (1885–1977) is credited for forming the Congressional Union for Woman Suffrage in 1913, which evolved into the National Woman's Party in 1917. See Shelia Tobias, *Faces of Feminism: An Activist's Reflections on the Women's Movement* (Boulder: Westview Press, 1997); Kerber and De Hart, *Women's America.*

39. Mabel Holcomb and Sharon Kay Wood, *Deaf Women: A Parade through the Decades* (Berkeley: DawnSignPress, 1989). This text is currently out of print.

40. Hilde M. Campbell, Jo-Anne Robinson, and Angela P. Stratiy, *Deaf Women of Canada: A Proud History and Exciting Future* (Edmonton, Alberta: Duval House, 2002).

41. There is only one known text describing the Cogswell family: Betty Young, *The Chain of Love* (Bloomfield, Conn.: P & S Services, 1997).

42. For more information about Georgianna Elliott Hasenstab, see B. E. Kraftt, *A Goodly Heritage* (Columbus, Ga.: Brentwood Christian Press: 1989), which is now out of print. While searching for this reference online, I came up with three listings for her reverend husband, Philip J. Hasenstab, however nothing on Georgianna herself. I ended up e-mailing a request to Archivist Michael Olson for the bibliographic information.

43. Many thanks to archivists Ulf Hedberg, Michael Olson, and Drew Budai.

44. Kay P. Meadow, M. T. Greenberg, Carol J. Erting, and H. Carmichael, "Interactions of Deaf Mothers and Deaf Preschool Children: Comparisons with Three Other Groups of Deaf and Hearing Dyads," *American Annals of the Deaf* 126 (1981): 454–68; Kay P. Meadow, M. T. Greenberg, and Carol J. Erting, "Attachment Behavior of Deaf Children with Deaf Parents," in *Annual Progress in Child Psychiatry and Child Development,* ed. Stella Chess and Alexander Thomas (New York: Brunner/Mazel, 1985), 176–87; Lynne S. Koester, "Intuitive Parenting as a Model for Understanding Parent-Infant Interaction When One Partner Is Deaf," *American Annals of the Deaf* 137 (1992): 362–69; Arlene Blumenthal Kelly, "Fingerspelling Interaction: A Set of Deaf Parents and Their Deaf Daughter," in *Sociolinguistics in Deaf Communities,* vol. 1, ed. Ceil Lucas (Washington, D.C.: Gallaudet University Press, 1995), 62–73; Patricia Spencer and Amy R. Lederberg, "Different Modes, Different Models: Communication and Language in Young Deaf Children and Their Mothers," in *Communication and Language Acquisition: Discoveries from Atypical Development,* ed. Lauren Adamson and Mary Ann Romski (Baltimore: Paul H. Brookes, 1997), 203–230.

45. I was recently invited to revise this chapter for a 2003 edition of *Odyssey* of which Dr. Jane K. Fernandes is the guest editor. In doing so, I revisited the girl featured in the chapter, now a teenager, to see how early fingerspelling acquisition had aided her academically and socially.

46. Kelly, "Fingerspelling Interaction"; Gaylene Becker and Joanne Jauregui, "The Invisible Isolation of Deaf Women: Its Effects on Social Awareness," *Journal of Sociology and Social Welfare* 8, no. 2 (1981): 249–62; N. Jones, "Don't Take Any Aprons to College!" (master's thesis, Gallaudet College, 1982); Janet MacLeod-Gallinger, "The Career Status of Deaf Women: A Comparative Look," *American Annals of the Deaf* 137 (1992): 315–25; Patti M. Singleton, "Leadership Style, Personality Types and Demographic Profiles of Deaf Female Administrators in Educational Programs for Deaf Students" (PhD diss., Administration and Supervision, Gallaudet University, 1994).

47. Tanis M. Doe, "Gender with Deaf Women and Their Sisters" (PhD dissertation, University of Alberta, Edmonton, 1993); Kelly, "How Deaf Women Construct Teaching, Language and Culture, and Gender."

48. The youngest informant in my study graduated in 1983, three years before the College became a University.

49. Examples include but not limited to Mary Belensky, Blythe Clinchy, Nancy Goldberger, and Jill Tarule, *Women's Ways of Knowing: The Development of Self, Voice, and Mind* (New York: Basic Books, 1986); Christiane Brusselmans-Dehairs, *Gender Differences in Learning Achievement: Evidence from Cross-National Surveys* (Paris: Bernan Associates, 1997).

50. John Van Cleve and Barry Crouch, *A Place of Their Own: Creating the Deaf Community in America* (Washington, D.C.: Gallaudet University Press, 1989).

51. Wayne Coffey, *Winning Sounds Like This: A Season with the Women's Basketball Team at Gallaudet, the World's Only University for the Deaf* (New York: Crown, 2002).

52. Carol Padden, *Interaction of Morphology and Syntax in American Sign Language* (New York: Garland, 1988); Holcomb and Wood, *Deaf Women: A Parade through the Decades;* Katherine Jankowski, *Deaf Empowerment: Emergence, Struggle, and Rhetoric* (Washington, D.C.: Gallaudet University Press, 1997); Brenda J. Brueggemann, *Lend Me Your Ear: Rhetorical Constructions of Deafness* (Washington, D.C.: Gallaudet University Press, 1999).

53. Robbin Battison, *Lexical Borrowing in American Sign Language* (Silver Spring, Md.: Linstok Press, 1978); Richard Winefield, *Never the Twain Shall Meet: The Communications Debate* (Washington, D.C.: Gallaudet University Press 1987); John Stanley Schuchman, *Hollywood Speaks: Deafness and the Film Entertainment Industry* (Urbana: University of Illinois Press, 1988); Oliver Sacks, *Seeing Voices: A Journey into the World of the Deaf* (Berkeley and Los Angeles: University of California Press, 1989); Jerome Schein, *At Home among Strangers: Exploring the Deaf Community in the United States* (Washington, D.C.: Gallaudet University Press, 1989); Harlan Lane, *When the Mind Hears: A History of the Deaf* (New York: Random House, 1984); Paul Preston, *Mother Father Deaf: Living between Sound and Silence* (Cambridge, Mass.: Harvard University Press, 1994); Douglas Baynton, *Forbidden Signs: American Culture and the Campaign against Sign Language* (Chicago: University of Chicago Press, 1996); Owen Wrigley, *The Politics of Deafness* (Washington, D.C: Gallaudet University Press, 1996); Harlan Lane, *The Mask of Benevolence: Disabling the Deaf Community,* 2nd ed. (San Diego: DawnSignPress, 1999); David Armstrong, *Original Signs: Gesture, Sign, and the Sources of Language* (Washington, D.C.: Gallaudet University Press, 1999); William C. Stokoe, *Language in Hand: Why Sign Came before Speech* (Washington, D.C.: Gallaudet University Press, 2001).

16. Queer as Deaf: Intersections

MJ BIENVENU

Identity: WHAT?

CAN A DEAF PERSON IDENTIFY as Lesbian or Gay and not as Deaf? Can we be one or the other and not both? At the 2002 Gallaudet Culture and Language Colloquium panel on "Culture within Culture," black Deaf storyteller Evon Black was asked the question, "Which are you first: black or Deaf?" She responded, "I expected this question. I think it is a very stupid question. There is no point in answering that." To this, I thought, "It's about time someone answers exactly that way." I have often been asked a similar question, "Do you feel more Deaf or more Lesbian?" What does this mean exactly? Does one identity preclude the other? From my experience, it seems one is not allowed to be both in the Deaf community. Perhaps this is true for other minority communities, too. You must choose to be either Deaf or a Lesbian. At least this has been the case historically. However, the concept of Deaf L/G is beginning to emerge in the Deaf community.

In 1969, the Gay community at large engaged in a profound event that would eventually change the place of Gay men and Lesbians in society today. In New York City the Gay community was tired of oppression, mistreatment by police in the city, and unnecessary raids of the gay bars. So in 1969, they fought back in what became known as the Stonewall Riots. The L/G community now has a more recognized place in society, even though we are not always offered a place at the table. Gay men and Lesbians are still stigmatized, we are still victims of hate crime, and we are still not allowed to have the status of marriage. There is a backlash going on now with threats of a U.S. Amendment banning Lesbian/Gay marriages. But progress has been made. More and more jurisdictions include Gay men and Lesbians in antidiscrimination laws. Gay men and Lesbians receive more media attention, albeit stereotyped. And, at long last a U.S. President (Bill Clinton) could use the word "Gay" and have it not sound dirty.

What about Deaf Lesbians/Gay men? Are we welcomed to take our place at the table of the Deaf community? We do not know for sure, but I'd think, no. Deaf identity is highly valued. To clearly assert one's L/G identity *might* be to jeopardize one's Deaf identity. Consequently, Deaf Gay men and Lesbians formed their own groups. One is the Rainbow Alliance of the Deaf, founded in 1977.[1] It seems the Deaf community has been slow to make room at the table. It was not until 1997 that we finally had a Deaf Lesbian caucus at the Deaf Women United (DWU) conference. (There were workshops on Deaf Lesbians and Homophobia in previous conferences, but not a formal caucus.)

Lest you think this accomplishment came easily, let me share a story about what happened in 1993. We had a special interest group for Deaf Lesbians at the DWU conference in New Jersey. The conference organizers directed me to where the meeting was to take place. When I went there, I found the room far from all of the rooms reserved for other special interest groups, and the door was closed. I entered the room, leaving the door open, thinking it had been closed by mistake. "No, no," they told me, I had to close the door because there were some Deaf women who were curious who we were and might spread the word. For three mornings, we met and debated (often heatedly) about whether to leave the door open or not. Finally, we agreed to all sit at the same table at the closing ceremony (and here I do mean literally amongst ourselves, not at the metaphoric table). The table was, as it happened, set in the middle of the large ballroom. (There were other tables reserved for some of the special interest groups, if they wished.) Ours grew from two tables to three to four and finally, if my memory serves me well, about six tables, holding about fifty or more of us. I casually observed women as they entered the room. Many of them asked, "Who are those tables reserved for?" Receiving the answer, it was amazing to see how quickly their hands dropped, as did their eye contact. Some remarked, "That many?" We were finally out of the closet and had a place at the table!

In 1995, there were two workshops on the topic of Lesbians. One was "Celebrating Deaf Lesbians" and the other was "Homophobia." Both were standing room only and the former was closed to Lesbians only. A few questioned why non-Lesbians weren't "invited," and it was made clear to them that, because it was the first time we could discuss Deaf Lesbians, we needed to have time to ourselves and express our pride without being stigmatized. There was no resistance to that. At that time, there were about seventy Deaf Lesbians at the conference (out of 249). Then in 1997, the Deaf Lesbian caucus finally met and proceeded to organize our first Deaf Lesbian Festival in Seattle in 1999. Of course, backlash occurred, not only from straight people, but also from many Deaf Gay men. Why would we want to have a festival for Deaf Lesbians only, excluding other Deaf people? It brings up the question again. Are we permitted to be both Deaf and Lesbian (Gay, black, Hispanic, etc.)? Or must we be Deaf and then something else secondarily? Why did Deaf Gay men feel betrayed when Deaf Lesbians had a festival of their own? Was it because, after all, both groups are Deaf? Did they fear their own position would be threatened by the possibility of the community becoming smaller? Is that why straight Deaf people want us not to have our separate meetings, because it supposedly diminishes our shared Deaf identity?

The continued presence of the Deaf Lesbian caucus and the successes of numerous Deaf Lesbian Festivals show we have our own community, albeit small—and fragile. The 2003 Deaf Women United conference had no workshops nor a caucus designed for Deaf Lesbians. The Deaf Lesbian Festival 2004 received a much smaller group although it was held in Washington, D.C., which has one of the largest Deaf Lesbian communities. There is a need for recognition, respect, and a political movement to fight homophobia within the Deaf community. But is the Deaf L/G community willing to risk the threat of being labeled "less Deaf" as a result?

Rejected Identity: Deaf

Often there are questions in addition to the question asked above. It is often questioned how open the Deaf community is to Deaf LGBTs, or is it not? Many Lesbians and Gay men fear to be stigmatized in the community of Deaf people. They value their identities as Deaf people and recognize quickly reactions of straight Deaf people, as illustrated in the following story.

At one of the conferences held in Canada sometime around the early 1990s, a group of us were discussing the Deaf and L/G communities when a straight Deaf person said, "I cannot understand why Deaf Lesbians and Gay men prefer to go to a hearing bar for New Year's Eve. The Deaf club needs money and they are Deaf, but they chose the hearing world. Why?" It is not that they choose the hearing world, I told her, but the comfort of being able to be who they are. She then added, "But I am an understanding person. I have nothing against them." Another question for her: "When the clock strikes twelve and everybody kisses, how do you think Deaf people will react when the L/G couples kiss?" To that, she clenched her teeth, squinted her eyes, and shook her head. Her non-verbal response itself was the answer to her own question. And, I am sure, to many others who ask the same question.

Such responses are one form that homophobia takes; yet there are others, sometimes more violent actions. There were two murders at Gallaudet University in the academic year 2002–2003. Both victims were male and freshmen. Eric Plunkett of Minnesota was the first victim killed in September and Ben Varner of Texas was found stabbed to death in February. A third male freshman, Joseph Mesa, was arrested for the murders and is now serving a life sentence in a California prison. As much as we hate to be reminded of the murders at the university, it is important to mention a noticeable change in people's reactions between the two murders. When Eric Plunkett, a Gay man who was just elected as secretary of the campus LGBT organization, was first murdered, Deaf L/G students were terrified. They immediately suspected it was a hate crime, especially when they found their message boards defaced with anti-Gay comments. The D.C. police made a wrongful arrest in October and charged a just-out Deaf Gay man with the murder of Eric Plunkett. Gay students at Gallaudet refused to believe one of their own (a Deaf Gay man) would do it. The administrators at Gallaudet responded accordingly and called for Gay awareness and sensitivity training on campus. They made it clear that anti-Gay behavior is not acceptable on campus. In general, faculty, staff, and alumni of Gallaudet who are Lesbians and Gay men felt the administration's response was professional and appropriate. Students and others on campus had a harder time responding to the idea of a hate crime on campus. When we speculated about comparing Eric, who had just come out as a Gay man, with Matthew Shepard, many asked who the latter was. Strangely, a hate crime would not have surprised many Lesbians and Gay men on campus. When Ben Varner was murdered, many wondered aloud if Ben was Gay. When it was "determined" (by whom, I wonder) that he wasn't, right away many straight people doubted Eric's death was Gay-related. The point here is even if Ben was not Gay, Eric still could have been murdered because he was Gay. And yet the community was all too willing to brush aside the possibility that a hate crime could be committed within the Deaf community. After all, aren't we all Deaf? Later, after Mesa was arrested and tried, he admitted that he chose his two victims because they seemed weak to him. Through L/G eyes, it was evident that Mesa could have thought Ben weak because he presumed him Gay, or vice versa. But no one (including the police) would recognize these atrocities as hate crimes because Ben wasn't Gay. It seems hard for the Deaf community to accept that there is a possibility of such hate toward another Deaf person.

Parallel Cultures

In various workshops on the topic of American Deaf Culture, speakers would compare Deaf Culture with black culture. They have their own language, they have their own values and norms, and they hold their own traditions. It often seems safe to compare Deaf Culture with black culture, although many don't agree with this. One of the common reasons is that black people acquire their values and beliefs from families, whereas only 10 percent of the Deaf population acquire them from their Deaf families. Nobody thought (or dared) to compare Deaf Culture with Gay culture until 1994. When the *New York Times Magazine* first published an article suggesting that Deaf culture might parallel with the Gay community[2] some Deaf people became upset. "We are not like Gay people!" said one at a Deaf bowling league. Another said, "I know, Gay was mentioned too often in that article, I worry people think Deaf people are the same as Gays." Members of both communities, Deaf and Gay, are stigmatized—and Deaf Gays are stigmatized within the Deaf community.

In 1998, I was asked to discuss the Deaf L/G community as a guest lecturer at one class meeting. Before the *New York Times Magazine* article, I had often discussed the Deaf community as it parallels to the black community. On this occasion, I decided to change the perspective and compare the Deaf community with the Gay community. This wasn't, I admit, exactly the same as discussing the Deaf L/G community, but it was a step, in my opinion, toward understanding the Deaf community through the eyes of the Gay community. This is still a preliminary work but enough to recognize the similarities between the two communities.[3] As I worked on this presentation, I couldn't help but think how Deaf straight people might react to this. They had already complained to me about being quoted and pictured in the article, even th̶o̶ ̶ ̶ ̶ in the Deaf community as a Deaf Lesbian.

Making the comparisons between Deaf and ̶ ̶ ̶ ̶ ep toward coming out for Deaf Lesbians and Gay men, an̶ ̶ ̶ ̶ ia in the Deaf community is getting out of the closet. I wa̶ ̶ ̶ ̶y com- parison at a Maryland Association of the Deaf con̶ ̶ ̶ ̶sting to see the reactions of Deaf people at the worksho̶ ̶ ̶ ̶eas- ing each other with "YOU G-A-Y!" in American Sign̶ ̶ ̶ ̶the comparison, I also discussed homophobia. When t̶ ̶ ̶ ̶, participants either became very quiet or just looked away. It is a difficult topic to discuss. When audism is brought up, Deaf people feel anger. Audism hits home, and Deaf people understand the oppression, but homophobia is just "them." Many Deaf people have argued that we need to focus our energies on the fight against audism, without watering it down by addressing other ills. Truth be told though, homophobia makes many of them the oppress*or*. Not a very comfortable position, when so close to home! However, to fight homophobia and audism hand-in-hand, one needs to be educated (again and again) about both negative isms.

Codes in the Deaf Closet

The power that comes from names and naming is related directly to the power to define others—individuals, races, sexes, ethnic groups. Our identities, who and what we are, how others see us, are greatly affected by the names we are called and the words with which we are labeled. The names, labels, and phrases employed to "identify" a people may in the end determine their survival. The word "define" comes from the Latin *definire*, meaning "to limit." Through definition, we restrict, we set boundaries, we name.[4]

Deaf, hard-of-hearing, deaf mutes, deaf and dumb, hearing impaired, those with hearing loss, those who move their hands, those poor people, hearing handicapped, dummy, monkey-like signers, apelike, Washoe.[5]

Lesbians, Gays, Queers, faggots, butch dykes, homosexuals, sissies, tomboys, fairies.

Labels also hurt. There have been discussions on how to sign LESBIAN and GAY and many found it uncomfortable. With more education and exposure, people are learning how to be politically correct when it comes to talking about Lesbians and/or Gay men.

A study was conducted on how we sign LESBIAN.[6] The question seemed simple, "Which contact point for the sign LESBIAN is the most acceptable?" As simple as it seemed, however, it caused great discomfort among Deaf people who were interviewed. Where the sign makes contact with the chin implies a person's attitude toward Lesbian. It is "less homophobic" if you make contact with the tip of your index finger on the chin, as opposed to a "stronger" contact on both the index finger and the thumb (see Figures 16.1 and 16.2). Choices between #GAY and the sign G̲A̲Y̲ (G on chin) were also surveyed. It seemed that the lexicalized form is the preferred choice among the Easterners, possibly because it seemed less negative.

Figure 16.1. Negative sign for LESBIAN.   Figure 16.1. Politically correct sign for LESBIAN.

There are codes used in the Gay community to indicate privately membership in the Gay community. The Deaf L/G community also has codes. Or at least we did. When I was in the closet, I saw many codes. Now that I am very out, I don't see them anymore. We had GOLF to mean Gay, BASEBALL to mean Bi, and we had this sign where one "pulls and wiggles" her/his ear lobe to identify as a Gay person (see Figure 16.3). Also, there was the use of the term GREEN AND YELLOW, an acronym for G-A-Y in English.

Often our codes were not manual, but just an eye gaze in the direction of a person, and accompanied by the yes/no question brow.

Lesbians and Gay men share numerous funny stories about straight people asking if we are L/G. One example includes a straight Deaf person fingerspelling, "A-R-E Y-O-U?" I'm not sure why the speaker switches to English for this kind of question, but it may be to distance the topic from the language of the Deaf world. Even my own Deaf Mom asked me in exactly that form! They seem unable to fingerspell G-A-Y or sign LESBIAN.

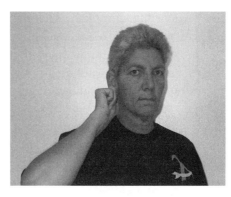

Figure 16.3. Closeted sign for GAY.

I witnessed this another time, when a Lesbian passed away at a Deaf residential school. A Deaf male staff member was telling me about the memorial service. He told me that there were about "fifty of them" in attendance. When I asked who the "them" was, he said, "You know what I mean." Although I did, I shook my head. He looked around, put his hand close to his waist, and fingerspelled, L-E-S-B-I-A-N-S. When I signed LESBIAN, it was as if I had I signed something very vulgar and not fit for public viewing. He quickly asked, "Are we allowed to use this sign?"

Rejected Identity: LGBT

Both Deaf and L/G communities do not have much power. But decisions made regarding L/G issues are made by those with more power—hearing Lesbians and Gay men. Even when Deaf and hearing work side by side toward empowerment on L/G issues, Deaf people feel like second-class citizens at Pride Days, parades, conferences, etc. It is clear that there is a power structure, or power hierarchy, at work.

Here's another story. There were about fifty Deaf people at a D.C. Pride Day festival. The organizers got volunteer interpreters and reserved a space for Deaf Lesbians and Gay men in front of the stage. The space was—no exaggeration here—about three feet wide by nine feet long. The interpreters were not allowed to stand on the stage because "they might steal attention away from the musicians and speakers," said the members of the Pride committee. Instead, the interpreters were located in a spot below the stage right next to a colossal loud speaker. The request by Deaf attendees to put the interpreters on stage and make their space larger was completely ignored. Letters of complaint were written to the planning committee. Lo and behold, the following year they had a Deaf person work on the committee. But when she suggested they might want to include Deaf speakers, she was told no. After all, what would Deaf speakers have to say? And didn't they already have a disabled Gay person on the program?

You've Come a Long Way Baby—But Longer to Go . . .

When the article on Deaf Lesbian mothers "designing" their deaf baby was printed in the *Washington Post Magazine*,[7] the overwhelming response was about the audacity of engineering a *deaf* baby. That the focus wasn't on the mothers being Lesbians was, I guess, indicative of the small strides made by the L/G community. This affirms my theory about which condition needs to be fixed, in the eyes of the general public.

In 1988 I wrote a short article for *TBC News*[8] about the label "prelingual Deaf." One paragraph reads as follows:

> For many years people have labeled me a pre-lingually deaf person because I was born deaf, meaning I was deaf before I "acquired language." I am not alone, and I am very aware of this. Those who were born hearing, but became deaf at the age of five or six or later are labeled post-lingually deaf. They are lucky: They acquired "language" before they became deaf; therefore, they are better adjusted to the world of language. If you look in the dictionary, you won't find either prelingual or postlingual, but if you look in many books on "deafness," you will find these terms. And while it is probably the case that such labels are being used less and less, they are still in the files of many Deaf people.

My "homosexual" condition was deleted from the *Diagnostic and Statistical Manual* by the American Psychological Association, but my "deafness" condition remains to be fixed by numerous surgeons today.

Where do Deaf Lesbians and Gay men fit in? In the hearing L/G community, we've not yet gained much power. We're still relegated to the little chair at the side table for the kids. It remains to be seen whether we've been welcomed to the big table in the Deaf community. But there are many Deaf L/G leaders in the Deaf community who are also educators, artists, and activists. The most outspoken of us tend to be Deaf-of-Deaf, so I guess it means "If you are strong Deaf, you run less risk that your Deaf identity will be compromised by also being Lesbian or Gay."

Deaf Lesbian/Gay Resources

There are minimal formal studies, if any, on the Deaf L/G community. This begs the question, how do so many Deaf Lesbians/Gay men allow this? What does a formal study mean to them? Outing themselves to the world? To the Deaf world? Being stigmatized again, and this time by formal studies? Personally, I'd love to teach a course on the Deaf L/G community, but where are my resources? It will mean I need to refer to the *hearing* L/G community to bring us to a discussion on the *Deaf* L/G community. Do we want to continue to do this? Like we have done with women, with persons with disabilities, and with blacks/African Americans? It is about time to develop more resources for Deaf LGBT to help academize Deaf Studies. It is believed that there are more out Lesbians/Gay men compared to ten to twenty years ago; therefore, there might be more written documents well suited for course work. Also, each time a course on Deaf LGBT is offered, students can do scholarly work, research, and more on that topic, which can be added to the list of references. There was, however, a reader written by Raymond Luczak in 1993 titled *Eyes of Desire: A Deaf Gay and Lesbian Reader* that can be used as a reference.[9] Still, it is clearly not enough.

Conclusion

For many years, Deaf people were "trained" to be ashamed of being Deaf. It was not until Stokoe's work in the 1960s that proved ASL is a language that more and more Deaf people became proud of who they are. There are many stories about Deaf people deciding not to sign in public because they were ashamed and didn't want to be stared at. Some

Figure 16.4. Queer/Deaf similarities. Created by Kendra Smith and MJ Bienvenu as a class handout, Gallaudet University, 1999.

QUEER	DEAF
Parents	
• Few parents of Gay/Lesbian are queer	• Only 5–10 percent of Deaf have Deaf parents
• Many parents don't accept	• Many parents don't accept
• Psychiatrist	• Therapist
• Seek cure	• Seek cure
Education	
• Denial	• Denial
Society	
• Normalization	• Hearingization
• Homophobia	• Audism
• Epithets	• Epithets
• Misconceptions (sex, sex, sex)	• Misconceptions ("can't" syndrome)
• Homosexuality	• Deafness
• Acceptance/tolerance	• Acceptance/tolerance
• Resistance to public identity based on community membership	• Resistance to existence of Deaf culture
• Denial of self-labeling	• Denial of self-labeling
• Lesbian/Gay Studies	• Deaf Studies
Culture	
• Denial/silence	• Denial/silence
• Coming out repeatedly	• Acknowledging repeatedly
• Misrepresentation (Andrew Cunanan)	• Misrepresentation (H. Whitestone)
• "Passing"	• Speech = more desirable
• Stereotypes (tomboys, sissies)	• Stereotypes (wild, emotional)
Identity	
• Defined by what we *do* (sexually)	• Defined by speech or dB loss

QUEER	DEAF
Language	
• Often the language of the majority	• ASL, BSL, etc.
Congress	
• Barney Frank, S. Gunderson, • G. Studds	• No Deaf Representatives
Media	
• Recognition	• Not much after DPN, unless attention is on gaining hearing (cochlear implants)
Age of onset	
• Genetic • Coming-out age	• At birth
Culture	
• Old envy young	• Young envy old

Figure 16.5. Queer/Deaf differences. Created by Kendra Smith and MJ Bienvenu as a class handout, Gallaudet University, 1999.

parents (both Deaf and non-Deaf) would tell them to put down their hands and not to embarrass them, or not to draw attention to themselves. Most of the stories are not written. Is it to "deny" admitting these things did happen to them? It is almost embarrassing to admit that one was not allowed to sign and that s/he complied with the oppressive commands.

Lesbians and Gay men were afraid of being out of the closet, and it was worse before the 1970s. It is still difficult for some of them to come out fully. Often those who came out experienced struggles with family and friends, but many of them don't regret their decision to be out of the closet. To protect many closeted members of the community many stories and pictures were not documented and/or destroyed. This probably explains why many of their stories were not written until the 1970s.

Following is an additional story to demonstrate a final example of what it is like for some Deaf Lesbians, even in 2004.

Deaf Lesbian Festival 2004, held in Washington, D.C. (as previously discussed in this chapter), turned out to be a huge success. During the closing ceremony there was a slide show of everybody at the festival, of various events, and everybody loved it. Some Deaf Lesbians asked to make copies of the slide show and additional pictures. No one asked questions and pictures were copied. One Deaf Lesbian told the group she would select some pictures and would paste them on her Web page. Still no reaction from anyone. That night there was a flurry of e-mails asking that she didn't publicize the pictures. Reasons given were that some were working in a deaf setting (e.g., residential school for the deaf, deaf service centers) and they wouldn't want to be exposed (their word) to the public.

In reference to responses from Deaf people when the *New York Times* articles came out, Kendra Smith and I did a study. We analyzed resources on American Deaf Culture and read articles on homophobia and racism. We then proposed that Deaf people are more similar to the LGBT community and came up with parallels (Figures 16.4 and 16.5). There is a great possibility there is a crossing between the Deaf and LGBT way—and that is sharing stories and staying safe from stigma.

Notes

1. For information, go to the Web page of the Rainbow Alliance of the Deaf, http://www.rad.org.
2. Andrew Solomon, "Deaf is Beautiful," *New York Times Magazine,* Section 6, August 28, 1994.
3. List of parallels in Figure 16.4.
4. Haig Bosmajian, *The Language of Oppression* (Lanham, Md.: University Press of America, 1983), 5.
5. In 1974, I was told of a poster shown at the Central Institute for the Deaf, in St. Louis, portraying Washoe, the first signing ape, with the caption "Do you want your child to be like him?" Unfortunately, I have never seen it, but fortunately I have not heard any more about it.
6. Mala Kleinfeld and Noni Warner, "Variation in the Deaf Community: Gay, Lesbian and Bisexual Signs," in *Multicultural Aspects of Sociolinguistics in Deaf Communities,* ed. Ceil Lucas (Washington, D.C.: Gallaudet University Press, 1996), 3–35.
7. Liza Mundy, "A World of Their Own," *Washington Post Magazine,* March 31, 2002, W22.
8. *TBC News* was a newsletter printed quarterly by The Bicultural Center, a for-profit organization founded in 1987 serving the Deaf community in areas of advocacy, bilingual education, interpretation, and ASL teaching headquartered in Riverdale, Maryland. It was closed in 1994.
9. Raymond Luscak, *Eyes of Desire: A Deaf Gay and Lesbian Reader* (Boston: Alyson Publications, 1993).

PART VI   *The Question of Disability*

17. Do Deaf People Have a Disability?

HARLAN LANE

RECENTLY I ASKED A COLLEAGUE, a university professor I'll call Archibald, whether he thought that Deaf people have a disability. "Of course they do," he answered. "It's common sense." I believe that most hearing people and some Deaf people, too, would say the same thing. When my colleague called the conclusion common sense, he implied that the meanings of the words themselves answered my question. A *disability* is a limitation of function because of an impairment. *Deaf* people are limited in some functions because of an impairment of hearing. Therefore, Deaf people have a disability. That nicely closes the issue for my colleague, but it closes it too soon for us. To travel this issue with the commonsense meanings of the words is to travel with too much a priori baggage. In particular, these meanings take *deaf* and *disability* to be physical attributes of individuals, like their blood pressure or eye color. A great deal follows from this biological understanding of *deaf* and *disability*, including much that Deaf people find hurtful and inimical to their interests. I propose, therefore, to suspend common sense on this issue long enough to explore the concepts of *deaf* and *disability* so we can see what was buried in both the question and the answer.

How did the concept of *disability* arise and what purposes does it serve in our societies? In several of his works, the French philosopher Michel Foucault showed how "bodies are the battlefield"—that is, how political and economic forces in the history of the Western world have fought for control of the human body and its functions.[1] By the eighteenth century, the Western tradition of esteeming the poor was replaced by a political analysis of idleness that continues to the present. To make productive citizens out of idle burdens on the state, it was necessary to distinguish those who *could* not work (the sick and disabled) from those who *would* not work (beggars, vagabonds, and thieves). In 1994 presidential aspirant Phil Gramm, a senator from Texas, confirmed this policy objective of separating the infirm from the indolent: "[We want able-bodied] people riding in the [welfare] wagon," he said, "to get out . . . and help the rest of us pull." The incoming Speaker of the House, Newt Gingrich, agreed.[2] Likewise, the British government has stated that the products of special education "should be productive if possible and not a burden on the state."[3] A 1993 Japanese law similarly aims to make people with disabilities independent and thus employable.[4]

To reduce the numbers of those who could not work and must be given a free ride, the state, starting in the eighteenth century, assumed great responsibility for ensuring the health of the population and could even penetrate the tightly knit family unit and prescribe what should happen to the child's body: hygiene, inoculation, treatments for disease, and compulsory education.[5] These practices are generally quite desirable, and they thus formed a continuing basis for the state's claim on the control of bodies. During this era of the rise of modern medicine and the growing intervention of the state in the health of the family, the first national schools for deaf people were founded. In order to ensure that those who could work would do so, a central purpose of those schools was to teach the deaf pupils a trade, removing them from their families where they were poor dependents and converting them into productive members of society. The deaf schools in Europe contained shops to teach trades such as printing, carpentry, masonry, gardening, tailoring, and so on. When schools for deaf people were founded in the United States, they followed this model.[6]

With the arrival of the Industrial Revolution, much larger numbers of people were marginalized; machinery, buildings, and transportation were designed for the normative worker. To separate the able-bodied who could work in these settings from those with disabilities who could not and to regulate the health of children and adults, it was necessary to measure, evaluate, create hierarchies, and examine distributions about the norm. For example, "mental defectives" were considered able to work at simple repetitive tasks, provided their impairment was not too severe. Moderate hearing loss (or unilateral loss) was not an obstacle to most employment, but severe bilateral loss was. Hence the state exercised a more subtle "technology of power" that replaced the brazen power of the king and nobles in feudal society. The technology that has been developed to aid in regulating and rehabilitating includes disciplines such as medicine and surgery, paramedical fields such as optometry and audiology, population studies and applied genetics, psychological measurement, physical anthropology, and rehabilitation and special education. In order to classify people as mentally handicapped, mentally ill, blind, deaf, lame, and so on and hence unable to work in varying degrees, the state requires techniques of measurement and specialists organized into agencies for making those measurements. The more elaborate these special services and benefits are, the greater the need for complex measurements.[7]

The Social Theory of Disability maintains, then, that the category of "people with disabilities" arises out of the work ethic of our capitalist society: People who are not working legitimately are those whose disability precludes employment; they have needs that the rest of society should meet. All other people, such as thieves, vagabonds, and the lazy, are not working for reasons that are illegitimate; they have no claim on our social solidarity, and they should work and be self-sufficient.[8] Over seventeen million Americans are considered disabled for work, so it is easy to see that the construct of "legitimately not working because of disability" is crucially necessary in our capitalist society.[9] Clearly, then, disabilities are not simply physical characteristics of the people who have them—they are not like blood pressure, for example. Social issues such as disability are constructed in particular cultures and at particular times in response to the efforts of interested parties. In the United States at present, we designate some forms of human variation as functional limitation arising from an impairment—therefore, a disability—whereas we consider other forms of human variation normal and not a disability at all. Thus we accept as normal human variation—and not disability—wide differences among people in height, but we consider very short people to have a disability;

we accept differences in weight as normal, but gross obesity is a disability; we accept differences in skin color as normal variation, but we consider albinos to have a disability. Differing degrees of alcohol consumption are not a disability, but alcoholism is. We all learn at different rates—that's normal human variation—but mental retardation is a disability. The following are not considered disabilities in the United States today: baldness, nearsightedness, halitosis, and addiction to cigarettes. Mood variation is normal, but we consider mania and depression as mental illnesses. An addiction to pipe smoking is not a disability, but an addiction to crack smoking is. Not only is it hard to tell disabilities from normal variation, but today's disability may be tomorrow's normal variation and vice versa. Alcoholism has gone from moral flaw to disability. Homosexuality from moral flaw to disability to minority rights. Child abuse from moral flaw to disability. Mild mental retardation from normal human variation to disability.

What then determines whether some form of human variation is a disability? The answer is—norms and the technologies of normalization. Take height, for example. What matters to a culture is not so much the physical attribute of so many feet or meters from head to toe but rather the cultural counterparts *short* and *tall,* which are relative to a norm. People who are much shorter or taller than the average *in a particular culture and a particular era* are viewed as having a disability in that culture and era. That is, they are seen as having an impairment—their very short or tall stature—that leads to restricted functioning. Very short people cannot readily reach keyboards, objects on standard countertops, parts of machinery, and so on. Very tall people cannot fit into airplanes readily, have difficulty driving standard cars, and the like. The view that people with abnormal heights have a disability sets the stage for the intervention of experts—the technologies of normalization. These experts will investigate the problem, teach others how to do so, propose remedies, administer medical and surgical treatment and rehabilitation, teach others how to do that, measure the remaining problem and determine eligibility for government-prescribed benefits, lobby government for those benefits, and so on.

Here is how the technologies of normalization have operated in the arena of height. In the United States and Great Britain nowadays, a large number of children are receiving injections of growth hormone, costing over $20,000 a year per child. Shortness was never viewed as a medical condition until the technologies of normalization came up with a treatment. Thus the disability did not lead to the treatment; rather, the treatment led to the disability. Shortness became a disability, once a treatment was available, because if doctors administered a treatment, there must be a disorder to treat. The synthetic growth hormone has some nasty side effects and is expensive. Nevertheless, the market for it in the United States is estimated to be $350,000,000 annually and growing.[10] Doctors working for Genentech, Inc., which manufactures the hormone, claim that the shortest 3 percent of the population needs their treatment. Ninety thousand children born annually make up the shortest 3 percent of the U.S. population, which corresponds to a potential annual market of $8–10 billion. Best of all for Genentech, there will always be children with this so-called impairment of growth, for no matter how tall our whole population becomes, there will always be a shortest 3 percent. According to Genentech doctors, however, treating these children is not a minor matter of cosmetics: statistics show that our society is "heightist," and short people do not get a fair deal.[11] Thus what sustains the whole enterprise is the biologizing of a social state of affairs. Discrimination against short people becomes rooted in *them,* not us, but we can treat the problem *they* have. Thus, socially rejected difference is reified as a treatable biological condition, and the responsibility for social inequality is shifted onto the individual who is said to have that treatable condition. This minimizes the need for change in the society at large, which pleases both the public, happy to leave the problem to the technologies of normalization, and also the technologies themselves, which, like all professions, tend to be self-perpetuating and self-promoting (audiology, for example, is on the threshold of having its services mandated for every child born in the United States from here on out).

The only group that clearly doesn't gain from the medicalization of social difference is its targets. In 1998 the British medical journal *Lancet* reported that short children whose height was increased two to three inches by treatment with the synthetic product Somatropin received no psychological benefits.[12] Researchers at Southampton Hospitals in England treated seven short girls with daily injections from age eight to fourteen. The cost of the treatment, paid for by drug companies, worked out to $46,000 per stimulated inch of growth—not to mention some 2,500 injections per child. A comparison group of short girls who did not receive the treatment was just as happy and well balanced as the treated girls although they were three inches shorter at age sixteen. The team is now repeating the investigation on short boys.[13]

Consider another example of a socially rejected difference reified for gain, thereby shifting the responsibility for inequality onto the individual. In this case, the socially rejected differences are differences in social class and skin color. In the late 1800s Francis Galton, son of a Birmingham banker, undertook a study of wealthy British families like his own and found that eminence ran in such families, which he attributed to superior heredity. He rejected the idea that a family with three generations of lawyers, for example, owed that success to superior education, family connections, and other such environmental explanations. Instead, much inspired by Charles Darwin's theory of evolution, Galton thought eminence to be mainly the result of biological differences in intelligence, the result of family heredity, and he tried to find biological correlates of eminence, such as head size, but was unable to. With the invention of Binet's IQ test at the turn of the century, scientists such as Galton, who believed that class differences were the result of innate differences in intelligence, finally had a measure of innate ability, and they found widespread evidence of a correlation between IQ scores and social success. For example, the unemployed and uneducated generally scored lower in IQ than people in the professions. Some modern-day scientists offer the same explanation for the disadvantaged condition of many blacks, attributing it to an innate deficiency in black intelligence.[14] To validate their claim, these scientists cite a fifteen-point difference in black and white scores on IQ tests. However, if such a difference exists, after correcting for the cultural bias in the tests, it may simply reflect the effects of being classed in our society as black rather than white: it may reflect social discrimination rather than heredity. Thus, a socially rejected difference—lower social class—has been reified as diminished innate intelligence, thereby shifting the responsibility for that difference onto the individual and minimizing the need for social change.

The technology of normalization organized around IQ is large indeed. IQ testing, especially the massive testing of two million recruits during World War I, changed psychology from a largely academic subject to one that was widely respected as having real social utility.[15] The IQ test was created by experts, administered by experts, and interpreted by experts. IQ testing of nearly two million World War I recruits yielded an alarming result: the average white American had the mental age of a thirteen-year-old; black Americans scored even lower. The IQ test, with these alarming results, helped to lay the foundations for special education. The experts in this technology of normalization computed a distribution around a norm and assigned those children who fell a specified number of units below the norm to specialized institutions on the grounds that technology had revealed their inner deficit, although that deficit frequently lacked any outer sign. The norm was arbitrary. In fact, other IQ tests would have classed as normal more than half of the children labeled as morons requiring institutional care.[16] The aggrandizement of the new "special education" proceeded rapidly in the following decades, encouraged by regular classroom teachers who were delighted with the resulting homogenization of their classrooms. The proportion of children enrolled in special education has grown a hundredfold in Finland in the last five decades;[17] in some states in Australia, it has grown fifteenfold.[18] In Great Britain, the *Warnock Report,* a comprehensive survey of special education "needs" in 1978, concluded that as many as one in five children would need those services and called for a major expansion of the special education establishment.[19] Thus is the majority protected from social deviation to the advantage of the technologies of normalization.

The technologies of normalization that developed around this particular reification in biology of social differences—IQ—included not just research, measurement, institutionalization, and rehabilitation but also eugenic measures to purge society of this unwanted burden. Early in this century, American psychologists found that the average intelligence of immigrants was declining now that their origins had shifted from northern to southern Europe—two out of five in steerage were feebleminded, they claimed—and they successfully urged stricter immigration policies.[20] They claimed that poorer people had not only lower IQ but also larger families so that over time the "bad germ plasm" would gain ground over the innate intelligence of the better classes. Thus, numerous eugenic societies sprang up in the United States and Great Britain, and many discussions of proposals for improving society through selective breeding ensued. Among them were sterilizing the unfit; educating the unfit so they would agree to voluntary sterilization; restricting marriage among the unfit and encouraging it among the fit; and tax rebates for maternity costs and child rearing in meritorious families.[21] The eugenic principle of selection on the basis of individual biological and mental quality was transformed into a principle of racial or ethnic-group selection in immigration, and behavior that was outside the bounds of prevailing middle-class standards was taken as evidence of biological and hence hereditary lack of fitness.[22]

With these reflections and the examples of height and IQ, we are in a position now to characterize *disability* more accurately and as it turns out in quite a different way from its dictionary definition. A disability is a classification of a physical, behavioral, or mental difference from the norm that is attributed to biological causes in a particular culture in a given era, as a result of the interventions of interested parties.

As with *disability*, we want to unpack the meaning of *deaf* and observe what the commonsense meaning of the word fences in and fences out. In everyday discourse, when we say that someone is deaf, we call on a socially constructed set of meanings. One of those meanings in common parlance is that deaf people lack a vital sense. Another meaning is that these are people whose choices are restricted. In many cultures when you say someone is deaf, you are understood to mean that that person can aspire to only a limited education and that their choices in employment will be severely restricted, too. In some countries, deaf is an explanation of why a child cannot go to school at all. In others, it is an explanation of why a child can profit from only elementary education; in still others it explains why university studies are not possible. Even in the United States, with its uniquely long history of higher education for deaf people, sentences such as "John didn't go to the university because he's short" strike us as illogical, but sentences such as "John didn't go to the university because he's deaf" do not. Likewise for the world of work. Sentences of the type "Because she's deaf, Mary couldn't be a politician like her mother" do not give most Americans pause. The underlying meanings that these explanations refer to have been called *audism*.[23] Like racism and sexism, audism insists that inherent biological factors determine individual traits and capacity. One of the greatest handicaps in being deaf is the reduced range of choices that is open to the deaf person. In many countries deaf people do not have the right to an education, to social services, to drive a car, to employment at the level of their skills, or to the free use of their language.[24] The loss of choices is largely the result of the social construction of what it means to be *deaf*—the result of audism—rather than of any sensory limitation that deaf people have. In that sense, our society largely creates the problems of being deaf.

The widespread tendency in our society to reify in individual biology what are in fact social conditions—the discrimination against short people, poor people, black people, Southern Europeans—alerts us at once to the hidden meanings of audist claims. In 1996 a leading American journal of ear surgery published the most extensive defense yet of the ethics of cochlear implant surgery on deaf children. Explaining why such surgery is necessary, the authors claim that deafness is "the most disabling of disabilities," that deaf children incur very high costs in education, and that deaf adults cost society a lot of money, too, because they need help gaining access to events and other help such as interpreters.[25] The message is that there is a serious problem because of the deviant physical makeup of the deaf child, and surgery is justified. The aim of normalizing surgery is to reduce human variation: to reduce or eliminate not only those differences that cause physical suffering but also those that underpin ways of life with which the concerned people are happy, people such as intersexuals, conjoined twins, dwarfs, and Deaf people.[26] Likewise blaming the child's hearing and asserting the need for technological services, a British audiology text contends that the entire family with a deaf child is a family with a disability and that the disabled family requires "saturation services" from numerous professionals like the authors of the book.[27] This is indeed claims making, the "politics of description." Nothing is said here of Deaf Culture, of the power and beauty of sign language, of the history of oppression of Deaf difference, of culturally Deaf people's above-normal abilities in spatial perception and cognition,[28] and so on.

Never is it mentioned that Deaf parents (and many hearing parents) raise Deaf children very well without surgery, without saturation services, and indeed without any special intervention.

The explanatory power of *deaf* is reinforced by the media. Movies and books have tragic deaf characters whose predicament is attributed to their being deaf. But positive images also reinforce the explanatory power of *deaf*. Deaf people are held up as admirable for having overcome or minimized their deafness. They took their deafness as a challenge that they successfully confronted. This image, too, reinforces the idea of *deaf* as an explanation. Both negative and positive images are emergent constructions of audism. What can this concept of *deaf* really explain? It cannot justify limited career choices because deaf people are found in virtually all fields. It cannot explain limited educational achievement because there are deaf PhDs, deaf professors, and so on. It cannot justify the livelihood of countless hearing professionals because, as mentioned, Deaf parents commonly raise Deaf children quite successfully without those professionals. The underlying idea is that mere sensory difference has vast explanatory power, yet it does not. The assumption that it does is reinforced by hearing politicians, doctors, and parents.

The stereotypes of audism are an expression of audism but not the audism itself. What is the source of the belief that being a deaf person entails an inherent biological limitation? Why is *deaf* associated with loss rather than difference and gain (different language, different culture, etc.)? I submit that it is because the society that has elaborated the concept of *deaf* is largely hearing and conceptualizes *deaf* as a loss of hearing. Indeed, the difference in hearing of a person born deaf and one born hearing is called "hearing loss," although the deaf person didn't lose anything. The idea that sensory difference is loss is reinforced by the limitations of hearing people who lose their hearing. Then, too, some authors have argued that deafness cannot just be mere difference because it involves the loss of a sense that is essential for survival. They believe that our species has survived because of its common features, including the five senses. In fact, the common features of our species, such as hearing, may reflect the vicissitudes of evolution eons ago, and, in any event, do not individuals with fewer common features have equal claim on our allegiance? Do they not have the right to value their atypical physical constitutions even if they were associated with less reproductive fitness?

Deaf organizations sometimes attack the manifestations of audism. They campaign against mainstreaming, against cochlear implant surgery on deaf children, and against discrimination in employment. The activism attacks the expressions of the audist beliefs but not the beliefs themselves, which are part of the meaning of the word *deaf* (deaf people are lacking; they have a biological flaw) and thus will continue to fuel oppressive practices. A similar sort of analysis applies to sign language. When people say that sign language is primitive or they express surprise that it is not universal, they are simply unfolding the socially constructed meaning of *sign language*, which is, according to *Webster's New Collegiate Dictionary*, "a system of hand gestures used for communication (as by the deaf); an unsystematic method of communicating chiefly by manual gestures used by people speaking different languages." Similarly, a campaign to allow sign language in the classroom can encounter determined resistance because it does not attack the source of the exclusion, which is the culturally constructed meaning of *sign language*.

Deaf organizations today have embraced the term *Deaf*, perhaps in part in the same "in your face" spirit that black people adopted *black* or that an organization of gay activists has adopted the name Queer Nation. Some Deaf leaders try to mark the distinct significance of *cultural* deafness—to set it apart from the general English usage of the word *deaf*—by capitalizing the *D*. The older terms for this cultural group were *deaf-mute* (as in the *Deaf-Mute Journal*) and *Silent* (as in the magazine *Silent Worker*). These terms, like the capital *D*, made a helpful distinction. Mute or Silent people are those who, for the most part, do not speak. This accurately excluded from the group hearing people who lost their hearing but who continued to speak and did not change cultural affiliation. An advantage of *mute* and *Silent* over the capital *D* is that the capital *D* is perceptible only in writing. Some culturally Deaf scholars have referred to the members of their culture as "the Visual People," but that label has not made inroads against *Deaf*.

I have argued that, for most hearing people, the term *deaf* has at the core of its meaning a loss, a flaw. Now, what does *deaf* mean to Deaf people? Because Deaf people have their own language and culture, and such ideas are culturally constructed, it is not surprising that different meanings, positive ones, are embedded in the term *deaf* in Deaf Culture. (If cultures dominated by hearing people value being hearing, must we not expect that cultures dominated by Deaf people value being Deaf? Indeed, is there any culture in the world that does not value the predominant physical makeup of its members?) According to my Deaf informants, *Deaf* means "like me"—one of us—in significant cultural ways. A Deaf person values being Deaf and possesses the other attitudes, values, mores, and knowledge particular to that culture. Thus, something positive lies at the core of the meaning of Deaf, and there is no implication of loss.

With these reflections and examples, we are in a position to characterize *deaf*, as it applies to members of the Deaf world, in quite a different way from its dictionary definition. *Deaf* refers to a member of a linguistic and cultural minority with distinctive mores, attitudes, and values and a distinctive physical constitution. We refer to the members of that culture as Deaf and to the culture itself as the Deaf world; these are glosses of the signs in American Sign Language (ASL) with which Deaf people refer to themselves and their culture, respectively. We also follow the Deaf world practice in referring to children of any age as capital-D Deaf who have, for whatever reason, the physical constitution characteristic of this minority—that is, they rely so much more on vision than on hearing that they communicate most readily, given the opportunity, in a natural sign language. This practice also reflects the logic of cultural attribution in hearing society, which is based on the child's likely life trajectory given its physical makeup. We call children Native American, African American, Asian American, and so forth long before they have learned any language or culture, and we do not ask to see their parents before deciding on their cultural membership, so such attributions are clearly based on physical makeup.

Poor Archibald! Asked "Do deaf people have a disability?" he answered that common sense says they do. But now we see that, far from common sense, the question makes no sense. A disability is a social classification in a particular culture at a particular time, the outcome of a power struggle among interested parties. And we see that Deaf, in the context of our present concerns, refers to a distinctive culture, not to loss or incomprehension. Perhaps Archibald would have been wiser to answer my question, "Do deaf people have a disability?" by saying "I can't answer your question because a disability is not something you have; it's a label you acquire." Well, then, *should* Deaf people seek this *disability* label assigned to them by the technologies of normalization or at least acquiesce in it, or should they actively resist it?

It seems to me (but then I'm not Deaf) that there are many reasons to resist the label of *disability*. In the first place, in the framework of their culture, Deaf people reject the suggestion that they have an impairment or a disability (the ASL sign that translates roughly as *disability* does not include being Deaf). In contrast, leaders in the disability rights movement say they themselves do have a disability (of course, there are exceptions in each group). These disability rights leaders call for ambivalence about their impairment; individually they want it positively valued as a part of who they are. At the same time, it is the result of poverty, war, disease, or accident, so they want it negatively valued and support measures that reduce the incidence of the impairment.[29] But the Deaf world is not ambivalent; its members characteristically think it is a fine thing to be Deaf and favor more of it. Unlike most expectant parents with disabilities, expectant Deaf parents characteristically hope to have children with whom they can share their language, culture, and unique experiences—that is, they hope to have Deaf children.[30]

So Deaf people are fundamentally unlike people who say they have disabilities, for to Deaf people the proposal that they have a disability "just doesn't compute."[31] Disowning the disability label would therefore be the honest thing to do. In the second place, consider what the disabilities rights movement seeks: above all, better medical care, rehabilitation services, and personal assistance services (e.g., help with personal hygiene, dressing, and eating).[32] Deaf people do not attach particular importance to any of these services—no more than any other able-bodied group. Whereas the disability rights movement seeks independence for people with disabilities, Deaf people do not have any more concern with independent living than people in general. Deaf people cherish interdependence with other Deaf people. Whereas people with disabilities seek total integration into society at large, Deaf people cherish their unique identity and seek integration that honors their distinct language and culture. Integration of Deaf children into hearing schools and classes is an anathema to the Deaf world. The specialized schools for Deaf people, especially the residential schools, were the setting in which most Deaf adults acquired fluent (manual) language and socialization. Those specialized schools and, after graduation, the Deaf clubs with their athletic, literary, political, and social programs have provided most Deaf people in America, despite their having hearing parents, with the generational continuity that is essential for a rich culture.

So Deaf people generally do not see themselves as disabled nor do they seek what people who say they are disabled seek. Disowning the disability label is therefore the prudent thing to do because the provisions that society makes for people with disabilities often do not suit the interests of Deaf people and may even run counter to them. Furthermore, because of the commonsense meaning of disability, when Deaf people embrace that label they encourage the untiring efforts of the technologies of normalization to reify in biology what are in fact social disadvantages of Deaf people. This deflects attention from the need for social reforms. Worse yet, this disability label encourages the technologies of normalization in their eugenic and surgical programs aimed at eliminating or severely reducing the ranks of culturally Deaf people. Because the hearing agenda for Deaf people is constructed on the principle that members of the Deaf world have a disability and because our society seeks to reduce the numbers of people with disabilities through preventative measures, hearing people have long sought measures that would reduce the number of Deaf people, ultimately eliminating this form of human variation and with it eliminating the Deaf world. The chairman of a U.S. National Institutes of Health planning group acknowledged this in an interview with the *New York Times:* "I am dedicated to curing deafness. That puts me on a collision course with those who are culturally Deaf. That is interpreted as genocide of the Deaf."[33]

Two measures that would reduce the numbers of Deaf people and are actively pursued today in many lands are eugenics and cochlear implant surgery on young Deaf children. The professions that advocate such extreme measures are clearly calling on the commonsense understanding of *deaf* as disability in promoting their programs.

Hearing efforts to eugenically regulate childbearing by Deaf people have a long history. The central purpose of the large-scale oral education of Deaf children that began in the last century and continues today in many lands was, according to U.S. leaders, to discourage reproduction by Deaf people by discouraging their socializing and marriage.[34] This was also a central goal of the day-school movement, a goal championed by one of the leaders of the American eugenics movement, Alexander Graham Bell. At first Bell saw in the oral education of Deaf people—based on speech and lipreading and prohibiting sign language—a means of encouraging them to marry hearing people. But it soon became clear that Deaf schoolmates intermarried no matter whether their residential school used ASL or spoken English. Thus, measures would be required to keep Deaf schoolmates apart physically so they would not marry and procreate more Deaf children. That meant boarding the Deaf pupils at home and instructing them in small classes to minimize contact among Deaf people. Bell told lawmakers that day schools allow "keeping deaf-mutes separated from one another as much as possible."[35] He warned of the dangers of Deaf congregation at the state residential schools.

Oral education and day-school classes are rather indirect methods of regulating Deaf childbirth. Hearing people have embarked on direct eugenics of Deaf people as well. The twentieth century witnessed movements in the United States and Germany, for example, to sterilize Deaf people by law and to encourage them to seek voluntary sterilization or abstain from childbearing. The legal initiative in the United States had limited success, but its well-publicized pursuit led untold numbers of Deaf people to abandon plans for marriage and reproduction or to submit to voluntary sterilization, and the clamor about Deaf eugenics also led untold numbers of hearing parents to have their Deaf children sterilized. Alexander Graham Bell, head of the Eugenics Section of the American Breeders Association (later the American Genetics Association), laid the groundwork for such efforts in his numerous statistical studies and censuses of the Deaf population in the United States and especially in his 1883 *Memoir upon the Formation of a Deaf Variety of the Human Race,* which he printed privately and distributed widely.

Moreover, he presented this broadside against Deaf Culture and Deaf intermarriage to the National Academy of Sciences on his election to that body, giving the false impression that it was sanctioned by the academy and was scientifically valid. In this memoir, Bell warned that "the congenital deaf-mutes of the country are increasing at a greater rate than the population at large; and the deaf-mute children of deaf-mutes at a greater rate than the congenital deaf-mute population." Bell attributed the problem to sign language, which "causes the intermarriage of deaf-mutes and the propagation of their physical defect."[36] The Eugenics Section prepared a model sterilization law and promoted it in the nation's state legislatures; it called for sterilization of feebleminded, insane, criminalistic, deaf, and other "socially unfit" classes.[37] By the time of the German sterilization program, some thirty states in the United States had sterilization laws in force. However, Bell's lobbying efforts were unsuccessful, and none of the laws specifically included Deaf people.

The purpose of the eugenics movement with respect to Deaf people, the measures aimed at discouraging their socialization, intermarriage, and reproduction, was not so much to achieve those goals, which were largely unachievable and would be ineffective if achieved. After all, most Deaf children have hearing parents, as Bell well knew, so even if he had had his way and no Deaf adults had Deaf children that would not seriously reduce the numbers of Deaf children. What then was Bell's purpose in promoting eugenic measures with Deaf people? I submit that it was to reinforce a certain conceptualization or "construction" of Deaf people, one that was linked to the construction of people with impairments such as feeblemindedness and to a particular technology of normalization—oralism—with its own authorities, legislation, institutions, and professions. Moreover, the eugenics campaign marked the Deaf world as an important social problem requiring expertise, one that had been previously overlooked, much to the danger of society. In this respect, the claims making closely paralleled the movement to awaken society to the dangers of mentally retarded people in our midst. As psychologists and superintendents of institutions for the feebleminded stood to gain from the recognition of the newly discovered social problem of mild retardation, so a competent authority that stood to gain from the construction of Deaf people as a newly discovered menace was the burgeoning organization Bell had founded, the American Association to Promote the Teaching of Speech to the Deaf (AAPTSD). In 1969 this association, now known as the Alexander Graham Bell Association for the Deaf, republished Bell's *Memoir,* praising its "perceptive insights."[38] The eugenics movement as it concerned Deaf people worldwide has received regrettably little study.[39] When National Socialism came to power in Germany, fully forty organizations of Deaf people in Berlin were combined into two; the treasuries of the original organizations were confiscated; the Jewish Deaf Association was prohibited; and Jewish members of all other Deaf organizations were expelled. Teachers of Deaf students advocated adherence to the hereditary purity laws, including the sterilization of congenitally Deaf people. Deaf school children were required to prepare family trees, and the school reported those who were congenitally Deaf or who had a Deaf relative to the department of health for possible sterilization. Leaders of the unified Deaf organization and the Deaf newspaper, themselves late-deafened, endorsed the sterilization campaign.[40]

The German sterilization law that went into effect in 1934 provided that "Those hereditarily sick may be made unfruitful [sterilized] through surgical intervention. . . . The hereditary sick, in the sense of this law, is a person who suffers from one of the following diseases . . . hereditary deafness."[41] The 1933 census showed forty-five thousand "deaf and dumb" persons in a total population of over sixty-six million. An estimated seventeen thousand of these Deaf Germans, a third of them minors, were sterilized. In 9 percent of the cases, sterilization was accompanied by forced abortion. An additional sixteen hundred Deaf people were exterminated in concentration camps in the 1940s; they were considered "useless eaters," with lives unworthy of being lived.[42] As in the United States, the medical profession was the certifying authority for forced sterilization. And as in the United States, such legislation may have been concerned more with constructions of social problems and the identification of competent authority than with measures for their practical resolution.

In 1992 researchers at Boston University announced that they had identified the "genetic error" responsible for a common type of inherited deafness. The director of the National Institute on Deafness and Other Communication Disorders [sic] called the finding a "major breakthrough that will improve diagnosis and genetic counseling and ultimately lead to substitution therapy or gene transfer therapy."[43] Thus a new form of medical eugenics applied to Deaf people was envisioned, in this case by an agency of the U.S. government. The primary characteristics of Deaf people with this genetic background are numerous Deaf relatives, sign language fluency, facial features such as widely spaced eyebrows, and coloring features such as a white forelock and freckling.[44] For such characteristics to be viewed not as normal human variation in physiognomy, coloring, and so on but as a "genetic error," some of the common features must clearly be construed as signs of a disease or infirmity. However, according to a leading medical geneticist, the "sole detrimental feature" of the syndrome is that some people with this gene are Deaf.[45] Within the culture of the Deaf world, then, this cannot be a disease.

The technologies of normalization seek not only to reduce Deaf births but also to change the physical makeup of the Deaf child through surgery so that that child is, to whatever extent possible, a little more like a hearing child or, to be more accurate, like a child with a hearing impairment. There is consensus among ear surgeons and audiologists that a child with a cochlear implant is "severely hearing-impaired,"[46] and some comparisons with hearing-aid users even place many of them in the category of those with a profound hearing impairment.[47]

If the Deaf child has a serious disability, then surely an operation that tries to reduce that disability is justified, even if it has limited success, even if its risks are not well understood, and even if it is very expensive. This consequence of the disability classification applied to culturally Deaf children is fraught with danger for those children and the Deaf world. The surgery is of unproven value for the main benefit sought, spoken language acquisition, while the psychological, social, and linguistic risks have not been assessed but appear ominous.[48] Thus the surgery is innovative, but innovative surgery on children is unethical.[49] Moreover, if there were highly effective implants—and one day there may well be—the ranks of the Deaf world would presumably diminish. It is unethical to take steps that tend to reduce the ranks of a minority culture, and it violates international law,[50] but the disability categorization of *deaf* is so intuitive here that few hearing people see the danger in allowing cochlear implant programs to proceed at an accelerating pace.

All in all, then, there are many powerful arguments in favor of Deaf people's resisting the disability classification that the technologies of normalization seek.[51] But therein lies a dilemma. Government and the technologies of normalization have linked granting Deaf people their fundamental rights as citizens to their colluding in classifying them as people with a disability. In those countries where Deaf people can get interpreters, those services are organized under a disability umbrella. In fact, able-bodied Deaf people in the United States and some other countries can get cash merely for agreeing that they are disabled and registering as such. Likewise, Deaf children can get schooling only under the disability classification. The dilemma is that Deaf people want access and as citizens in a democracy have a right to access—access to public events, government services, and education—but when they subscribe to the disability definition in order to gain access, they undermine their struggle for other rights, such as an education for Deaf children using their best language, an end to implant surgery on those children, and an end to efforts to discourage Deaf births in the first place. The technologies of normalization, through extensive lobbying, have shaped those government policies that have created this dilemma for Deaf people. With enough disincentives to change, Deaf people may tolerate the misclassification and indeed may even appear to support it, as when they demand their rights under the Americans with Disabilities Act. The stronger the link between Deaf and disability, the better the prospects for the professions predicated on that link.

Yet, Deaf activism may turn things around. The constructions of numerous social groups are different today from what they were generations ago because of the groups' activism in changing social understanding. Blacks in America are no longer property—they are citizens. Gays and Lesbians are no longer distinguished by a defect but rather are seen as a minority set apart by a characteristic of their birth, like blacks and women. Native Americans are no longer understood as savages; women are no longer thought to be inherently the weaker sex, whose life roles must center around child rearing. Deaf people can come to be understood not as a disability group but as the possessors and protectors of a great cultural heritage, a beautiful language, numerous art forms, and an eloquent history. That will require Deaf people to mount a vigorous effort to oppose the claims making of the technologies of normalization. Indeed, many in those professions and in the social sciences and humanities would join Deaf people in their opposition. Is an antidefamation league needed to promptly rebut such self-serving disparagement of Deaf people as "a catastrophe,"[52] a people in need of saturation services, implant surgery, and eugenic gene therapy? Is the time right for Deaf people to mount a major marketing effort, one that involves, for example, advertising, public service announcements, celebrity spots on TV, stories for the media, and a source of pro-Deaf information for the nation? Such an effort would target outreach to parents, doctors, and legislators as well as the general public, helping them to understand the positive value of this form of human variation. In the nineteenth century, black leader Frederick Douglass said this about a comparable effort for his minority: "Oh, had I the ability, and could I reach the nation's ear, I would today pour out a fiery stream of biting ridicule, blasting reproach, withering sarcasm, and stern rebuke. For it is not light that is needed, but fire; it is not the gentle shower, but thunder."[53] Unless Deaf people challenge the culturally determined meanings of *deaf* and *disability* with at least as much vigor as the technologies of normalization seek to institutionalize those meanings, the day will continue to recede in which Deaf children and adults live the fullest lives and make the fullest contribution to our diverse society.

Notes

1. Michel Foucault, *Power/Knowledge: Selected Interviews and Other Writings, 1972–1977* (Brighton, Sussex: Harvester Press, 1980).
2. "Welfare Helps Kids," *USA Today,* November 16, 1994, 12A.
3. Department of Education and Science, *Special Educational Needs (Warnock Report)* (London: Her Majesty's Stationery Office, 1978).
4. Osamu Nagase, "Disabled Persons' Fundamental Law in Japan" (paper presented at the Disability Rights Symposium of European Regions, Southampton, England, 1995).
5. Foucault, *Power/Knowledge.*
6. Harlan Lane, *When the Mind Hears: A History of the Deaf* (New York: Random House, 1984).
7. Susan Gregory and Gillian M. Hartley, eds., *Constructing Deafness* (London: Pinter, 1991).
8. Paul Abberley, "The Concept of Oppression and the Development of a Social Theory of Disability," *Disability, Handicap and Society* 2 (1987): 5–19. M. Oliver, "Multispecialist and Multidisciplinary: A Recipe for Confusion? Too Many Cooks Spoil the Broth," *Disability, Handicap and Society* 6 (1991): 65–68.
9. U.S. Department of Commerce, *Statistical Abstract of the United States* (Washington, D.C.: Superintendent of Government Documents, 1999).
10. "Teva to Market," *Business Wire,* March 30, 2000, http://www.businesswire.com.
11. Beth Werth, "How Short Is Too Short?" *New York Times Magazine,* Section 6, June 16, 1991, 14–17, 28–29, 47.
12. E. McCaughey, J. Mulligan, L. Voss, and P. Betts, "Randomised Trial of Growth Hormone in Short Normal Girls," *Lancet* 351 (1998): 940–44.
13. "Researchers at Southampton University Hospitals," *Science News,* April 25, 1998, 271. A. B. Downie, J. Mulligan, E. S. McCaughey, R. J. Stratford, P. R. Betts, and L. D. Voss, "Psychological Response to Treatment in Short Normal Children," *Archives of Disorders of Childhood* 76 (1996): 92–95.
14. Richard Herrnstein and Charles Murray, *The Bell Curve* (New York: Free Press, 1994).
15. M. L. Andersen, "The Many and Varied Social Constructions of Intelligence," in *Constructing the Social,* ed. T. R. Sarbin and J. I. Kitsuse (London: Sage, 1994), 119–38.
16. S. A. Gelb, "Social Deviance and the 'Discovery' of the Moron," *Disability, Handicap and Society* 2 (1987): 247–58.
17. J. Kivirauma and O. Kivinen, "The School System and Special Education: Causes and Effects in the Twentieth Century," *Disability, Handicap and Society* 3 (1988): 153–65.
18. G. Fulcher, "Australian Policies on Special Education: Towards a Sociological Account," *Disability, Handicap and Society* 1 (1986): 19–52.
19. Department of Education and Science, *Special Educational Needs.*
20. Stephan Chorover, *From Genesis to Genocide* (Cambridge, Mass.: M.I.T. Press, 1979). H. H. Goddard, "Mental Tests and the Immigrant," *Journal of Delinquency* 2 (1917): 243–77.
21. Lane, *When the Mind Hears.*
22. Daniel Kevles, *In the Name of Eugenics: Genetics and the Uses of Human Heredity* (New York: Knopf, 1985).

23. Tom Humphries, "Communicating across Cultures: Deaf/Hearing and Language Learning" (PhD diss., Union Graduate School, Cincinnati, 1977). Harlan Lane, *The Mask of Benevolence: Disabling the Deaf Community,* 2nd ed. (San Diego: DawnSignPress, 1999).

24. M. Joutselainen, *World Federation of the Deaf Survey of Deaf People in the Developing World* (Helsinki: World Federation of the Deaf, 1991).

25. Thomas Balkany, A. Hodges, and K. Goodman, "Ethics of Cochlear Implantation in Young Children," *Otolaryngology: Head and Neck Surgery* 114 (1996): 751.

26. Alice Dreger, *Hermaphrodites and the Medical Invention of Sex* (Cambridge, Mass.: Harvard University Press, 1998). A. Draeger, "The Limits of Individuality: Ritual and Sacrifice in the Lives and Medical Treatment of Conjoined Twins," *Studies in the History and Philosophy of Biological and Biomedical Sciences* 29 (1998): C:1–29. Joan Ablon, *Little People in America: The Social Dimensions of Dwarfism* (New York: Praeger, 1984). Harlan Lane, "The Cochlear Implant Controversy," *World Federation of the Deaf News* 2, no. 3 (1994): 22–28.

27. Ivan Tucker and Michael Nolan, *Educational Audiology* (London: Croom Helm, 1984). Quoted in Gregory and Hartley, *Constructing Deafness,* 97.

28. Karen Emmorey, *Language, Cognition, and the Brain: Insights from Sign Language Research* (Mahwah, N.J.: Lawrence Erlbaum Associates, 2001).

29. Abberley, "Concept of Oppression."

30. Gaylene Becker, *Growing Old in Silence* (Berkeley and Los Angeles: University of California Press, 1980). R. Saltus, "Returning to the World of Sound," *Boston Globe,* July 10, 1989, 27, 29.

31. Tom Humphries, "Deaf Culture and Cultures," in *Multicultural Issues in Deafness,* ed. K. M. Christensen and G. L. Delgado (White Plains, N.Y.: Longman, 1993), 14.

32. Joseph P. Shapiro, *No Pity: People with Disabilities Forging a New Civil Rights Movement* (New York: Times Books, 1993).

33. "Pride in a Soundless World," *New York Times,* May 16, 1993, section 1, p. 1.

34. John V. Van Cleve, "Nebraska's Oral Law of 1911 and the Deaf Community," *Nebraska History* 65 (1984): 195–220.

35. Robert V. Bruce, *Alexander Graham Bell and the Conquest of Solitude* (Boston: Little, Brown, 1973).

36. Alexander Graham Bell, *Memoir upon the Formation of a Deaf Variety of the Human Race* (New Haven: National Academy of Sciences, 1883; repr. 1969), 40, 44.

37. Harlan Lane, "Cochlear Implants: Their Cultural and Historical Meaning," in *Deaf History Unveiled,* ed. John Van Cleve (Washington, D.C.: Gallaudet University Press, 1993), 272–91.

38. Victor Goodhill, "Foreword," in Bell, *Memoir upon the Formation of a Deaf Variety of the Human Race,* unnumbered page.

39. But see Horst Biesold, *Crying Hands: Eugenics and Deaf People in Nazi Germany,* trans. Will Sayers (Washington, D.C.: Gallaudet University Press, 1999). Donna Ryan and John Schuchman, eds., *Deaf People in Hitler's Europe* (Washington, D.C.: Gallaudet University Press, 2002).

40. J. Muhs, "Followers and Outcasts: Berlin's Deaf Community under National Socialism, 1933–1945," *Collage* 33 (1996): 195–204.

41. W. W. Peter, "Germany's Sterilization Program," *American Journal of Public Health* 243 (1934): 187.

42. Biesold, *Crying Hands.* Cited in W. Higgins, ed., "La Parole des Sourds," *Psychoanalystes* 46–47 (1993): 1–216.

43. "BU Team Finds Genetic Cause of Waardenburg Syndrome," *Deaf Community News,* March 1992, 6.

44. G. R. Fraser, *The Causes of Profound Deafness in Childhood* (Baltimore: Johns Hopkins University Press, 1976).

45. George R. Fraser, "Hearing Loss: Genetic Causes," in *Gallaudet Encyclopedia of Deaf People and Deafness,* ed. John Van Cleve (New York: McGraw-Hill, 1976), 20–23.

46. Mary Joe Osberger and D. Kessler, "Issues in Protocol Design for Cochlear Implant Trials in

Children: The Clarion Pediatric Study," *Annals of Otology, Rhinology and Laryngology* 9, suppl. (1995): 337–39.

47. R. T. Miyamoto, K. I. Kirk, S. L. Todd, A. M. Robbins, and M. J. Osberger, "Speech Perception Skills of Children with Multichannel Cochlear Implants or Hearing Aids," *Annals of Otology, Rhinology and Laryngology* 104, suppl. (1995): 334–37.

48. Harlan Lane and Ben Bahan, "Effects of Cochlear Implantation in Young Children: A Review and a Reply from a DEAF-WORLD Perspective," *Otolaryngology: Head and Neck Surgery* 119 (1998): 297–308.

49. Harlan Lane and M. Grodin, "Ethical Issues in Cochlear Implant Surgery: An Exploration into Disease, Disability, and the Best Interests of the Child," *Kennedy Institute of Ethics Journal* 7 (1997): 231–51.

50. United Nations, *Rights of Persons Belonging to National, or Ethnic, Religious and Linguistic Minorities,* Resolution 47/135 (New York: United Nations, 1992).

51. Harlan Lane, "Constructions of Deafness," *Disability and Society* 10 (1995): 171–89.

52. Claude-Henri Chouard, *Entendre sans Oreille* (Paris: Laffont, 1978).

53. Frederick Douglass, Public Address on Independence Day, 1852, http://www.historyplace.com/speeches/douglass.htm.

18. Beyond Culture: Deaf Studies and the Deaf Body

DOUGLAS C. BAYNTON

THE CONCEPT OF DEAF CULTURE is fundamental to the field of Deaf Studies. In recent decades, the distinctive cultural attributes of the American Deaf community have been documented and described at length, among them a shared history, a rich literary culture, rules of etiquette and naming practices that differ from those of the larger hearing society, a strong tendency to marry within the group, a unique means of transmitting cultural knowledge between generations, and of course a complex visual language. In addition, like other cultural minority groups, Deaf people have established a variety of social, political, and economic organizations, as well as a periodical press, dating from the mid-nineteenth century. Perhaps most importantly, Deaf people share fundamental values that differ from those of the hearing Americans around them, in particular having the value of American Sign Language (ASL) and the Deaf world. The existence of a deep, rich, and long-standing culture of American Deaf people is now beyond reasonable dispute.[1]

As important and useful as it has been, however, the concept of Deaf Culture increasingly appears inadequate by itself as an explanation of the Deaf community and the experiences of Deaf people. For example, recent research has shown that Deaf people process visual information differently than hearing people, and in some ways more efficiently. This has complemented a growing emphasis in recent years on the centrality of vision to Deaf experience, with some Deaf people suggesting that they instead be referred to as "Seeing people" or "Visual people."[2] The statement by George Veditz that Deaf people "are facing not a theory but a condition, for they are first, last, and all the time *the* people of the eye," has become a popular aphorism among Deaf activists.[3] Deaf people now often speak of "deaf eyes," a characteristic and recognizable way Deaf people have of using the eyes. Under an exclusively cultural model, how do we discuss such phenomena? What, moreover, is the implication of arguing, as Deaf people long have argued, that it is in the *nature* of deaf people to use signed languages, a view that has been given support by linguistic research into language acquisition and development among deaf children? All of these suggest that Deaf people differ from hearing people in physical (or, more precisely, sensory) ways that are not explained by culture.

This is not to say that sensory difference by itself is sufficient to explain Deaf identity. For example, many people identify themselves as hearing impaired, hearing disabled, deaf, or hard of hearing who are not culturally Deaf: they do not share the values of Deaf people, they are not (or only partially) fluent in the language of the community, and they do not identify as Deaf and are not seen as Deaf. The cultural distinction between deaf and Deaf, while sometimes ambiguous, is nevertheless a crucial one.

Consider, however, another kind of outsider to Deaf identity: hearing people who grow up within a Deaf family, marry into the Deaf community, or for whatever reason immerse themselves in the Deaf world. They may be as fluent in ASL, cognizant of Deaf cultural beliefs and etiquette, familiar with Deaf folklore, and involved in the social life of the Deaf community as any Deaf person. They may be accepted, respected, well liked, included in the community "as if" they were Deaf, and they may even be referred to as "Deaf" in certain circumstances. Yet they are recognized as not *really* Deaf. As Padden and Humphries note in *Deaf in America*, "Hearing children of Deaf parents represent an ongoing contradiction in the culture: they display the knowledge of their parents—skill in the language and social conduct—but the culture finds subtle ways to give them an unusual and separate status." Cultural explanations by themselves are insufficient to explain Deaf identity.[4]

The cultural model also fails to adequately account for the stories Deaf people commonly tell of their first weeks at the residential school, of feeling that they had found their true home. Culture cannot explain that experience, for they are not yet "Deaf" when they arrive. Similarly, many young deaf people grow up in oral schools or in mainstream programs who do not encounter ASL or Deaf Culture until adulthood, yet as young adults (often as students at Gallaudet University) choose to learn ASL as best they can, to principally associate with Deaf people, and to identify themselves as culturally Deaf. This includes many people who were considered to be "oral successes" by their teachers and parents. Under a simple cultural model, this ought not to happen with such frequency. Children raised in the hearing world are culturally hearing, not Deaf, yet in large numbers choose to join the Deaf world. An explanation of why they make this choice must point beyond culture.

Moreover, how do we explain the strong connections that Deaf people often feel to other Deaf people from outside their own country, to people from very different and distant cultures? Deaf cultures, like hearing cultures, vary a great deal from country to country.[5] Carol Padden is currently studying the Bedouin deaf, who are fully integrated in a hearing community where everyone signs, and who consequently have not created a distinct Deaf Culture. Yet Padden sees her research as part of Deaf Studies and of interest to American Deaf people. Why should that be, if culture alone is what defines Deaf people and binds them together? Indeed, in spite of major cultural differences, Padden tells me that upon meeting the Bedouin deaf, she felt the same sense of commonality and connection that Deaf people typically feel upon meeting.[6] The cultural model needs a great deal of stretching to cover such phenomena. A more plausible and straightforward alternative is to posit that Deaf people are different from hearing people in ways other than cultural.

It has become standard practice in Deaf Studies to speak of the Deaf community as an ethnic group. While that term fits in many ways, in other ways it can be misleading. As Jeffrey Nash pointed out in 1987, "in conventional ethnic groups, members of the first generation have the ethnic mother tongue as native, and . . . second and third generations shift from the ethnic to the dominant language."[7] In other words, ethnic groups in America typically assimilate during the second and third generations. Deaf people do not. Nor do Deaf people tend to marry outside the group, as do second- and third-generation children of ethnic groups. Furthermore, ethnicity is typically an identity shared within families, while deafness is typically not. Recent research estimates that only about 3 percent of Deaf people have two Deaf parents. Ethnicity, then, offers a misleading model for the childhood experiences of 97 percent of Deaf people (and of that 3 percent, a majority have hearing siblings, again an experience unlike that of most ethnic groups).[8]

When I wrote my book *Forbidden Signs: American Culture and the Campaign against Sign Language,* I worked within the cultural model. One of the criticisms I encountered from historians who read my early drafts, however, was that I argued that deafness was a cultural construction while simultaneously contending that oralism was *necessarily* harmful to deaf people. They pointed out to me that if deafness was truly just a cultural construction, there were no grounds for taking the position that deaf people everywhere in all times *needed* signed language. In making that claim I was necessarily making a claim about the *nature* of deafness. In response to that criticism, I wrote the following in my introduction to the book:

> Deafness is . . . very much a cultural construction that changes over time. But it is also a physical reality. The hearing people who have traditionally made most of the decisions concerning the education of deaf children can spend entire careers contented within these constructions of deafness, unconstrained by physical reality, but deaf people cannot. When the cultural climate of the nineteenth century changed to make sign language objectionable, hearing people could simply say, "Away with sign language," and imagine that this could be accomplished. Deaf people could not, for they are both members of a species that by nature seeks optimal communication, and inhabitants of a sensory universe in which that end cannot be achieved by oral means alone.[9]

In the book's conclusion I added that being deaf "is more than a cultural construction. It means most fundamentally that one occupies a different sensory world from those who hear, and this has certain consequences that cannot be *constructed* away. This physical reality (upon which culture works, certainly, and with which culture intertwines and interacts) transcends culture."[10] I did not pursue the matter any further, however. Constrained by the cultural model, I simply did not know what to do with these ideas. Increasingly, I have become convinced that if the field of Deaf Studies is to progress, it must move beyond the culture model to talk about the body, about the significance of living in a different sensory world.

There is an understandable resistance among Deaf people and Deaf Studies scholars to focusing on the physical aspect of deafness. In the past, such a focus has meant defining deafness in terms of defect and deficiency. It has meant talking about what Deaf people have in common with other disabled people, which has seemed a dangerous path to start down, given that most people think of disability in terms of inability, absence, and loss. Many Deaf people have tried to distance themselves from this image by distancing themselves from any notion of disability and insisting that their identity is based on cultural rather than physical difference from the hearing majority. They explain that being Deaf is not a defect, that being Deaf offers no less rich and rewarding a life than being hearing, and that being Deaf is neither a pathology nor a medical matter. Most of us in Deaf Studies have correspondingly defined our work as a branch of ethnic studies, separate and distinct from disability studies.

However, what most people have in mind when they think of disability is a medical model (a.k.a. the functional limitations or pathological model). According to this model, disability is simply a physical, mental, or sensory impairment. It resides solely or largely in the individual with the impairment. Prevention, cure, and rehabilitation are of primary importance. When Deaf people say that "disabled" does not describe them, it is generally this model that they reject.[11] It is precisely this model, however, that Disability Studies scholars (and disability rights activists) also reject. In recent decades they have advanced a social model that locates disability not in individual bodies but rather in social structures and practices that do not take account of normal human variation. Just as gender and race are not merely matters of bodily difference, so is disability not simply inherent in bodies but rather a way of interpreting human differences. People with particular physical differences from the majority are *disabled* by the prejudicial beliefs and actions of the majority. When buildings, technology, and media are designed for certain types of people but not others, when communication is carried out in ways accessible to certain types of people but not others, or when school curricula are designed for certain types of learning but not others, disability results. Disability, in short, is a product of oppression.[12]

In this, disabled people have followed a trajectory similar to other oppressed groups. It was once also generally accepted that the bodies of women and members of "inferior races" limited their capacity to participate in social and economic life. As Harlan Hahn has noted, "unlike other disadvantaged groups, citizens with disabilities have not yet fully succeeded in refuting the presumption that their subordinate status can be ascribed to an innate biological inferiority." They have made considerable progress in recent years, however. People with physical differences from the majority have increasingly moved away from the notion that they *have* a disability, or are persons *with* a disability, and instead refer to themselves as *disabled people* to indicate its centrality to their identity, and speak of "disablement" to refer to the social process of becoming disabled. Many people find it difficult to understand that anyone would willingly embrace the identity of "disabled person," since disability in our culture seems self-evidently a personally discrediting label. Just as most hearing people simplistically translate "deaf" into "cannot hear," so do most people equate *dis*abled with *un*able. By claiming disability as an identity, however, disabled people name the oppression under which they live, declare solidarity with others similarly oppressed, and set themselves in opposition to it.[13]

Our bodies matter because they shape how we experience, understand, and interact with the world, and because they affect how others view us. On both counts, the body is intensely relevant to Deaf people. The appropriate vocabulary is that of difference, however, not loss. Just as deafness brings into being new ways of using the other senses, so does any physical difference result in a new configuration of abilities. Merely equating disability with impairment reduces a way of life, a complex relation to the environment, and a web of social relationships and cultural meanings to a simple and concrete absence. It fails utterly to account for the human experience of disability. Like Deaf people, disabled people experience disability in terms of social relations rather than as personal deficiency, and it becomes just one aspect of the world in which they live, in all its complexity.

This does not mean that disabled people experience no limitations, but rather that the experience of limitation is a universal one, not characteristic merely of a subset of humanity. Relative to most of the animal kingdom, after all, humans live in a flat and unvariegated scent world. Their vision is severely impaired by the standards of, say, a hawk, and their night vision is abysmal compared to an owl or a cat. They are deaf to frequencies heard well by dogs, bats, whales, and elephants. They are poor swimmers, slow runners, and incapable of flight absent assistive technology. The list of abilities that other creatures enjoy and that humans lack is long indeed, yet somehow the human species manages to limp along without nursing feelings of grief or loss. The reason we do not consider ourselves disabled is that the term is relative to notions of normality around which we structure our societies. Radio programs do not employ frequencies beyond normal human hearing, jobs do not demand the eyesight of an eagle, and schools do not require students to stand all day like horses without sitting. We establish expectations based on what is normal for the majority and design our built environment to serve that norm—and to exclude, often, any who fall outside it. Deaf people are disabled in the sense that they fall outside most cultures' notions of normality and are on that basis denied equal access to social and economic life.

Culture

The common argument that Deaf people are a cultural and linguistic group and *therefore* are not disabled wrongly characterizes culture and disability as mutually exclusive. Saying that Deaf people share a culture says nothing about the usefulness or validity of speaking of Deaf people as disabled. The social model of disability is entirely compatible with an understanding of Deaf people as a cultural minority group and, as a complement to the cultural model, accounts for much about Deaf experience that the cultural model cannot. Not only is it entirely possible for Deaf people to be both a distinct cultural group *and* disabled, it is necessary if Deaf and Disability Studies scholars are to provide a coherent account of the Deaf community.

What do we mean when we say that people "have" a culture? If there are any words with fixed, definite, and unchanging meanings, this one is certainly not among them. Until fairly recently, "culture" referred to a quality acquired through education, an elevated and learned ability to discern the finer from the baser aspects of the world. It was acquired through *cultivation*. Only in the twentieth century did its current anthropological meaning become prevalent, and that meaning is still by no means standardized. Speaking of *a culture* is a shorthand way of saying that a defined group of people share certain distinctive beliefs, practices, and ways of interpreting the world that persist across generations. It refers, in essence, to what a group of people typically think (as expressed in language) and what they typically do.

Some have resisted the term Deaf Culture, arguing that Deaf Americans partake in the larger American culture and therefore constitute a *sub*culture within it. The flaw in this reasoning is that it assumes the nation-state to be the natural level on which culture operates, and cultures on a smaller scale to be necessarily subordinate. The concept of culture, however, has no necessary affiliation with the nation-state. It would make equal sense to speak of "Western culture," to assume "the West" to be the level on which culture resides and national cultures as subcultures. Alternatively, one might situate "culture" on the level of region or ethnicity, and argue that modern nations are too diverse to claim a unitary and cohesive culture. The distinction between culture and subculture is an arbitrary one. We make the distinction as a matter of practical utility not of logical or natural necessity. "Culture" is variously used to describe national linguistic groups (even when these share languages with other, distinct national cultures), stateless linguistic groups, supranational and subnational groups with or without shared languages (including *movement cultures* when these involve significant, shared structures of thought). It has been used in these diverse ways because in each case *it has proved useful* in understanding the attributes of a given group. Describing the distinctive beliefs and practices of the American Deaf community in terms of culture has been tremendously productive in a variety of ways, both for Deaf people themselves and for the academic study of their community. It is a powerful idea and therefore has, in the pragmatic sense, truth value. While there is still resistance to the idea of Deaf Culture in some quarters, it now seems to be an idea that is here to stay.[14]

It may also turn out to be useful to speak of a disability culture. A number of disability activists and scholars think so and have been busy developing an argument for it in recent years. If it helps us to understand the experience of disability and the lives of disabled people—if it turns out, that is, to have truth value—then the idea will have staying power. If it does not, if it distorts or obscures more than it clarifies, then it will not. The evidence for such usefulness is not very strong yet, in my opinion, but it is still a relatively new idea and its proponents have not yet elaborated it to any great extent, so it is too early to judge. The idea of Deaf Culture, after all, took a couple of decades to work out and to begin to make sense to both scholars and Deaf people. And unlike Deaf Culture, which is understood to date in the United States from the nineteenth century, disability culture is usually understood as something that has emerged only in recent decades, in part as a movement culture.[15]

Whether or not the concept of disability culture turns out to have merit, the point here is that there is no inherent contradiction in identifying a group as both disabled and as a cultural group. The terms do not describe mutually exclusive states of being. "Disability" describes a particular kind of relationship between a majority and a minority, between socially constructed notions of normality and deviance. "Culture" describes a set of values and beliefs within a group. Saying that Deaf people share a culture says nothing about the usefulness or validity of speaking of Deaf people as disabled. It is not necessary to say that Deaf people are *either* a cultural group *or* disabled. It is entirely possible to be both.

Pragmatic Considerations

Considered as a purely practical matter, what good and what harm come from Deaf people aligning themselves with disabled people and the concept of disability? This is by no means a simple question. In the past, the emphasis of the disability rights movement on educational inclusion or mainstreaming has been a point of serious contention. Disability rights activists have increasingly come to understand and respect the Deaf position on this question, in addition to increasingly questioning the often ideologically rigid, one-size-fits-all approach of the early years of the movement. *Disability Watch*, the periodic assessment of the status of disabled people in the United States published by Disability Rights Advocates, pointed out that while inclusion has been good for most disabled people, it "is proving disastrous for deaf children." It went on to describe how "the Deaf community has vigorously opposed these ill-considered practices, but its cogent dissent has gone largely unheeded" by school authorities.[16] Of course, as with any coalition made up of groups with diverse interests and experiences, disagreements are unavoidable. Still, cooperation between Deaf and disability rights groups has accomplished much good, most notably the Americans with Disabilities Act. The constant refrain heard from the Deaf community that "we are not disabled," however, threatens to undermine the basis for that cooperation. Disabled and nondisabled people alike increasingly respond that if Deaf people really don't want to be considered disabled, then they ought not to claim the protections of that designation.

In any case, alignment with disabled people clearly holds more promise than one with ethnic groups. If there are differences among disabled groups, they pale in comparison with the distance between Deaf and other ethnic communities. Can we imagine the Chinese American community agitating in favor of Deaf teachers? What reason would hearing Spanish speakers have for supporting residential schools for deaf children? (After all, in California a majority of Hispanic-American voters recently joined other citizens in voting to end bilingual education.) In battling the resurgence of eugenics, are disabled people or Cuban Americans going to be more steadfast allies? Who have been powerful allies of Deaf people in the past, ethnic Americans or disabled Americans?

If the disability model tends to have a bias toward assimilation, contrary to the interests of the Deaf community, the ethnic model in the United States does as well, but without accommodations for physical differences from the majority. The rights and services that Deaf people demand are of the kind demanded by disabled people not ethnic groups. Interpreters, for example, are provided to linguistic minorities in the United States only in a limited number of unusual situations, such as court appearances and medical emergencies. Those who wish to attend college or take up a profession are expected to master and use the national language. College instructors and graduate students whose first language is not English must pass an exam demonstrating their ability to make themselves clearly understood in spoken English before they are permitted to teach. Deaf people, on the other hand, rightly demand subsidized interpreting services that allow them to participate in cultural, social, and economic life on an equal basis with hearing people. The demand for captioning and relay services is even less compatible with the ethnic group model. To the extent that these services are provided, it is in the name of disability rights, not ethnic group rights, since no other minority requests, let alone asserts a right to, such services. The principle at work in the provision of these services is that it is wrong to construct, for example, a phone system that serves some people and excludes other, or to offer a college education that is accessible to some but not others, merely on the basis of physical, sensory, or mental differences. As far as I am aware, every useful law in the United States protecting Deaf rights has been based on this principle, rooted in the demand for disability rights rather than in protections for ethnic minorities. Furthermore, aside from the pragmatic considerations of political efficacy, the ethnic model fails conceptually even to explain the kinds of rights that Deaf people assert.

In the struggle to provide a decent education for deaf children, the cultural model also falls short, and in fact is counterproductive. Hearing parents of deaf children are rarely persuaded of the value of ASL by being told about Deaf Culture, and often resist the notion that their children ought to be part of a culture other than their own. In fact, they frequently express fears of "losing their children to the Deaf Culture." More persuasive arguments stress the importance of ensuring linguistic input via the eyes while children are still very young, to achieve their fullest social and intellectual development. That is, it focuses on the ways in which their children's sensory needs differ from those of hearing children.

The Deaf Culture model by itself has always posed a troublesome incongruity when used to discuss deaf children. When we speak of deaf adults who are not culturally Deaf, no one objects to referring to them as disabled. However, when we speak of mainstreamed deaf children in hearing families, we often speak of them as Deaf even when they have had no contact with Deaf Culture, in part because we think that they *ought* to be Deaf, and in part because they are likely to become Deaf at some point in the future. Some of them, however, will never be culturally Deaf, and it is clearly contradictory to speak of deaf children as Deaf, only to reclassify some of them as disabled when grown, when nothing substantive has changed other than their age. We are stuck with making this incoherent argument because, under the cultural minority model, there is no other logical way to assert their linguistic rights as children. To claim, however, that children who have no connection to or even knowledge of the Deaf community are culturally Deaf is unpersuasive to say the least. It is utterly unpersuasive to their hearing parents, who often view it as presumptuous as well as absurd, and it is intellectually implausible to scholars to suggest that Deaf people, unlike any others in the world, might somehow be born with a culture inherent within them.

An alternative that resolves the incongruity, as well as offering a more plausible line of argument in favor of early ASL for all deaf children, is to take seriously the truism that (in Padden and Humphries's words), "Deaf people are both Deaf and deaf."[17] That is, Deaf people are both a cultural minority *and* disabled. This allows us to say that a deaf child is physically different from hearing children, therefore has fundamentally different needs from hearing children, and therefore if denied access to effective bilingual education *is disabled by that denial*. It allows us to say, further, that both Deaf and hard-of-hearing persons are disabled by social practices designed to accommodate only hearing people, and to demand arrangements that accommodate them as well as hearing people.

Indeed, those writing within the Deaf Culture model often do say that deaf children who are denied access to ASL and to the Deaf community by parents and schools are disabled by that denial.[18] This is precisely in line with the social model of disability. The Disability Studies model would go further, however, to argue that even Deaf children who attend bicultural/bilingual educational programs and are fully acculturated in the Deaf community *continue* to be disabled by discriminatory practices that extend beyond secondary school. It is disabling to be denied equal access to television, movies, theater, or civic and public events. It is disabling to be denied reasonable accommodations, in higher education or on the job, such as competent interpreting services. According to the social model of disability, both deaf and Deaf people are disabled not because they do not hear, but because society is structured and everyday business is conducted in ways that exclude them: mass media and public services are often inaccessible; education is generally inferior; information in public places comes over aural but not visual channels; prejudice, demeaning stereotypes, and discrimination are widespread; and in general the hearing majority assumes a hearing norm and doesn't accommodate those who deviate from it.

Thus when disability activists claim that Deaf people are in the same boat with them, they do *not* mean to suggest that Deaf people are afflicted with a defect that ought to be fixed or eliminated, or that they are not whole, or that something is wrong with them, as Deaf people often seem to assume. Rather, they mean that Deaf people have a sensory difference from the majority that requires a different way of life; that the majority hearing population often tries to obstruct or thwart that way of life, or at the least does not make reasonable accommodations for it; and that the hearing majority thereby disables Deaf people. It is understood that if Deaf people were to live entirely in a Deaf world they would not be disabled, just as it is understood that the same is true of many other disabled people. This way of understanding disability does not seem to contradict in any fundamental way how Deaf people already view themselves.

The cultural model also has had little practical relevance to the debate over cochlear implants. Even if all hearing people were to become convinced that Deaf people are "not disabled" and constituted a cultural minority, would that affect the implanting of deaf children? After all, minority cultures in the United States come and go without much fanfare. There used to be strong Italian American communities in many cities, for example, that have mostly disappeared. There were once thriving Scandinavian cultures across the rural upper Midwest and Polish American communities in the cities. Asian Americans and Jewish Americans are increasingly assimilating today. A marked and distinct ethnic identity usually persists only to the extent that majority prejudice prevails over the tendency toward assimilation, as has been the case for most African Americans. The charge of "ethnocide" sometimes raised in the case against cochlear implants is not a persuasive one in the United States, for the disappearance of minority cultures—whatever opinion one may hold about this—is not only commonplace but has often been held up as an ideal. Not only are Americans generally unwilling to offer bilingual education for the purpose of preserving ethnic cultures, opposition to the persistence of minority cultures is one of the main arguments deployed against bilingual education, which is on the defensive and in decline across the country. If it is true that implants threaten Deaf Culture (which is a subject of debate within the Deaf community), hearing Americans seem unlikely to support the idea of preserving deafness in order to preserve Deaf Culture when they have shown no widespread concern for preserving other minority cultures.

Medicalization of difference is as much an issue for disabled people generally as it is for Deaf people. Disabled people are equally concerned about the attitudes that lead to excessive, risky, and often ineffective surgeries performed on children in valiant attempts to restore "normal function"—for example, to enable someone to walk about with difficulty, rather than modifying public spaces in ways to enable them to roll about with ease. The problem Deaf people face is not that they are not recognized as an ethnic group, but rather, as Alice Dreger has written, that in the modern West "the most prevalent myth is that an unusual anatomy must be considered a medical pathology." It is equally a problem for deaf and all disabled people that "most children with unusual anatomies are born to parents who do not share the unusual trait, and so the parents' reaction often involves fear, confusion, shame, guilt, and distress. . . . The parents often can't imagine living 'that' way."[19]

Like Deaf people, many disabled people see disability as central to their identity and have no desire whatsoever to join the nondisabled "other."[20] This is particularly true of those born disabled or disabled from an early age. Disabled people are in fact very similar to Deaf people in this way, and use similar language when they speak of disability as their norm, as something in which they have pride, as essential to their identity. The question is not so much whether one is Deaf, blind, or a wheelchair user, but rather whether that is an integral part of one's identity, which is in large part a question of time and life stage. People who grew up with an atypical body or set of senses tend to see themselves as "normal" and experience little or no desire to change. Those who experience a dramatic change in bodily or sensory configuration go through a period, some longer than others, of wishing they could return to their earlier norm, but in most cases this sense of inhabiting an abnormal body passes with time. As Susan Triano told a reporter at the 2004 International Disability Pride Parade in Chicago, "We're trying to unite all people with all different kinds of disabilities to send a message that disability is a natural and beautiful part of human diversity. We don't need to be cured. We don't need to be fixed. We are whole human beings just the way we are."[21]

Although I have long known that disabled people routinely express satisfaction with their identity and way of life, I was nevertheless surprised to learn recently that only once in history have conjoined twins expressed a desire to be separated. Of course, parents and surgeons routinely decide to surgically separate them in infancy, but when conjoined twins reach an age at which they can speak for themselves, they nearly always express satisfaction with their lives. Why was I surprised? Because I had imagined what it would be like to live such a life and concluded that it would be intolerable. That is the problem. Hearing people imagine what it must be like to be deaf, and envision a gray and lonely existence. Walking people imagine life as a wheelchair user, and see only limitation and constraint. Deaf people know that deafness is not deprivation, but imagine other disabilities much as hearing people do. Blindness looms especially large in the Deaf imagination as the negation of their identity as visual people, and has been a felt presence in the Deaf community in the form of Usher Syndrome. John Lee Clark, however, writes that while Deaf people fear blindness and blind people fear deafness, they need not, for "we all share the same capacity for human experience. And that capacity can be filled in infinite ways, from a bank of small spigots to a fewer but larger ones. However the reliance on senses are distributed, we all hold equal access to living full lives."[22]

Resistance to technological normalization flies in the face of powerful social forces and is an uphill battle no matter what arguments are deployed. Nevertheless, the disability critique of the modern tendency to homogenize human experience, to regulate human appearance and behavior, and to lessen human variation is a broad and powerful argument. Claiming that implanting deaf children constitutes ethnocide is not, for the children who are implanted are neither culturally Deaf nor members of an ethnic group. As individuals, they possess no elements of a minority culture. What they do possess is a different sensory relationship to the world around them. It is the value of *that* difference that is at issue. If an effective counterargument is to be constructed, it is more likely to be based upon the good that comes from preserving sensory and physical diversity rather than upon ethnic identity.

Ethnicity

The desire among Deaf people to be defined only by cultural and not physical difference has striking parallels with the mid-twentieth-century campaign by European immigrants to be redefined as ethnic groups. In the nineteenth and early twentieth centuries, what we now term "ethnic groups" were typically referred to as "races." It was common to speak of a multiracial Europe populated by the Irish race, the Italian race, the Jewish race, the Slavic race, and so on. The concept of race denoted *both* body and culture, inherited *and* environmentally influenced characteristics, nature *and* nurture, which were all seen as inextricably linked. A study of immigration in 1926, for example, identified fifty-six races of people employed in American industry. Among those described as distinct races were Poles, Slovaks, South Italians, North Italians, Magyars, Lithuanians, Croatians, French-Canadians, Hebrews, Spanish, and "native-born White Americans." The study described how the "bodily form" and "shape of the skull," as well as the temperament and personality, varied from race to race.[23]

Proponents of immigration restriction, such as Edward Ross, sociology professor at the University of Wisconsin, maintained that recent immigrants to the United States tended to be physically inferior: "South Europeans run to low stature," he wrote. "A gang of Italian[s] . . . filing along the street present, by their dwarfishness, a curious contrast to other people. The Portuguese, the Greeks, and the Syrians are, from our point of view, undersized. The Hebrew immigrants are very poor in physique . . . the polar opposite of our pioneer breed. . . . The physiognomy of certain groups unmistakably proclaims inferiority of type."[24] This is why restricting the immigration of these "inferior types" was so important to eugenicists at the time, because their "defects" were seen as inherent racial traits. Eugenicists stigmatized both disabled people and "inferior races" as prisoners of defective bodies, and sought to exclude immigrants who were "degenerate," whether due to racial characteristics or to individual disabilities. In effect, both racial and disabled minorities came under the purview of a medical model. From this medical model came increasing attacks on the liberties of disabled people and racial minorities, including widespread institutionalization, sterilization, and exclusion from American economic and social life.

A similar kind of medicalization of difference was prominent in the justification of slavery and, after slavery's demise, of other forms of racial oppression. For example, an article on the "diseases and physical peculiarities of the negro race" in the *New Orleans Medical and Surgical Journal* explained, "It is this defective hematosis, or atmospherization of the blood, conjoined with a deficiency of cerebral matter in the cranium, and an excess of nervous matter distributed to the organs of sensation and assimilation, that is the true cause of that debasement of mind, which has rendered the people of Africa unable to take care of themselves."[25] African Americans were assumed to become ill or disabled more easily than whites, especially under the stressful conditions of freedom. Diseases of blacks were generally attributed to "inferior organisms and constitutional weaknesses," which were claimed to be among "the most pronounced race characteristics of the American negro." Women's physical differences, as well, have been endlessly medicalized (to a lesser degree still are today). One of the important strategies of the opponents of women's suffrage was to attribute various disabilities to women, among them irrationality, uncontrolled emotionality with a tendency to hysteria, and constitutional weakness. The supposed tendency among "inferior races" to feeblemindedness, mental illness, deafness, blindness, and other disabilities has been repeatedly invoked in arguments for racial inequality and discriminatory immigration laws. Time and again, when categories of citizenship are in question, a medicalized notion of disability has been called upon to discredit and to stigmatize.[26]

European American minorities began arguing that they should be considered ethnic groups rather than races in the 1930s to escape the imputation of physical and biological inferiority. Ethnicity suggested that all European Americans were members of the "white race," and therefore culturally but not biologically different. The ethnicity model excluded African, Asian, and Native American minorities, who continued to be stigmatized by a medical model that associated them with disabled people: prisoners of defective bodies, degenerate by nature, and likely to pass on their defective characteristics to future generations. European American minorities, on the other hand, were so successful at shedding the notion of race and becoming "white ethnics" that most people soon forgot that they had ever been considered members of different races at all.[27]

The claim today that disabled people differ from the nondisabled by dint of physical difference, while Deaf people differ from the hearing only by culture, mirrors the division of ethnicity from race. Just as the decision of European Americans early in the twentieth century to identify themselves as ethnic groups rather than racial groups was in part a political decision, and just as the identity of "white person" is in part a political choice, "Deaf" and "disabled" are also, at least in part, political choices. These are constructions of history—always contested, never settled, and always open to question. There is nothing timeless or "natural" about them.

This is not to argue that the idea of ethnicity is disreputable, but rather that it is a construct that arose under particular historical conditions and was used for particular purposes. Whatever the particular origins of the concept and its problematic relationship with the notion of race, ethnicity is a useful model because it provides a framework for exploring the ways in which Deaf Americans have maintained distinct community institutions and have passed down, over many generations, a common history, language, and culture. Nor is this to say that Deaf people should not be conceptualized as an ethnic group, or that Deaf Studies scholars cannot learn much from Ethnic Studies (not to mention Women's Studies, Race Studies, and Queer Studies). It is undeniable that the cultural/ethnic group model has been extraordinarily useful and beneficial in many ways to both Deaf Studies and the Deaf community. It is nevertheless useful to reconsider in light of its history what purposes the model is serving today, and whether an exclusive reliance on the cultural model serves ends that scholars and Deaf people wish to pursue.

Historically Created Identities

The statement that "Deaf people are not disabled" suggests that current definitions of Deaf and disabled are natural, timeless, and universal categories. These are not fixed definitions, however, but rather historically created and impermanent identities. Padden and Humphries put the matter more accurately when they wrote in *Deaf in America* that "'disabled' is a label that historically has not belonged to Deaf people," but still they left open the question of which historical period they meant.[28] My preliminary research suggests the possibility that the "Deaf people are not disabled" claim *may* be of fairly recent origin.

In the nineteenth century it seems to have been common to talk of Deaf people as disabled. Laurent Clerc, one of the founders of the American School for the Deaf, in an 1818 address, spoke of "the infirmities of the bodily organization, such as deafness, blindness, lameness, palsy, crookedness, ugliness." In 1835, John Burnet wrote of his deafness as one of the "long catalogue of infirmities which flesh is heir to." He went on to explain that,

> [Our] misfortune is not that [we] are deaf and dumb, but that *others* hear and speak. Were the established mode of communication . . . by a language addressed not to the ear, but to the eye, the present inferiority of the deaf would entirely vanish; but at the same time the mental and social conditions of the blind would be far more deplorable, and their education far more impracticable, than that of the deaf is now.[29]

This seems a perfect expression of the social model of disability, applied to deafness and blindness.

In 1855, John Jacob Flournoy argued that Deaf people should abandon the hearing world that oppressed them and establish their own state, and at the same time saw no contradiction in describing Deaf people as disabled. Responding to William Turner's statement that a Deaf man was as unsuited to serve in a legislature as a blind man was to lead an army, Flournoy wrote (in his wonderful phrasing): "The old cry about the incapacity of men's minds from physical disabilities, I think it were time, now in this intelligent age, to *explode!*" He made his case by referring to great disabled military heroes and blind philosophers: "Have you ever heard how Muley Moloch had himself borne in a litter, when lamed by wounds, to the head of his legions . . . ? So much for a *lame* man. Then, as for a *blind* one. . . ." Flournoy described Deaf people as a distinct and oppressed community *and* as sharing a common oppression with other disabled people.[30]

Nor does it seem to have been very common for Deaf people to reject the association with disability (at least in print) through most of the twentieth century. In *Illusions of Equality,* Bob Buchanan describes two significant instances, during the 1908 battle over the hiring of deaf people for the Civil Service, when Deaf community leaders objected to an association with disability: George Dougherty wrote that being classed in Civil Service regulations with "the insane, the crippled, and criminals" might prejudice employers against them, and George Veditz warned, "Once let the government brand deafness as a disability that renders us ineligible for its service, and it will not be long before the prejudice will spread among the employers at large." Both of these instances, however, had to do specifically with concerns over employment discrimination rather than a general aversion to being thought of as disabled. The Veditz quotation is ambiguous in that he does not reject the idea that deafness is a disability, but specifically that deafness is *a disability that renders us ineligible for employment.* The term "disability" at the time was often used in this more specific sense to refer to a trait that disqualified a person for certain rights and privileges. Buchanan also documents occasions on which Deaf leaders decided against collaboration with disability groups, but while this *may* suggest a rejection of the concept of disability, it does not do so necessarily. The ethnic group model, after all, is not weakened by the fact that Deaf people do not typically collaborate with other ethnic groups.[31]

Susan Burch, in *Signs of Resistance,* suggests that Deaf people began to reject the association with disability in the early twentieth century. It is a plausible suggestion, but Burch provides only one significant source for the claim. An editorial in the *Empire State News,* supporting a proposal for a labor bureau for deaf people and responding to an argument that it ought to serve all disabled people, asserted that "the average deaf worker belongs in the classification of foreign-language groups rather than that of the physically handicapped." This would appear at first glance to be an endorsement of the cultural model and rejection of the disability model. However, the editorial then went on to explain that a worker's "deafness is sure to raise difficulties of communication which may hinder his effectiveness until he becomes accustomed to the routine of work in that particular place. Hence, some follow-up work would be necessary in a placement service for the deaf. This is an additional detail which the regular service cannot handle." That is, the editorial is focused entirely on the issue of *what deaf people need from a labor bureau,* not their identity. Deaf people have employment needs that are distinct from those of "other handicapped groups," the editorial continued, because "one has to have effective communication between the placement officer and the deaf applicant. No such difficulty exists in the case of the blind, the crippled, and other groups, for all of these possess in common with the director and his assistants the great blessing of combined hearing and speech, which facilitate the interview." The point is the specific employment needs of deaf people, nothing broader. Moreover, the editorial twice refers to "*other* groups of handicapped people," which suggests no aversion to being thought of as one of those groups.[32]

In my (admittedly not exhaustive) research so far, I have found no unambiguous and explicit examples of Deaf people rejecting association with disability before the 1970s in the United States.[33] While it would not be surprising to find such examples, it does seem suggestive that I have come across no published examples so far, while I have found numerous examples of Deaf people who referred to themselves as disabled or handicapped. For example, in 1930, Albert Ballin, in *The Deaf Mute Howls,* referred to deafness as a "handicap," as did Thomas Ulmer, a Deaf contributor to the *American Annals of the Deaf,* in 1945. In 1941, Tom Anderson, then president of the National Association of the Deaf (NAD), urged President Roosevelt to "give handicapped persons a break in working for the defense program," by which he clearly meant to include Deaf people. He was quoted in a *New York Times* opinion column by a disabled man writing in favor of greater employment opportunities for disabled people, and in 1942 the *Empire State News* approvingly reprinted that piece. The president of the California Association of the Deaf, Toivo Lindholm, in 1953 referred to Deaf people as handicapped. In 1970, NAD president Frederick Schreiber wrote of Deaf people having a "disability." In 1974, in his book *A Deaf Adult Speaks Out,* Leo Jacobs described Deaf people as a minority group and simultaneously as people who have a "handicap."[34]

Clearly more careful research than what I have done here is needed. The history of Deaf people's relationship with the concept of disability is no doubt far more complex than I am able to describe in this essay. However, if these preliminary findings are borne out, it is possible that the argument that Deaf people are not disabled came to prominence alongside the Deaf rights movement and the rise of the culture model in the 1970s and 1980s. If so, the claim that Deaf people have long rejected identification as disabled might be an example of an "invented tradition," a common phenomenon in all cultures but particularly those reacting to rapid change. Historians have become increasingly interested in recent years in the ways that societies seek to reinforce the legitimacy of their values by projecting their origins back in time and defending them as long-standing cultural traditions.[35]

The rejection of disability since the 1970s seems mainly intended as a refutation of the demeaning focus on deafness as defect. In their desire to avoid the focus on the ear to the exclusion of all other aspects of Deaf experience, and to emphasize the legitimacy of their culture, Deaf people increasingly denied that physical difference had any significance in the formation of Deaf identity. Just as early ASL studies downplayed the importance of fingerspelling, iconicity, and any other element that seemed to make signed languages less like "true languages" (that is, conforming to definitions and standards derived from the study of spoken language), so also did early Deaf Studies deny the importance of sensory difference in order to emphasize the cultural aspect of Deaf identity. Just as it was thought that a "true language" would not rely on iconicity or the spelling of borrowed words, a "true culture" could have nothing to do with physical difference. However, just as ASL scholars now have enough confidence to explore the significant place of iconicity and fingerspelling in the language, so too has Deaf Studies begun pointing toward the significance of physical difference in defining the Deaf community.

Conclusion

Nothing I have written here should be construed as an argument against the cultural model. It has been and continues to be a powerful tool in Deaf Studies, as well as in the struggle for Deaf rights and community pride. Ethnicity is a crucial concept because it provides a framework for exploring the ways in which Deaf Americans have maintained distinct community institutions and have passed down, over many generations, a common history, language, and culture. As Ella Mae Lentz recently pointed out to me, it may also more closely reflect the way in which Deaf people experience their relationships with hearing people. When encountering a nonsigner, she maintained, a Deaf person does not think, "I cannot hear and therefore cannot communicate with this person," but rather, "Our languages are different and therefore we cannot communicate with each other." In this way, the Deaf individual's experience is that of a linguistic minority.

However, the social model of disability can account for much that the cultural model cannot. The disability model allows us to explore how sensory differences between hearing and deaf people shape their worlds, as well as how the concept of normality shapes both hearing people's attitudes toward Deaf people and the development of Deaf children's sense of identity. It provides an explanatory context for the medicalization of deafness, and a theoretical framework for the argument that Deaf people are not disabled by hearing impairment, but rather by the oppression of difference. It provides powerful arguments for ASL in Deaf education. It shows us that the response of hearing people to deafness is not unique but rather part of a larger response to disability. It makes sense of the fact that Veditz wrote *not* that Deaf people were people of sign language, but that they were people of the eye.

Moreover, the disability model should not pose a threat to Deaf people's sense of identity any more than does the ethnic model. After all, until fairly recently most Deaf people would have strongly objected to being identified with ethnicity. Once Deaf people in the 1970s and 1980s began to identify themselves as an ethnic group, they felt no less Deaf than they had before, and they felt no compulsion to merge their identities with Vietnamese Americans, Italian Americans, or other ethnic groups. Deaf Americans (or for that matter Chinese Americans) are not expected to feel a close affinity for Cuban Americans just because, for purposes of explaining their experiences as minorities, we describe both as ethnic groups. The same holds true for disability. Deaf people will doubtless always feel far more affinity for other Deaf people than for other disabled people (or for other ethnic groups). It is not a question about identity but rather about the need for a coherent category of analysis for scholars, for a unified, broad-based movement for effective activism, and for explanations that the general public, in particular the parents of deaf children, can find both plausible and persuasive.

Most groups who now identify themselves as disabled have done so only recently. Blind people in particular long resisted both the label and association with the larger universe of disabled people. People with mental disabilities and those with physical disabilities have long had an uneasy relationship. Those with acquired disabilities, such as disabled war veterans, often have resisted association with people who have lifelong disabilities. The tendency of those with lesser stigmatized disabilities to distance themselves from those with more highly stigmatized disabilities is a common phenomenon. Throughout American history, disabled people have been more likely to identify themselves in terms of a specific group than as disabled.

Only recently has the identity of "disabled person" been widely embraced. This is in part a conscious political decision, in part the product of a new consciousness of shared experience, and in good part due to increasing awareness of the social model of disability. It was once common to hear wheelchair users say, "Just because I use a wheelchair doesn't mean you should treat me like I'm retarded." Today it is more common to hear something like, "Nobody, regardless of their disability, should be treated that way." Some disabled people are far more vulnerable to discrimination, institutionalization, and eugenic assault than others, but a tenet of disability solidarity is that those less threatened should not abandon the more vulnerable. Disabled people differ significantly from one another, but they share common experiences resisting the medicalization of their identity, coping with inferior "special" education, fighting for autonomy and self-determination—in short, they share a common experience of oppression and of struggle against it. Thus, sharing a common oppression, they have undertaken to forge a common liberation.

Indeed, one of the remarkable aspects of the pan–disability rights movement is its ability to bring together diverse groups of people into common action. It is a fractious coalition, riven by identity politics and conflicting agendas to be sure. Nevertheless, its very existence and dramatic growth is testament to a powerful idea—that the goal ought not to be for any one group to find liberation for itself, in effect merely reshuffling the deck, but rather to resist and disrupt the systematic translation of *difference* into structures of privilege and oppression.

Notes

The author wishes to thank Robert Buchanan, Bryan Eldredge, William Ennis, Christopher Krentz, Anna Mollow, and Joseph Murray, as well as the participants in the 2002 Deaf Studies Think Tank at Gallaudet University, for their helpful comments on earlier drafts.

1. American Deaf Culture has been described in a number of books and articles. See, for example, Carol Padden and Tom Humphries, *Deaf in America: Voices from a Culture* (Cambridge, Mass.: Harvard University Press, 1988); John V. Van Cleve and Barry A. Crouch, *A Place of Their Own: Creating the Deaf Community in America* (Washington, D.C.: Gallaudet University Press, 1989); Harlan Lane, Robert Hoffmeister, and Ben Bahan, *A Journey into the Deaf-World* (San Diego: DawnSignPress, 1996); Robert Buchanan, *Illusions of Equality: Deaf Americans in School and Factory, 1850–1950* (Washington, D.C.: Gallaudet University Press, 2002); Susan Burch, *Signs of Resistance: American Deaf Cultural History, 1900 to 1942* (New York: New York University Press, 2002).

2. Lane, Hoffmeister, and Bahan, *Journey into the Deaf-World,* 111–16. Brice Alden, "Visualist Theory 101," *Tactile Mind,* Spring 2002, 8. Ben Bahan, "Notes from a 'Seeing Person,'" in *American Deaf Culture: An Anthology,* ed. Sherman Wilcox (Silver Spring, Md.: Linstock Press, 1989), 30, 31.

3. George Veditz, "President's Message," in *Proceedings of the Ninth Convention of the National*

Association of the Deaf and the Third World's Congress of the Deaf, 1910 (Philadelphia: Philocophus Press, 1912), 30.

4. Padden and Humphries, *Deaf in America*, 3. Bryan Eldredge has a wonderful discussion of the complicated place hearing people occupy in the Deaf community; see chapter 1 in "The Role of Discourse in the Formation and Maintenance of Deaf Identity and the Deaf-World" (PhD dissertation, Department of Anthropology, University of Iowa, 2004). Some Deaf people, most notably World Federation of the Deaf president Markku Jokinen and the editors of *The Tactile Mind*, have argued recently for thinking in terms of "sign language users" rather than "Deaf persons," as this would emphasize culture and language rather than lack of hearing. See Markku Jokinen, "'The Sign Language Person': A Term to Describe Us and Our Future More Clearly?" in *Looking Forward: EUD in the Third Millennium—The Deaf Citizen in the 21st Century*, ed. Lorraine Leeson (Coleford: Douglas McLean, 2001), 50–63. Paddy Ladd, in his recent and important book *Understanding Deaf Culture: In Search of Deafhood* (Clevedon, UK: Multilingual Matters, 2003), suggests that in the absence of oppressive relations Deaf people would welcome culturally Deaf hearing people as full members of the community. I would maintain that sensory differences matter, regardless of the cultural setting. Ladd, in another section of his book, suggests this point by arguing that "blindness, being a sensory impairment, might well involve certain psychological patterning which, when reinforced by time spent together, might add up to a phenomenon with some notable cultural features" (194). Human beings are cultural beings, and they are also physical beings. To deny one or the other, to say that our fates are entirely decided by our bodies, or conversely that we are all culture and that our bodies do not shape who we are, is equally wrong.

5. Arkady Belozovsky, for example, spoke at the 2004 Deaf Studies Today conference about cultural differences between Russian and American Deaf people, such as attitudes toward physical contact and ways of introducing people. Arkady Belozovsky, "Learning Foreign, Linguistically Related Sign Languages: What Are the Benefits to ASL/Deaf Studies Instructors" (paper presented at the Deaf Studies Today conference held at Utah Valley State College, April 12–14, 2004).

6. Carol Padden, "A New Language" (paper presented at the Deaf Studies Today conference held at Utah Valley State College, April 12–14, 2004). Joseph Murray suggested to me that Padden's experience of a sense of connection might also be explained by her *expectation* that Deaf people should feel such a connection with one another. This indeed suggests an alternative explanation in general for Deaf experiences of kinship across national lines; biological kin often feel a similar sense of connectedness and mutual responsibility in spite of cultural divides. Still, I would argue that the shared experience of sensory difference from the majority, and the knowledge that another's experiences of the world are in this fundamental way like one's own, would be likely in itself to produce a sense of commonality.

7. Jeffrey E. Nash, "Policy and Practice in the American Sign Language Community," *International Journal of the Sociology of Language* 68 (1987): 11. Nash also points to important similarities between Deaf and other ethnic groups.

8. Ross E. Mitchell and Michael A. Karchmer, "Chasing the Mythical Ten Percent: Parental Hearing Status of Deaf and Hard of Hearing Students in the United States," *Sign Language Studies* 4 (2004): 138–63.

9. Douglas Baynton, *Forbidden Signs: American Culture and the Campaign against Sign Language* (Chicago: University of Chicago Press, 1996), 10.

10. Ibid., 160.

11. Ladd, in *Understanding Deaf Culture*, acknowledges the significance of the disability model, writing that Deaf people should be "seen as intrinsic 'dual-category members'—that is, that some of their issues might relate to issues of non-hearing whilst others relate to language and culture" (16). He notes that the concept of "access" has provided a rationale for important services to Deaf people such as interpreting services, text telephones, captioning, and the like (while it has also created problems, as in the debate over separate versus mainstreamed education). On the whole, however, he downplays deafness and focuses almost entirely on what he aptly terms "Deafhood."

The emphasis is understandable, given that he is trying to reach a public ignorant of Deaf Culture and that views Deaf people simply as people burdened with nonfunctioning ears. Nevertheless, it leads him to understate the importance of sensory difference in constructing the Deaf community and determining its membership (41–42, 74 n. 8) And while he gives a serviceable description of the social model of disability, he then goes on to equate recognition of "physical deafness" with "the medical concept," which is precisely the equation that the social model rejects (16, 166–69).

12. On the social model of disability, see Mike Oliver, *The Politics of Disablement* (New York: Palgrave McMillan, 1990); J. Swain et al., eds., *Disabling Barriers—Enabling Environments* (London: Sage, 1993); Harlan Hahn, "Antidiscrimination Laws and Social Research on Disability: The Minority Group Perspective," *Behavioral Sciences and the Law* 14 (1996): 41–59; Tom Shakespeare and N. Watson, "Defending the Social Model," *Disability and Society* 12 (1997): 293–300; Len Barton and Mike Oliver, eds., *Disability Studies: Past Present and Future* (Leeds, UK: Disability Press, 1997); Mark Priestley, "Constructions and Creations: Idealism, Materialism and Disability Theory," *Disability and Society* 13 (1998): 75–94; Len Barton et al., eds., *Disability Studies Today* (Cambridge: Polity Press, 2002). For recent examples of disability studies in the humanities, see Paul K. Longmore, *Why I Burned My Book and Other Essays on Disability* (Philadelphia: Temple University Press, 2003); Rosemarie Garland Thomson, *Extraordinary Bodies: Figuring Physical Disability in American Culture and Literature* (New York: Columbia University Press, 1997); David T. Mitchell, and Sharon L. Snyder, eds., *The Body and Physical Difference: Discourses of Disability* (Ann Arbor: University of Michigan Press, 1997); Lennard Davis, *Enforcing Normalcy: Disability, Deafness, and the Body* (London: Verso, 1995); Paul Longmore and Lauri Umansky, eds., *The New Disability History: American Perspectives* (New York: New York University Press, 2000). For overviews of recent work in the field, see my essay "Bodies and Environments: The Cultural Construction of Disability," in *Employment, Disability and the Americans with Disabilities Act: Issues in Law, Public Policy and Research*, ed. Peter Blanck (Evanston, Ill.: Northwestern University Press, 2000), 387–411, and Catherine J. Kudlick, "Disability History: Why We Need Another 'Other,'" *American Historical Review* 108 (June 2003): 763–93.

13. Hahn, "Antidiscrimination Laws and Social Research on Disability," 43. Simi Linton defines disability as "a marker of identity" that has brought together a coalition of people stigmatized by physical, sensory, and mental differences from the majority, in *Claiming Disability: Knowledge and Identity* (New York: New York University Press, 1998). Anna Mollow suggested to me that the social model assumes a false opposition between the medical and the social, and excludes disabling conditions that originate in progressive, chronic, or terminal illnesses such as AIDS, cancer, and diabetes. She argues that some disabilities are best understood as both social and medical. While I think that a conceptual distinction can be made between illness and disabilities associated with illness, Mollow's point may well indeed indicate a need for a more nuanced model of disability. However, since it does not directly affect the argument I present here, I have to plead the standard excuse that it is a question beyond the scope of this essay.

14. Lawrence Goodwyn's *Democratic Promise: The Populist Moment in America* (Oxford: Oxford University Press, 1976) is a prominent example of this use of "movement culture." Ladd, *Understanding Deaf Culture*, has a useful discussion of culture and subculture in which he posits language as a crucial element in distinguishing the two.

15. On disability culture, see Longmore, "The Second Phase: From Disability Rights to Disability Culture," in *Why I Burned My Book;* Sharon Barnartt, "Disability Culture or Disability Consciousness?" *Journal of Disability Policy Studies* 7, no. 2 (1996): 1–20; James I. Charlton, *Nothing About Us Without Us: Disability Oppression and Empowerment* (Berkeley and Los Angeles: University of California Press, 1998); Susan Crutchfield and Marcy Epstein, eds., *Points of Contact: Disability, Art, and Culture* (Ann Arbor: University of Michigan Press, 2000); Kenny Fries, *Staring Back: The Disability Experience from the Inside Out* (New York: Plume, 1997).

16. Reprinted in Longmore, *Why I Burned My Book,* 26.

17. Padden and Humphries, *Deaf in America,* 3.

18. See for example, Harlan Lane, *The Mask of Benevolence: Disabling the Deaf Community* (New York: Alfred Knopf, 1992), and Jan Branson and Don Miller, *Damned for Their Difference: The Cultural Construction of Deaf People as Disabled* (Washington, D.C.: Gallaudet University Press, 2002).

19. Alice Dreger, *One of Us: Conjoined Twins and the Future of Normal* (Cambridge, Mass.: Harvard University Press, 2004), 77, 55.

20. Joseph Shapiro, *No Pity: People with Disabilities Forging a New Civil Rights Movement* (New York: Random House, 1994), 14.

21. Jim Ritter, "650 Walk, Roll and Bike in City's First Disability Pride Parade," *Chicago Sun-Times,* July 19, 2004.

22. John Lee Clark, "On Sensory Unloss," http://www.johnleeclark.com/mainthing2.html#ci (site discontinued).

23. Joel M. Sipress, "Relearning Race: Teaching Race as a Cultural Construction," *History Teacher* 30 (February 1997): 179.

24. Edward Alsworth Ross, *The Old World and the New: The Significance of Past and Present Immigration to the American People* (New York: Century, 1914), 285–90.

25. Samuel A. Cartwright, "Report on the Diseases and Physical Peculiarities of the Negro Race," *New Orleans Medical and Surgical Journal* 7 (1851): 693.

26. George M. Fredrickson, *The Black Image in the White Mind* (New York: Harper and Row, 1971), 250–51. On the ways in which the concept of disability has been used to justify discriminatory practices against women and minority groups, see my essay, "Disability and the Justification of Inequality in American History," in Longmore and Umansky, *New Disability History,* 33–57.

27. On the social construction of ethnicity and of "whiteness," see Matthew Frye Jacobson, *Whiteness of a Different Color: European Immigrants and the Alchemy of Race* (Cambridge, Mass.: Harvard University Press, 1998); Karen Brodkin, *How the Jews Became White Folks and What That Says about Gender and White Supremacy* (New Brunswick: Rutgers University Press, 1999); Noel Ignatiev, *How the Irish Became White* (New York: Routledge, 1996); Sipress, "Relearning Race," 175–85.

28. Padden and Humphries, *Deaf in America,* 44.

29. Laurent Clerc, "Address to the Connecticut Legislature," and John Burnet, "What the Deaf and Dumb Are before Instruction," in *A Mighty Change: Deaf American Writing, 1817–1864,* ed. by Christopher Krentz (Washington, D.C.: Gallaudet University Press, 2000), 17, 40.

30. John Jacob Flournoy, "Mr. Flournoy's Plan for a Deaf-Mute Commonwealth," *American Annals of the Deaf* (1858), reprinted in Krentz, *A Mighty Change,* 166.

31. Buchanan, *Illusions of Equality,* 42.

32. Burch, *Signs of Resistance,* 121. Burch cites two other issues of the *Empire State News,* but I could find nothing in them related to this question. The first briefly alludes to dissatisfaction with the work of the New York State Employment Service and endorses the idea of a deaf labor bureau. The other discusses concerns that the New York State Employment Service "claims to have 19 specially trained interviewers for the handicapped, but that none of these specially trained interviewers are equipped by experience or training to deal intelligently with the problems of the deaf." Again, the point is to address the particular needs of deaf people, not to make any conceptual distinctions between them and other "handicapped" persons.

33. A Deaf Frenchman, Henri Gaillard, did write in 1893 that, "Infirm we are not. In order to be infirm in the true sense of the word, it is necessary to be deprived of a limb, be bandy-legged, one-armed, crippled, blind or blind in one eye." *Proceedings of the World Congress of the Deaf and the Report of the Fourth Convention of the National Association of the Deaf* (Chicago, 1893), 176. This is the kind of unambiguous statement that has not yet been produced from research on the American Deaf community. The extent to which American Deaf people (or French Deaf, for that matter) agreed remains to be established. Thanks to Joe Murray for bringing Gaillard's statement to my attention.

34. Albert Ballin, *The Deaf Mute Howls* (1930; repr., Washington, D.C.: Gallaudet University Press,

1998), 57. Thomas A. Ulmer, "A Review of the Little Paper Family for 1944–45," in *Deaf World: A Historical Reader and Primary Sourcebook,* ed. Lois Bragg (New York: New York University Press, 2001), 260. Anderson was quoted in Jay McMahon, "Rehabilitation Urged," *New York Times,* April 28, 1941, E6; reprinted in a regular column by Charles Joselow, "For Your Record," *Empire State News,* January–February 1942, 3; both cited in Buchanan, *Illusions of Equality,* 175 n. 10. Toivo Lindholm, "Place of the Adult Deaf in Society," in Bragg, *Deaf World,* 272. Frederick Schreiber, "What a Deaf Jewish Leader Expects," in ibid., 34. Leo M. Jacobs, *A Deaf Adult Speaks Out* (1974; repr., Washington, D.C.: Gallaudet University Press, 1989), 13, 23. For a more recent example, see Tom Willard's 1998 essay in which he wrote of his frustration with "the misconception that people with disabilities are not happy or whole until they have overcome their disability." Tom Willard, "What Exactly Am I Supposed to Overcome," in Bragg, *Deaf World,* 273.

35. See for example, Eric Hobsbawm and Terence Ranger, eds., *The Invention of Tradition* (Cambridge: Cambridge University Press, 1983).

19. Postdeafness

LENNARD J. DAVIS

ARE DEAF PEOPLE HANDICAPPED? Impaired? Disabled? A race? An ethnic group? A minority? These are questions posed in an ongoing way by both Deaf people themselves and by the hearing world. A brief history of the context of these labels might be in order. Before the eighteenth century, prelingually deaf people were widely regarded in a category that included madmen, lunatics, and idiots—that is, people who were seen as having lost their senses or wits. In this sense, particularly as "mute" people, they had the status of children or animals. In Catholic countries they were thus treated as people who could not receive the sacraments and legally as people who were not responsible for their actions. In this sense, they were constructed as lesser people, childlike, and without the full rights of citizens.

In the eighteenth century, schools for the deaf began to flourish and with the attempt to universalize local sign language dialects into national and transnational languages, deaf people were able to participate in the public and civil sphere. With the notion of universal rights endowed by a creator, deaf people were increasingly allowed by a hearing majority to partake in citizenship and the rights that it conveyed and in religion. Education could lead to that goal or end, so a project to humanely educate the deaf, along with curing the insane and helping educate people with mental retardation, was begun.

With the advent of the "scientific" eugenic study of humans in the nineteenth century, and with the accompanying attempt to improve the human race through such studies, deaf people moved from being seen as childlike or mentally deficient to being seen as diseased and degenerate beings, less highly evolved than their normalized counterparts in the hearing world. Of course, deaf people were not alone in this construction. Anyone who was not in the dominant group, which tended to define itself as the norm, was seen as abnormal. Such people included in this abnormal status were the working classes, criminals, people with disabilities, people with mental and cognitive disabilities, people of short stature, people from Africa, India, Southern Europe, Ireland, the Middle East, and Asia, among others. The program here was not necessarily to create a class of people to be discriminated against, although that did happen, but to improve the human race by decreasing the occurrence of disease and degeneracy. Linked to this program was another related endeavor that aimed to classify and study human variety; so anthropology, sociology, comparative anatomy, and psychology, what have been called "disciplines"—in both senses of the word—of the human sciences, came about as specializations in this project.

Inherent in this movement was the idea that desirable and undesirable traits were inherited in groups in ways that were called "racial." Although the mechanism of this inheritance was not understood, animal breeding had allowed a rough understanding of the process by which traits could be inherited and in which that inheritance could be shaped by selective mating. Linked to this idea was Charles Darwin's discovery of evolution, which implied that species (and by extension races within species) could evolve or degenerate. Gregor Mendel, at the end of the century, came up with mathematical models for inheritance that included the distribution results of dominant and recessive traits, although he did not understand or explain the mechanism of this transmission of traits.

This scientific study aimed at description, diagnosis, and remediation or cure. Deaf people, like these other groups, were assembled into entities in schools and institutions, subjected to statistical studies, and were part of a project to educate them into oral language, whose lack was seen as a deficit. This institutionalization had its negative impacts, but in the case of deaf people, it helped to form a culture and a community with a common (although subversive at this point) language. Just as prosthetics became a major industry following the Civil War, oral education was seen as a prosthetic device that would make people who were lacking a part of their human body whole.

During this time, the deaf began to be called a "race," particularly in the by-now infamous proposal of Alexander Bell to avoid the creation of a deaf race. Deaf people were seen as a race along with many other races because of the idea of inherited traits. Indeed the nineteenth-century researchers had developed many more races than we now usually think of when we speak of race. Proposals for separating the deaf from the hearing races came from within the Deaf community as well with the idea for a separate state or nation for Deaf people encouraged by diverse Deaf people in the nineteenth century.

The general project of eugenics, that is, good breeding, was a successful one for many years, most notably in England and the United States, where it was pushed quite aggressively, concentrating on "positive" eugenics—that is, the encouragement of breeding between members of "fitter families." And notions of racial categories and of degenerative races held fast until the Nazi era. The Nazis' project, borrowed quite late from the Anglo-American project, employed "negative" eugenic measures that emphasized the active elimination from the gene pool of degenerate races through sterilization and mass executions. We are only too aware of the consequences of that endeavor. In keeping with the discussion here, it is important to point out that before the mass execution of Jews and Gypsies, seen as diseased and degenerate races, the T-4 program killed tens of thousands of people with disabilities, deaf people, people with mental illnesses, and homosexuals. It is important to recall that these were also considered "racial" killings since deaf people and the other groups were all seen as people carrying inherited and inheritable traits.

The defeat of Nazi Germany had two effects for the purposes of this discussion: it eliminated eugenics as a viable intellectual and social pursuit and it gave a bad name to the concept of "race." In addition, the abolition of slavery in the United States and the incipient development of a civil rights movement also contributed to an avoidance of the concept of race. Eugenics morphed into genetics, and race morphed into ethnicity. The general position on race in contemporary research is clearly stated by one analyst:

> Genetic surveys and the analyses of DNA . . . show that human races are not distinct lineages . . . human "races" are not and never were "pure." Instead human evolution has been and is characterized by many locally differentiated populations coexisting at any given time, but with sufficient genetic contact to make all of humanity a single lineage sharing a common evolutionary fate.[1]

To offset the negative side of racial categories, the idea of ethnicity was invented. Ethnicity would do double duty by allowing the categorizing of human populations while seeming to avoid the absolute biology of race. Ethnicity allowed the inclusion of cultural, socioeconomic, religious, and political qualities, language, diet, dress, customs, kinship systems, and historical or territorial identity. But ethnicity has also been used "as a surrogate for biological difference"[2] in various kinds of research. A dictionary of epidemiology makes the familiar conflation in defining race: "Persons who are relatively homogenous with respect to biological inheritance (see also ethnic group)."[3] Despite the attempt to detach ethnicity from race, many people including academics blur the line. For example, the journal *Nature Genetics* defines "race" as "a distinct *ethnic* group characterized by traits that are transmitted through their offspring," and includes in its definition of "ethnicity" "A social group or category of the population that, in a larger society, is set apart and bound together by common ties of *race,* language, nationality or culture."[4] Indeed, even the U.S. government system of classifying identity mixes racial and ethnic categories. Four racial categories and two ethnic categories in the census include the racial groups American Indian or Alaskan Native, Asian or Pacific Islander, black, and white. Ethnic groups are divided into two categories: "Hispanic origin" and "Not of Hispanic origin." While the government allows Hispanics to be of any racial category, many who self-define ethnically as Hispanic check "Other" when responding to the race question, indicating widespread confusion about the meaning of such terms as race and ethnicity.[5] That confusion is inherent in the idea of ethnicity, which itself seems fraught with the inherited baggage of racial categorization.

Using the concept of a minority is an alternative to ethnicity. It would seem that minority groups were coined as a way of avoiding the idea of ethnic groups. And identity groups were developed to move away from the idea of minority status since, for example, women or whites are not minority groups.

I have given this brief and by definition limited history as a way of placing the discussion about the status of Deaf Studies and by extension the role of Deaf people and their social construction. Harlan Lane, for one, has suggested that we consider Deaf people as an ethnic group; others have proposed that Deaf people be thought of as a linguistic minority. While these proposals are attractive in many ways, most particularly in removing the biological stigma of defining a group by its supposed lack or inability or association with disease (i.e., Deaf people *can't* hear; Deaf people *can't* speak; they can be cured by medical means). With the minority or ethnic model, as opposed to the "handicapped," "disabled," or "medical" models, Deaf people and community get to be a sociological group like any other—African American, Armenian, Jewish, etc.—although it is unclear if all those groups are races, ethnicities, or minorities.

The idea of ethnic group or even minority is so tinged with the history of racial politics that one wonders if that stream of categorical consciousness is the best one to choose as a model. Indeed, with the recent reexamination of identity politics under way in the United States, and with the concomitant rethinking of the category of identity, is the best choice to go with a model that is increasingly antiquated and outmoded?

When we talk about identity, we do speak of social identities, but the bedrock identities of this culture—racial, gendered, sexual, and so on—seem to have been, at least historically, defined by the fact that they, like disability, have been necessarily rooted in the body. Race and gender have been the strongest component of these body-centered identities. How tightly linked to the essence of the body these identities have remained is an interesting question. Historically, gender and race before and through the eighteenth century was often thought of as a product of the environment's effects on the body. Phenotypical traits were believed to be produced by harsh sun, diet, and custom. Likewise, gender characteristics were thought to be assigned by birth, but subject to change throughout life, as Tom Lacquer and others have argued.[6] From the nineteenth century on, with the rise of medicine and science, identity became founded on the bedrock of inherited traits. While these traits could be inherited by various unclearly explored mechanisms—whether "blood" or "germs"—what was clear was that the overriding theory was essentially a eugenic and Darwinian one. Indeed, many if not all medical theories of the nineteenth century coalesced around identities—physiological, mental, sexual, etc.—which became the basis for theories of improvement of the human race and produced various kinds of oppression in the process. After Mendel, genes have most clearly been seen as the originating points of such transmitted traits.

The point is that, historically, the era of identity is connected fundamentally to a notion of inherited traits linked to groups of people who carry such traits. That is, race, sexual orientation, gender, ethnicity, national origin, along with deafness, were pinpointed for improvement and correction (and likewise discrimination) from the mid-nineteenth century on in the name of eugenics and later genetics. Thus, there has been since that time an intimate connection between disease and identity—with each stigmatized group seen as the repository of bad blood, bad genes, disease, and qualities that were a product of or could lead to the degeneration of the human race.

In that sense identity has remained fairly fixed in the body until the advent of postmodernism. The only scientific refinement has been in identifying more clearly the mechanism of transmission of inherited traits. Postmodernism has sought to destabilize grand categories and metanarratives. Philosophers like Jacques Derrida, Jean-François Lyotard, Judith Butler, and others have chipped away at the idea that you could in fact ever describe in words anything in its fundamental essence. Likewise, the idea of a complete and coherent narrative was made to seem impossible. And the same with any notions of universal ideas or tenets, as we have heard from philosophers like Richard Rorty and critics like Stanley Fish. As postmodernist ideas began to interpenetrate ideas of identity, a kind of crisis has arisen.

The first target of this deconstructing of identity was the critique of "essentialism."

In effect, the notion of a human body with inherited and inherent traits tied to identity was put under scrutiny. Feminist critics like Judith Butler and Eve Kosofsky Sedgwick put forth the notion that the gendered body was a social construction or a performance—likewise identity. In this notion, one is not essentially a female, for example, but one performs femininity. The onus is then placed on a social construction argument rather than any innate sense of "being" feminine that would be tied to hormones, genitalia, secondary sexual characteristics, and so on. In race studies, ideas like passing, signifying, and so on gave a subtlety, and also perhaps a lack of clarity, to older notions of identity based on phenotype or "blood." Postmodernism also included a cultural idea of pastiche or kitsch in which icons of race, nation, and ethnicity became all mixed up. You had African American kids wearing Hilfiger as a sign of being down, and white kids wearing Hilfiger and listening to hip-hop while Korean kids were eating McDonalds and listening to hip-hop. Universal symbols of particular "races" or "genders" got all mixed up. The old advertisement used to say "You don't have to be Jewish to love Levy's Rye Bread." Now, you'd have to say "You don't have to eat rye bread to be Jewish."

Dovetailing with notions of performativity and constructionism were various scientific and medical "discoveries." Thus far, no one has been able to identify a person as belonging to a specific "race" through DNA analysis. In fact, DNA analysis has let us understand that the category of race is one that does not exist in physiological terms. Further, since difference in skin color, often the basis of racial thinking, developed rather late in human development, a mere one hundred thousand years ago, it turns out there is ten times more genetic variation within a group we have called a race than within the entire human gene pool. So, for example, a Chinese person may have less in common genetically with another Asian than with a German. Indeed, no one is even able to tell us how many races there are, and fine distinctions between phenotypes tend to dissolve even more actively any notion of categorical racial identities.

In some cases of deafness, a genetic component is involved. For example, the so-called Connexin 26 gene is responsible for some kinds of inherited deafness. In this sense, one could try to define deaf people as a race, but this would work only if people with two copies of this specific gene were so defined. However, it is obvious that so many more people than just the genetically deaf are included in the concept of Deafness that this racial view cannot really be said to be relevant.

The Human Genome Project offered up the possibility of mapping with certainty the complete sequence of approximately 3.2 billion pairs of nucleotides that make us human. But the project has left us with more questions than it has answered. For example, scientists are puzzling over the relatively low count of genes in the human genome. It had been estimated that humans would have approximately one hundred thousand genes, but the study yielded a paucity of thirty thousand, putting Homo sapiens on a par with the mustard cress plant (twenty-five thousand genes) for genetic complexity.[7] More annoying, and less known, is the fact that the two groups who analyzed the genome, the privately owned Celera group and the government-financed consortium of academic centers, have come up with only fifteen thousand that they jointly agree on. Fifteen thousand more genes do not overlap in either analysis.[8] Considerable doubt exists as to whether these genes found are "real."

The issue of race is complicated too by the use of in vitro fertilization. In a recent case of "scrambled eggs," a fertility doctor implanted in a woman's womb not only her own fertilized embryo but that of another couple as well. The resulting birth was of fraternal twins, one white and the other black.[9] Such complications of reproductive technologies will certainly lead to other kinds of choices being made by parents and physicians, intentional as well as unintentional, with the effect of rendering even more complex racial or even gender identity.[10] We are also familiar with attempts, most recently of a Deaf lesbian couple, of Deaf people to try to have deaf children. Questions will have to be asked about whether such attempts are radical ways of fighting against oppression by dominant groups or technological fixes in the service of a conservative, essentialist agenda. Finally, the patrolled area of "mixed race" is being interrogated. The fact that multiracial identifications have been prohibited on national censuses is now being challenged. The reasons for keeping single-race check-off boxes is itself a highly politicized and tactical arena in which, understandably, oppressed groups have gained redress and power by creating a unified subject. Where censuses allow a mixed-race check-off box, the statistical stronghold of race may well become weakened with questionable results. The fact is that some 1.5 million Americans are in mixed-race marriages, and that number is doubling every decade. About 40 percent of Asian Americans and 6 percent of African Americans have married whites in recent years.[11]

One can legitimately ask if race has anything to do with Deafness, considering the emphasis that Deaf activists and scholars have put on notions of culture and shared history. While we don't tend to think of the Deaf as a race anymore, that label would have been applied not just by Alexander Graham Bell but also by anyone interested in eugenics. Their notions of race were far more expandable than our current ones are. But the use of ethnicity, with its idea of culture and world, has to become suspect since it relies on an essentially racial model, as I am arguing.

In the area of gender, we are also seeing confusions in otherwise fixed categories. A culture of transgendered peoples is now being more widely permitted, and the right to be transgendered is being actively fought for. The neat binaries of male and female are being complicated by volition, surgery, and the use of pharmaceuticals. Intersexuals, formerly known as hermaphrodites, were routinely operated upon at birth to assign them a specific gender. That move is now being contested by groups of adult intersexuals. Some feel they were assigned the wrong gender, and others feel that they would have liked to remain indeterminate. Transsexuals now routinely occupy various locations along a gender continuum demarcating their place by clothing and other style-related choices, surgical corrections, and hormonal therapy. Even on the genetic level, both females who are genetically male and males who are genetically female are a naturally occurring phenomenon. The gender determination is suppressed or enhanced in these cases of what are called "Turner's syndrome" and "Klinefelter's syndrome" so that the genetic markers do not express the expected sexual phenotypes.[12]

What we have called "nature" is not universal but can be modified in fundamental ways through biotechnology, prosthetics, genetic manipulation, hormone treatments, and so on. Thus the ground—the bedrock—of the "body" began to seem as if it were less reliable.

The very idea of a singular, unproblematic identity is crumbling. The response by various sides has varied. Some theorists have adopted a more global, cosmopolitan sense of identity, allowing hybridity and mixed categories some play. Others have barricaded the classic idea of identity and fought from or against those unitary ramparts.

So, given these complexities and attacks on identity, why should Deaf people now choose to see themselves as fitting into the kind of identity politics now being reexamined by society at large? The big problem related to trying to make Deafness into a socially constructed ethnic or minority group is that in order to shore up the concept, certain kinds of very unpostmodern moves need to happen. The firewall between Deaf and non-Deaf has to be patrolled in very serious ways. Let us examine how.

First, the linguistic model presented in which Deafness is defined as a minority language group has, by definition, to rule out all non–ASL (American Sign Language) users as "other." This model, while helping to include Deafness in the minority language model, has the effect of excluding or at least marginalizing Deaf people who are orally trained or who never had the chance to learn sign language. One can imagine many people who grew up in non-ASL settings in the 1950s and 1960s thinking of themselves, quite happily, as Deaf until they were informed that since they were non–ASL users they were not Deaf. Likewise, it includes hard-of-hearing people who have learned ASL but expels those who have not. Ironically, the model punishes the victims of oral education rather than including them into the society of Deafness. The other flaw in the model is that signing Codas should be defined as being Deaf, but those who follow the minority model often do not see Codas in this light. To be true to its intention, the minority language model would have to say that signing Codas were fully fledged, strongly Deaf people. One can argue that Codas aren't Deaf because they can hear and aren't actively discriminated against by the hearing world; but if one takes that tack, then one has to abandon the idea that language is the defining term in Deaf.[13] If you let language go, then you are back to hearing loss, that is, either some kind of phenomenological model or the more prevalent and insidious audiological/medical model.

As for the ethnic group model, while the argument about a shared common history, language, social customs, and organizations had been historically true, with the advent of the Internet, mainstreaming, the decline of residential schooling, and the demise of the Deaf club it is harder to make this argument. And, of course, one of the key notions of an ethnic group is ethnic cuisine, often the last thing to go in assimilation, according to Steven Steinberg.[14] Alas, there is no Deaf cuisine—unless we consider replication of residential-school menus as filling that bill.

The ethnic argument sets up a model of the true or "pure" Deaf person, in imitation of the worst aspects of racially defining a people. In this ethnic group model, there is an in-group and an out-group. Those most "in" are Deaf of Deaf people, that very small percentage (only perhaps 5 percent of all congenitally born deaf) who come from a Deaf family and who often make up the elite of the Deaf world. Those "in" include people lucky enough to have gone to Gallaudet, National Technical Institute for the Deaf, and other Deaf schools. Excluded are hard-of-hearing, oral, Codas, urban poor or third-world rural poor who never had a chance to learn sign language, and deaf people with limb impairments or spinal injuries that affect their limb and digit mobility. Further-

more, Deaf people on the Internet or using pagers, while obviously talking about subjects that are of common interest, may not appear dramatically different in their language usage than any other ESL group with its own specialized jargon and idioms. And
if a Deaf person doesn't choose to talk the talk or walk the walk, does that exclude that
person from the ethnic group? This same question could be asked about African Americans who speak standard English and do not code switch.

The ethnic model is also dubious because of the association now between ethnic
groups and violence. In the old days of the 1960s and 1970s, nationalism used to be
considered the bad thing and ethnicity the good thing. But since the growth of what
Hardt and Negri call "empire,"[15] and with the weakening of some national entities, re-
gionalism, tribalism, and ethnicity have lead to interethnic warfare like that found in
Uganda, Rwanda, Bosnia, Serbia, Croatia, and Afghanistan, and between the ethnic
Kurds and the Turks or Iraqis. While it may be true that some ethnic groups have managed to refrain from this kind of violence, although I can't think of any at the moment,
we might want to wonder if the model of ethnic pride is something so desirable as opposed to a more cosmopolitan internationalism. Are the kinds of distinctions ethnic
groups make between self and other necessarily the models that we want to follow in
defining Deafness?

One of the key notions in an *ethnos,* a people, is the idea of an extended kinship system. People within an ethnic group are related not only by language, history, and culture but also by a family structure that passes along a genetic inheritance. But the vast
majority of Deaf people do not come from Deaf families. According to often-cited statistics, over 90 percent of Deaf people are born to hearing families. The Deaf, Codas, people with disabilities, and queer folk are, as Robert Hoffmeister has said of Codas, only
"one generation thick." In this sense, these four groups have more in common with each
other than with any ethnic group. Indeed, one could argue that without the extended
kinship system, you can't have an ethnic group. Even large groups, like Americans, may
have shared cultural, linguistic, historical, geographical, and other characteristics but
are not, properly speaking, an ethnic group. So how can the Deaf make a claim with less
than 10 percent of Deaf people being born into Deaf families? Given the laws of Mende-
lian distribution in relatively new mutations like Connexin 26, the mathematical model
will continue to insure that even a second or third generation of deafness within the
same family is unlikely. Thus, although there are a small percentage of deaf families that
pass on deafness, no significant familial system exists with any significant similarity to
the absolute regularity of family based on consanguineous, multigenerational kinship
of other ethnic groups. One can always emphasize that Deaf people pass along their
culture by a nonkinship system, but then you are talking about a rather different kind of
social organization than an ethnic group.

The other problem with the ethnic or minority group model is that usually being
part of an ethnic group defines one in a totalizing way. You usually can't be Jewish, for
example, and be Japanese. If you happen to be of mixed ethnicity, then each ethnic category is diluted. So one can be Jewish and black, but you'd be 50 percent of each. Deaf
people can and do belong to some other ethnic group. But, as we know, Deaf people
don't feel that their Deafness is diluted by their ethnicity, which means that being Deaf

isn't really like being Jewish. One doesn't feel 50 percent Deaf and 50 percent Jewish but rather all Deaf and all Jewish. This shows us that the attempt to make Deafness an ethnic group doesn't work because the category doesn't operate in the same way as does ethnicity.

The problem with ethnic or minority status is that in having that status a group is letting a dominant majority make the definition of what you are or should be. It is true that such groups then take the victimization and turn it into a kind of cultural resistance, but at base the terms are still defined by the oppressor. In adopting the language of race, a language of victimization, various groups have been able to build pride and power into their social organization, but given the choice, should Deaf people begin to call themselves an *ethnos* when that idea includes the idea of minority (including the sense of marginal, minoritized) status and the adoption of the language of the oppressor? Indeed, one could say that all the racial and some ethnic categories were defined by those who wished to rid the world of those categories. The social construction of various human populations performed by those who were dominant often aimed at creating categories of inferiority for the purposes of exploitation, institutionalization, remediation, or elimination.

Related to this point is a strategic question. Are the protections built into the law for ethnic groups effective? Does one want to choose the category of ethnic group as the regnant defining term and then seek protection or redress under the law under that status? Or is it better to allow protections and rights under the law to apply under the statutes that cover disability? Would you rather be protected by the Americans with Disability Act, Section 504, and other protections built into the law, or will you take your chances with affirmative action, hate-crime legislation, and so on?

The concept of DEAF-WORLD or DEAF-CULTURE has been used by many Deaf people, and there is something attractive about the concept. It does not have any associations with medical imperatives or racialized discourses. The problem with the terms is that they are perhaps too general and elastic. If you start defining what you mean by either, you immediately fall back into categorical generalizations of the kind we have been discussing. Who is Deaf? Who belongs in the DEAF-WORLD? How do you get into it? Who are the gatekeepers? As for DEAF-CULTURE, you again have to define what makes it different from any other culture. What if we were to substitute "WHITE WORLD," "BLACK WORLD," "JEWISH WORLD," or "NON-JEWISH WORLD"? Would one be happy to celebrate and analyze the meaning of those terms? What if we said "ASL-ONLY USERS WORLD"? Or "40 PERCENT–100 PERCENT HEARING LOSS WORLD"? The problem with such concepts is that they tend to fall back into the older categories designed to exclude people, reduce their rights, and create marginalized communities. It's just a question of who gets to set up the barriers and checkpoints. In the past, it was the hearing people who did; now it is segments of the Deaf community. Of course, no group of people can exist without some kind of cultural and social distinctions. But in thinking through, in the best theoretical sense, new directions for Deafness, we have to look at the problems and the solutions with a high degree of rigor.

This last point brings me to the issue of disability. Deaf people are not alone in this reconsideration. They do not have to build the house of theory around identity alone.

As I mentioned earlier, what brings together all the social injustices of the past two hundred years is the idea that people with various bodily traits have been discriminated against because of those traits. This is not a medical model, but rather a model based on biopower analysis along the lines of the founding work done by Michel Foucault and others. The extension of this work is the postmodern assault on identity that has critiqued the fundamental assumptions of that kind of discrimination by saying that you can't base identity on these putative bodily traits because you can't justify the existence of these markers anymore. The grand categories of race, gender, etc. have no validity as categories with rigid firewalls. I've also pointed out that Deafness, too, is subject to this critique. You can only create the category of Deafness if you build these rigid firewalls; otherwise you've got a continuum of hearing-impaired, hard-of-hearing, partially deafened, profoundly deaf, and so on. You've also got a range of people with oral abilities, and a range of ASL abilities, including a range of ASL usage among Codas. The concept of Deafness can get very messy unless you perform a kind of "commonsense" purifying of the category that may work, but it has the pitfalls of the "common sense" of racial categories, for example. Common sense, in reality, is actually socially constructed truisms that are never really common at all.

The argument then is why use the outdated, outmoded, and potentially dangerous categories of ethnicity, minority status, nationhood (including "world" and "culture") when one might do better to use the category of "one-generation" identities to redefine the nature of social identity. Rather than trying to force the foot into the glass slipper, why not make a new shoe that actually fits?

In this scenario, people with disabilities, Deaf people, gay people, and Codas can say "we represent the way out of the identity politics dead end." We are social groups that are not defined solely by bodily capabilities. We are not a group that has been defined in advance by an oppressor, but we choose to unite ourselves together for new purposes. We are not defined by genetic qualities or inherited traits. We are, precisely, not an ethnic group or a minority but something new and different emerging from the smoke of identity politics and rising like a phoenix of the postmodern age.

Disability is one way of talking about this kind of postmodern identity. At this point, there is a fairly elaborated theory of disability emerging. Queer Studies also offers various approaches to identity that do not have to imitate the identity categories of the past. The key to both is that identity is part of a continuum. It is malleable and not grounded in the traditional medicalized or essentialized views of the body. It does not have to rub shoulders with racialized ways of thinking or divisive views of what it is to be human based on tribal or parochial points of view.

Deaf people have argued that disability doesn't fit their experience of being Deaf. Many Deaf people have said, "I'm not disabled like a crippled person or a mentally retarded person." But the problem with that refutation is that it uses ableist concepts. It implies that each Deaf person would be diminished if they considered themselves disabled. This position, in my opinion, does not allow for the fullest sense of disability that has been elaborated in disability theory. The point has always been that people with disabilities are not disabled by their impairments but that the society surrounding them creates the disability when it denies or impedes accommodation. There is nothing diminished or disabled about a person with a disability where there is access and accommodation. Likewise, there is nothing disabled about a Deaf person who is surrounded by people who are in their language community or when interpreters are freely provided in other public and private venues.

I have come to see the position made by some Deaf people that disability is not a desirable umbrella under which to group Deaf people at this point. That may be the case, but I also think that minority status, ethnicity, or exclusive worlds don't work either. If disability and ethnicity are rejected, what is left? I would hope that Deaf Studies would develop a theory of Deafness, an explanation of Deaf identity, that had its own inherent and internal cohesion in some kind of connection with other minoritized people. But I would caution that the errors of previous identity politics not be repeated. The simple attempt to adopt linguistic minority status, as has been done, or ethnic status, or exclusionary worldviews will be antiquated by contemporary thinking and will appear in the long run as making Deaf people be wannabes in an outmoded game. Further, the attempt to rigidify Deafness by making rules—must be Deaf, must be ASL user, must participate in Deaf Culture, must adopt Deaf ways, and so on—will create a system of microenforcements and identity requirements that will seem parochial, oppressive, and unbending. Tellingly, Gallaudet University itself accepts students who run the gamut from hearing to Deaf. A better course for Deaf Studies would be to examine the situation in identity politics now, learn from the past, think about the beyond-identity issues floating in the public sphere, come up with flexible and nonhierarchical models of being, and lead the way out of the dead end of identity thinking. As African Americans and feminists took the lead in the past to help the larger society to theorize subjecthood in the 1970s and 1980s, so can the Deaf, the disabled, and queer folk help postmodern society to imagine what subjectivity looks like in a postidentity period. This process is necessarily collective and situational, and it would be presumptive of me to suggest how that discussion should go. Those discussions are proceeding even now, and they will benefit from an awareness of the regnant issues and ideas that are disturbing and intriguing all identity groups not only in the United States but throughout the world.

Notes

1. Alan R. Templeton, "Human Races: A Genetic and Evolutionary Perspective," *American Anthropologist,* n.s., 100, no. 3 (1998): 632.

2. Sandra Soo-Jin Lee, Joanna Mountain, and Barbara Koenig, "The Meaning of 'Race' in the New Genomics," *Yale Journal of Health Policy, Law, and Ethics* 1 (2001): 33.

3. John Last, ed., *A Dictionary of Epidemiology* (New York: Oxford University Press, 1988), 110.

4. M. A. Rothstein and P. G. Epps, "Pharmacogenomics and the (Ir)relevance of Race," *Pharmacogenomics Journal* 1, no. 2 (2001): 108n (emphasis mine).

5. Judith C. Barker, "Cultural Diversity: Changing the Context of Medical Practice," *Western Journal of Medicine* 157 (1992): 248.

6. Thomas Lacquer, *Making Sex: Body and Gender from the Greeks to Freud* (Cambridge, Mass.: Harvard University Press, 1990). See also Leslie Feinberg, *Transgender Warriors: Making History from Joan of Arc to Dennis Rodman* (Boston: Beacon Press, 1996).

7. Let us not even consider the further problem that in order to locate a gene, we have to cordon off "good" DNA from "junk" DNA. Now, with the advent of relatively low numbers of genes for

humans, scientists are beginning to posit that so-called junk DNA may have a role to play in "influencing" the good DNA. Thus the exact science of genetics begins to resemble other explanatory systems requiring influence such as earlier models based on humors, astrological causes, and so on. Indeed, many human traits are polygenic, involving several different genes working in coordination with each other and with other processes.

8. *New York Times,* August 24, 2001, A13. Also note that in a *New York Times* article from March 5, 2002, we see a report that a new paper written by Robert Waterston of Washington University, Eric Lander of MIT, and John Sulston of the Wellcome Trust Sanger Institute claim that Celera's decoding "incorporated key sequences already developed by the public effort to complete their map" (A18). If this is the case, then the fifteen thousand that supposedly overlap actually do not since some of that number is from the international public consortium. The study, published in the National Academy of Science's proceedings states that "Celera did not produce an independent draft of the genome as it had claimed."

9. *New York Times Sunday Magazine,* March 25, 2001.

10. Although as Dorothy Roberts has pointed out, prenatal technology is still very much a site of racial discrimination. See "Race and the New Reproduction," *Hastings Law Journal* 47, no. 4 (1996): 935.

11. Nicholas D. Kristof, "Love and Race," *New York Times,* December 6, 2002, A35.

12. For more on this subject, see Feinberg's *Transgender Warriors.* Also see Bob Beale, "New Insights into the X and Y Chromosomes," *The Scientist* 15, no. 15 (2001): 18.

13. The story of Christy Smith is telling. The *Philadelphia Inquirer* of March 22 reports that Ms. Smith, currently on the television program *Survivor,* is Deaf but not using sign language on the program. The Deaf community is described as "split" between pride about her being on the program and disappointment or outrage about her not using ASL. Regardless of the merits, the issue is this: if you define Deafness as about ASL then she must use ASL, otherwise she is not Deaf. This position creates a dilemma for people like Ms. Smith who are pressured to act in a particular way in all situations whether or not the situation itself warrants it.

14. Steven Steinberg, *The Ethnic Myth: Race, Ethnicity and Class in America* (Boston: Beacon, 2001).

15. Michael Hardt and Antonio Negri, *Empire* (Cambridge, Mass.: Harvard University Press, 2000).

Postscript: Gallaudet Protests of 2006 and the Myths of In/Exclusion

H-DIRKSEN L. BAUMAN

ON OCTOBER 13, 2006, the Washington, D.C., Metropolitan Police Department arrested 133 Gallaudet University students, staff, and alumni, the largest number of university arrests in the United States since the 1960s. The arrests occurred amid weeks of building and campouts lockdowns, hunger strikes, a sprawling tent city, rallies, and a two thousand–person march to the Capitol. At a time when many university faculty across the nation lament apathy on campus, Gallaudet University students orchestrated a massive protest that garnered national media attention and forced the Board of Trustees to meet their demand that the president-designate be removed before taking office.

What could possibly have sparked such widespread activism? The very causes of the protest were themselves a principle site of vigorous debate. Unlike the 1988 Deaf President Now (DPN) movement, which rallied behind the well-defined issue of selecting a deaf president for a deaf university, the 2006 protests were far more complicated and overdetermined. The Gallaudet Protest of 2006 could only be fully explained through a feature-length documentary film or book-length analysis with writers from all perspectives engaged in a critical collaboration with the issues. Such a volume would be able to lay out the escalation of events from the initial protests in May to the campus lockdown in October and the Board's capitulation. Such a volume would also describe the relevance of the protest in this particular historical moment. What *do* the protests say about Deaf political life in 2006 and beyond?

While it is still early to define the legacy of the 2006 protests, they do clearly dramatize issues simmering throughout the pages of *Open Your Eyes*. In fact, many of the contributors to this volume were deeply involved in the protest—on both sides. Some were members (and even president) of the Board of Trustees, while others were Gallaudet faculty members who played significant roles in the coalition of protesters, the Faculty Student Staff and Alumni (FSSA) coalition. What's more, the figure at the center of the controversy, then-Provost Jane Fernandes, provided financial support for, and participated in, the Deaf Studies Think Tank that gave rise to this volume.

Given that many of the debates and issues in this volume were dramatized before a national audience when the manuscript had already been delivered to the publisher, it seems only fitting that a postscript be added—not to advocate for one side or the other, not to delve into the minutiae of this or that event, but to take a wide-angle lens on the protest, to place it in a historical, cultural, and political context.

One of the most striking and relevant issues is the widespread disagreement on the very reasons for protest in the first place. The University administration asserted that the protest erupted out of a deep cultural anxiety about radical changes wrought by medical and technological advances, such as cochlear implants, that offer deaf people opportunities to become immersed into the hearing world rather than in the separate culture revolving around American Sign Language (ASL). Dr. Jane Fernandes, who is deaf though she grew up speaking and did not learn ASL until the age of twenty-three, symbolized a future that her critics were resisting. According to this line of reasoning, she was not culturally "Deaf enough" to be the public face of Gallaudet University.

Protesters denied these claims, citing the fact that 82 percent of the faculty asked for the president-designate's resignation or removal from office, which is especially significant given the fact that only 38 percent of the faculty are deaf, out of which only a small portion are native users of ASL. Instead, the protesters' grievances included a long list of concerns: the lack of diversity among the finalists, the Board of Trustees' lack of responsiveness to students of color, the persistence of audism on campus, and the appearance of an unfair search process that led to the appointment of a widely unpopular, internal candidate. These issues brought together a broad-based coalition of students, faculty, staff, and alumni who decided that the problems with the administrative system of Gallaudet that surfaced through the search process were worthy of vigorous dissent. As Deaf lawyer Kelby Brick writes, "The Deaf President Now protests in 1988 installed a deaf person as president, but they did not reform this almost 150-year-old entrenched bureaucracy of paternalism."[1]

Whether one accepts the administration's or the protesters' version of the sources of the protest—or some mixture of the two—the fact is that, for a short time, much of the nation did indeed open their eyes to Deaf Culture talking. Concepts like *audism* and *d/ Deaf cultural wars* entered American households. From the outside, issues such as "not being deaf enough" must have puzzled and troubled readers. Articles and editorials in *Time, Newsweek, USA Today,* the *Washington Post,* and the *Boston Globe-Mail* excoriated the protesters for engaging in a radical form of identity politics. The view from the inside of Gallaudet, however, reveals a far more complicated view of the protests, one that undeniably involves, but does not revolve exclusively around, identity politics.

The critique of identity politics, especially as described in this volume by Lennard Davis, is that identity is not a fixed, stable notion, rooted in a single defining element, such as ethnicity, race, gender, sexual orientation, or language skill. Upon closer observation, the protest did not revolve around any one single axis of identity. While the Deaf President Now protest was led by four white, Deaf of Deaf student leaders, the 2006 protests were led by a coalition among whose prominent figures were hearing, hard-of-hearing, late deafened, late learners of ASL, and ASL-fluent individuals. The dissenters know as well as anyone that there are many ways to be d/Deaf (and to be hearing, for that matter). Some protesters pointed out the irony that DPN was more rooted in single-axis identity politics than the 2006 protests that included resistance to racism and paternalism and a lack of shared governance and administrative transparency. It has been argued that the 2006 protests were a result of coalition politics more than identity politics.

While this may be the case, paternalistic administrations are present on many campuses, and yet there have been no comparable protests. Even when nearby American

University President Benjamin Ladner was dismissed from his position for improper expense accounting and was given a severance package of 3.75 million dollars, there were no widespread protests. So what is unique about the Gallaudet activism? What would go so far as to politicize the football team, which was responsible for escalating the protest from a single locked-down building to the entire campus? What would inspire over seventy tent-cities to be erected across the nation? Why would so many alumni return for a homecoming celebration that was cancelled by the administration, only to be replaced with a march on the nation's Capitol?

In order to understand this unique phenomenon, one has to appreciate the near mythic role that Gallaudet University plays within the Deaf world. It is the only plot of land in the entire world where Deaf people may have direct access to higher education through a signed language. Historically, Gallaudet has been a bastion of signed-language instruction even during a time when all residential schools in America banned ASL, promoting the possibility that Deaf people could be educated in a manner, as Joe Murray would put it, *coequal* with hearing counterparts. Further, Gallaudet's position is unique in the history of ideas, as it appears to fulfill an enduring human dream of a society that exists without recourse to the voice. In the seventeenth century, John Bulwer speculated on the benefits of an institution of learning based exclusively in gestural language. In the eighteenth century, Rousseau mused on the possibilities of a society in which "we would fully express our meanings by the language of gesture alone."[2] In the nineteenth century, when philanthropist Amos Kendall donated land for the founding of the National Deaf-Mute College, which would become Gallaudet University, he helped create a homeland where a signed language would flourish. Placed in this historical backdrop, we can begin to appreciate why Gallaudet serves as a sacred space—an Aztlan or Mecca—within global Deaf and signing communities.

Given the deep cultural connection to Gallaudet, the protests of 2006 bring into focus the larger dreams and desires of a people as they are elaborated through a vision of what Gallaudet should and could become. Whether or not the protesters were justified in pinning the future of their vision on the dismissal of Jane Fernandes is a complex and contentious question that is beyond the purview of this postscript. Yet if we are to understand the current Deaf cultural climate, we must recognize and name the deep yearning for a better Gallaudet that was expressed through the protest. There is an undeniable sentiment that the disruption of the presidential selection process was the first step in a larger reformation, not only for Gallaudet University but for the future of Deaf education in America and beyond.

The vision of the future is for Gallaudet to become a truly bilingual institution that explores and promotes the cognitive, cultural, and creative benefits of a bilingual education (in this case, ASL/English) to the wider world—both d/Deaf and hearing. As such, Gallaudet should explain, through example and research, to parents, educators, and doctors the wisdom of nurturing, rather than suppressing, ASL in deaf people's lives. The message coming from Gallaudet should be seen, loud and clear: signed languages are a vast human resource, and there is no better place to witness their wealth than on the ninety-nine-acre plot of land in northeast Washington, D.C.

The problem, however, is that Gallaudet University had never taken a clear position on ASL/English bilingual education. With the Deaf community looking to Gallaudet as a beacon of bilingual education, they received nothing but mixed messages. Twenty years after Deaf President Now, many administrators, staff, faculty, and students are only marginally literate in ASL—and worse, many hearing people do not even bother to sign in public, rendering Gallaudet at times no different than any other hearing university. The lack of ASL skills and basic Deaf cultural protocol at Gallaudet is a systemic problem that has been buttressed by long-standing curriculum and policy issues. There had never been a requirement that students—or faculty and administrators for that matter—formally study ASL. Ironically, Gallaudet students are expected to write college-level English, but many of their teachers often cannot produce elementary school–level ASL.

Critics charged that the lamentable state of communication on campus is a result of the adminstration's unwillingness to take a clear position about the mission and strategic goals of the university as they relate to ASL/English bilingualism. When it became clear that the university would be under the long leadership of another administrator who had presided over years of hand wringing over what to do with ASL on campus, protesters felt that it was time for a change. Members of the Deaf community could not sit idly by for another couple of decades without taking a clear position on difficult issues affecting the lives of deaf people for generations to come. Dissenters were much less concerned about when Jane Fernandes learned ASL than they were with her commitment to ensuring that children in future generations would learn it earlier than she did. As Provost, Fernandes oversaw the creation of a Strategic Plan for the university that failed to take a position on bilingualism, and worse, critics charged, that she unnecessarily pitted inclusion against bilingualism.

Under Provost Jane Fernandes, the university's Strategic Goal number one was for Gallaudet to model "what it is to be an inclusive deaf university in all aspects of its operations, academic and community life." To clarify, the strategic objective offered a definition of "inclusive deaf university" that was longer than the objective itself:

> The term inclusive deaf university refers to an academic institution of higher learning that is comprehensive and recognizes the diversity among deaf and hard of hearing people—in cultural identification, language and communication choices, audiometric measures, age of onset, use of amplification technology, school experiences—and in age, gender, disability, racial and ethnic background, religion, sexual orientation, and social-economic class.

Clearly, no one would argue against the spirit of inclusivity; after all, the authorizing legislation for Gallaudet University—the Education of the Deaf Act (EDA)—mandates that Gallaudet educate the nation's deaf and hard-of-hearing population; significantly, this mandate exists regardless of cultural or educational background. Shifting demographics show that fewer deaf students are educated in residential schools, while more are receiving cochlear implants and educated with little exposure to signed languages. Given these cultural shifts, an "all-inclusive deaf university" appears to be a wise and well-intentioned position to take.

However, the objection was not about inclusivity itself, but about what was *not* included in the strategic objectives and mission of the university: that Gallaudet was, in "all aspects of its operations, academic and community life, an all-inclusive *bilingual* university." While many other universities, such as the University of Ottawa and the University of Fribourg, openly embrace bilingualism as a defining element, Gallaudet seemed poised for another president and Board to skirt the issue under the banner of inclusion.

With the assistance of the *Washington Post* editorial staff, the Gallaudet administration of I. King Jordan and Jane Fernandes was able to frame the discussion that protesters who argued for a stronger presence of ASL were being exclusionary cultural "absolutists" who wished to retreat into a bunker of signed language. When pitted against the feel-good rhetoric of inclusion, defenders of bilingualism faced a difficult rhetorical task—to point out the perils of inclusivity as envisioned by the Gallaudet administration, and to demonstrate that bilingual education, if done correctly, actually means greater inclusion and enhanced academic rigor and accountability.

The perils of Gallaudet's approach to its all-inclusive strategic plan and mission were identified not only by protesters but also by commissioners from Gallaudet's accrediting body, the Middle States Commission on Higher Education (MSCHE). Noting the fragmentation over the mission of the university, commissioners sensed that the university mission lacked focus as it was "trying to be all things to all people."[3] A concrete indication of the perils of inclusivity could be found in the university's Communication Policy, which defined ASL in the following way: "*The term American Sign Language is to be used in an all-inclusive sense and includes signs expressed in English word order, with or without voice*" (emphasis added).[4] Such a definition is not only symbolic of the systemic denigration of ASL, critics charged, but academically embarrassing. Clearly, ASL and English are in daily contact at Gallaudet, but they are distinct languages, a revelation that came about, ironically, at Gallaudet University over four decades ago. Researchers in the hundreds of linguistics programs across the country who work on signed languages would scoff at Gallaudet's definition of ASL. Gallaudet's historic unwillingness to commit to a position, critics claim, has potentially harmed its image as a prestigious, let alone credible, institution. Imagine the public consternation if Gallaudet were to define English "in an all-inclusive sense that includes words expressed in ASL word order."

The Communication Policy, which was revised in the spring of 2007,[5] was indicative of a larger, systemic problem of accountability fostered under a spirit of trying to be all things to all people. Faculty who were deficient in ASL skills and who voiced could simply claim that they were meeting the needs of students under an anything-goes policy. If faculty, staff, and students were never held accountable for communicating clearly—certainly a worthwhile goal at a university—then how could a climate of academic rigor be cultivated? Clearly, it is not radical to claim that sound pedagogical strategies would include using an intelligible, grammatically correct language. Though students' skills may not be up to par, they should have the benefit of being guided toward more sophisticated expression. Thus, while the rhetoric of inclusivity often sounds good, if it is not infused with higher standards and accountability, the result is often lack of effectiveness.

Due to its unique status, Gallaudet could afford to proceed on its own terms for nearly a century and a half. Without a culture of assessment and improvement, Gallaudet gradually lost touch with higher education's movement toward a more rigorous and systematic collection of direct evidence of student learning. While reports of student learning were generated, the Gallaudet administration did little with them, as they did not always paint the desired picture. Rather than centralizing and focusing on institutional assessment, the Jordan/Fernandes administration failed for two years to replace the director of institutional research who retired in 2004. Further, a 2001 MSCHE report required Gallaudet to overhaul its undergraduate general studies curriculum and reform its faculty governance system. By the time of the Periodic Review Report in 2006, it had become clear that the administration and faculty had failed to follow these mandates of the university's accrediting body.

Then came the protests and the media reports of low academic standards. Suddenly this venerable institution, and progressive federal experiment signed into being by Abraham Lincoln, was under the scrutiny of news watchers across the nation, including members of the MSCHE. This negative publicity came at a time when the U.S. Department of Education (located within a fifteen-minute walk from Gallaudet) was threatening to take over accreditation from regional bodies and Gallaudet had received an unfavorable evaluation from the federal Office of Management and Budget (OMB). One particularly damaging news article in the *Washington Post* ended with a Gallaudet administrator pointing out, in response to the negative evaluation from OMB, that at least Gallaudet is fully accredited.[6] Now the very credibility of independent accrediting bodies was brought into public view. Not surprisingly, Gallaudet received notice that it would be visited by the MSCHE. After two site visits and various reports, MSCHE voted in June to place Gallaudet on probation—while recognizing that significant progress had occurred under interim President Robert Davila, it was not enough and the pace of change was not sufficiently rapid.

While nine months' time is too soon to be writing the legacy of the 2006 protests, clearly the most dramatic and far-reaching legacy is not the removal of Jane Fernandes, but the catalyst of sweeping reform at Gallaudet University. While no university wishes to be placed on probation, there is clear sentiment that such negative attention may be the best thing that could have happened to Gallaudet. No longer can this acclaimed institution afford to operate under the immunity of its uniqueness. It must reinvent itself if it is to remain relevant in the twenty-first century.

Change at Gallaudet University: Toward Inclusive Bilingualism

As a result of the MSCHE's demands that Gallaudet address issues of mission, shared governance, campus climate, and academic rigor, Gallaudet must find its way out of the existential crisis in a big hurry. It is now doing so, with the help of an ultimatum—without accreditation students will not come, and the United States Congress would likely not grant appropriations to an institution without students. Suddenly Gallaudet found itself with a rare opportunity: with the imperative that it must begin anew, faculty, staff, students, and administration have banded together in a cluster of working groups. In the course of a few months, Gallaudet University has undergone a thorough review of its mission and vision statements and has completely overhauled its undergraduate general studies curriculum. During this intensely productive, all-hands-on-deck time, Gallaudet is redefining itself for the future, which has implications for the future of the Deaf world.

As the Working Group on the University Mission met for the first time, we looked at ourselves, we looked at Gallaudet, and we asked: Who are we? Who do we serve? How do we serve them? In answering these questions, two answers became very apparent: we are bilingual and we are diverse. What emerged from community feedback were mission and vision statements that proclaim what we have been all along: a bilingual university. The new mission, which was approved by the Board of Trustees in August 2007 reads:

> *Gallaudet University, federally chartered in 1864, is a bilingual, multicultural institution of higher education that ensures the intellectual and professional advancement of deaf and hard of hearing individuals through American Sign Language and English. Gallaudet prepares its graduates for career opportunities in a highly competitive, technological, and rapidly changing world* (emphasis added).

In order to emphasize its mandate to educate all eligible deaf and hard-of-hearing students, Gallaudet's vision statement commits the institution to

> offer a welcoming, supportive, and accessible bilingual educational environment for teaching and learning through direct communication, and to embrace diversity within the deaf community by respecting and appreciating choices of communication while guiding students through their process of linguistic and cultural self-actualization.

The spirit of the new mission of Gallaudet is to create a model of *inclusive bilingualism,* where Gallaudet welcomes all qualified students from the wide variety of educational backgrounds, with varying degrees of proficiency in ASL and English. The difference, however, is that the university commits to supporting its members in developing bilingual proficiency during their time at Gallaudet. This would place Gallaudet directly in line with a host of other bilingual universities. As the European Centre for Higher Education notes, "significant proportions of students in the bilingual institutions are not bilingual when they enter the university. The university can play an important role in helping individuals from both language groups to become bilingual. . . . Part of the challenge is therefore to ensure that students can quickly operate in a bilingual environment, which requires a number of special measures, including intensive language courses when necessary."[7]

While there was strong support indicated for the new mission of Gallaudet, among its faculty, staff, students, and alumni, there are those who claim that any embrace of ASL is tantamount to cultural segregation, placing Gallaudet out of step with the rest of the world. The *Washington Post* editorial staff, for example, counsels that Gallaudet "must expand its mission in an era when many deaf children receive cochlear implants and have options beyond sign language."[8] Michael Chorost, author of *Rebuilt: How Becoming Part Computer Made Me More Human,* goes so far as to claim that the signing Deaf community and Gallaudet should resign itself to the death of ASL and focus on "innovating new ways for everyone to hear, using technology."[9] While these authors would defend their positions based on current and projected demographics, they operate under the false opposition of technology and signed languages. They betray a deep cultural fear that somehow learning a signed language has detrimental effects for deaf people and should be avoided if at all possible. In an age when parents are responding to research showing the benefits of bimodal bilingualism for their children, when hearing college students are learning ASL at unprecedented rates, and when hearing linguists are conducting sophisticated research on signed languages, deaf people are routinely counseled against learning signed languages. If signed languages are good for hearing people why would they be detrimental to a deaf person with a cochlear implant? Wouldn't it better to have two languages than one? The ironies of such positions are obvious: advocates of an English-only education are claiming that a bilingual education for deaf people is exclusionary. However, as the European Center for Higher Education claims, "the continuous use of two working languages is viewed as a central element in the mission of the university to promote a broad intellectual and social outlook."[10] Those who become bilingual in English and ASL would have access to two languages, one of which is capable of rich and clear visual and spatial discourse, a boon to students fortunate enough to watch a master signer describe photosynthesis or map out macroeconomic theories in clear grammatical space.

By building a greater presence for ASL, Gallaudet is not segregating itself for cultural or political reasons, but expanding the rigor of its curriculum, pedagogy, and standards. The evolving reasons for a defense of ASL, then, are not only about cultural preservation, but about critical pedagogy, visual-spatial cognition, and the economic vitality of Deaf people, which together will bring about a strong *Deaf public voice* that commands an audience.

Yet this is only the beginning of a cultural and academic exchange that must put Gallaudet firmly on the map of intellectual life in America. As Frank Bechter writes in this volume: "Indeed, even standing on the public stage is not enough. For deaf life truly to be heard there (for a subaltern voice truly 'to speak' and no longer be subaltern) the very terms of discourse on that stage—its very 'alphabet'—would need to be transformed." Such a transformative public voice, it is believed, may only come about when ASL gains a presence that demands attention. This future vision of Gallaudet is one that will incubate and encourage all of the ways that Deaf ways of being and signed languages can deeply affect a wide spectrum of academic and creative practices.

Instead of repeated curriculum and ways of knowing, Gallaudet should be out in front, taking the lead in understanding the unique insights that Deaf people and other sign language users have on, among a host of topics, visual language, visual learning, filmmaking, art, graphic and Web design, theater, literature, architecture, anthropology, philosophy, psychology, communication studies, public "speaking," and the rhetorical art of gesture. Each of these fields could be transformed by opening up to Deaf ways of being.

Gallaudet University, for example, has recently received a prestigious National Science Foundation Learning Center grant, known as Visual Language and Visual Learning, the purpose of which is to "gain a greater understanding of the biological, cognitive, linguistic, sociocultural, and pedagogical conditions that influence the acquisition of language and knowledge through the visual modality."[11] Clearly the National Science

Foundation considered the insights from Deaf people to be a scientific and empirical asset; otherwise it would not have awarded Gallaudet a grant of 35.5 million dollars over the next ten years. This learning center will contribute insights into this overlooked realm of human learning from the institution that should know more about visual learning than any other. In addition, Gallaudet University has invested in a three-year project to explore the notion of a Deaf architecture—not on the functional ADA level, but on deeper phenomenological and aesthetic levels where building designs may embody Deaf ways of being. How could such designs—the hallmarks of which are open spaces, special attention to light, and curvilinear form—be welcoming and splendid designs for all humans?

These two projects mark only the beginning of a Gallaudet University that assumes a much larger role in the intellectual life of higher education. Through the lens of the particular phenomenology of a Deaf being-in-the-world, what other fields of inquiry and creative production could be transformed at their base? The first and perhaps most significant will be a more thorough and sustained investigation into Deaf/sign language filmmaking. What could all filmmakers learn from the insights and practices of those who live, think, and love in signed languages that bear homological affinity to film language? One may ask, given such potential, why hasn't Gallaudet produced more accomplished filmmakers? The answer to this question also contributed to the protests of 2006. Jane Fernandes was widely criticized for effectively dismantling the film production program at Gallaudet. Given that film is now the only way to document ASL, a lack of support for a film program was interpreted as lack of support for the growth of ASL.

Part of the impatience on the part of protesters is the feeling that Gallaudet has been squandering its greatest resource, its raison d'être. With the appointment of Fernandes, Gallaudet seemed poised to continue its lack of commitment to signed languages evident under the Jordan administration. Protesters thought that, by now, Gallaudet should have been been able to correct what Pierre Desloges described in 1779 as a human irrationality: "I cannot understand how a language like sign language—the richest in expressions, the most energetic, the most incalculably advantageous in its universal intelligibility—is still so neglected and that only the deaf speak it (as it were). This is, I confess, one of those irrationalities of the human mind that I cannot explain."[12] For better or worse, there is a desire that the leader of Gallaudet University become the spokesperson, the *surdus vox populi* who would embody the future of deaf education through a fluent and eloquent signed language—to demonstrate the academic benefits of signed language in deaf education nationally and internationally, and to instill in the cultural climate of America that Deaf people and their signed languages are largely misunderstood and underutilized human resources. More than ever, the Deaf community senses the urgency to make the case, not only why America needs Gallaudet University, but why the world needs Deaf people and their signed languages.

Notes

I would like to thank David Armstrong for his feedback on this postscript.

1. Kelby Brick, "First Step in Gallaudet Revolution," *Baltimore Sun*, November 2, 2006, Opinion page.

2. Jean Jacques Rousseau, *Essay on the Origin of Language,* trans. John Moral and Alexander Gode (Chicago: Chicago University Press, 1966), 9.

3. Commissioner Sweeney, Middle States Commission on Higher Education, January 11, 2006, Gallaudet University.

4. The former Communication Policy is no longer available to read on the Gallaudet University Web site, but can be accessed at http://blog.deafread.com/mishkazena/2007/05/14/gallaudets-new-communication-policy-psd-survey/.

5. The new policy, which appears in the Gallaudet University Faculty Handbook, 2.2, reads: "The University Faculty recognizes that our community is comprised of deaf, hard of hearing, and hearing individuals who depend on a variety of communication modalities. Gallaudet's mission as a unique educational institution is inextricably bound to the need for direct, comprehensible and accessible communication among students and faculty. To that end, all members of the University Faculty are committed to promoting bilingual (American Sign Language and Written English) communication. The University is committed to providing training and resources, as needed, to support all members of the Faculty in developing the necessary language skills." This policy is not prescriptive, allowing considerable latitude with regard to acceptable communication on campus; the only restrictions are that the communication be direct, comprehensible, and accessible.

6. Mary Pat Flaherty and Susan Kinzie, "A Conflict in Integrity Surfaces," *Washington Post,* November 9, 2006, B1.

7. European Centre for Higher Education, "The Bilingual University, a Focus for a Multi-Cultural Europe," http://www.cepes.ro/hed/policy/bilingual_universities/Default.htm.

8. "On Probation: Change is Central to Gallaudet's Survival," *Washington Post,* July 14, 2007, A16.

9. Michael Chorost, "Politics, Technology and the Future of Deafness," March 21, 2006, Gallaudet University. Paper accessed at http://www.michaelchorost.com/?page_id=35.

10. European Centre for Higher Education, "The Bilingual University," http://www.cepes.ro/hed/policy/bilingual_universities/Default.htm.

11. Visual Language and Visual Learning Center, Gallaudet University, http://vl2.gallaudet.edu/.

12. Pierre Desloges, "A Deaf Person's Observations about *An Elementary Course of Education for the Deaf,*" in *The Deaf Experience: Classics in Education,* ed. Harlan Lane, trans. Franklin Philip (Cambridge, Mass: Harvard University Press, 1984), 46.

Contributors

Benjamin Bahan is professor of Deaf Studies at Gallaudet University. He is a coauthor (with Harlan Lane and Robert Hoffmeister) of *A Journey into the Deaf-World* and coauthor (with Carol Neidle, Judy Kegl, Dawn MacLaughlin, and Robert Lee) of *The Syntax of American Sign Language: Functional Categories and Hierarchical Structure*. He has appeared in numerous American Sign Language videotapes.

H-Dirksen L. Bauman is professor of Deaf Studies at Gallaudet University, where he directs the graduate program. He is coeditor of the DVD and book project *Signing the Body Poetic: Essays on American Sign Language Literature*.

Douglas C. Baynton is associate professor of history and American Sign Language at the University of Iowa. He is the author of *Forbidden Signs: American Culture and the Campaign against Sign Language*.

Frank Bechter is a PhD candidate in sociocultural and linguistic anthropology at the University of Chicago.

MJ Bienvenu is chair and associate professor of American Sign Language and Deaf Studies at Gallaudet University. She is the director of the forthcoming *American Sign Language Dictionary* and has lectured throughout the United States on Deaf Culture and American Sign Language. She was codirector of The Bicultural Center.

Brenda Jo Brueggemann is associate professor of English, Women's Studies, and Comparative Studies at Ohio State University, where she coordinates the American Sign Language program and the Disability Studies minor. She is the author of *Lend Me Your Ear: Rhetorical Constructions of Deafness*; coeditor of *Enabling the Humanities* and *Women and Deafness*; and editor of *Literacy and Deaf People: Cultural and Contextual Perspectives*.

Lennard J. Davis is professor in the departments of English, disability and human development, and medical education at the University of Illinois at Chicago, where he is also director of Project Biocultures. He is the author of several books, including *Enforcing Normalcy: Disability, Deafness, and the Body*; *My Sense of Silence: Memoirs of a Childhood with Deafness*; and *Bending over Backwards: Disability, Dismodernism, and*

Other Difficult Positions. He edited *The Disability Studies Reader* and *Shall I Say a Kiss: The Courtship Letters of a Deaf Couple, 1936–38.* His two most recent books are *Obsession: The Biography of a Disease* and *Country of Lost Children: A Natural History of Artificial Insemination.*

LINDSAY DUNN is the special assistant to the president for diversity and community relations at Gallaudet University. He has published numerous articles and has lectured widely on issues of race, colonialism, deafness, and ethnicity. He has been instrumental in forming advocacy programs for minority communities within the Deaf community.

LAWRENCE FLEISCHER is the founder and chairperson of the nation's first Deaf Studies program at California State University at Northridge. He has been a longtime advocate for Deaf persons in educational and legal institutions.

GENIE GERTZ is assistant professor of Deaf Studies at California State University at Northridge. She has lectured on the topic of internalized oppression in the Deaf community.

HILDE HAUALAND is a researcher at FAFO Institute in Norway.

ROBERT HOFFMEISTER is the director and cofounder (in 1981) of Programs in Deaf Studies at Boston University and the director of the Center for the Study of Communication and the Deaf. He is the coauthor (with Harlan Lane and Ben Bahan) of *A Journey into the Deaf-World,* and he has published and lectured widely on Deaf education and literacy.

TOM HUMPHRIES, associate director of the Teacher Education Program at the University of California, San Diego, holds a joint appointment in the department of communication. He is coauthor (with Carol Padden) of *Deaf in America: Voices from a Culture, Inside Deaf Culture, A Basic Course in American Sign Language,* and *Learning American Sign Language.*

ARLENE BLUMENTHAL KELLY is associate professor in the Department of ASL and Deaf Studies at Gallaudet University. Her areas of interest are cultural studies, linguistics, and Deaf history.

MARLON KUNTZE is codirector of the Programs in Deaf Studies in the School of Education at Boston University. He taught English high school Deaf students before he went to Stanford University, where he earned a PhD in educational linguistics. His area of interest is on language and literacy development and how the process may differ for children who are bilingual as well as for children who do not have access to spoken language; he is most interested in Deaf children who grow up with ASL and written English.

PADDY LADD is director of graduate programs at the Centre for Deaf Studies, University of Bristol. He is the author of *Understanding Deaf Culture: In Search of Deafhood.* An internationally recognized writer and Deaf activist, he received the Deaf Lifetime Achievement award by the Federation of Deaf People in 1998. He has been a pioneer of Deaf television programming in Britain.

Harlan Lane is Distinguished University Professor at Northeastern University. He is the author of several books, including *The Wild Boy of Aveyron: Foundations of Special Education*; *When the Mind Hears: A History of the Deaf*; *The Mask of Benevolence: Disabling the Deaf Community*; and (with Robert Hoffmeister and Ben Bahan) *A Journey into the Deaf-World*. He is the recipient of the John D. and Catherine T. MacArthur Foundation Fellowship, the Distinguished Service and Literary Achievement Awards of the National Association of the Deaf, and the Order of Academic Palms from the French government.

Joseph J. Murray is Director of the Projects Division at the Ål folkehøyskole og kurssenter for Deaf people in Norway and a doctoral student in history at the University of Iowa. His dissertation explores transnational interconnections among Deaf people in the late nineteenth century.

Carol Padden is professor in the Department of Communication at the University of California, San Diego. She is coauthor (with Tom Humphries) of two sign language textbooks and two books about Deaf culture, *Deaf in America: Voices from a Culture* and *Inside Deaf Culture*. She has been the recipient of numerous grants and awards, including a John Simon Guggenheim fellowship and grants from the National Science Foundation, the U.S. Department of Education, the Spencer Foundation, and the National Institutes of Health.

Index